JOHN BETJEMAN

Reading the Victorians

JOHN BETJEMAN

Reading the Victorians

GREG MORSE

sussex
ACADEMIC
PRESS

BRIGHTON • PORTLAND

2 4 6 8 10 9 7 5 3 1

First published 2008 in Great Britain by
SUSSEX ACADEMIC PRESS
PO Box 139
Eastbourne BN24 9BP

and in the United States of America by
SUSSEX ACADEMIC PRESS
920 NE 58th Ave   Suite 300
Portland, Oregon 97213–3786

British Library Cataloguing in Publication Data
A CIP catalogue record for this book is available from the British Library.

Library of Congress Cataloging-in-Publication Data
Morse, Greg.
John Betjeman : reading the Victorians / Greg Morse.
    p.cm.
Includes bibliographical references and index.
ISBN 978-1-84519-271-6 (h/c : alk. paper)
1. Betjeman, John, 1906-1984—Criticism and interpretation.
2. Literature and society—Great Britain—History—20th century.
3. Influence (Literary, artistic, etc.) I. Title.
PR6003.E77Z78 2008
823′.912—dc22

                                                                        2008013637

Mixed Sources
Product group from well-managed
forests and other controlled sources
www.fsc.org Cert no. SGS-COC-2482
© 1996 Forest Stewardship Council

Typeset and designed by SAP, Brighton & Eastbourne.
Printed by TJ International, Padstow, Cornwall.
This book is printed on acid-free paper.

Contents

Foreword by Norman Vance

We are just beginning to realise how important John Betjeman was as poet and as public figure. It is entirely appropriate that his sculpted image now presides over the revitalised St Pancras station. Not only has he become an emblem of Englishness for international travellers: he was one of the first to make us see that the great Victorian stations were noble social spaces which could be studied like churches. He loved engine-sheds as he loved bell-towers and rood-screens, with a discriminating passion. Without him, the twentieth century would have been duller and the nineteenth century an enigma. Greg Morse's fine, wide-ranging study of the formation and achievement of John Betjeman breaks new ground by exploring the complexity and imaginative richness of his evolving Victorianism. It also demonstrates that the distinctive blend of dignity and domesticity, feeling and function in Victorian poetry and Victorian architecture is more resilient and enduring, and more open to creative transformation, than we may have thought.

Victorian patriarchs, oppressively righteous or sometimes just oppressive, were not unnaturally resisted, and sometimes resented, by the next generation, particularly in Bloomsbury. Betjeman's own relations with his Victorian father were not easy. Lytton Strachey's brilliantly disrespectful caricatures in *Eminent Victorians* (1918) were part of a prolonged literary reaction which can be traced back to the studied impieties of Swinburne and the licensed wickedness of Wilde. Self-conscious modernity in the 1920s and 1930s and later rather conspired against Victorian brick and Victorian Gothic. As Morse demonstrates, Betjeman's initial preference seems to have been for Georgian architecture and his early journalism on the *Architectural Review*, responsive to editorial policy, showed little overt sympathy for the Victorians. But first in his poetry and then in his other writing, and eventually in his radio and television work, he assimilated and celebrated the heritage of Victorianism and other neglected aspects of the English past in town and country, particularly the West Country. Morse shows us that he was not just an immensely popular and often undervalued poet but, from the days of *Ghastly Good Taste* (1933) onwards, an increasingly influential cultural commentator who could change the way people saw things all around them.

He helped to lead the reaction against anti-Victorianism which gradually rehabilitated and conserved all things Victorian and stimulated the development of Victorian studies. But in a sense Victorianism had never gone away. C. F. A. Voysey among the architects, Thomas Hardy among the poets, and among the historians G. M. Young, author of the seminal *Victorian England: Portrait of an Age* (1936), were all Victorians who survived well into the twentieth century to overlap with Betjeman and his generation. Betjeman interviewed Voysey in 1931. He liked the Victorian hymn-tunes that Hardy had liked, the cadences and verse-forms Hardy adapted from Tennyson, and the Victorian churches which Hardy's employers had built or restored. The conventional literary history of the interwar years, dazed by dictators and pylon poets, minimises such continuities, celebrates W.H. Auden and rather ignores the young Betjeman. But Morse's meticulously researched study indicates a richer and more complex history, in which Auden admired and envied Betjeman's work, like Philip Larkin a little later. Thanks to Morse, we can now sense more clearly than ever before that in verse and prose Betjeman is a significant voice, for his own times and for ours.

UNIVERSITY OF SUSSEX, *March 2008*

Acknowledgments

I was on the Isle of Anglesey, that jewel of the North Wales coast, when my love of Betjeman's work began . . .

Like all good yarns, this one isn't quite true. I'd heard of him long before this – he was part of the nation's fabric, after all, and I'd written about him in my mock 'A' level exam. It was during that Cambrian holiday in 1994, however, that I called my mother as she was watching a repeat of *Time with Betjeman*. 'It's on again next week,' she said, 'you ought to watch it.' So I did.

As I sat in our living room the following Saturday, sipping clip after clip from the poet's considerable back catalogue, I was enraptured. It was partly his enthusiasm, partly his eccentricity, but mainly his love of things that I too adore: railways, old buildings, the landscape, the country of my birth. This was around the tenth anniversary of Betjeman's death, so there were many other programmes from which to choose. I watched, and loved, them all. Then came the books – letters, poems and prose in all manner of editions, as I devoured as much of the late Laureate's output as I could. Finally, there came study – and the volume you have before you now. It is for this reason that I must thank my mother, Marna Francis, for suggesting Betjeman to me, and she, my step-father, Sam Francis, and my partner, Julia Williams, for their unstinting support as the Great Victorian took over my life.

I also take this opportunity to thank Professor Norman Vance (University of Sussex) for writing the superb Foreword, and for his advice and encouragement as my D.Phil supervisor. Roger Badger's splendid photographic and montage work, which makes the statue of Betjeman 'read' Barlow's Victorian train shed at St. Pancras, is a testament to his skill and understanding of the project; his efforts are much appreciated. I would like to thank Tony Grahame at Sussex Academic Press too, for publishing the book in such fine fashion.

Similarly, I am grateful to Virginia and John R. Murray. Virginia worked for John Murray the publisher when I started and the John Murray Archive when I finished; she could not have been more helpful in answering my many queries. John acted as a most gentlemanly advisor and conduit between myself and Hodder, the current owners of Betjeman's poetic work. With that in mind, I also thank Loreen Brown of Hodder for her kindness and forbearance throughout our correspondence. I have also been fortunate to have received much support from the following:

Will Adames, Amanda Alcock (*Private Eye*); Kathryn Badger; Blackwell's Rare Books, Oxford; John Bodley (Faber & Faber Ltd.); Peter Cowley (The Telephone Museum, Milton Keynes); Peter Daniels (Assistant Librarian, The Religious Society of Friends in Britain); The Doric Arch; Dr. Ian Dungavell (Director, The Victorian Society); David Farmer; Stephen Games; Bridget Gillies (University of East Anglia Library); Jim Goddard MA; John Heald (Chairman, The Betjeman Society); Christopher Hunt (Imperial War Museum); Kay Kershaw (SPCK); the Trustees of the Mass-Observation Archive, University of Sussex; Charlotte Marwood (The Plunkett Foundation); Ian McFarlane (The Religious Society of Friends, Clerk, Jordans MM); Valerie McFarlane (Clerk to Old Jordans Trust); David Pearce; Deborah Stevenson (Dorset Record Office); R&SI; Dr. Terry Rogers (Marlborough College Archive); Mrs. Patricia Sedgwick; The Society of Authors; Terry Silcock (Railway Correspondence & Travel Society); Francis Smith; Alison Swann; David Tabraham-Palmer (Highgate School); Roger Trayhurn and Terry Tuey (McPherson Library, University of Victoria, Canada).

John Betjeman's *Collected Poems* and *A Pictorial History of English Architecture* are, as indicated above, reproduced by permission of John Murray (Publishers). The uncollected writings and collected letters of John Betjeman are reproduced with the kind permission of the Estate of Sir John Betjeman. Quotations from Olive Cook's *The Stansted Affair: A Case for the People* appear with kind consent of Pan Macmillan. (Copyright © Olive Cook, 1967.) Extracts from Wordsworth's *The Prelude* are cited from *The Prelude: 1799, 1805, 1850* by William Wordsworth: A Norton Critical Edition by William Wordsworth, edited by Jonathan Wordsworth, M. H. Abrams. Copyright © 1979 by W. W. Norton & Company, Inc. Used by permission of W. W. Norton & Company, Inc. All other copyright holders are acknowledged in the appropriate endnotes, though I record my gratitude to each of them here in addition.

Throughout the course of my work, the following libraries were consulted, to whose staff I also extend my thanks: the Centre for Buckinghamshire Studies, Aylesbury; Bodleian Library, Oxford; Library of the Religious Society of Friends in Britain; McPherson Library, University of Victoria, Canada; National Monuments Record Centre, Swindon; Swindon Central Library; Swindon Reference Library; University of Bristol Library and the University of Sussex Library.

Finally, I pay tribute to my fellow Betjeman Society members and those who have written about Betjeman in the past – all have proved to be an inspiration, but I must extend especial thanks to Dennis Brown, Timothy Mowl, John Press, Derek Stanford, Patrick Taylor-Martin and (of course!) Bevis Hillier.

List of Abbreviations

The following volumes, all of which are referred many times throughout this book, have been abbreviated thus in the notes:

YB   Bevis Hillier, *Young Betjeman* (London: John Murray (Publishers) Ltd., 1988)

JBNFNL   Bevis Hillier, *John Betjeman: New Fame, New Love* (London: John Murray (Publishers) Ltd., 2002)

BTBOL   Bevis Hillier, *Betjeman: The Bonus of Laughter* (London: John Murray (Publishers) Ltd., 2004)

L1   *John Betjeman – Letters Volume One: 1926 to 1951*, ed. by Candida Lycett Green, 2nd edn (London: Reed International Books Ltd., 1995)

L2   *John Betjeman – Letters Volume Two: 1951 to 1984*, ed. by Candida Lycett Green, 2nd edn, (London: Reed International Books Ltd., 1996)

CH   *John Betjeman: Coming Home – An Anthology of Prose*, ed. by Candida Lycett Green, 2nd edn (London: Vintage, 1998).

Textual Note

Publication dates for Betjeman's writings are quoted from the Betjeman Society's own bibliography.[1] For the most part, poems are discussed in their volume groupings, but, if different, the original publication date is given in parenthesis in order to minimise false assumptions about historical context. Furthermore, first editions of said volumes have been consulted in *all* cases

---

[1] Peter Gammond (with John Heald), *A Bibliographical Companion to Betjeman* (Guildford: The Betjeman Society, 1997).

and textual variants noted where the versions included in *Collected Poems* (1958) fail to correspond.

Quotations from Betjeman's verse-autobiography, *Summoned by Bells* (1960), are cited from Murray's second edition (1976).

Betjeman's prose works are cited from the original where possible, or from *First and Last Loves* (2nd edition, 1969) or *John Betjeman: Coming Home – An Anthology of Prose* (2nd edition, 1998).

JOHN BETJEMAN

Reading the Victorians

CHAPTER ONE

Introduction

Teddy Bear to the Nation

This is how *The Times* chose to describe John Betjeman – the most popular Poet Laureate since Tennyson – in 1982.[1] For many, the phrase epitomised the 'cuddly', unthreatening pillar of the establishment that the creator of 'Miss J. Hunter Dunn' had become. And, of course, *everyone* knew about Archibald . . .

In fact, the carrying of that childhood toy from tutorial to tutorial was a calculated gesture of defiance during those undergraduate days of the 1920s. By the mid-80s, however, the thought of a grown man keeping a stuffed bear on his bed led poet-critic Tom Paulin to deem *this* Laureate an 'absurd', 'utterly ridiculous figure'.[2]

As the celebrated Warden of Wadham, Maurice Bowra, described Betjeman as having 'a mind of extraordinary originality', perhaps Paulin had failed to see the joke; perhaps by 1985 it was no longer funny.[3] Whatever the case, the image has stuck, and though there have been a few recent references to the lack of 'cosiness' in Betjeman's work, most commentators continue to see him as the shambolic 'parodist of [. . .] *Hymns Ancient and Modern*' that Geoffrey Grigson felt him to be.[4]

The current critical mood is caught best by Andrew Sanders who, in *The Short Oxford History of English Literature* (1996), notes that Betjeman's success was based not only 'on easily comprehensible, generously rhymed, and meticulously scanned verse, but also on a calculated projection of himself as a celebrity'.[5] Thus *Summoned by Bells* (1960) is dismissed as 'gushy', while the volumes spanning the 1950s, 60s and 70s are described as showing little more than the poet's 'further refining [of] the techniques and forms he had evolved in the 1940s'.

Sanders' subsequent valedictory shrug that 'most of Betjeman's readers, Larkin included, did not read him for surprises' may cause students of H. R. Jauss to dub him a 'culinary lightweight' and seek edification elsewhere.[6] In his essay 'Literary History as a Challenge to Literary Theory' (1967), Jauss had used this term to describe 'irresistible, convincing and enjoyable [. . .] art' which nevertheless has an aesthetic distance of zero (meaning that no difference exists between what the reader anticipates from a work – the 'horizon of expectations' – and what it delivers). In *John Betjeman: Reading the Victorians*, initial audience reactions to each verse collection will be analysed by drawing on contemporary sales figures and reviews. This will facilitate a deeper understanding of the original 'horizon of expectations', which should in turn aid assessment of whether Betjeman was, or has become, a lightweight of *any* sort.

Regardless of the 'culinary' allegation, Larkin commented – on the same radio programme Paulin aired his opinion – that Betjeman did seem to bring 'a new kind of poetry' into being: namely, 'places in terms of people', 'people in terms of places'.[7] Kingsley Amis added that while he had indeed thought the verse 'light' and 'entertaining', 'Croydon' (1931), with its closing revelation that 'Uncle Dick' is dead, came to typify for him 'that horrible dig in the ribs' one frequently finds in Betjeman. 'Very often,' he went on, 'the message is: in the midst of life, we're in death.' Auden would probably have agreed: writing in the preface to *Slick But Not Streamlined* (1947), the book which launched his friend in America, he had generously remarked that he found it 'difficult to write [. . .] judiciously about a poet whose work [made him] violently jealous'.[8]

But while the case of Auden may be more complicated than the above suggests, it is clear that Betjeman is a poets' poet of sorts. Bill Ruddick demonstrated this in *Critical Quarterly* by examining the relationship between the Laureate and Larkin's 'Church Going' (1955) (and – to a lesser extent – 'The Whitsun Weddings' (1964)).[9] Betjeman recognised the worth of the earlier piece, having included it in his 1959 anthology *Altar and Pew*, but while Ruddick concludes that Larkin used details from his predecessor's poetry in a 'healthily active and independent' manner, he most certainly '*absorbed*' it first (my italics). Moreover, in *The Bonus of Laughter* (2004), the final part of his masterly three-volume biography of Betjeman, Bevis Hillier lists Seamus Heaney (1939–) and Craig Raine (1944–), two poets from the generation after Larkin, as being among those whose work continues to ring a familiar chime.[10] In particular, the latter's 'Baize Doors' (1984) is likened to 'Death in Leamington' – and not without reason:

> a *Reynolds News* between her floor
> and the opened skull [. . .]
> :   :   :   :   :
> A pair of bellows prayed in the hearth.
> The kitchen fire fell to its death.
> (RAINE, 'BAIZE DOORS', LL. 22–23; 29–30)

> Beside her the lonely crochet
>   Lay patiently and unstirred,
> But the fingers that would have work'd it
>   Were dead as the spoken word.
> (BETJEMAN, 'DEATH IN LEAMINGTON', LL. 4–8)

Hillier also discusses the ways in which his subject adheres to the characteristics of the Romantic, as outlined by Anita Brookner in *Romanticism and its Discontents* (2000). He acknowledges the familiarity of 'nostalgia and terror', but realises that the trait which most befits Betjeman is his '"conviction of a secret destiny or calling"'. This is supported by a quotation from *Summoned by Bells*:

> I knew as soon as I could read and write
> That I must be a poet [. . .].[11]
>
> (BETJEMAN, *SUMMONED BY BELLS*, P. 16)

The Napoleonic Wars (1792–1815) essentially prevented those pioneer Romantics, Wordsworth and Coleridge, from travelling abroad to drink in the world's delights. For them, there was little choice but to appreciate the joys of their own landscape. Betjeman, though he visited America and Australia (among other short trips), instinctively loathed continental travel and one could argue that this self-imposed restriction placed him in the same sphere of tradition as his earlier counterparts. It does not follow, however, that he was influenced by Romantic *poetry* to any great extent.

A Question of Upbringing

'No Poet, no artist of any art,' wrote T. S. Eliot, 'has his complete meaning alone [. . .]; you must set him, for contrast and comparison, among the dead.'[12] Harold Bloom adds that poets 'undo' the power their predecessors hold over them, but this can result in the rather unhelpful idea that 'the meaning of a poem is another poem'.[13] It is also not true of Betjeman, who *embraced* his antecedents. True, he revered the architecture of the Georgian period, but its poets were not his 'dead': despite his liking for Cowper (1731–1800) and Crabbe (1754–1832), it would be later exponents – such as Tennyson (1809–1892) and Hardy (1840–1928 – Victorian by nurture, if not publication date) – who inspired him the most. I believe that a central part of Betjeman's identity rests on his interest in the Victorians, and to miss the significance of this interest is to miss what he represented. 'Missing something' is also a risk if one focuses solely on the poetry: Betjeman was a 'complete writer' in that he came to use virtually all media to disseminate his message to as wide an audience as possible; his prose, television appearances and radio broadcasts will therefore be considered here too.

Betjeman's nineteenth-century tendencies are explained when one considers his background. Born in 1906, his parents were certainly Victorian, and his upbringing is therefore likely to have embodied vestiges of the 'Victorianism' that was to some extent demonised by Lytton Stratchey's Oedipal attack in *Eminent Victorians* (1918). But his love of the unfashionable largely delivered him from such conventional assaults and led him naturally to colour his undergraduate writing with a distinctly Tennysonian tint while his contemporaries were basking in the glow of T. S. Eliot and the

Sitwells. This is part of his reaction to the previous generation's intellectualism – a general state that is considered at length by Humphrey Carpenter in *The Brideshead Generation* (1989). Yet even if Betjeman were the 'silly young man' that Carpenter portrays, he was clearly as creative a reader of nineteenth-century verse as Wilfred Owen was of Keats; his earliest work is not only peppered with references to Tennyson and Hardy, note, but also D. G. Rossetti, Father Prout, Calverley, Meredith and Allingham.

The wider culture of that period had as profound an effect on his opinions as the poetry. This is reflected in his interest in faith (and doubt), his 'gaslight and steam' Englishness, and his love of the countryside.[14] However, it was not always thus and in the 1930s his writing displayed elements of both modernism *and* traditionalism. He felt that Victorian buildings were risible and wrote much in praise of the Bauhaus style. This was in some respects channelled by the editorial stance of the *Architectural Review* (for which he worked between 1930 and 1934), although he did seem to throw himself into the role by joining the seminal Modern Architectural Research Society (MARS); it is also possible that his short-lived Quakerism may be relevant, given the puritan nature of that sect (an attribute which also extended to the architecture of its meeting houses). CHAPTER TWO will plot the poet's growth through this turbulent decade and will show that the outbreak of war in 1939 was something of a watershed, after which Betjeman's appreciation of nineteenth-century buildings (never *fully* extinguished) became more obvious.

This shift was aided by his awareness of the dangers of post-war urban redevelopment, which created an urgency that lent those traditional verse forms an increasing poignancy, seeming, as they do, to critique their present via the poetics of the past. Betjeman's co-founding of the Victorian Society in 1958 further emphasizes his changed attitude, which continued into the 1960s and 70s through his multifarious multimedia campaigns, and waned only when age and infirmity overpowered him.

In short, just as he had changed his own mind, Betjeman also managed to alter *public* perceptions of beauty; without him, it is unlikely that Sir Gilbert Scott's St. Pancras station hotel (1873) – to name but one example – would still exist, let alone be respected in the manner it is today. Indeed, it is partly with Victorian architecture in mind that the adjectives 'Betjemanic', 'Betjemanesque' and 'Betjemanish' now reside in the *Oxford English Dictionary*. These alone signal the need to explore exactly what 'Betjeman' signifies.

Betjeman Today

If half the problem of the poet's status is his perceived 'cuddliness', then the other half is surely time. We are now on our second Laureate since his demise and the fuss surrounding the appointment of Andrew Motion and the revelations about Ted Hughes's relationship with Sylvia Plath have helped to distance him from our collective consciousness. And while impressive sales figures did nothing to mar the reputations of Tennyson or Elizabeth Barrett Browning, such success appears to have done little but condemn Betjeman to be forever associated with writers of populist doggerel. His contemporaries – Auden, Eliot, Yeats and Larkin – continue to be studied and analysed, quite rightly, yet the fact is that Betjeman's work is perhaps more affecting and 'relevant' now than it has ever been. When one considers the main themes of his verse, it becomes clear that he has left us with a poetic legacy which has much to say about the world we currently live in.

None of Betjeman's satiric targets are more perennial than the 'Executive', first immortalised in 1971.[15] Today's white-collar wanderer may drive a Laguna or Mondeo instead of the 'firm's Cortina', but he continues to talk in jargon and has little respect for anything over ten years old. He is a materialist and dwells in the same materially defined world as Browning's Duke (cf. 'My Last Duchess', 1842). In this sense, 'Executive' reaches back some one hundred years *and* looks forward to twenty-first century consumerism. Similarly, while we may meditate on the M25 rather than the A30 (cf. 'Meditation on the A30', 1966), the road rage that bubbled just under the surface then is increasingly apparent in Britain now. How many people, like the man 'on his own in a car', open the throttle with anger at something wholly unconnected with driving? How many allow their minds to empty to such an extent that the bend in the road, if not accepting its 'kill', comes very close to doing so? But the petulant motorist, more interested in the Mini or Jag ahead, is unlikely to consider the rape of the fields alongside until seeing the television news in the evening:

> We spray the fields and scatter
> The poison on the ground
> So that no wicked wild flowers
> Upon our farm be found.
> ('HARVEST HYMN', 1966, LL. 1–4)

For the original audience, this was a poem about pesticides; the modern audience should also be moved to consider the state-of-the-art threat from GM crops.

The scholar-critic Nicholas Shrimpton has recently stated that, in 'Death in Leamington' (1932), the poet reaches the profound through the trivial.[16] Betjeman himself claimed that death is perhaps the only thing that gives life a sense of proportion and, in concentrating on minutiae as he does here, and in 'Devonshire Street, W.1' (1954), 'Remorse' (1954) and many other poems, he shows how such profundity is all around us. This sense of mortality is what links him with poets like Tennyson, Christina Rossetti and Clough, and what links them all with us. Betjeman has also said that a day never passed in which he did not think about how he would die – a fear that goes hand-in-hand with his inherent sense of religious doubt. This is, of course, essentially a Victorian debate: it was during the nineteenth century that Christian belief came under attack both from scientific discovery (epitomised for many by Darwin's *The Origin of Species* [1859]) and Biblical textual criticism (as in David Friedrich Strauss's *Das Leben Jesu* [translated by George Eliot in 1846]). From the 1830s onwards, poetry became increasingly sensitive to this conflict, as Matthew Arnold's 'Dover Beach' (1867), Emily Brontë's 'No Coward Soul is Mine' (1850) and Clough's 'Easter Day. Naples, 1849' (1865) prove.

In his 1974 volume in the *Writers and Their Work* series, John Press commented that whereas Hardy 'disbelieved the Christmas story [but] hoped it might be true', Betjeman 'affirms his faith while fearing that it may be false'; a poem such as 'Before the Anaesthetic or A Real Fright' (1945) illustrates this 'dialectic' between an affirming and a rejecting spirit perfectly:

> And in the colour-shafted air
> I, kneeling, thought the Lord was there.
> Now, lying in the gathering mist
> I know that Lord did not exist;
>
> ('Before the Anaesthetic', ll. 45–48) [17]

There can be no doubt that this topic is central to any study of Betjeman and vital to setting his poetry in a post-Victorian context. His idealised Britain (typified in poems like 'Pot Pourri from a Surrey Garden' (1940)), where the Church of England is all-powerful and where it is perpetually Sunday afternoon in summertime, is merely the calm surface to a maelstrom of deeper angst. That angst continued to grow as Betjeman grew older and it is a tragic irony that, in 1972, just as his footsteps were starting to falter, he was appointed Poet Laureate. The pressures of this particular office were great for a man who believed in the power of Inspiration, and this meant that many of the poems relating to Royal Events (and so written 'to order') were not among his best. But the Betjeman oeuvre is a parabola of uneven form, for though it describes an arc through his development towards maturity, his zenith and ultimate decline, we will see that light would occasionally shine out until the very end.

This short introduction clarifies the importance of taking a chronological approach to Betjeman. Despite Sanders' judgment (cited at the beginning), the poet's approach to what he wrote *did* change over time, as did his subject matter – particularly in prose. However, after a decade-by-decade analysis, I will return to the 1960 verse-autobiography, *Summoned by Bells*. This may be seen as a 'memento, advertisement, and anthem for male youth', but it is also the most appropriate end point as, in many ways, it encapsulates the whole ethos of Betjeman, his make-up and the main emphases of his work.[18]

CHAPTER TWO

The 1930s

The Opening World[1]

While viewing a decade in isolation can be problematic, there are many critical works about the poetry and politics of the 1930s that accentuate its apparent independence. For Malcolm Muggeridge, it began with a 'phoney peace', ended with a 'phoney war' and thus 'fell neatly into one theme'.[2] But, as Valentine Cunningham reminds us, it was in 1930 that D. H. Lawrence died, the *Daily Worker* was founded, and Spender's *Twenty Poems*, Waugh's *Vile Bodies* and William Empson's *Seven Types of Ambiguity* were published; similarly, 1939 saw *New Verse* and *New Writing* both fold, W. B. Yeats pass away, and MacNeice produce his *Autumn Journal*, Spender his *Still Centre* and Isherwood his *Goodbye to Berlin*.[3]

It was also during the 1930s that John Betjeman began to flourish as a writer. Amid countless newspaper and magazine articles, he published two volumes of verse (1931 and 1937), an impassioned account of architectural taste (1933) and a collection of essays on the University of Oxford (1938); he became Assistant Editor of *The Architectural Review* (1930–34), conceived the *Shell Guides* (1932) and was employed as film critic on the *Evening Standard* (1934–35). This followed a term as a schoolmaster in Gerrard's Cross (1928), a brief spell as Private Secretary to Sir Horace Plunkett (1929) and a session of teaching at Heddon Court Prep School (1929–30). The start of Betjeman's literary life, then, clearly coincided with the start of the decade, though it was a start that at once jarred with the political writing of Auden, Spender and MacNeice, and aligned him more closely with contemporary novelists like Waugh.[4] Rather than the poet enlarging our sense of the 1930s, however, it will become apparent that what we know of the 1930s will enlarge our sense of the poet.

The Victorian nature of Betjeman's background and the relevance of his love of the unfashionable were clarified in CHAPTER ONE, but education also played a part in stimulating his taste. It was probably at Highgate School, between the ages of nine and eleven, that he first read Tennyson's *Idylls of the King* (1859), for example (he would go on to memorize much more by the great Laureate at the Dragon School in Oxford [1917–20]).[5] Furthermore, the Highgate archive holds a copy of Palgrave's *Junior Golden Treasury*, several of which were given as prizes in 1919. Though he missed the chance of winning one, it was here that his long relationship with the anthology doubtless began (by his death in 1984, he owned four different editions of the "adult" version, which he also named as the book choice for his 1975 appearance on BBC Radio 4's *Desert Island Discs*).[6] In contrast, the Dragon School produced its own poetry collection for pupils, which, though not published until 1935, nevertheless gives an idea of the poems that Betjeman would have been taught there fifteen years before. Among its pages are many favourites, such as William Allingham's 'Up the Airy Mountain' (1850) and C. S. Calverley's 'Waiting' (1872).[7]

In his early reading of Victorian verse, Betjeman was no doubt no different from tens of thousands of his contemporaries. However, the deviation in his 1930s attitudes towards nineteenth-century literature and architecture is interesting when one considers that just a few years before, while at Marlborough College (1920–1925), he seemed to favour neither. He admits in the preface to the second edition of *Ghastly Good Taste* (1970) that the era became a fascination at this time, but adds that he saw its buildings as 'purely imitative and rather vulgar'.[8] In 1923, Philip Harding recorded in the college's literary society minutes how Betjeman had read a paper proving 'to what artistic depths the Victorians had debased themselves'.[9] Of course, one has to know about something in order to mock it, but he also heaped scorn on the 1851 Great Exhibition and wrote (though did not publish) an 'Ode on a Mid-Victorian Centre Ornament', which began:

> Oh thou maid of buxom beauty!
>   Lifting up to hold the cake,
> An impossible creation,
>   Which is surely a mistake,
> I have often wept in thinking
>   How terribly your arms must ache.
>
> ('ODE ON A MID-VICTORIAN CENTRE ORNAMENT', LL. 1–6)

This was in spite of the Swinburnian stanzas that he claimed were then filling his brain (*Summoned by Bells*, p. 71). Hillier tries to rationalise the seeming inconstancy by suggesting that Betjeman 'passed through all the stages that James Laver has ascribed to style revivals: hostility, amused tolerance, romantic appreciation and scholarly investigation'. But, for the adolescent, *everything* is funny and humour can be such a good weapon against enemies and unpopularity that even one's loves can become valuable shield-targets. Indeed, the first part of Hillier's biography, *Young Betjeman* (1988), paints a picture of an individual who saw humour in so much that he must, on occasion, have been most irritating company. So, while mocking nineteenth-century literature (or at least some of it), note that it was also at Marlborough that Betjeman read, quoted, and corresponded with Lord Alfred Douglas.[10] It was here too that he discovered the poetry of fellow Old Marlburian William Morris, and James Elroy Flecker, whose brother Oswald taught English at the college.

Oxford, however, was to be entirely different. Here Betjeman met Auden, who came up to Christ Church in 1925 at the same time he arrived at Magdalen. Both would eventually study English, but as Betjeman wrote in 1938 (with some scorn), the subject in those days: '[was] really Anglo-Saxon, Northumbrian dialect and tedious mediaeval poems'.[11] Auden's interest in Anglo-Saxon put him closer to the 'beer and Beowulf' C. S. Lewis than Betjeman, his tutee, could ever have hoped to come. It was at Oxford that *he*, conversely:

> [. . .] learned to love
> That lord of landscape, Alfred Tennyson;
> There first heard Thomas Hardy's poetry,
> Master of metre, local as his lanes,
> The one expressive village fatalist.
>
> (*SUMMONED BY BELLS*, CHAPTER IX, P. 102)

Though Betjeman did not say so, the syllabus of the Oxford English school ended with the Romantics at that time, so by reading Victorian literature, he was a radical whether he liked it or not (and Lewis did *not* like it). An unsent letter to Lewis (dated 13 December 1939) pinpoints the disparity between the two:

> [t]he difference of our views comes out clearly in your book on Spenser. Nowhere in that excellent book do you say anything appreciative about Spenser's amazing powers of topographical description [. . .].
>
> :   :   :   :   :
>
> Probably to you, the opening of Tennyson's 'Princess' is just funny, while to me it is moving and good. Probably you prefer the 'Wreck of the Deutschland', which I cannot understand, to [Hopkins's] 'Epithalamion' [. . .].[12]

While Humphrey Carpenter claims that Harold Acton invented the post-Great War 'Victorian renaissance' in 1922, and despite Betjeman's (much) later assertion about Tennyson and Hardy, it is evident that he had an independent, broad (if not totally well-disposed) knowledge of nineteenth-century matters before he came up to Magdalen.[13] By the time his first volume of verse appeared in 1931, his connoisseur interest in Victorian *poetry*, at least, was clear.

Chapel and Spa

It was in the May of that year that Edward James, artist and patron, announced his intention to publish his old Oxford friend, whom he saw as 'the only real literary talent' of his generation.[14] With such a co-conspirator, it was perhaps natural that great importance would be placed on how the book would look on the shelf. After dismissing the idea of using 'a type in awfully bad taste –

possibly an abortive gothic', due to its suitability for only '60 or 70 per cent' of the poems, James thus settled on two options.[15] The first was that a selection of typefaces be used, tailored to each piece ('which would be extremely amusing if successfully carried out'); the second, less preferable idea, was to use 'one dull, sober, non-commital type' throughout. Betjeman opted for the latter, and while James may have mildly disappointed, the end product undoubtedly imparted the feeling of quality that he had sought. As he wrote:

> I suggest that the paper be fairly good and the cover nicely executed, so that while the book may present an epitome of everything that is the worst taste in type and decoration, yet there be an underlying feeling that the whole is well-produced. We must not allow the outside world one moment to doubt the deep intensity of our sophistication.

One wonders whether anyone else would have got the joke, but, as *Summoned by Bells* implies, it probably didn't matter:

> At William Morris how we laughed,
>   And hairy tweeds and knitted ties:
> Pub poets who from tankards quaff'd
>   Glared up at us with angry eyes-
> For, Regency before our time,
> We first found Cheltenham sublime.
>
> Ah how the trivial would enchant!
>   On our Botanic Gardens walk
> We touched the tender Sensitive Plant
>   And saw the fronds enfold the stalk
> At each light blow our fingers dealt-
> So very like ourselves, we felt.
>
> (SUMMONED BY BELLS, CHAPTER IX, P. 108)

The cover shows 'a Persian engraving of a tight-waisted lady telephoning'.[16] Two separate editions were available and both – lady aside – were equally eye-catching: the deluxe, retailing at a hefty 12s 6d, was limited to 100 copies and included patterned end papers and blue and gold quatrefoil paper binding; the more modestly priced version (5s 6d) had a simpler red and black striped paper lining. Comparing this with the 1931 figures for weekly unemployment pay (17s for a man; 9s for his wife, plus 2s for each child) shows that *Mount Zion* would have been an expensive luxury indeed. This is surely one reason why it did not sell widely, which in turn partly explains why, to James's despair, Betjeman gave away so many copies gratis.[17]

The book's internal appearance was as startling as its exterior: as Pryce-Jones noted in his *London Mercury* review, it was 'printed on alternate, or roughly alternate, sheets of pink, or roughly pink, and green paper, bound up in those papers which are usually seen on indoor fireworks, and printed in blue and brown inks'.[18] It was originally to be called *Chapel and Spa*, which, being shrewdly indicative of the contents (and much of the rest of Betjeman's oeuvre), should perhaps have been retained.[19] But while we may wonder why the change of heart, Hillier speculates that Gwendolen Green's 1930 volume of the same name may have inspired the final choice, just as the subtitle was doubtless derived from Ralph Waldo Trine's *In Tune with the Infinite* (1898).[20] Of course, 'Mount Zion' is also a hymn tune by Arthur Sullivan, and is one of several cited by Thomas Hardy in his poem 'The Chapel-Organist' (l. 46). Betjeman was surely aware of this, but his interest in printing, binding and design overshadows the possibility of the reference and suggests that he was more a pseudo-1890s aesthete who had failed to grow up at this point. Yet the material within often belies such posturing, as the opener, 'Death in Leamington' (1930), illustrates.

This famous 'spa' piece, with its 'death on the one hand, [. . .] precise place on the other', encapsulates what Philip Larkin felt to be the quintessential Betjeman.[21] The building therein, with 'stucco [. . .] peeling' (l. 21) as plaster drops from its 'yellow Italianate arches' (l. 23), seems to be in sympathy with the central character in what can only be described as an architectural pathetic fallacy. It also provides a good example of how Victorian poetry formed Betjeman's early verse, for though the 'chintzy cheeriness' (l. 19) could be a fleeting reference to Morris, it is Dante Gabriel Rossetti's 'My Sister's Sleep' that may be detected most strongly here.

Unfortunately, proving that Betjeman read this poem is difficult. First published in *The New Monthly Belle Assemblée* for September 1848, it reappeared in *The Germ* in January 1850 and (with several emendations) in the 1870 edition of Rossetti's poems. The problem is that there are no records of Betjeman having ever owned copies of these works – nor any of the anthologies in which it was included.[22] However, he did own a first edition of Evelyn Waugh's 1928 biography, *Rossetti: His Life and Works*, which contains a reference to 'My Sister's Sleep' on page 155.[23] Though signed and dated by the author in 1946, Hillier notes that Betjeman's visit to Rossetti's Birchington grave may have been due to his being 'alerted to its existence' by Waugh's study.[24] The trip was made during Betjeman's employment as Private Secretary to the Irish politician and agricultural reformer, Sir Horace Plunkett, so it must have occurred between January and March 1929; this makes the case for claiming that 'My Sister's Sleep' was on his mind as he wrote 'Death in Leamington' a touch stronger.

While they do not share poetic form (Rossetti uses that later made famous by *In Memoriam*; Betjeman employs a simple ABCB rhyme scheme), the subject matter is common to both verses and is differentiated only by age, 'Leamington' describing the demise of an old woman, 'My Sister's Sleep' that of a comparatively young one. Furthermore, the reader enters the narrative *after* the deaths have occurred in each case:

> She died in the upstairs bedroom
>   By the light of the ev'ning star
> That shone through the plate glass window
>   From over Leamington Spa.
>
>   ('DEATH IN LEAMINGTON', LL. 1–4)

> She fell asleep on Christmas Eve:
>   At length the long-ungranted shade
>   Of weary eyelids overweigh'd
> The pain nought else might yet relieve.
>
>   ('MY SISTER'S SLEEP', LL. 1–4)[25]

Only the reader has the advantage of the characters at this moment: in 'Leamington', the nurse does not realise that her ward is dead until she sees the 'gray, decaying face' at the 'silent bedstead' in the penultimate stanza; similarly, Rossetti's Margaret falls asleep 'on Christmas Eve', but it is not until the after Twelve has struck (l. 25) that the mother notices her daughter's state is permanent.

It is also clear that Margaret is more fortunate in terms of love and consideration: she has a mother who had 'leaned all day / Over the bed from chime to chime' and a brother so upset at his sister's death that he has to hide his face (l. 49); moreover, there is a hint that more family members are waiting in the room above (ll. 37–40). The Leamington woman has only a nurse, who goes about her business 'alone with her own little soul', working automatically, as the repetition of the feminine pronoun in the fourth stanza indicates:

> She bolted the big round window,
>   She let the blinds unroll,
> She set a match to the mantel,
>   She covered the fire with coal.
>
>   ('DEATH IN LEAMINGTON', LL. 13–16)

Although the 'Half dead and half alive!' refrain at the end of Betjeman's next stanza doubtless refers to the link between decaying building and decayed owner, it is difficult to suppress the feeling that it is about the nurse herself, who seems to be wrapped up in routine. Indeed, it is at this point that the tone of 'Death in Leamington' changes, with the narrator breaking off from description before breaking in to the narrative:

> Do you know that the stucco is peeling?
>   Do you know that the heart will stop?
> From those yellow Italianate arches
>   Do you hear the plaster drop?
>
>   ('DEATH IN LEAMINGTON', LL. 21–24)

Here is the inherent bond between people and place that Larkin recognised, and it is immediately after this impassioned exhortation that the nurse at last looks at 'the silent bedstead'. Thus 'the table of bottles' is moved away and, 'tiptoeing gently', she turns down the gas in the hall – an old-fashioned gesture of respect for the dead (though Derek Stanford's note that this is 'a ritualistic touch' may indicate a still-prevalent degree of detachment).[26]

Close attention to detail is another common factor between the poems. In *The Poetry of Dante Gabriel Rossetti* (1981), Joan Rees quotes her subject's own memoir in which he wrote that he had deliberately used '"homely externals"' in 'My Sister's Sleep' to 'bring out "the inner soul of the subject"'.[27] This is evident in the bedroom where the scene takes place:

> Through the small room, with subtle sound
> Of flame, by vents the fireshine drove
> And reddened. In its dim alcove
> The mirror shed a clearness round.
>
> ('MY SISTER'S SLEEP', LL. 17–20)[28]

This is intimate, warm and even cosy – reflecting the love of the family in contrast to the cold December night outside. In 'Death in Leamington', Betjeman too employs the minutiae, the every day items no longer required, to emphasise the situation, showing at the same time that he was capable of using more than architecture to reflect the people in his poems. Thus we have the 'tea-things' and the 'stands and chairs' in addition to the 'table of bottles'. Most striking, perhaps, is the 'lonely crochet' which 'Lay patiently and unstirred', and which will now remain so.

Such consideration of the elderly served to distance Betjeman from the Auden set. As Cunningham notes, it was during the 1930s that the concept of 'the youth' arrived, and Auden's *The Orators*, published in May 1932 when he was just 25, was undeniably 'for youths, about youths, by a youth'.[29] Betjeman's counter to this is furthered by the highly sympathetic piece 'For Nineteenth-Century Burials':

> This cold weather
> Carries so many old people away.
> Quavering voices and blankets and breath
> Go silent together.
> The gentle fingers are touching to pray
> Which crumple and straighten for Death.
> These cold breezes
> Carry the bells away on the air,
> Stuttering tales of Gothic, and pass,
> Catching new grave flowers into their hair,
> Beating the chapel and red-coloured glass.
>
> ('FOR NINETEENTH-CENTURY BURIALS', LL. 1–11)

As the breeze carries away the lives of the elderly, so it beats the chapel and scatters 'grave flowers'. Indeed, the poem seems to challenge the ability of religion to offer succour: the sound of the bells is not spread by the wind, note, but *dispersed*. This points to Betjeman's later wrangles with Faith and Doubt, but there is also more than an echo of Hardy's 'Afterwards' (1917) here, which, with its reference to 'the wind-warped upland thorn' (l. 7), covers similar ground, although Hardy's 'crossing breeze cuts a pause' in the 'outrollings' of the 'bell of quittance' in *his* last stanza. Betjeman, however, clearly used to notice such things.

In 'Competition', he notices something quite different and reveals himself to be something of a schism-spotting satirist:

> The Independent Calvinistic   1810
>   Methodist Chapel is gone,
> Dust in the galleries, dust on the stairs,
>   There was no one to carry it on.
> And a Norman New Jerusalem Church   1840
>   Was raised on the sacred site,
> Where they praised the Lord and praised the Lord
>   By incandescent light.
> ('COMPETITION', LL. 1–8)

From this glow, we progress to the Gothic of 1860, go on to a Wesley Memorial Church and end up at 'Mount Carmel Baptists (Strict)' of 1875. Betjeman's knowledge of the varieties of English Protestantism – and their architecture – is clear, while references to electric lighting and central heating presage the satires on non-spirituality in *Poems in the Porch* (1954 – see CHAPTER FOUR). But the touch of 'Competition' is light and one gets the impression that Betjeman, though mocking nineteenth-century sectarian rivalry, is more than half in love with the diversity it created.

Half-love is certainly not evident in the poem now known as 'Hymn', however. Neither chapel nor spa, it is one of the rare instances in *Mount Zion* where Betjeman the architectural critic and Betjeman the poet become one. Unfortunately, the present title seems to play into the hands of those who agree with Grigson that he was no more than a 'parodist of the modes of *Hymns Ancient and Modern*'.[30] In fact, Betjeman's compositional process often involved melodies. Writing to Frank Rutherford in 1954, for example, he listed those which were in his head 'constantly': as well as indeed 'a good many tunes' from *A&M* and the *Methodist Hymnal*, were also 'Hyfrydol', 'Tea For Two' and 'Over the Sea to Skye'.[31] Grigson's further accusation that the form is 'limited in its aims and expressions, and disfigured by sentimentality, inflexible metres, self-congratulation, and religiosity', is also inappropriate to 'Hymn', which is set quite deliberately to the tune of 'The Church's One Foundation' in order to produce ironic effects.[32]

It was first published in *Isis* on 24 October 1928 as 'To the Blessed St

Aubin', but its satiric force came fully to the fore on its second appearance in *The Architectural Review* (February 1930). Here, it was introduced with the idea that, while the 'Roman Church' 'is a good patron no longer', '[i]n the English Church [. . .], we can look back to those wonderful 'eighties, when all the artistic talent of England united in bringing about a second and more glorious Restoration'.[33] While *Isis* readers were requested to sing the piece 'as reverently as possible', the more knowledgeable audience of the 'Archie Rev' was merely incited to sing 'loudly'. The punning title was also unnecessary: *they* knew the target was the architect and church "restorer" J. P. St. Aubyn (1815–95) and his ilk. But the change to 'The Church's Restoration' was not mirrored by any change in content, for the original, hard-hitting, third stanza remained intact:

> Church furnishing! Church furnishing!
>> Come, MOWBRAY, swell the praise!
> He gave the brass for burnishing,
>> He gave the thick red baize,
> He gave the new addition,
>> Pull'd down the dull old aisle,
> – To pave the sweet transition
>> He gave th'encaustic tile.

Both 'brass' and 'down' are very emphatic in the melody, falling on stressed high notes, and this serves to accentuate the parody very compellingly. In the 1970 preface to *Ghastly Good Taste*, Betjeman explained why the second line was changed to 'Sing art and crafty praise!' (which is how it appeared in the *Shell Guide to Cornwall* (1934)): 'Mowbrays [sic] at the time objected to their name being used, because they thought it detrimental to their church-furnishing business.'[34] Betjeman's irritation is understandable from a poet's point of view (the amendment reads like a flimsy criticism of Morris & Co) but not from a businessman's: the firm is clearly indicted throughout the rest of the stanza, despite the fact that, in terms of the poem's internal logic, its only crime is to supply the "restorer" with contemporary fittings.

The Reverend Samuel Stone wrote 'The Church's One Foundation' in 1866, during the controversy over Bishop Colenso of Natal's heresy. Its 7.6.7.6 metre is, for J. R. Watson, a 'stomping' rhythm (respected by S. S. Wesley's very foursquare tune 'Aurelia'), which provides 'a formidable example of a strong Anglican hymn'.[35] Colenso had doubted the accuracy of the Pentateuch and, although he was acquitted in 1869, Stone was inspired to look at the Church as it might be perceived from the outside.[36] 'Hymn' sees Betjeman attempt to look at the church from the *inside*, with the emphasis this time on *architectural* schism. There is thus a parallel between Betjeman and Stone beyond the similarity of form, although that similarity is also worthy of attention. Aside from the obvious opening line ('The church's restoration/one foundation') connection, for instance, consider the endings of the respective first verses. That of 'Foundation' closes with this reference to Christ:

> From heaven he came and sought her
> To be his holy bride,
> With his own blood he bought her
> And for her life he died.

Betjeman finishes his first stanza with the sarcastic comment that the restored church is a 'Memorial of the good work / Of him who planned it all'. When read side-by-side with 'Foundation', the effect somewhat stronger than mere sarcasm: who, after all, could compare favourably with Christ? And though this is verging on the profane, it certainly makes the point that the restoration work is the real blasphemy.

Stone's rhyming of 'glorious' with 'victorious' (verse 4) is alluded to by Betjeman's coupling of 'uproarious' with 'glorious', once again showing that the poem's bathos is more pronounced when read in conjunction with its model. In addition, the 'encaustic tile' is, like the 'varnishéd pitch-pine', a practical detail that threatens to puncture the rhetoric, and so re-assert the notion of secularity. The message is hammered home at the end as, when sung to the original tune, the 'humble' of Betjeman's final stanza provides a counterpoint by falling on the highest (and thus most emphatic) note. This gives it a disconcerting prominence, and one wonders whether anyone has ever been able to sing 'The Church's One Foundation' with sincerity after reading 'Hymn'.

As its title suggests, Betjeman also applied religious metre to 'An Eighteenth Century Calvinistic Hymn', which follows an anapaestic 8.9.8.9 rhythm. The main lyrical inspiration, however, seems to have come from William Gadsby's *Selections: A Selection of Hymns for Public Worship* (1814). Hillier recognises this, singling out the work of Joseph Hart (1712–68) as being the writer closest to the poem in tone:

> Poor wretched worthless worm!
> In what sad plight I stand!
> When good I would perform
> Then evil is at hand.[37]

The resemblance is redolent:

> I am not too sure of my Worth,
> Indeed it is tall as a Palm;
> But what Fruits can it ever bring forth
> When Leprosy sits at the Helm?
> :　　　:　　　:　　　:　　　:
> Oh! I bless the good Lord for my Boils
> For my mental and bodily pains,

For without them my Faith all congeals
And I'm doomed to HELL'S NE'ER-ENDING FLAMES
('An Eighteenth Century Calvinistic Hymn', ll. 5–8; 13–16)

The blessing of the Lord for one's 'Boils' is probably a reference to Job, while the final block capitals recall a fanatical "fire and brimstone" preacher, the like of whom would once have terrified small children. In truth, the language is so overdone that it is difficult to read the poem with a straight face; never was the phrase "grimly jocular" more appropriate, and the effect is only increased by the proximity of 'Leprosy' (l. 8) and 'Backgammon' (l. 11) to those boils.

It is also significant that the rhythm goes well to 'Trewin', a Welsh tune set to several hymns by the staunch Calvinist, Augustus Montague Toplady (1740–78) – including 'A Debtor to Mercy Alone'. So well does it fit in fact that Toplady *must* have been on the poet's mind at the time of composition. Indeed, Candida Lycett Green has revealed that her father nurtured a 'lifelong interest' in the man.[38] His bookshelves 'groaned' with Calvinistic writings generally, but would Betjeman have needed so many volumes just to affirm what must, given the tone of the poem, have been disdain? Well, perhaps so: writing about R. S. Thomas in 1955, he commented that a number of 'good Welsh writers' had been 'driven to satire and contempt by the narrow Calvinism of mercenary peasantry'. Moreover, 'Poor Morgan' (of Thomas's 'The Minister' – 'well versed' in said theology) 'mistrusted beauty in scenery [and] women'.[39] Hardly Betjemanian, one must concede! Later still, in 'N.W.5 & N.W.6' (1958), he would describe his relationship with a Calvinist nursemaid, from whom he caught his 'terror' (l. 30) and 'guilt at endlessness' (l. 27). This was to have a lasting significance, as we shall see.

It should be clear that Betjeman enjoyed a mastery of poetic technique, using metre for pastiche and parody with considerable élan. Carpenter adds that by cloaking 'his most serious observations in comic form', Betjeman was ensuring 'that people would at least listen to them'.[40] Dennis Brown takes this further, claiming that the poet's 'traditional (finally oral) modes of linguistic communication' allow for 'a comfort structure [. . .], even when the content is disturbing'.[41] As noted in CHAPTER ONE, for Kingsley Amis this quality was encapsulated first in 'Croydon', which, as Patrick Taylor-Martin agrees, 'is not simply a facile piece of mock-Victorian sentimentalising, as a superficial reading might suggest':

> In a house like that
>   Your Uncle Dick was born;
>   Satchel on back he walked to Whitgift
>   Every weekday morn.
>
> ('Croydon', ll. 1–4)[42]

Here we have 'people and place' again, as well as a link to childhood in the form of the satchel. However, in his review of *Mount Zion*, Alan Pryce-Jones used the poem in an attempt to explain Betjeman's 'new attitude', which, he said, 'is a variation of what the late eighteenth century called "horrour"'. That is, at the thought of 'Croydon, the Low Church, gas, an Irish peer in a bog [etc.]', Betjeman's sensibility 'becomes horrid'.[43] 'Westgate-on-Sea' is then cited as an example of an instance where this horror 'bristles' as Betjeman becomes 'amused at the spectacle of himself in a rage'. Yet the 'Happy bells of eighteen-ninety' in that piece also recall the 'laurel, shrubs and privet. / Red geraniums in flower' of Croydon, while the 'minarets' of the first stanza remind us of those that reach a 'tapering summit' in Father Prout's 'The Bells of Shandon' (1834, l. 31).[44] Pryce-Jones remained oblivious to this, and quotes the following in order to make his point:

> Church of England bells of Westgate!
> On this balcony I stand,
> White the woodwork wriggles round me,
> Clock towers rise on either hand.
>
> For me in my timber arbour
> You have one more message yet,
> "Plimsolls, plimsolls in the summer,
> Oh goloshes in the wet!"
>
> ('WESTGATE-ON-SEA', LL. 21–28)

In fact, this collapse into bathos is closer to C. S. Calverley's 'Waiting' (1872):

> "Hush! Hark! I see a towering form!
> From the dim distance slowly rolled
> It rocks like lilies in a storm,
> And O, its hues are green and gold:
>
> "It comes, it comes! Ah rest is sweet,
> And there is rest, my babe, for us!"
> She ceased, as at her very feet
> Stopped the St. John's Wood omnibus.
>
> (CALVERLEY, 'WAITING', LL. 21–28)[45]

As with 'Croydon', there are references to childhood in 'Westgate-on-Sea', but here they prepare us for that final joke on the rhythm of the bells, as in the third stanza, where the focus shifts from describing the church itself to the children that the narrator can see from his vantage point in the tower. Thereafter, those to whom the feet 'that scamper on the asphalt' belong slowly start to take over. Their concerns are for 'prunes and suet' and keeping a perennially running nose in check, and Betjeman's neat juxtaposition of the 'wire around their glasses' and the 'wire across their teeth' gives a clearer indication that a "punchline" is imminent than the reader gets from Calverley. It does not come as *much* of a surprise, therefore, that the woodwork 'wriggles' and that the tone has been coloured to such an extent by childhood memories that the peal of bells merely provides the tune for a daft ditty (ll. 27–28).

Like Pryce-Jones, many of Betjeman's first reviewers were also his friends; thus the most sympathetic notice came from his old Oxford chum, Randolph Churchill.[46] 'If you like the genuine sublimation of the ridiculous,' he wrote, 'you should read these poems,' adding that '[the] book contains some of the wittiest satires that have been produced for some time.' The anonymous critic of the *Times Literary Supplement* agreed, noting that some of the 'humours of ecclesiastical life in the period [. . .] are touched off in a delightful hand'.[47] However, he also refers to the work as 'a little book of verse' with a quaint title. Betjeman was quite happy to make such comments himself (he had written to Tom Driberg on 10 November 1931 to present him with 'his precious little work'), but would not have enjoyed a similar remark coming from another quarter.[48] There, of course, is the rub, for those who exist in an attitude of humour are apt to be plagued by it even when being serious. It also tends, in poetic terms, to be associated with the lightweight and ephemeral; and on the whole, Betjeman's acquaintances *did* tend to regard *Mount Zion* as a purely comic creation (even in the present century, old friends like Wilhelmine Harrod feel happy to describe him as a 'sort of joke we all knew').[49]

Yet it seems that he enjoyed playing up to this in his work, many of the poems, such as 'The 'Varsity Students' Rag', conforming to the expectation. 'The Wykehamist' is another piece in this idiom, though Betjeman was not alone in lampooning Winchester scholars. In 'A Happy New Year' (1933), for instance, Auden also mocked the extreme intellectual arrogance once associated with the breed.[50] Betjeman's 'rather dirty' academic obliterates the autumn glow 'with heavy baize', happy to settle down to the edifying subject of Norman fonts; such were favourite targets of Betjeman's circle (including Maurice Bowra, who, as an undergraduate at New College, would have met all-too-many Wykehamists). But humour is a many-faceted trait, as its emphasis in 'Camberley' illustrates. This poem, though first published in *Mount Zion*, has a direct link to its author's work for *The Architectural Review*; for entertainment, Betjeman and his colleagues at the journal often submitted correspondence purporting to be from angry readers – a device used mainly to send up what was generally regarded as good taste. One of their characters was H. Bardsley Brushing, of Poonah Punkah, Kenilworth Avenue, Camberley, who was obviously a near neighbour of the poem's Kittiwake family (of Enniscorthy Drive, Poonah Punkah Park).[51]

Colonel Kittiwake is a caricatured imperialist, who bears an unusually striking resemblance to Field-Marshal Lord Chetwode, Betjeman's future father-in-law (though the poem is slightly too early for this to be more than coincidence). The setting is lushly suburban – the 'cosy little bungalow' being set beneath 'Surrey pines' – but there is a tangible harshness about the place: visitors are reminded to 'mind the terrier' (notoriously tenacious beasts), while the monument to Clive of India also gives the impression of a family (or at least a *man*) who would be happier keeping the natives in order. The choice of 'Enniscorthy' as a street name is interesting too, as this is in County Wexford, Ireland, which seems to be at odds with the almost serene calm of the setting and may indicate a certain Celtic fervour about the Colonel. Poor Mrs Kittiwake, who clearly needs the friend that the narrator is trying to find for her, is the veritable underclass of 'Coolgreena': hers may be the pink and mauve décor, but even the maid 'is less likely to take the blame' than she. This reference to gender/class emancipation is unexpected – the maid has power, and the poem makes it plain that spillages caused by visitors who ring the doorbell at inopportune moments will not be cleared up by *her*. Another discernible sting in the tail, but such sophistication was not enough to ensure that *Mount Zion* sold – there were simply too few (rich) people who wanted to laugh with Betjeman as he wallowed in 'horrour'. This, however, was soon to change.

Bourgeois Verses

Like Edward James, John Murray had been a friend of Betjeman's at Oxford. The two had kept in touch and, though there were problems to overcome (not least the poet's agreement with both James and one Reginald Hutchings, who had been told the next book would be his), by September 1936 Betjeman was in a position to send Murray a list of verses for consideration.[52] *Continual Dew*, the volume that arose from these negotiations, was duly published on 2 November 1937.[53]

It retailed at 7s 6d and comparing this once more with the level of weekly unemployment pay (17s for a man; 10s for his wife, plus 3s for each child in 1939 – scarcely above the 1931 figures cited earlier) shows that Betjeman's product was still being aimed at the wealthy.[54] If Julian Symons's figures are accurate, this policy was not nearly so lucrative as Auden's, whose *Poems* (1930) had sold 1,000 copies by 1933. Issued in simple paper covers, it also cost only 2s 6d – five shillings less than *Continual Dew*. Its augmented and cloth-bound second edition, published that November (5s), sold so well that an extra print run of 1,500 was required by September 1934, followed by another for 1,517 three years later.[55] *Continual Dew* nevertheless reached many more people than its predecessor: 2,014 were printed, of which, after deductions for the author, libraries, the press and so on, 1,913 were available for retail. The start was promising, with 538 having been sold by the end of the year, followed by a further 220 during the next. The early stages of the war witnessed a dip to an average of 114 copies every twelve months, although things picked up in 1943 (273 copies) and 1944 (355), after which the book was sold out.[56] Betjeman was evidently starting to attract readers who were neither reviewers nor friends.

The hint of surrealism that coloured *Mount Zion* was to remain. E. McKnight Kauffer's cover, for instance, shows a hand with leaves sprouting from the wrist, reaching down thorough a rainy sky. This is presumably another pun, the title itself being derived from *The Book of Common Prayer*: 'pour upon us the continual dew of thy blessing'.[57] While the picture may also refer to the fecundity of the poetry within, the joke is sustained on the title page, which includes a section drawing of a tap. Removing the dust jacket reveals the publisher's binding, on which, in a mock-Victorian font, the title is emblazoned in gold block lettering (along with stylised gilt clasps at the corners). The page-edges are gilded, and there is a central section printed on thin Indian paper of a type often used for prayer-books. The poems on the blue bond that constitutes the rest of the volume begin with the sort of illuminated capital that one would also find in a book of hymns. The importance of religion is apparent in the poetry as well, but such visual punning follows on from the previous book in a way that is fitting, given the overlap of content between the two: no fewer than fourteen *Mount Zion* poems found a home in *Continual Dew*. Many are not as funny today as they probably were to a late 1930s audience, but what kind of audience would this have been?[58]

The *New Statesman and Nation* published the first review of the book (by Peter Quennell) on 13 November 1937. Its title, 'Flowers of Mediocrity', was presumably a nod to Baudelaire's *Les Fleurs du mal* (1857), a play which suggests mediocrity to be worse than evil.[59] Quennell, though, was referring not to the verses, but the 'the characteristic eeriness of modern life' about which he writes at length. It is in *this* world that he felt 'the modern poet finds an epitome of horror' (that word again). Indeed, when he finally gets round to the work he is reviewing, he notes that Betjeman's speciality is to use his 'remarkable wit and facility' to observe the 'second-rate' and uncover 'the deep essential vulgarity, of modern industrial civilisation'. A 'mixture of love and hatred is the poet's strength', thus 'Slough' – with its vitriolic invective – is much less successful than 'Death in Leamington' (which Quennell 'cannot refrain' from quoting).

Evelyn Waugh, writing in *Night and Day*, appreciated that '*Continual Dew* contains all that was best in *Mount Zion*'.[60] He felt it was in the new poems that '[t]he same limited range of mood and subject matter finds rather more finished expression', despite the fact that '[n]o poem, except "Tunbridge Wells" [an old one], comes within measurable distance of artistic finish'. This is typical Waugh, though he is wise to recognise that much of Betjeman's verse is at its best when recited (in a style which should near, in his opinion, an 'epileptic animation'): 'only thus can the apostrophic syntax, the black-bottom rhythms, the Delphic climaxes, the panting ineptitude of the transitions be seen in their true values'. This seems unnecessarily snide: the reference to jazz time signatures has merit, but while one must admit that not every poem is brilliant, 'panting ineptitude' is perhaps going too far. However, as all but one brief paragraph of this review of *two* books is devoted to *Continual Dew*, it is clear that Waugh does favour Betjeman's second offering to an extent.

A seemingly better notice came from 'Beachcomber' (aka J. B. Morton), who remarked in *The Listener* that the poet wrote 'in a manner which is a blend of the early Sitwells and an intelligent Oxford don (if such not be a contradiction in terms)'.[61] There is worthy praise in the shrewd remark that 'he has a vigour of his own, and a trick of sudden contrast' and while seeing that the tone of *Continual Dew* 'is never serious for long', Morton correctly observes that, in 'Croydon', 'the joke is deferred, and many a Croydon exile in lands beyond the waves, reading these lines, will see, through a mist of tears, the dear old gasworks, the goods-yard and the public library'. An early hint of the Laureate of the future, perhaps. Shame, then, that Morton concludes by admitting that he felt the poet to be 'painfully self-conscious'.

The most interesting point about these three reviews is not so much what they do say, but what they do not. Generalisations apart, there are almost twice as many references to ex-*Mount Zion* poems as purely *Continual Dew* examples. This makes it hard to assess the audience reaction to Betjeman's mid- to late-1930s output specifically, but it does give the impression that the book was a sort of *Collected Poems*-in-miniature. The implication is that Betjeman had not developed in the intervening six years, and though the work does not always bear this out, the religious poems do illustrate where the overlap shows an *extension* rather than a progression. Thus 'Competition', 'The Sandemanian Meeting-House in Highbury Quadrant', 'An Eighteenth-Century Calvinistic Hymn' and 'For Nineteenth-Century Burials' are repeated, while 'Our Padre' (a newer piece) spoofs a generic ex-forces chaplain, who still 'wears medals and a stole' and who still has the strength and resolve to 'Row like smoke' for the shore. Similarly, 'Exchange of Livings', a dialogue between two "incumbents", hints at clerical commercialisation.[62] 'Undenominational', however, is from quite a different mould:

> UNDENOMINATIONAL
> But still the church of God
> He stood in his conventicle
> And ruled it with a rod.
>
> ('UNDENOMINATIONAL', LL. 1–4)

For Derek Stanford, this is a 'small but apt postscript on revivalist religion', but the tone is actually very difficult to gauge: do the lamps which 'within their brackets shook' indicate the volume of the hymns being sung or a certain religious trepidation, for example?[63] The opening stanza, and indeed the title itself, undoubtedly suggests that sectarianism is unimportant to God. This is a theme to which Betjeman would return in 'Remorse' (1953):

> Protestant claims and Catholic, the wrong and the right of them,
> Unimportant they seem in the face of death–
>
> ('REMORSE', LL. 9–10)[64]

'Undenominational' also has a hint of Calvinism about it, yet while the 'lone conventicle' is an acknowledged 'beacon in the dark', and while the poem ends with glory in the narrator's soul, the idea of 'Revival' running 'along the hedge' conjures thoughts of fire – an oddly hellish image in this context. There is *more* than a hint of Hardy here, though, as the hymn tunes listed in the third stanza betray:

> "Glory" "Gopsal" "Russell Place"
> "Wrestling Jacob" "Rock"
> "Saffron Walden" "Safe at Home"
> "Dorking" "Plymouth Dock"
>
> ('UNDENOMINATIONAL', LL. 9–12)

Compare this with those named by Hardy in 'The Chapel-Organist' ('the Old-Hundredth, Saint Stephen's, / Mount Zion, New Sabbath, Miles-Lane, Holy Rest, and Arabia, and Eaton', ll. 45–46) and note that Betjeman does not repeat any of his forebear's selection. It is possible that this was deliberate, so that, while using Hardy's technique, Betjeman retained his individuality by choosing more obscure hymns – at least in comparison to 'the Old-Hundredth'.

Given this religious emphasis, it is reasonable to assume that the three poems printed on prayer-book paper have special significance, particularly as they are lifted further from the rest by the lack of page numbers.[65] Sadly, such ethereality is not supported by the poetry. 'Calvinistic Evensong', for instance, simply revisits familiar ground, while 'Exeter' is most interesting for its architectural references, as in 'Wulfric's altar and riddel posts' ('riddel posts' being a 'signature' of Ninian Comper – of whom more later).[66] Both are enhanced by Osbert Lancaster's artwork (which owes a little to Morris's Kelmscott Press), but it is the first of the trio, 'Dorset', which is most noteworthy as it continues the Hardy theme. For Donald Davie, it is an 'imitation' of 'Friends Beyond':[67]

> RIME Intrinsica, Fontmell Magna, Sturminster Newton and Melbury Bubb
> Whist upon whist upon whist upon whist drive, in Institute, Legion and Social Club.
> Horny hands that hold the aces which this morning held the plough
> While Tranter Reuben, T. S. Eliot, H. G. Wells and Edith Sitwell lie in Mellstock
>   Churchyard now.
>
> (BETJEMAN, 'DORSET', LL. 1–4)

> WILLIAM DEWY, Tranter Reuben, Farmer Ledlow late at plough,
>   Robert's kin, and John's, and Ned's,
> And the Squire, and Lady Susan, lie in Mellstock Churchyard now!
>
> (HARDY, 'FRIENDS BEYOND', LL. 1–3)[68]

Betjeman uses the setting of Mellstock (Stinsford), the essence of the last line of Hardy's first stanza and Tranter Reuben (who also appears in *Under the Greenwood Tree* (1872)) to indicate his poem's provenance, but, as we shall see with 'Love in a Valley', he adopts this framework in order to set a totally different scene. Thus in Hardy the narrator imagines a 'group of local hearts and heads' (l. 4) whispering to him in the churchyard: they converse, offer advice even, and play a proactive role in the proceedings. In Betjeman, Tranter Reuben *et al.* are relegated to giving a sense of constancy and *inevitability*: the gloved hands that 'hold the hymn book', and which earlier 'milked the cow' (l. 7), will eventually join those luminaries in the cemetery, all equal in the eyes of God: 'From the aisles each window smiles', note, 'on grave *and* grass *and* yew tree bough' (l. 11 – my italics).

Donald Davie is infuriated by Betjeman's footnote that the names he quotes are 'not put in out of malice or satire but merely for their euphony'.[69] This 'puffs such a dense vapour of self-consciousness about the poet's relationship to his readers that behind it the lineaments of the poem as in any way a considered utterance entirely disappear'. However, the comment makes too much of a juvenile squib intended mainly to amuse his friends – the poem was first published in December 1932, when Betjeman was still only 26, after all.[70] Indeed, the real euphony surely comes from the chiming Dorset village names (was ever a place more deserving of poetic immortality than Rime Intrinsica?)[71] Written during a visit to the county in July 1928, it reads like a future guide-book writer's view of the place: names are espied from road signs as they whiz past (Betjeman was fined for speeding during the trip), while traditional pastoral scenes are both noted and imagined as he allows himself to be receptive to the sorts of things that his Wykehamist would probably have missed.[72]

This, of course, is a world apart from the first poem in *Continual Dew*. 'The Arrest of Oscar Wilde at the Cadogan Hotel' actually dates from 1933, when it appeared in the *Oxford and Cambridge* magazine's Summer Number, having been famously rejected from *New Verse* by Grigson for being too 'smart and frivolous'.[73] Though Betjeman preferred to remember Wilde's halcyon days, and though humour does play an undeniable part in the proceedings, the figure of Wilde is tragic enough to suggest a parallel between the poem and 'Death in Leamington'.[74] Technically, the two share both rhyme and three-stress rhythm, but the connections are such that 'The Arrest' might equally be called 'The Death of Oscar Wilde'. There is a similar attention to detail in the hock and seltzer, the astrakhan coats, the hansom and so on, but note that both protagonists also expire in upstairs bedrooms; the difference is that the Leamington woman's demise is as a private figure, while Wilde's is as a public one. The evening light of the earlier poem becomes the artificial 'morning gaslight' here, hinting cleverly at the inevitability of the downfall: gas, like fame, runs out, and the failure of the staff to answer Wilde's bell perhaps suggests an audience that is already starting to wane. By the poem's conclusion his fall is complete – those rheumy, drunken eyes may have been poetically 'bees-winged' to begin with, but they have become 'terrible' by the end.

Though the Cadogan is more opulent than the Leamington villa, both buildings are prisons from which neither inmate can escape without sacrifice. And though Wilde has the unseen 'Robbie' (Robert Ross) as his 'Nurse', it is the policemen who offer the only audible contact:

> A thump, and a murmur of voices–
> ("Oh why must they make such a din?")
> As the door of the bedroom swung open
> And TWO PLAIN CLOTHES POLICEMEN came in:
>
> "Mr. Woilde, we 'ave come for tew take yew
> Where felons and criminals dwell:
> We must ask yew tew leave with us quoietly
> For this *is* the Cadogan Hotel."
> ('The Arrest of Oscar Wilde', ll. 25–32)

This is where the "frivolity" comes in. Stanford claims the use of block capitals to be 'in the best undergraduate tradition' – yet it is also theatrical, like a stage direction, and this reflects the antic disposition that made up much of Wilde's life.[75] The cockneyisms of the detectives offer more humour, but it is only fleeting, serving 'to make the descent into tragedy effective by contrast':

> He rose, and he put down *The Yellow Book*.
> He staggered – and, terrible-eyed,
> He brushed past the palms on the staircase
> And was helped to a hansom outside.
> ('The Arrest [. . .]', ll. 33–36)

Factually, 'The Arrest' is quite accurate: Richard Ellmann's account of the event shows that there were indeed two detectives, though a waiter preceded them into the room. On hearing the charge against him ('committing indecent acts'), Wilde rose and 'grasped unsteadily at his overcoat and for a book with a yellow cover'; it then became 'suddenly evident' that he had been drinking heavily. After asking Ross to have a change of clothes sent on to him, he was taken to Bow Street in a cab.[76] There had been a half-packed suitcase on the bed, which Ellmann describes as an 'emblem of contradictory impulses', though it is fair to say that Wilde was tired of the fight by this time.

Carpenter refers to the bourgeois architecture and decoration in Betjeman's poem, noting that Pont Street, 'in her new built red', exemplifies a middle-class degradation of fine architecture.[77] But while the idea of Buchan appearing in the 'latest *Yellow Book*' (ll. 13–14) may symbolise the 'commercialization of what the Nineties had stood for', Wilde's tome could easily have been a French novel (which usually sported yellow paper covers). The point is that people *wanted* it to have been *The Yellow Book*: it was risqué, notoriously decadent – dangerous, even. Assuming its presence in the hotel room also allows Betjeman to go further by showing that the world had moved on since Wilde's heyday. The ambitious Buchan had specifically requested to study at Brasenose because of its connection with Walter Pater. Yet, as author of *The Thirty-Nine Steps* (1915), among other works, he was in himself almost *counter*-decadent. Betjeman's implication is that, by 1895, even *The Yellow Book* had become respectable, and with the domestication of decadence thus complete, the 'Happy bells of eighteen-ninety' started to ring a different tune. That Buchan did not actually appear in the periodical until January 1896 shows that the poet was quite determined to make this point.[78]

To the Bright Young Things of the 1930s, the *fin de siècle* was no more remote than the early Larkin, the Liverpool Poets, or even The Beatles are from us, and, though hardly an obscure figure like Calverley or Prout, critics generally saw Wilde as no more than a decorative entertainer. At Marlborough, Betjeman had found that he 'was someone one ought not to mention', and the 'great attraction' this engendered led him not only to read *Lady Windermere's Fan*, but also correspond with 'Bosie'.[79] There is an irony circling above this interest, for it was not really until the 1960s that Wilde began to be taken seriously by the academy.[80] His admirer still waits his turn, yet the point must be made that Betjeman did not view this era through rose-tinted spectacles. In his introduction to Martin Secker's *The Eighteen Nineties* (1948), for example, he observed that it was also a world which, in addition to Wilde's imprisonment, ended in 'suicide for Crackanthorpe and John Davidson, premature death for Beardsley, Dowson, Lionel Johnson, religion for some, drink and drugs for others'.[81]

'Distant View of a Provincial Town' (1935), the poem that follows 'The Arrest', represents a change in tone. Its middle stanzas refer again to Church of England subdivision, but the first and last have a further significance:

> Beside those spires so spick and span
>   Against an unencumbered sky
> The old Great Western Railway ran
>   When someone different was I.
>   :   :   :   :   :
> The old Great Western Railway shakes
>   The old Great Western Railway spins
> The old Great Western Railway makes
>   Me very sorry for my sins.
>
> ('DISTANT VIEW OF A PROVINCIAL TOWN', LL. 1–4; 21–24)

As the GWR ages, so does the narrator and Betjeman is thus using the railway as a metaphor for life. The sympathy between it and the narrator's decline and fall also has an interesting link with Tennyson, who used the verb 'to spin' in 'Locksley Hall' (1842):

> Let the great world spin for ever down the ringing
> grooves of change,
> (TENNYSON, 'LOCKSLEY HALL', L. 182)[82]

As his son Hallam recorded in *Tennyson: A Memoir* (1897), when the poet travelled on 'the first train from Liverpool to Manchester' (1830), he thought that the wheels 'ran in a groove' (it was a very dark night and this, coupled with the crowd round the train, prevented anything below the underframes from being seen).[83]

This is one of Betjeman's earliest references to Tennyson. Here, of course, it serves no critical purpose, being simply an allusion to a favourite poet. A more explicit example of the technique may be found in 'Love in a Valley', which shares its trochaic rhythm with Meredith's similarly named 'Love in the Valley' (1851, though Betjeman bases his work on the revised version, first published in October 1878). As Betjeman would later write in *The Spectator*: 'if Tennyson is the poet of Lincs, Hardy of Dorset and Arnold of Oxon, then Meredith is the poet of Surrey'.[84] To quote Meredith's biographer, David Williams, 'Love in the Valley' is also 'about physical passion expressed through imagery drawn from [. . .] the earth-mother, and the cyclic seasons'.[85] Betjeman clearly appreciated the connection, though where Meredith's narrator is male and unrequited, his is female, with a loving relationship that is about to be ended by outside forces:

> Portable Lieutenant! that they carry you to China
> And me to lonely shopping in a brilliant arcade;
> (BETJEMAN, 'LOVE IN A VALLEY', LL. 21–22)[86]

These important differences show that, again, Betjeman was not trying so much to copy or parody Meredith, but write his own poem in the same idiom. Indeed, his is a very skilful update, emphasising the woman's about-to-be-lost love through both the natural and the suburban landscape:

> Tall, tall, above me, olive spike the pinewoods,
> Olive against blue black, moving in the gale.
> (BETJEMAN, LL. 7–8)

> Deep the spliced timber barked around the summer house,
> Light lies the tennis court, plantain underfoot.
> (BETJEMAN, LL. 11–12)

Betjeman's foregrounding of adjectives ('Tall [. . .] Olive', 'Deep [. . .] Light') is archaic, and an obvious nod to Meredith, but note how the 'blue black' sky and the gale signpost the heartache which only becomes obvious at the end of the poem. Line 13 of the earlier piece also mentions the 'squirrel that leaps among the pine-tops', which, on its own, is a simple topographical reference point: no poet writing about Surrey could really avoid pine trees.[87] Betjeman's work is peppered with similar quotations, half-quotations, allusions to the sunset (Betjeman, l. 17; Meredith, l. 63), crimson hues (Betjeman, l. 19; Meredith, l. 54) and the like, but while similar triplets occur in his second ('Deep [. . .], / Deep [. . .], / Deep [. . .]') and Meredith's fifteenth ('Yellow [. . .]; / Yellow [. . .]; / Yellow [. . .]') stanzas, the following example illustrates the most noticeable structural parallels:

> Oh! the metal lantern and white enamelled door!
> Oh! the spread of orange from the gas fire on the carpet!
> Oh! the tiny patter, sandaled footsteps on the floor!
>   (BETJEMAN, LL. 14–16)

> O the golden sheaf, the rustling treasure-armful!
> O the nutbrown tresses nodding interlaced!
> O the treasure-tresses one another over
> Nodding! O the girdle slack about the waist!
>   (MEREDITH, LL. 153–156)[88]

As well as the 'Oh'/'O' connection, note that the warm sensuality of the 1878 girl's 'nutbrown tresses' has become the warm, orangey glow of the hearth by 1937 – another instance of Betjeman's modernising of Meredith. Note too that where there was a 'golden sheaf', now sits a 'metal lantern', while the nineteenth century's 'treasure-armful' becomes the twentieth's 'enamelled door'.

Comparing the two poems like this shows a natural, bucolic world replaced (if not usurped) by suburbia. However, this is only emphasised by juxtaposition, for the picture painted by Betjeman here would seem to be much at odds with the piece for which *Continual Dew* is most famous: 'Slough'. For Cunningham, this is an unnecessarily snobbish poem, in which bomber pilots are urged to 'make free with the mortgaged homes of ordinary people'.[89] Humphrey Carpenter goes further, believing it to encapsulate the hatred of the Waugh circle for suburban existence:

> Betjeman wants to destroy not merely Slough itself, but the businessman who has created it. [. . .] A whole section of British society is being written off in much the same way as the Nazis were currently writing off the Jews.[90]

But of course there are really two suburbias: *this* one, and the posher Pooterlands of Camberley, Croydon *et al.* Betjeman would send up the latter in his later poem, 'Group Life: Letchworth' (1940), whose diction proves his target was not the working class, but the worthless factions of his own:

> "[. . .]Wouldn't it be jolly now,
>   To take our Aertex panters off

> And have a jolly tumble in
> The jolly, jolly sun?"
> ('GROUP LIFE: LETCHWORTH', LL. 21–24)

In fact, the violence of 'Slough' fools Carpenter into missing the point slightly. To quote from the poet's *Buckinghamshire Guide* (1948), the town was 'used as a dump after the 1914–18 war, [. . .] and hence [its] valuable market-gardening suburb became a centre for light industry'. This, coupled with later 'Egyptian and jazz-modern factories', along with 'multiple stores and acres of new villas' represented 'the new industrialism which makes one county look like another'.[91] Such notions would be revisited in his preface to *First and Last Loves* (1952) but, as he commented in 1967, 'the Slough Trading Estate was [also] built on some of the most valuable agricultural land in England'. This explains the emphasis of the last stanza:[92]

> Come, friendly bombs and fall on Slough
> To get it ready for the plough.
> The cabbages are coming now;
> The earth exhales.
> ('SLOUGH', LL. 37–40)

Here, Betjeman recalls William Morris, who had made a similar plea in *The Earthly Paradise* (1868–1870):

> Forget six counties overhung with smoke,
> Forget the snorting steam and piston stroke,
> Forget the spreading of the hideous town;
> Think rather of the pack-horse on the down,
> And dream of London, small and white and clean,
> (WILLIAM MORRIS, *THE EARTHLY PARADISE*, 'INTRODUCTION', LL. 1–5)[93]

In his 1972 volume, *A Pictorial History of English Architecture*, Betjeman gave another insight into the rationale behind 'Slough'. With an allusion to line 10, he describes the 'bow-windowed two-storey houses [of the 1920s] with half-timber in the gables, which could be bought through a building society for so much a week down'. These dwellings were poorly constructed by builders (as opposed to architects), who wanted to squeeze as much money from a site as possible by building 'as close together as the by-laws would allow (sometimes closer)'. '[P]eople,' he added, reiterating the point he had made in the *Guide*, 'began to think there would be no country left anywhere in England, except for those areas where land was so unprofitable that it could safely be defined as "national park".'[94] So 'Slough' is also a diatribe against the 'speculative builder', whose aim was 'not solidity or value for money, but an outward appearance that made it impossible for a visitor to mistake his products for council houses'.[95]

A potentially dangerous sham, but those 'tinned minds' (l. 8) have also become stagnant; why else would they prefer the radio to birdsong (l. 26) and 'bogus-Tudor bars' (l. 30) to the night's sky? The architectural historian Timothy Mowl is thus *half* right when he writes that it was 'not the architecture of 'Slough' that disgusted [Betjeman] but the shallow lives and loose morality of its inhabitants'.[96] Yes, their lives seem 'shallow', but the 'loose morality' is clearly more relevant to 'Group Life: Letchworth'; the hapless Slough dwellers are in fact *moulded* by the double-chinned boss and have no choice, given what he pays them, to live where they do. In such light it may be seen that this semi-socialist poem is also about compartmentalization – a circumstance emphasised by the line drawing that accompanies the *Mount Zion* poem 'The Garden City' (reproduced in *Continual Dew*), which shows a row of identical plots, with tenants in identical poses, 'In close and garden delving' (l. 4). This idea is recurrent in Betjeman: his 1963 television film on Bath, for example, satirised a generic developer who wants to build 'a lot of little cells for us to live in'; seven years later, Peter Fleetwood-Hesketh's illustration for the second edition of *Ghastly Good Taste* (1970) included a tower block divided by light pencil lines that created a similar effect.

Architectural Revue[97]

So much for Betjeman's attitude to the architectural landscape of his own century; what about the development of his thoughts on Victorian styles? The poetry gives precious few clues. There *may* be a snipe at Pont Street Dutch in 'The Arrest of Oscar Wilde', 'The Outer Suburbs' (1931) *may* lampoon the 'blackened blocks' (l. 5) of the country's myriad Rosslyn Avenues, but such references are too few and further between for us to extrapolate any firm opinion from them. Betjeman's early preferences are outlined more clearly in a letter he sent to Ward, Lock & Co. on 11 November 1928: while criticising the firm's guide to Leamington, he mentions the 'stucco villas and terraces', which were, he felt, 'very good examples of late Georgian Architecture' (note, however, that the Gothic parish church is defended as being 'not as bad as [the book] makes out').[98] A letter to the BBC the following January also refers to a liking for '*early* nineteenth-century' design (my italics).[99]

Through 'Hymn' we already know what Betjeman thought of the post-Georgian period's penchant for church restoration, but how can we reconcile the later protector of all things Victorian with he who had laughed at its buildings and would go on to join the ultra-Modernist Modern Architectural Research Group (MARS)?[100]

Both 'Archie Rev' writer Philip Morton Shand and editor Hubert de Cronin Hastings were evangelists for the radical Modern Movement, which held that freeing the mind of traditionalism would pave the way for human progress. Any young, unknown writer entering the organ's offices in Queen Anne's Gate, as Betjeman did in October 1930, would have been expected to tow the editorial line. This, of course, meant espousing the best contemporary work, and Mowl's description of Hastings' ruling 'by a kind of terror at long distance, with sudden telephoned diktats [and] sensational ideas posted from his holiday retreats' depicts a man not easily resisted.[101] Similarly, Shand had the power to make 'a stylistic theory read like a logical extension to the Sermon on the Mount'. All heady stuff for an impressionable novice, which is what Betjeman essentially was, despite his impressive "Assistant Editor" title. By all accounts, however, he got on extremely well with his new mentors, although he admitted that the workload could be tiresome. 'I write and I write and I write,' he commented in 1933, 'under different names and in different styles [. . .]. I must have written the word architecture more times than there are people in England who can pronounce it properly.'[102] He also submitted poems, such as the omnipresent 'Hymn', and 'The Electrification of Lambourne End' (1933), a mock-heroic in the style of Crabbe:

> How ALBERT SPARKE has licences to sell
> Both beer and spirits in his new Hotel:
> :   :   :   :   :   :
> How Albert's income rose from night to night,
> From fifty pounds to fifteen hundred quite
> Largely because of *the Electric Light*.
>
> ('THE ELECTRIFICATION OF LAMBOURNE END', LL. 1–2; 7–9)[103]

Though cracks would appear in the Modernist veneer, Mowl suggests that there was more than just the influence of Hastings and Shand keeping any latent admiration for Victorian architecture in check.[104] For him, Betjeman's short-lived membership of the Religious Society of Friends was one of the agencies that helped the poet brainwash himself 'into stylistic sympathies which he would later have to disown and attack'.[105]

Betjeman's religious upbringing was Church of England; this, despite a brief flirtation with atheism at Marlborough, developed into the staunch Anglo-Catholicism for which he is remembered.[106] The conversion, which can, therefore, only be described as unexpected, seems to have been suggested by Gerald Heard, principal secretary to Sir Horace Plunkett, who, though not himself a member, believed the Society to be '"the most promising force for spiritual regeneration within the Christian Church"'.[107] Plunkett's diary shows that the poet was attending Quaker meetings by 1929: in the entry for 17 February, for example, he describes how he 'had to fetch John Betjeman from his Meeting House of the Society of Friends at Esher', adding wryly that '[f]our Quakers and he communed (mostly in silence)'.[108] However, Plunkett also reported that his new employee had worshipped in Margate only the week before 'at some strange sect – Countess of Huntingdon's Connection, I think'.[109] This is an offshoot of Methodism, so was Betjeman enjoying a whistle-stop tour of Non-Conformist beliefs when Heard alerted him to the specific advantages of Quakerism? A difficult question to answer, but the appeal of the Society may have been increased by the poet's pacifism, confirmed by the journal he kept between August 1935 and April 1936: '[d]amned if I will fight,' as he wrote in October. 'Rescue work yes, but not killing. Dread death. Thoughts of Ernie [Betjemann] all alone in that waste of marble at Highgate. How he must hate it if he knows.'[110]

This reference to his father (who passed away in June 1934) implies that the wish to avoid battle had been heightened by bereavement. Regardless of any animosity there may have been, nothing brings home one's own mortality like the death of a parent. Betjeman was also part of the generation which rebelled against battle, having been all-too-aware of the losses sustained on the fields of Belgium. Yet this conviction was not to last, so it is probable that the disinclination to fight, if bolstered by Quakerism, was not a consequence of it. Neither did it bring about a palpable increase in sober piety: it was, after all, after leaving Plunkett's employ that he became a highly irresponsible (though doubtless entertaining) schoolmaster at Heddon Court, spent most weekends away with rich friends at enormous country houses, and wavered romantically between several women while enjoying their lavish hospitality. He even proposed to Wilhelmine Cresswell during his engagement to Penelope Chetwode (whom he would later marry)![111]

Betjeman may have begun attending Quaker meetings in the late 1920s, but he did not join formally until 12 February 1931.[112] This was three months after he started work for *The Architectural Review*, and two years after he had written to Alan Pryce-Jones that he was 'joining the Society of Friends for a time'.[113] This sounds more like a toe being dipped into water than a full immersion. Unfortunately, his letter of application seems to have been destroyed, but Quaker records show that it was sent on 15 January 1931 (from The Fife Hotel in Charterhouse Square, London). The request was discussed at the following Westminster and Longford Monthly Meeting and two Friends, Cuthbert Dukes and George B. Jeffery, were duly appointed to visit him. It is important to stress that getting this far was by no means a guarantee of membership – many entries in the Meeting minutes show that applicants who did not fulfil certain criteria were requested to reconsider. Betjeman clearly suffered from no ambivalence or lack of sincerity in the eyes of his inter-viewers, at least.[114]

In April 1932, he moved to the Quaker settlement of Jordans in Buckinghamshire, where he stayed until his marriage in July 1933.[115] This is not as significant as it seems, for most weekends continued to be spent away and the published letters reveal that most (if not all) his contemporaneous correspondence emanated from the *Architectural Review*.[116] Indeed, the evidence suggests that Betjeman's membership was fairly undistinguished and anonymous: while at Jordans he raised no concerns, sat on no committees, and warranted no appointed Quaker presence at his wedding.[117] He must have sustained a *certain* presence at Westminster and Longford, as a letter from fellow Friend Mildred Alston, sent with good wishes after he had resigned, conveys the hope that 'the floods [had] avoided Uffington'.[118] This Berkshire village became Betjeman's home during February 1934, so at least one member got to know him well enough to learn his private address. However, one has to admit that this confirms little more than his personable nature.

Yet for all this, the Quaker interlude does seem to have had an effect on his poetry, as the verses in *Continual Dew* indicate. The references to old Sandemanians, Calvinists, Padres and the like do fit in with our knowledge of a poet who revelled in the Church's 'narrow-gauge' (to quote Mowl), but the emphasis, as I suggested earlier, is most often satirical: in 'Exchange of Livings', for example, the incumbents are more interested in the deal being offered (an attitude more forcefully conveyed in 'Competition'), while 'The Sandemanian Meeting-House in Highbury Quadrant' shows with some significance how the old Sandemanians are *'hidden from the sun'* (my italics).[119] Despite this, the burning question remains: how did Quakerism affect Betjeman's views on architecture? There are few explicit references to it in his writing of the period, though one of the earliest comes in *Ghastly Good Taste* (1933). Here, the Quakers are listed among those Non-Conformists who shout (circa 1863) against '"the ritualism, the class distinction, the idleness and the waste of money at the Hall"' – this being the fictitious Great House Betjeman had concocted to show the changing architectural attitudes and influences down the ages.[120] Thus the group forms part of the author's argument against the post-Industrial Revolution rise of the middle-class 'when "architecture" was considered something to stick on to a building afterwards to make it "showy" or upper class'.[121] Indeed, the Quakers' (and others) 'humble brick meeting-houses [. . .] were a chastening influence' at this time, while by the *fin-de-siècle*, '[t]here is an atmosphere of [. . .] Quakerism and sober gaiety that marks the beginning of emancipation in the early twentieth century'.[122]

Ironically, the other major clue comes in '1837 – 1937', published in *The Studio* in February 1937, the month before his resignation was accepted. This is divided into a number of dated sections – 1837, 1867, 1907 and 1937 – each illustrating the architectural deterioration of Boggleton, a small market town that expanded with the coming of the railways. Compare the following entries:

(1837)
Down one of these alleys is the Quaker Meeting House, a simple affair in limestone with scrubbed benches and white walls within and nicely graded tiled roof distinguishing its plain exterior.[123]

(1867)
[. . .] the only remains of Old Boggleton were the Town Hall and the Quaker Meeting House [. . .].[124]

(1907)
Only the Quaker Meeting House remained the same.[125]

Such continuity seems to imply that Quakerism may have represented the 'unity of ideals', the new Christendom, which Betjeman had expounded in *Ghastly Good Taste*.[126] This recalls William Morris, who believed that building design would only become possible again when socialism prevailed: 'until such a change comes about,' he insisted, 'there will be no real modern architecture'.[127] Morris also felt that '[t]here is only one style of architecture on which it is possible to found a true living art, which is free to adapt itself to the varying conditions of social life, climate, and so forth, and that style is gothic architecture'. With this in mind, it is perhaps no surprise that Betjeman, writing under his pseudonym Lionel Cuffe, felt able to assert that Morris was 'indeed the leader of the modern movement'.[128]

It may be that this apparent acceptance of Modernism, with its clean, uncomplicated lines was assisted by the creed, with its clean, uncomplicated meeting houses. As he wrote in the *Architectural Review* (December 1940), 'the doctrine of the society demanded no worldly ostentation whatever', thus 'the buildings have the quality of a well-scoured farmhouse kitchen [. . .]. One might say the Quakers were the Cistercians of Nonconformist builders'.[129] The same piece includes the telling note that he had 'attended numerous small country meetings where a scrubbed and white-washed austerity still recalls the strictness of old Friends'.[130] It must be clarified, however, given the timing if nothing else, that Betjeman is unlikely to have joined the Society of Friends *deliberately* to mould himself into an aesthetic position which seems so alien to what we know of him now. Remember that, until January 1935, he was *employed* by the *Architectural Review*, and surely understood his obligations. An example of his boss's style may be discerned in his editorial for the journal's April 1930 issue, in which he explains that '"what Mr John Betjeman calls the Awf'lly Modern Movement"' (in 'Still Going Strong', published the following month), was actually 'a mocking reference to Art Deco' (which Hastings loathed) and not to the continental Modern Movement (which he did not).[131] This accounts for the article's rather uncomfortable connections between Sir John Soane and Modernism amid Betjeman's survey of Victorian decorative arts. Such was very much in the vein of the William Morris article and, as Hillier wryly commented, here we see (again) a man 'trying to reconcile what he likes with what he is required to like':[132]

[Soane's] first lecture, delivered at the Royal Academy, contains these memorable words, and since we are only just starting again where Soane left off I shall begin and conclude with his remarks.[133]

[. . .] the truly simple efforts of Le Corbusier and Dufy are hardly appreciated. They are merely regarded as "jazz" [i.e. Art Deco] gone a little too far. But the work that the French, Germans, and Swedes are doing speaks for itself when we bear in mind the axioms of Soane in that their simplicity is the result not of whim but of logic.[134]

'Still Going Strong' may be the first clear sign of the Hastings effect on Betjeman's architectural writing. By the October 1931 issue, however, he had come up with another way of playing the journal at its own game. The poet realised that C. F. A. Voysey (the Victorian/Edwardian architect-designer) was still alive, thanks to a letter of complaint he had sent to the editorial office.[135] A visit was arranged and this led to 'Charles Francis Annesley Voysey: The Architect of Individualism', which appeared immediately after Voysey's own piece, '1874 & After'. The latter was in praise of Gothic, a genre Voysey felt to be a practical, 'broad principle' that did not depend necessarily on 'the imitation of familiar Gothic detail'.[136] It was also evident that he hated what he saw as the commercialisation of a style whose aesthetic qualities had manifestly become 'quite unimportant to those who built' in it.[137] These opinions made it difficult for Betjeman to discuss him as another pioneer of the Modern Movement, though there was one comment Voysey made which provided a point of ingress: '[t]he 1851 Exhibition awakened the idea of unity as the basis of Art. All that was necessary for daily life could be, and ought to be, made beautiful'.[138] Pugin designed the Medieval Court at this landmark event, so it was clearly a Gothic high point. Voysey's remark also echoes William Morris's maxim: '[h]ave nothing in your houses that you do not know to be useful or believe to be beautiful', which itself echoes Ruskin's idea that '[t]he variety of the Gothic schools is the more healthy and beautiful, because in many cases it is entirely unstudied, and results, not from mere love of change, but from practical necessities'.[139] By coupling all this with the idea that Gothic did not *have* to mean pointed arches, Betjeman was able to claim that the emphasis on 'necessity' heralded a return to 'simplicity' from 'the complex and futile revivalism in which many architects still remain'. As this was the 'Archie Rev', the point had to be made, of course, that such reawakening had 'made itself felt at least on the Continent'.[140]

Betjeman's next article, 'The Death of Modernism' (published two months later), takes up the mantle once again, claiming that Voysey's use of the term 'Gothic' in '1874 & After' had probably been misunderstood 'by those whose minds are not yet rid of "period" taste'. He felt compelled to explain the Gothic-equals-necessity equation once again, immediately following it by stating that:

[t]he Crystal Palace is Gothic, far more Gothic than the St. Pancras Hotel.[141]

This rather painful notion was in well keeping with the precepts of the MARS Group and one can understand why Mowl feels the piece to be the product of a 'hack journalist'. Yet it also shows how that journalist squirmed beneath the weight of Hastings' editorial diktats.[142] A further example of this may be seen in a radio talk that Betjeman gave in February 1932. In his script, he had described the St. Pancras Hotel as 'that fantastic Baronial palace', but in the actual broadcast dismissed it as a 'ridiculous-looking' edifice, which was 'half cathedral and half Baronial hall and like neither'.[143] Stephen Games, anthologist of this piece, speculates that the programme's producer probably forced the amendment, but for me it has the touch of Hastings about it. If so, one can clearly see how the idea that Modernism was a natural progression from traditional architecture would have made Betjeman's situation much more tolerable. It also doubtless helped him to justify references in the magazine to Voysey, Morris *et al.* – even if, like Voysey, those forerunners did not always agree with the pigeonhole into which they had been placed.

Elsewhere in 'The Death of Modernism', the poet lashes out at suburban homes, which are debunked for their architectural dishonesty:

> [h]ardly a villa rises without its half-timber, hardly a front door without its stained glass to hide the world. Hardly a monumental building is erected which is not masking some honest English face behind.[144]

In 'The Outer Suburbs', also published in 1931, Betjeman described how 'A stained glass window, red and green, / Shines, hiding what should not be seen' (ll. 9–10). In the *Architectural Review*, this effect is disliked for being fake; here, it is a false façade. Yet by 1937 – despite 'Slough' – his opinion was somewhat different; note how the 'Leaded [. . .] windows lozenging the crimson' of 'Love in a Valley' (l. 19), for instance, are used to paint an evocative picture of young love. The reason for this change of heart will become apparent later, but the opening paragraph of 'The Death of Modernism' nevertheless betrays a certain lack of accord with both these earlier strands of thought:

> [r]apidly every inhabitable part of the world is becoming industrialised, and communities which formerly possessed a creative art of their own, by coming into contact with the rest of the world, imbibe another culture – the culture of industrialisation. Nor should we despair that there is no longer a city which is unexplored, no longer a country replete with eighteenth-century towns of mellow houses and spacious streets, nor even an island of medieval towers and fortresses that is not strung across with wires and scarred with tarmac roads. Only the swamps and thick tropical forests remain and on them it is impossible to build. We have prepared and planned the world beyond recognition and can hardly be blamed for not turning our attention to the rubbish heap.[145]

So, was Betjeman's description of a pylon's 'functional beauty' at a 1932 lecture what he *really* felt?[146] Also, note the contrast between the 'mellow houses' and 'spacious streets' of the eighteenth century and the modern tarmac roads that *scar* the landscape. Note too the overpowering negativity of the syntax:

> *[n]or* should we despair that there is no longer a city which is *unexplored, no* longer a country replete with eighteenth-century towns [. . .] (my italics).

Perhaps Betjeman was *trying* to say that we should not feel despondent as industrialisation marches ever onward, but the writing betrays a certain contempt of it. Indeed, the effect of industrialisation on architecture is one of the central themes of *Ghastly Good Taste*.

Betjeman's daughter, Candida Lycett Green, comments that the panoply of typefaces employed on the cover of this volume gave it the look of 'a Victorian music-hall programme'.[147] As noted earlier, at Marlborough Betjeman was amused by Victorian buildings, but by the time he reached Oxford in 1925, he had grown bored by Gothic 'whether it was genuine or false'.[148] Scouring second-hand bookshops at that time led to purchases which 'gave [. . .] a vision of Georgian England which was utterly different from those seen in the big Batsford books or [those] published by A. and C. Black' – hence the letter to Brereton.[149] Yet perhaps the most telling sentence comes at the end of the 1970 preface:

[i]t was in this muddled state – wanting to be up to date but really preferring all centuries to my own – that I wrote this book [. . .].[150]

Here again is proof of the battle between true opinion and editorial policy, which Betjeman had doubtless felt obliged to respect even in this ostensibly independent production.

His general argument is that a lack of education was responsible for the worst post-1860 architectural horrors. The treatise proper begins with a history lesson, and, after claiming eighteenth-century work to be beautiful (because 'people minded about architecture and took a pride in it'), Betjeman then goes back further, to before the Reformation, when 'all Europe was Christendom', 'united in an age of faith', and 'the Church was the dominant force in architecture'.[151] Following the Renaissance, 'and a vague hankering after classical learning', fear of education lessened; then came 'the architecture of the age of reason – the work of Wren, of Gibbs, of Kent, of Chambers'.[152] This led to a system of class-consciousness, with the consequence that structural design 'fell into the hands of the upper classes' (by which he meant 'the educated, not necessarily the well-born').[153]

The problem really came, Betjeman felt, with the post-Reform Bill, post industrialisation, rise of the Middle Class, whose members decided they needed something that would show them to be 'a station above the mere manual workers in the factory and assistants in the shop'.[154] It was then that mistakes were made. These may have been 'good, vulgar mistakes', but the end was nevertheless in sight.[155] In 1874, work began on G. E. Street's new Law Courts, which were, for Betjeman, a 'colossal failure', sounding 'the death knell of the old-fashioned scholarly Gothic'.[156] From here on, architecture became self-conscious and even the 'healthy breeze' of William Morris failed to affect anything other than domestic work.[157] Now, presumably, the individualism that would have threatened the earlier age of unity was welcome if it came in the shape of Charles Francis Annesley Voysey, for, as Betjeman wrote, Voysey considered 'the training of character to be of far greater importance than any knowledge of styles and books'.[158] Alas he was but one man: the aesthetic self-consciousness of the 1930s – institutionalised and stale – was a step too far.[159] What was needed was co-ordination:

> [t]he only hope I that can put forward is that England will emerge from its present state of intense individualism and become another Christendom. Not until it is united in belief will its architecture regain coherence. That union cannot come until a return of Christendom. Whether that Christendom will be a Union of Soviet Republics, a League of Socialist Nations or an Ecclesiastical Union, it is not for me to say.[160]

The possibility of Quakerism providing this unity was alluded to in '1837 – 1937', of course, although Betjeman would cover similar ground in his 1937 lecture, 'Antiquarian Prejudice' (published 1939). To Humphrey Carpenter, this is 'a rare serious moment'; to Mowl it is 'brash and foolish'.[161] There is certainly plenty of evidence to suggest that Betjeman was playing to his audience. As with '1837 – 1937', he employs a daft place name to help win them over. There it was Boggleton; here it is Tickleby Tomcat. He also uses the first person, and his opening sentence ('I come to you fresh from Evensong and with my outlook widened') reveals his key return to the Church of England (he had recently accepted a position as People's Warden of St. Mary's, Uffington).[162] Again, his preference for the Georgian style is made clear, and again the modern architect is lambasted for his mediocrity. But, interestingly, there are additional references to the 'arrogant, staring, badly-planned travesties of Queen Anne architecture', which 'flare up in place of the decent Early Victorian stucco' in St. John's Wood. The loathing of 'jazz-modern' may still be strong, but the presence of this decidedly un-antiquarian genre simply adds to the 'muddled' sense that Hillier highlights.[163] In addition, we can see how the Hastings/Morton Shand promotion of contemporary building materials had yet to be extinguished:

> [f]or an antiquarian reason, to which the present state of architecture in U.S.S.R. gives the direct lie, an honest, plain structure of steel, glass, and/or reinforced concrete is considered Bolshevistic or international.[164]

This notion would reappear in *An Oxford University Chest* (1938), for while recognizing the Radcliffe Camera (1737–49) to be among James Gibbs's best work,

> one cannot but admire the courage of an architect boldly building in the style of the time right in the midst of some of the grandest work of past ages.[165]

This echoes the more Shandian comment in *Ghastly Good Taste* that:

[t]he man who had the courage to place the great round classical dome of the Radcliffe Camera, hemmed in on every side by Gothic fronts and towers and spires, [. . .] would also have had the courage to build today as sincere an essay in modern materials in its place.[166]

The Camera stands in front of the partly medieval University Church of St. Mary the Virgin, with the seventeenth-century Bodleian Library behind and Hawksmoor's eighteenth-century All Souls at its flank, so does this mean that Betjeman would have approved of the glass pyramid that currently stands outside the Louvre? Surely not. And Gibbs did at least build his masterpiece in stone – considered by William Morris (after Ruskin) to be the 'most noble' of construction materials.[167]

Readers would have to wait until 1970 for Betjeman to footnote that his earlier theory was 'fallacious', though by 1938 he was prepared to admit that the Camera was very different from 'the half-hearted attempts to blend the ancient with the modern which characterize post-war Oxford architecture'.[168] As Carpenter recognizes, *An Oxford University Chest* is largely dismissive of the 'repulsive' and 'unfortunate' Victorian work in the city.[169] However, his note that Betjeman only praises Butterfield's Keble College (1870–78) because it is 'an "honest expression" of the age of gaslight' is a little inaccurate. True, the poet feels the 'uncompromising colour of the brickwork', while 'skilful', has given rise to 'unlovely patterns'; but the college itself,

[a]s an essay in the right arrangement of masses, in good proportion and originality in the Gothic manner, [. . .] is by far the best Gothic Revival work in either Oxford or Cambridge.[170]

Though he commented in 1935 that the Houses of Parliament were a 'masterpiece of early Victorian Perpendicular', the progression in Betjeman's thinking regarding Victorian architecture is revealed most clearly in the differences between the first and second editions of his *Shell Guide* to Cornwall (1934 and 1964).[171] The original version, introducing what was conceivably Betjeman's favourite county, was odd to say the least. Spiral-bound down the left hand side like an exercise book ('very Modern Movement' according to Hillier), the front cover displays not a photograph of the landscape as its successor would, but a hoary, hairy old gent smoking a pipe (an image which one cannot help but feel caused the author no end of mirth at the time).[172] Betjeman claims his work to be 'more of an anthology' than a traditional guide, although the title page gives the unfortunate impression that it is more an anthology of typefaces than topography.[173] It also suffers from having the information on towns and churches in separate sections. There are two words to describe the latter: one is jargonistic; the other, in spite of the author's professed contempt for the man, is *Pevsnerian*.[174] Were he alive, he would undoubtedly protest with the utmost vehemence, but note, for example, the entry for St. Juliot:

Romantic situation : 15th cent. : bench ends : restored.

This is very stark, very unromantic and very un-Betjeman, although it does show one way in which the poet's thinking did not change: the gazetteer is prefaced by the telling note that 'Cornwall suffered from pious and ill-considered restoration by Victorians, even more than other counties'.[175] Indeed, as 'A Song for those Interested in Churches', 'Hymn' is reproduced yet again. The entirely rewritten second edition of the guide makes his position even more clear, however. The 1934 entry for Cornelly may note that its church was '[o]ver-restored', but in the 1964 version we are told much more explicitly that 'J. P. St. Aubyn *ruined* the church's interior in 1886' (my italics). The 1964 volume contains many similar references to St Aubyn's 'brutal' lack of historical empathy, but it should be noted that "restoration" and all its variants are almost always denied the literal meaning by being encased in double inverted commas.[176]

Yet the later Betjeman was by no means blinded by fury, there being reason as well as rage: the second edition of *Cornwall* recognises St. Aubyn's 'pretty village school' at Ladock, for instance, while St. Juliot's rather Spartan 1934 entry (as above) is replaced by an account of Thomas Hardy's work there, the overall effect of which is described as 'pleasant and Cornish'.[177] "Restoration" was nevertheless a subject to which Betjeman would frequently return, in subsequent *Shell* (and later *Murray's*) guides, as well as numerous broadcasts and articles.

In spite of this continuation of thought, and despite Hillier's comment that it was 'very successful', the 1934 guide is generally regarded as a poor effort.[178] Mowl makes a case for showing that even Pevsner's 1951 paperback guide to the county (*Cornwall*) is more perceptive: here Callington is described as a 'little town, not specifically attractive, [. . .] dominated by the great chimney of a disused mine on Kit Hill, looking from the distance like one more Wellington testimonial'. For Betjeman in 1934, the town's chief virtue was that its 'unimportance [. . .] will commend it to those who need a rest'. Pevsner uses history, and even a little irony, to give *some* idea of what the place was like; Betjeman, by contrast, seems detached and sarcastic. By 1964, he had altered his approach, noting that that 'which used to be a small town of houses built of dark slate' had become a sort of casualty of progress:

> [n]ow what houses of the little town on its declivity remain are covered with cement paint and the gaps between them filled with parked cars.
>
> Just below the church a fine Georgian house front has been murdered by the modernistic extension of a shop. The inhabitants of the town have mostly moved into bungalows and council estates on the outskirts.

At least the fifteenth-century church had been 'de-St Aubynised a little'.[179]

But this change came sooner rather than later. The Devon guide of 1936 shows that, perhaps influenced by Edith Olivier (who had provided the gazetteer for Robert Byron's *Wiltshire*, 1935), Betjeman quickly started to inject a little of himself into the proceedings. Thus, where *Wiltshire* refers to ghosts, *Devon* has pixies, and so on.[180] Mowl quotes one particularly amusing example, which is worth reproducing:

> Cranmere Pool. On Dartmoor, is said to be difficult to find. It is not worth finding, a dull, small puddle in a dull large bog. There is a visitor's book which makes good reading in the way of invective.[181]

With mild controversy, Betjeman noted that 'the Cathedral is the most disappointing thing about Exeter', although he did add that Sir George Gilbert Scott restored it 'with considerable sensibility for a Victorian'.[182] In fact he was trying to encourage those who would 'go to Exeter, park their cars in the close, look at the Cathedral, and conclude that they have "done" Exeter' to see the other sights, most notably Southernhaye (1800–06), which appeared in the original version of the poem named after the city:[183]

> Once those bells, those Exeter bells
> Called her through Southernhaye
> By pink, acacia-shaded walls
> Several times a day
> To Wilfric's altar and riddel posts
> While the choir sang STANFORD in A.
> ('Exeter', ll. 7–12)

(Note that in the Exeter bells, we also hear 'those Shandon bells' of Father Prout once again.)

The artist John Piper, whom Betjeman had met when J. M. Richards recommended his typographic skills, paid tribute to *Devon*, calling it 'the model *Shell Guide* for all time'.[184] Mowl in fact credits Piper with bringing out the 'true' Betjeman, exemplified by the article that arose from a '*Shropshire Guide*' research trip, during which the pair caught a stopping train that stopped rather longer than the timetable decreed at Whittington. For this, 'The Seeing Eye or How to Like Everything' (1939), Piper sketched the Victorian stucco station building, while the poet fantasised about how it might inspire the opinions of the clergy (personified by Mr Squinch), professional architects (Mr Quantity) and architectural journalists (Young Camshaft).

Camshaft's ideas are perhaps the most disturbing, embodying a vision 'beyond the carriage window view, beyond Whittington, beyond England': 'a place of soaring crystal towers among spacious parks dotted with motor cars [where] the sky is flecked with noiseless aeroplanes'.[185] One feels that people would contaminate this ultra-clean future, but as well as Piper's, Betjeman tempers such views with his own:

> [w]e see in Whittington Station the heyday of steam architecture. Such a building as this might have come straight from Bassett Lowke and the

locomotive puffs as proudly away as did that on the cover of *The Wonder Book of Railways*.[186]

The feature concludes with a look at six different architectural styles, including 'the doctor's italianate [sic] house in the suburb, the model dwelling on the edge of the village, the Gothic gate-lodge, the Baptist chapel, the decaying Victorian terrace in the spa where, as the old ladies and the gas go out, the flats, the orange paper and the electric light come in'. Each is described by Squinch, Quantity, Camshaft and finally (and most reasonably), by Piper. Betjeman tells the reader that the artist 'has made us look a second time', and that in following his example, 'by taking scenery as it is and not what we have been told it ought to be, we will be getting all the good we can out of the war'. We should accept buildings at 'façade value' and perhaps, if we do,

> those of us who are alive will emerge with a deep sense of jazz-modern and a genuine desire to preserve the bogus Tudor of the new industrialism. I hope so. In any other direction madness lies.

Despite the sting-in-the-tail sarcasm (could it really be anything else?), the article's 'pure Piper aesthetics' is evidence that the Seeing Eye was happiest when its gaze fell – in common with Betjeman's best poems – on *people*.[187] The obverse may be seen in 'Antiquarian Prejudice', when he puts forward the daft idea that that Lord Nuffield could have produced pressed-steel prefabs for the masses at Oxford.[188] He would almost certainly have tempered this view had he actually met any of Oxford's working class. But while there can be no doubt that Piper was instrumental in encouraging Betjeman to step away from Hastings and Shand, as Mowl also recognises, the ability to see the world in this way was already within him.[189]

In fact, it surfaced as early as October 1933, when the *Architectural Review* published 'Leeds – A City of Contrasts'.[190] And what a contrast it was:

> [t]o understand Leeds, to understand its Civic Hall and the regrettable Headrow, one must acquire a Leeds sense of proportion. And this is done by realising two things about Leeds. First, it is a Victorian city. Secondly, it is parochial. These two qualities are far more blessed than is generally supposed.[191]

One wonders how Betjeman got away with the somewhat unexpected assertion that to be Victorian is to be blessed! And from the 'large, gas-lit stations' out into the 'industrialised communities', the tone is at once romantic, realistic and sympathetic. So, Brodrick's Town Hall (1858) is 'fine', and the 'nineteenth-century mills and warehouses [. . .] are the cathedrals of the industrial north'.[192] But the 'appalling' housing of the working class is not considered on purely aesthetic grounds:

[o]n the deaths from tuberculosis, the infant mortality, and the results of compulsory constipation it is needless to expatiate.

:   :   :   :   :

You have to know your neighbour opposite on the first floor when you want to string a clothes line across the street to dry your washing.[193]

Commenting on the high turnout for a recent royal visit, Betjeman wrote: 'I think a city which has such remarkable people should take better care of them.'[194] The situation was particularly bad in the Hunslet area of South Leeds, described by Richard Hoggart in *The Uses of Literacy* (1957):

[t]o a visitor they are understandably depressing, these massed proletarian areas; street after street of shoddily uniform houses intersected by a dark pattern of ginnels and snickets (alley-ways) and courts; mean, squalid, and in a permanent half-fog; a study in shades of dirty-grey, without greenness or the blueness of sky; degrees darker than the north or west of the town, than 'the better end'.[195]

Over dinner, Betjeman learns that local opinion holds the Civic Hall to be 'the most beautiful [. . .] in the world'.[196] This is a view of Leeds not as a potential work of art, but a place where people *live* – people who have feelings and opinions. Thus the last word is given to a Yorkshire builder, who dismisses Vincent Harris's new Civic Hall as a 'structure of steel'. Brodrick's Victorian Town Hall, however, was a different matter: 'that's architecture, that's craftsmanship,' says the artisan, '[i]t's *grown up*'.[197] There is a sense that this article is too.

In the same year that the *Architectural Review* published 'The Seeing Eye', it also produced 'A Note on J. N. Comper', 'the first article on his work that [had] appeared in any architectural magazine'.[198] Betjeman may have first become aware of Comper when he saw Molesworth Chapel (in Little Petherick Church) as a boy.[199] As the years wore on, the two men became friends, the younger going on (successfully) to campaign for the elder's knighthood.[200] Though he may have been 'the most gloriously high camp' of architects, Comper shared Betjeman's (now re-surfaced) Anglo-Catholicism and impressed the poet with the idea that a church should 'bring you to your knees when you first enter it'.[201]

In the article, Betjeman extolled Comper as 'the logical outcome of the Gothic Revival', a man who had 'gone on from where Bodley, his master and to whom he was articled, [had] left off'; indeed, '[w]hat Voysey did for small houses, Comper has done for churches'.[202] Betjeman's fears for the future of British architecture – outlined at length in *Ghastly Good Taste* – are allayed to an extent by Comper's refusal (like Bodley) to join the R.I.B.A. Instead, he advocated the system of apprenticeship, claiming that '"Schools of Art have been a complete failure. They give their pupils a smattering of everything and proficiency in nothing".'[203] Crucially, the lecture which spawned 'Antiquarian

Prejudice' was given the same year that the two met – hence the notion therein that:

> [t]he time-honoured system of apprenticeship and practical experience, of being articled to an architect who either repulses you so much you react against him as Bodley did to the elder Gilbert Scott, or evolve from him out of admiration as Soane did from the younger Dance – that system is over. That system created individualists, great men of whom Comper, Voysey, Ashbee, Lutyens, Baillie Scott and a few others survive.[204]

Clearly, this was not mere affectation, but an opinion based on the sound knowledge of one who understood the full implications of what he believed. Just as Leeds became attractive when he could see the people, just as Whittington had done when Piper steered him towards the same conclusion, Betjeman's theorising hit home with greater force when he could see a man.

Onward and Upward

For Hillier, Betjeman's conversion to Victorian architecture was 'well advanced' by 1937. Indeed, it was in this year that he warned John Summerson that the 'magnificent' Mary Ward settlement at Tavistock Place, London, was to be demolished and lamented the destruction by fire of the Crystal Palace.[205] Perhaps it was more a case of admiration rising to the surface, for, as we have seen, there had been glimpses of a sneaking regard throughout the decade (and even before). Certainly by now his MARS membership was long gone, and the 'Quaker period' was drawing to its official close. But while the latter *might* have assisted his Modernist stance, the former may have been little more than a deft piece of role-playing: the Pritchard Archive of the University of East Anglia holds a number of MARS Group papers; Betjeman's name does not appear *anywhere* in those for the 1930s. In fact, the distance that quickly grew between the two sides is revealed in a 1941 letter from Tim Bennett to Jack Pritchard, in which Bennett refers to a Puginesque room as a potential source of delight for 'the Betjeman-Piper front'.[206]

This was the direction of the future, but it is plain that Betjeman's architectural vacillation was not duplicated in his attitude to Victorian *literature*, which had remained much the same since Oxford. Many would nevertheless argue that this early Betjeman resembles a schoolboy in a sweetshop, littering his verse with a dash of Prout here, a twist of Meredith there, and half a dozen Hardyisms everywhere else. C. S. Lewis might have loathed this interest, but Maurice Bowra knew that it was not simple pretence.[207] In fact, it provided the crucial basis of his verse, as a letter to Frederick Booker (31 January 1948) shows:

> [d]o let me advise a course of Pope. His *Essay on Criticism* is brilliant and so

useful. And then turn to some master technician like Tennyson (particularly his 'Audley Court', 'The Lady of Shallot', 'In Memoriam', 'The Kraken', 'Aylmer's Field', 'The Dying Swan') and read them out *aloud*.[208]

This implies that Betjeman checked himself continually against those he believed to be worthy of emulation. Sometimes the effect of this influence is subtle ('Death in Leamington', 'Westgate-on-sea'), sometimes it is based on biographical interest ('The Arrest of Oscar Wilde at the Cadogan Hotel'). Often, the use of form and technique is more obvious and more dextrous ('For Nineteenth-Century Burials', 'Love in a Valley'). Yet part of the problem with gauging Betjeman's stance is that his use of humour often clouds the truth. Where it is used for satiric purposes ('Hymn', 'Slough'), the results are at once incisive and impressive, but a number of the early verses – like the dreadful call-and-answer 'Public House Drunk' – are too similar in emphasis to the 'Funny Poems by Clever John Betjeman', written to impress Vera Moule during his brief spell as a master at Heddon Court.[209]

Freud noted that one 'motive force' for exercising wit is to flaunt one's own intelligence.[210] Indeed, it was also at Heddon Court that Betjeman asserted his superior knowledge with 'an exhibitionist relish', ex-pupil Paul Miller confirming that he '"never hesitated to mock our enthusiasms for all they were worth"'.[211] Moreover, in *Laughter: An Essay on the Meaning of the Comic* (1911), Henri Bergson wrote that mirth is the price extracted from those whose behaviour has become rigid and inflexible – hence the Wykehamist and his interminable Norman fonts.[212] But, and this is a point well worth making again, humour also assists those wishing to be popular among their fellows. On this subject, Morton Shand wrote a very telling letter to Penelope Chetwode on 12 July 1933:

> I hope John will start to write when he marries. "Being Amusing" which I fancy (though no doubt I'm wrong) is a phase drawing to a close, is his great danger. Marriage should cure it. Many imbeciles only know him in that light, and John usually does nothing to open their eyes. In fact the contrary.[213]

The 1930s were a decade of discovery for Betjeman, but as his theories on buildings and belief would develop, so would the promise he had shown in his first two volumes of verse. Shand and the readership would not have long to wait.

CHAPTER THREE

The 1940s

Home Fires

As Britain edged closer to its darkest hour, Betjeman – no longer the pacifist he had been – did all he could to get into the armed forces. Unlike Auden and Isherwood, who decamped to America with some speed after the declaration, he had offered his services to the Ministry of Labour as early as September 1938.[1] But while Evelyn Waugh's string-pulling led to a commission, by March 1940 Betjeman found himself trapped in the restrictive, and somewhat boring, world of the Ministry of Information.[2] Despite this, it is clear that his war effort was in many ways more effective when it involved his skill with words. The next salvo came on the 14th of that month, when *Old Lights for New Chancels*, his third volume of verse, was published.

It was a manifest departure from *Mount Zion* and *Continual Dew*, showing Betjeman in the ascendant – an established poet, growing in confidence, less reliant on esoteric references and coterie humour than before. He now seemed to be invoking the great triumvirate of Tennyson, Hardy and Browning more deliberately, leaving behind some of the second XI versifiers who had dominated his earlier work. This lent his literary Victorianism a greater sense of purpose, transforming him from precious humorist into propagandist. Stirred to expound the virtues of his homeland, he also achieved an increasing sense of cohesion during this period, which grew when the dangers of post-war urban redevelopment heightened the need to critique the present via the poetics of the past.

Austerity measures meant that the appearance of *Old Lights* was new too – there could be no lavish inserts or expensive coloured paper now. Betjeman understood this and wrote to Murray that he favoured 'a small, chaste octavo printed very simply' on 'creamy brown' paper, with binding of 'dark blue cloth' so that the whole resembled a 'sort of pocket book'.[3] And so it did. In fact, the basic design of these volumes was to remain the same for the rest of Betjeman's life, a move which had a twofold effect, for not only did it help focus the reader's mind on the work (as opposed to mannered production values), but also lowered the retail price to 5s – the same as the second edition of Auden's *Poems* and a full 2s 6d less than *Continual Dew*.[4]

More importantly, *Old Lights* was the first – and, as it turned out, the only – collection to include a proper preface. Ostensibly, it was a riposte to the adverse review of *Continual Dew* that had appeared in *The Draconian* (the magazine of the Dragon School, Oxford). This was hardly *Harpers and Queen* and would have had few readers, but within what was probably both a send-up of the literary reply and an expression of anger that an 'old boy' could have been treated thus, Betjeman set out the reasoning behind his work.[5] 'Poets who have been brought up in the country,' he explained, 'are entitled to write on these subjects, for they are their natural visual outlet.'[6] So Hardy was 'the poet of the small provincial town', who 'looks at London [. . .] as someone with a return ticket in his pocket', while Tennyson 'saw England from the Rectory Library or out on the gravel above the arboretum, or up in the family museum, or where the pines rock at the bottom of the garden'.[7] In fact, 'the English or Irish background' was precisely what endeared a poet to Betjeman. Browning was too cosmopolitan a writer by half, thus he is labelled 'unsympathetic'; yet, as we shall see, dramatic monologues in the Browning style would be a feature throughout his career.[8]

The topographical poems that form the bulk of *Old Lights* represent Betjeman's own attempts 'to catch the atmosphere of places and times' in his homeland – very apt for wartime. Each is preceded on the contents page by the locale with which it deals, and it is interesting to note that 'Pot Pourri from a Surrey Garden' (with its 'bountiful' Pam) is considered not as an 'Amatory' verse, but as a reflection of its setting, there being, Betjeman felt, 'no harm' in trying to describe that 'overbuilt' county in verse.[9] Furthermore,

> [t]he suburbs, thanks to Punch which caters for them, are now considered 'funny'. Some people still think Victorian industrial scenery is only fit for invective. Churches are always 'funny' unless they are written about by a devotional writer. Gaslight is funny, Pont Street is funny, all sorts of places and things are funny if only the funny writers are funny about them. I love suburbs and gaslights and Pont Street and Gothic Revival churches and mineral railways, provincial towns and Garden cities. *They are, many of them, part of my background* (my italics).[10]

Hillier, for one, believes much of this to be 'disingenuous', pointing out that Pont Street had also been satirized by Osbert Lancaster.[11] Indeed, Betjeman did mock its pseudo-Dutch style in 'Cheshire', a short verse considered for *New Bats in Old Belfries* (1945), but not published until *Uncollected Poems* (1982):

> Infirmaries by Aston Webb
> On ev'ry hill surmount the pines;
> From two miles off you still can see
> Their terra-cotta Dutch designs,
>
> ('Cheshire', ll. 1–4)

He dismissed this as 'very early work' when the volume was being compiled, but while the infirmaries clearly jar with the landscape, in an urban setting such as Pont Street, surely the effect would be less unpleasant to the eye?[12] The same architecture was described in *Vintage London* (1942) as the 'largest incursion into conscious stylism' of the 'later Victorian builders', which provided 'the inspiration for many a corbelled, balconied, stone-dressed, french-windowed block of solid pre-war flats, known in their luxurious days as "mansions"'.[13] This rattled-off list of attributes does sound disparaging, as though Pont Street were being blamed for the many pale imitations that followed it, but note that the blocks are *solid*. It may also be contended that the hapless street as it appears in 'The Arrest of Oscar Wilde', towering in its 'new built red / [. . .] hard as the morning gaslight' (ll.6–7), could have been contrived to convey the attitude that a bleary-eyed Wilde might have had to his hotel room vista.

Assume for the moment that Betjeman's preface *is* sincere and that maybe this post-Piperian preface is as heartfelt and 'moving' as Jock Murray found it.[14] Certainly a man who repeats the word 'funny' seven times in a mere 82 words would seem to be heartily sick of being referred to as such. Yet Betjeman's unpredictable attitude to comedy could still cause problems and create ambivalence where there should have been certainty. Though he had chosen *Old Lights for New Chancels* for a title in November 1939, for example, by the following January he had decided it was 'too humorous' and ran the risk of cancelling out his introduction.[15] This is seemingly sat odds with Hillier's revelation that he had wanted to include a joke beneath the silhouette of himself which appears on the facing page. Whatever this was, Murray thought it would have been as detrimental to the tone of the book as its author did the title. He therefore quashed it in the same way he did Betjeman's last-minute suggestion to release *Old Lights* with a band round its dust-jacket which read 'NOT RECOMMENDED BY THE BOOK SOCIETY'.[16] The naughty schoolboy in Betjeman would always remain, although it could be that, by this time, he had become embarrassed by the passion of his essay and felt it needed to be tempered.

Aside from those members of the canon already mentioned, Betjeman names a number of other poets who fuelled his imagination. From the eighteenth century, Dr Watts, Swift, Robert Lloyd, Thomson, Cowper and Burns are among his 'favourites', but those from the nineteenth include

PRAED, HOOD, CLARE, EBENEZER ELLIOTT, CAPT. KENNISH, NEALE, [. . .], CHARLES TENNYSON TURNER, CLOUGH, WILLIAM BARNES, MEREDITH, WILLIAM MORRIS and a score or so more.[17]

This is Betjeman setting himself 'among the dead' and it is clear that the concept of influence is pivotal. Tennyson might have been buried clutching a copy of *Cymbeline*, but his admiration for Keats and Shelley can come as no ·surprise to those familiar with his early lyrics.[18] The same is true of Betjeman and the Victorians, and this underlines the point made in the last chapter about connoisseurship. He may have claimed to derive 'great pleasure in what is termed minor poetry' and 'long epics which never get into anthologies', but the scope of his knowledge was plainly much wider than that.[19] There is a growing sense right through the book of a mind discerning in its tastes and a writer able to incorporate them into his own work either subconsciously or as overt homage.

The first poem is an Old Light shining brightly. 'Cheltenham', which had been published in *The Listener* over a year before (22 December 1938), at once reflects and reverses the first poem of *Mount Zion*, though where in Warwickshire there was decay, in the Gloucestershire spa town there is hope:

> *Floruit, floret, floreat!*
> *Cheltonia's children cry.*
> ('CHELTENHAM', LL. 1–2)

With its references to 'elm trees', 'distant carriages' and the celebrated batsman C. B. Fry, 'Cheltenham' seems to be all middle class tea-and-cricket Englishness. The opening also recalls the public school anthem *Floreat Etona* and is a neat pun on the flower festivals for which the town is known. But there is more than a hint of the fêted late-Victorian anthology *Lyra Heroica* (1891) here too. W. E. Henley, who edited this collection, wanted, among other things, to 'set forth [. . .] the beauty and the joy of living, the beauty and the blessedness of death [and] the sacred quality of patriotism'.[20] This philosophy is clearly appreciated by Betjeman and though the poem originally appeared before even the so-called Phoney War, by March 1940 its optimism would have undoubtedly been welcome amid the despair of looming destruction. Betjeman owned a copy of Henley's second edition (1892), and one might speculate that the social upheaval of the 1930s inspired him to re-read it; its presence may be felt throughout *Old Lights* – even some of those poets listed in the preface (Cowper, Burns, Elliott, Meredith, Morris etc.) feature therein.[21]

From 'Cheltenham' we travel northwards via the old Midland Railway to Salop, where we find 'A Shropshire Lad' to be strangely ambivalent in its portrayal of the region's industrial landscape. The poem obviously gestures ironically towards the ruralism of Housman's well-known work and Patrick Taylor-Martin suggests that it 'raises the question of how seriously Betjeman could really be taken'.[22] Indeed, the note at the head that it should be *'recited with a Midland accent'* was undoubtedly mocking: the poet and John Piper had, after all, greatly enjoyed mimicking the local inflection when working on the *Shell Guide* to the area in 1939 (published 1951); Betjeman's friend Stuart Piggott noted in particular that the pair '"kept up conversations in a comic Shropshire accent, full of flat vowels and hard "g's" [. . .]"'.[23] This accounts for the repetition of 'Swimming along' and 'Dripping along' in the first two stanzas, though Betjeman seems to have tired of the joke by the end where Captain Webb is described, in entirely unfunny terms, as 'Rigid and dead'. As Goronwy Rees observed in his review for *The Spectator*, '[i]n the sophisticated this [poem] is calculated to create a *frisson*; in a far greater number, brought up on Moody and Sankey, it might inspire the kind of emotion, the associations, the nostalgia, aroused in others by, let us say, *Inside of King's College Chapel*.[24] Quite so, and some of the description is at least as sympathetic as that which we saw in the poet's 1933 article, 'Leeds – A City of Contrasts':

> The sun was low on the railway line
> And over the bricks and stacks,
> And in at the upstairs windows
> Of the Dawley houses' backs,
>
> ('A Shropshire Lad', LL. 13–16)

Whether he intended to or not, Betjeman was beginning to write poetry that connected with the life of the nation.

Rees's highly favourable piece concludes with an interesting note on 'Myfanwy at Oxford', in which he draws a parallel between the poet and an august antecedent:

> [i]s it an accident, given their common architectural tastes, that in his amatory ecstasies Mr Betjeman sometimes strongly reminds one of Ruskin; and what is the influence of Butterfield on sex?[25]

As his devotees will doubtless know, Butterfield is to sex what Carlisle United is to the Premiership. The reference to his counterpart, however, presents us with two possibilities: is Rees referring to Ruskin's unconsummated marriage to Effie Gray (and thus a sort of sexless aesthetic appreciation of femininity) or his passion for Rose La Touche (his nine-year-old cousin)?[26] Such ambiguity is in fact reflected in the verse itself: 'Myfanwy' may not be a 'double poem', but it does come close to being two separate pieces.[27] The opening and closing stanzas, for example, are plainly written from the perspective of a child:

> Kind o'er the *kinderbank* leans my Myfanwy,
> White o'er the play-pen the sheen of her dress,
> Fresh from the bathroom and soft in the nursery
> Soap-scented fingers I long to caress.
> :   :   :   :   :   :
> Then what sardines in the half-lighted passages!
> Locking of fingers in long hide-and-seek.
> You will protect me, my silken Myfanwy,
> Ringleader, tom-boy, and chum to the weak.
>
> ('Myfanwy', LL. 1–4; 25–28)

The narrator, who is granted his wish at the end of the poem, *is* the child in the play-pen. Where then is the "perversion" that Rees can see, and what does it tell us?[28] Two Victorian poetic theories (among the many) may help. The first, and perhaps the most famous, is John Stuart Mill's belief that 'all poetry is of the nature of soliloquy', expressing feeling close to 'the exact shape in which it exists in the poet's mind'.[29] The second centres round Robert Browning's idea that a poem can be staged as 'an expressive fiction or psychological moment'.[30] With Mill, if a writer writes it, then he or she must think it – a concept developed by Arthur Hallam, who added that 'the emotions of a poet, during composition, follow a regular law of association'.[31] So even a mask, by its very construction, can betray the idiosyncrasies of its maker. From such a perspective, and confining the analysis to the lines quoted above, Myfanwy may be seen as a sort of doughty older sister, worshipped by a younger and feebler narrator than Betjeman himself. However, the rest of the poem is a strange diagonal between childhood reminiscence – with its familiar shop names ('Home and Colonial, Star, International') and symbols of comfort ('Rackham's Hans Andersen' and 'Robertson's marmalade') – and the eroticism conveyed by the girl's 'Black-stockinged legs', peddling away at her 'fortunate bicycle'. As much of the work demonstrates (to say nothing of his choice of wife), Betjeman *did* perceive himself as weak and he *did* idolise strong women. Sex can never be far away in these circumstances, thus in the case of both 'Myfanwy' and its sequel, 'Myfanwy at Oxford' (1938), the Browningesque role-playing is obviously coloured by Betjeman's own feelings. It *would* be 'perverted' if he, a 34-year-old man, were truly lusting after a schoolgirl, but truth belies the insinuation: the muse in this case *was* a woman; no less than the blond, attractive, intelligent wife-of-the-artist, Myfanwy Piper (neé Evans – hence the 'Sancta Hilda, Myfanwyatia / Evansensis' of 'Myfanwy at Oxford').[32] Indeed, it is in this second poem that Betjeman's interest is made even clearer, for here he considers the same woman from a different point in her life. However, it is little less than ironic that Rees did not pick up on the footnote to 'A Shropshire Lad', which gleefully claims that its opening ('The gas was on in the Institute') was derived from a line in *Boyhood* (1930), a novel in verse by the Rev E. E. Bradford, the "paedophile poet" whose work was known to reduce Betjeman and Auden to tears of laughter.[33]

Hillier cites the 'Myfanwy' diptych as another example of the influence of Arthur Machen's *The Secret Glory* (1922), which also features a 'golden Myfanwy' in one its so-called Welsh Poems.[34] There is also a tenuous link to Tennyson's *The Princess* (1847), which was quoted by Betjeman in his preface. The Prologue of this medley includes a reference to 'sweet girl-graduates in their golden hair' (l. 142) – recognizably Myfanwy types, although echoes may also be detected in 'Pot Pourri from a Surrey Garden'. The biographer recognises the use of Tennysonian 'scene-setting' and 'sensuous imagery' here, although in some respects the 'petulant' (l. 4) Pam is a comic amalgam of the 'petulant' Lilia (*The Princess*, Prologue, l. 152), the Amazonian sentinels of Princess Ida's court, and the ethos of the Princess herself.[35]

Pam, I adore you, Pam you great big mountainous sports girl,
    Whizzing them over the net, full of the strength of five:

That old Malvernian brother, you zephyr and khaki shorts girl,
    Although he's playing for Woking,
      Can't stand up
    To your wonderful backhand drive.
      ('POT POURRI FROM A SURREY GARDEN', LL. 13–18)

               close behind her stood
Eight daughters of the plough, stronger than men,
Huge women blowzed with health, and wind, and rain,
And labour. Each was like a Druid rock;
      (THE PRINCESS, IV, LL. 258–261)[36]

The presence of Tennyson is certainly strong, but a closer reading also discloses other allusions. It may be noticed, for instance, that Betjeman employs a similar, accentual version of the classical metre used by Clough in (among other things) *Amours de Voyage* (1858):

WHICH of the three Misses Trevellyn it is that Vernon
    shall marry
Is not a thing to be known; for our friend is one of those
    natures
Which have their perfect delight in the general tender-
    domestic,
So that he trifles with Mary's shawl, ties Susan's bonnet,
Dances with all, but at home is most, they say, with
    Georgina,
Who is, however, too silly in my apprehension for Vernon.
    (CLOUGH, AMOURS DE VOYAGE, I.VI [CLAUDE TO EUSTACE], LL. 115–120)[37]

Clough's accentual hexameters not only highlight the difficulties of translating "ancient" into "modern" sensibly, but also give rise to a conversational style more closely (if ironically) related to the classical epic than that of 'Pot Pourri'.[38] Betjeman's alternation of hexameter and pentameter in the first three lines of his stanzas recalls more readily the so-called "elegiac" metre used by Ovid in his love lyrics. Of course, true classical poetry does not rhyme and Clough follows this rule, choosing to use diction to mock Eustace's rather pompous mode of speech. Betjeman, on the other hand, accentuates the humour with some quite outrageous examples of rhyme – 'Hendren's' and 'rhododendrons' in the fourth stanza and 'casement', 'enlacement' and 'embracement' in the fifth.[39] This (in part) spoofs Betjeman's own classical education, but he seems to have taken it further quite deliberately by basing the poem on ironic models; the aural repetition in lines 3 and 4, for instance, betrays a similar interest in the phonetic qualities of verse that Calverley displays in 'In the Gloaming' (1872):

> Miles of pram in the wind and Pam in the gorse track,
>> Coco-nut smell of the broom and a packet of Weights
> Press'd in the sand. The thud of a hoof on a horse-track –
> A horse-riding horse for a horse-track –
>> Conifer county of Surrey approached
> Through remarkable wrought-iron gates.
>> (BETJEMAN, 'POT POURRI FROM A SURREY GARDEN', LL. 1–6)

> Love, you dear delusive dream, you! Very sweet your victims
>> deem you,
> When, heard only by the seamew, they talk all the stuff one can.
>> (CALVERLEY, 'IN THE GLOAMING', LL. 11–12)[40]

The interest in Amazonian women is echoed later in *Old Lights* by 'Senex', where the girls wholly to Betjeman's liking are tennis-playing, 'golden hiking' cyclists. The poem is based on the story of Actaeon, the young hunter who saw Artemis naked and was turned into a stag and torn to pieces by his own dogs for his trouble. However, Hillier is probably right to assert that inspiration (and the title) came from the work of another *Lyra Heroica* poet, Thomas Campbell (1777–44), whose 'Senex's Soliloquy on his Youthful Idol' was first published in 1842.[41] Campbell was an old man by this time, but Betjeman was still in his early thirties when his poem first appeared, and while much more concerned with the purging of lust, his opening refrain is certainly indicative of the ageing process and the distance from sexual encounters that it often enforces:

> Oh would I could subdue the flesh
>> Which sadly troubles me!
> And then perhaps could view the flesh
> As though I never knew the flesh
>> And merry misery.
>> ('SENEX', LL. 1–5)

The obsessive repetition of 'flesh' is suggestive of the pain that only unconsummated passion can bring; in this context, the poor individual (who clearly *has* known the flesh) is a definite forbear of the protagonist of later pieces more obviously connected with superannuation, like 'Late-Flowering Lust' (1950) and 'The Olympic Girl' (1954). But while the poet may have wished himself above carnal sin, he cleverly reveals his lowly status in relation to the girls by placing them atop two-wheeled cycles: *his* character, note, needs the stability that only a tricycle can bring.[42] Betjeman may also have taken his cue from Hardy, for despite its references to 'wasting skin' (l. 12), Hardy's 'I Look into my Glass' (1898) is really a lament for 'hearts grown cold' (l. 6). Time is cast as the enemy here because it 'Part steals, lets part abide' (l. 10). Betjeman, though influenced by this, is less subtle: Hardy ends with the mere hint of sex in the 'throbbings of noontide'; in 'Senex', we are treated to the full-blown (and hugely evocative) images of underwear, suspenders and buttocks.

We find the sentiment of Hardy's churchyard poems more specifically in 'On a Portrait of a Deaf Man', a piece that has been the cause of some difficulty for many commentators, since it involves the death of Betjeman's father in 1934.[43] The problem derives from the widely known fact that the relationship was an uneasy one; consider stanza 4:

> And when he could not hear me speak
>   He smiled and looked so wise
> That now I do not like to think
>   Of maggots in his eyes.
>   ('On a Portrait of a Deaf Man', ll.13–16)

Is this funny? Ghastly? Horrifying? What does it say about the relationship between father and son? The man with the 'kind old face, the egg-shaped head / The tie, discreetly loud' (ll. 1–2) does not sound like an object of hatred. This is the same man, after all, who 'liked the rain-washed Cornish air' (l. 17), and who liked to paint the 'big and bare' (l. 19) landscape – interests that strike one as very similar to those of his son. We are, conceivably, meant to laugh at the maggots in the eyes, the clay-filled mouth and the rotting fingers: the jaunty, ABCB rhyme tells us we should, as does the rigid 8.6.8.6 metre with its alternating four- and three-stress lines. But the clue is in the ambivalence for, as is so often the case, the truth revealed at the last makes us feel perhaps a little ashamed:

> You, God, who treat him thus and thus
>   Say "Save his soul and pray."
> You ask me to believe You and
>   I only see decay.
>   ('On a Portrait of a Deaf Man', ll. 29–32)

Line 29 conveys something of the raging argument in Clough's 'Is it true, ye gods, who treat us' (1849), but the last harks back to 'Abide with Me' ('change and decay in all around I see'). While the tone of that hymn is ultimately positive, however, Betjeman can only see decomposition. Yet 'On a Portrait of a Deaf Man' is a poem which also evokes the same idea that features in much of Hardy's work: "in the midst of life, we are in death". This is evident in 'Life and Death at Sunrise' (1925, although associated with 1867), where we find a similar mixture of humour, mortality and continuity:

> 'And what have you got covered there?'
> He nods to the waggon and mare.
> 'Oh, a coffin for old John Thinn:
> We are just going to put him in.'

'– So he's gone at last. He always had a good constitution.'
'– He was ninety-odd. He could call up the French Revolution.'
(HARDY, 'LIFE AND DEATH AT SUNRISE', LL. 19–24)[44]

Hardy's 'The Choirmaster's Burial' (1917) also has a recognisable collapse
into pathos, while his 'Voices from Things Growing in a Churchyard' (1921)
captures a similar image of the rotting corpse so vivid in Betjeman: 'In shin-
gled oak my bones were pent; / Hence more than a hundred years I spent /
In my feat of change from a coffin-thrall / To a dancer in green as leaves on
a wall' (ll. 11–14). In terms of a structural model, however, Betjeman may
have been influenced by 'The Dead Quire' (1901), which has both a similar
rhyme scheme to 'On a Portrait of a Deaf Man' (ABAB, against ABCB), and
a similar metre (Hardy's second line having one stress more than
Betjeman's):

> 'The singers had followed one by one,
> Treble, and tenor, and thorough-bass;
> And the worm that wasteth had begun
>   To mine their mouldering place.
> ('THE DEAD QUIRE', IV, LL. 13–16)[45]

As we saw in the last chapter, Betjeman's earlier religious poems had
concentrated on sending up the clergy; 'On a Portrait of a Deaf Man' is the
first piece to convey any serious sense of religious doubt. John Press has
commented that where 'Hardy disbelieved in the Christmas story [but] hoped
that it might be true; Betjeman affirms his faith in it while fearing that it may
be false,'[46] Such fear would seem to have plunged to the depths here as
Betjeman torments himself with the issue that so troubled Matthew Arnold,
Christina Rossetti, Clough and Robert Browning *et al.* Yet like all good
debaters, he also gives us the other side of the argument in 'Olney Hymns'
(whose lines, 'With words of Grace which Thou didst choose', recall both John
Newton and Cowper) and 'Saint Cadoc', a paean to him who breathed the
breath of God.[47] Here, the fear of war – 'Some cavern generates the germs /
To send my body to the worms' (ll. 19–20) – is assuaged by a mixture of faith
and the comfort offered by the Cornish coastline:

> Here where St. Cadoc sheltered God
> The archaeologist has trod,
> Yet death is now the gentle shore
> With Land upon the cliffs before
>   And in his cell beside the sea
>   The Celtic saint has prayed for me.
> ('SAINT CADOC', LL. 31–36)[48]

By the last stanza, Betjeman is sufficiently reassured to feel that 'death is now the gentle shore'; as 'Saint Cadoc' is the final poem of *Old Lights*, this per-haps suggests that he had come down on the side of Belief for now.

The collection's Hardy theme makes the omission of 'The Heart of Thomas Hardy' seem surprising. Its absence is explained by the fact that Betjeman felt it to be 'below standard', although it did appear in the first edition of *Collected Poems* (1958). For Donald Davie, despite ultimately being a 'hyperbolical compliment' to Hardy, its reference to 'several unmarried mothers' (l. 8) is 'flippantly knowing' and merely representative of 'shallowly competitive conversation'.[49] He concedes that the verse form (a 'sort of English hexam-eter') is handled 'with something approaching Hardy's inventiveness', but the rhythm (again, close to an English hexameter) is actually more subtle than Hardy usually managed:

> There, in the heart of the nimbus, twittered the heart of Hardy
> There, on the edge of the nimbus, slowly revolved the corpses
> Radiating around the twittering heart of Hardy,
> Slowly started to turn in the light of their own Creator
> Died away in the night as frost will blacken a dahlia.
>
> ('THE HEART OF THOMAS HARDY', LL. 14–18)

In fairness to Davie, it must be said that 'twittering' does not convey the sort of reverence that a writer likened to God should command. Though the basic idea for the poem derives from Dante's *Paradiso*, it does employ a similar semiology to Hardy's graveyard poems, yet the fact that Hardy's creations – 'Tess and Jude and His Worship' *et al.* – are ephemeral, is no compliment to the master either. Perhaps Larkin summed it up best when he referred to the poem as 'totally eccentric'.[50] Perhaps indeed it was an experiment that did not go entirely to plan, too at odds with the Hardy who suffused the preface and poetry of *Old Lights for New Chancels*.

While Betjeman dragged himself successfully away from the abyss of contradiction here, he fails regarding his somewhat perplexing opinion that Browning lacked sympathy. There are, in short, too many allusions to, and examples of, Browning's work in the volume for this view to hold up. As we have seen, 'Myfanwy' loosely follows the pattern of a monologue; similarly, 'In Westminster Abbey' uses the form for satirical purposes: 'Gracious Lord, oh bomb the Germans. [. . .] / But, gracious Lord, whate'er shall be, / Don't let anyone bomb me.'[51] And, 'Bristol and Clifton', though a *dia*logue, is a defi-nite relative of Browning's quintessential dramatic *mono*logue, 'My Last Duchess' (1842).

Admittedly this is more a meeting of feeling than form, for where the Duke speaks in obscured rhyming couplets, Mr Battlecock, Betjeman's church-warden, is given a conversational blank verse style. But, as a replacement for the Count's envoy, note that Betjeman gives us a church visitor, who, while preventing the poem from being a monologue *per se*, speaks only to punctuate the speech of the warden himself. The Duke, apart from being murderous, is also chiefly interested in his wealth and all it says about his good taste; in Betjeman, this corresponds to the effect that money is hoped to have on God's beneficence, illustrated by the stained glass window, which is said to be superior to the one in Battlecock's home, and which is, of course, Betjeman's version of the Fra Pandolf portrait. (Pandolf himself is represented by the 'Bristol firm' that executed the window, and that made 'The figure of the lady on the left' resemble Battlecock's own Duchess-wife).

The church is naturally the Battlecock power base: *he* donates its oak, and points out the brass plaque commemorating the fact; *his* was the decision to have radiators fixed along the walls to hamper the work of a Ritualist (should one be inducted) and it is *he* who fulfils the vital role of counting out the money. He is, in fact, the 'Duke of Clifton' and Betjeman keeps the connection going until the bitter end when the warden tries to impress his audience of one by telling him that he knows 'the Inskips very well indeed'.[52] This was a real family, but it nevertheless allows a humorous phonetic connection to Browning's coda:

> Notice Neptune, though,
> Taming a sea-horse, thought a rarity,
> Which Claus of Innsbruck cast in bronze for me!
> ('My Last Duchess', ll. 54–56)[53]

With the associations between past and present, and people and place in *Old Lights for New Chancels*, there is a clear sense of Betjeman becoming the Betjeman familiar to his popular audience of the 1960s. But the book is only a stepping-stone in some respects, for, as well as showing a great deal more confidence, he continued to hark back to his earlier work by drawing out oddities from childhood reading and elsewhere. So, as well as the references to Clough, Browning, Tennyson and Hardy, Betjeman also quotes Bradford, for example, and includes his 1938 pamphlet *Sir John Piers*, a quintet based on a true-life Obscure Irish Peer.[54] Ironically, the phrase 'black in rain', which appears in the first line of 'The Attempt' (No. II in the *Sir John Piers* cycle), is put to use again in 'Trebetherick'. In this way, it serves to highlight the poet's climb, a climb which is encapsulated by the Cornish poem more than any other of the period:

> But when a storm was at its height,
> And feathery slate was black in rain,
> And tamarisks were hung with light
> And golden sand was brown again,
> ('Trebetherick', ll. 21–24)

Here, the nostalgia for childhood hinted at in 'Myfanwy' is abundant. Our formative years will forever be associated with carefree holidays, with their 'Sand in the sandwiches, wasps in the tea' (l. 7), yet Betjeman manages to convey too a sense of growing-up, both in the reference to 'an early cigarette' (l. 10) and the tacit awareness of the violent dominance of man (represented by the pheasant and rabbit that 'lay torn open at the throat' (l. 20)).

However, 'Trebetherick' not only lies in Hardy's Lyonesse, but also in the land of Tennyson. The 'tamarisks' of lines 10 and 23 may have been suggested by a reading of *The Princess* (where they appear with some frequency), but the sensuality of the language in the above extract is also indicative of Betjeman's respect for the late Laureate's mastery of technique: observe the redolent combination of the 'feathery slate', the illuminated foliage and the 'golden sand', for example. Indeed, it is in this poem that Betjeman reveals the first vestiges of his Tennysonian interest in the sea.[55] His forebear's 'Break, break, break' (1842), for example, conveys a similar marriage between child and ocean:

> Break, break, break,
> On thy cold gray stones, O Sea!
> And I would that my tongue could utter
> The thoughts that arise in me.
>
> O well for the fisherman's boy,
> That he shouts with his sister at play!
> O well for the sailor lad,
> That he sings in his boat on the bay!
>
> ('BREAK, BREAK, BREAK', LL. 1–8)[56]

The perspective may be somewhat different, but the reader may discern that the sea remains a place of happiness and adventure for the youngsters, just as it does for 'Ralph, Vasey, Alastair, Biddy, John' and Betjeman in 'Trebetherick', where, even after a storm, the waves bring 'treasure' as they roar majestically up the beach:

> Then roller into roller curled
> And thundered down the rocky bay,
> And we were in a water world
> Of rain and blizzard, sea and spray,
> And one against another hurled
> We struggled round to Greenaway.
>
> ('TREBETHERICK', LL. 31–36)

In addition to Goronwy Rees's favourable notice, *Old Lights for New Chancels* was reviewed in *The Times Literary Supplement* (*TLS*), *The New Statesman and Nation* and *The Listener* (among others). Both the *TLS* and "Senex" in *The New Statesman* noted the references to childhood and quoted from 'Trebetherick', the *TLS* drawing particular attention to its 'sensitively handled, [. . .] precise detail'.[57] "Senex" called it 'one of [the poet's] most successful metrical experiments', but the most insightful remark came from the *TLS*, which closed with the observation that the wit of *Old Lights* was 'humorously revealing, because [Betjeman] has an attachment for places and people which others would overlook or even despise'. The sales figures would seem to support the general critical view: 629 copies were sold in the first three months, with the total for the year reaching 787 – almost 250 more than the first year sales of *Continual Dew*. In fact, the new volume sold out within three years (about half the time of its predecessor), and though this is partly due to the print run being some 600 copies fewer, the faith Murray had in his author to publish something as palpably unimportant as poetry at such a crucial point in the war is clear.[58] Furthermore, there is no doubt that the quality of Betjeman's work had increased over the past three years. The same was true of his profile, thanks, as we shall see, to an increasing number of radio broadcasts. Despite this, it would be inaccurate to claim that the public was starting to buy copies of his work simply because he was becoming what would now be called a media celebrity. Such status would not really be a factor until the later 1950s and '60s, when Betjeman began to augment his output with television appearances. Steady sales mean that an author has attracted a certain following and an early surge such as *Old Lights* enjoyed implies a certain level of anticipation (and, perhaps, acceptance of critical opinion). Despite the fact that he was still not selling enormous numbers of copies, Betjeman was now reaching a much wider public than the arcane audience of the previous decade.

Ireland

In 1941, after his stint at the Ministry of Information, Betjeman moved on to become the United Kingdom's Press Attaché in Dublin. He worked under Sir John Maffey and there is some speculation that he became one of Maffey's so-called "spies" in that department. Bevis Hillier plays this down, suggesting that any intelligence role would only have been a small part of the poet's work.[59] It was certainly not enough to get his name in the infamous Nazi 'Black Book', which listed all those the invading forces would exterminate if Britain's last line of defence crumbled.[60] But in spite of the lack of importance that this implies, a 2000 television documentary did include facsimiles of various reports that Betjeman had written on potential collaborators and sympathisers. It must be said that there was nothing childish or "funny" about them. From the general public's point of view, however, Betjeman's most important war work continued to centre on the media.[61] It was now, after all, that he successfully assisted Laurence Olivier in his quest to film the battle scenes of *Henry V* (1944) in the Republic – a propaganda coup if ever there was one.[62]

In similarly patriotic fashion, much of the prose from this period was written in celebration of Britain. In 1942, William Collins published *Vintage London* and here, amidst numerous colour plates, Betjeman endeavoured to show where the old city's gems could 'still be rediscovered'.[63] The book was 'an escape', and though he later claimed to have written it 'at a time of financial stress', it does show the emphasis he was placing ever more on encouraging people to look about them.[64] Such patriotic propaganda was vital in two senses: first, in combating the anxieties of those who were unable to fight on the front line (which would help ensure that the country carried on functioning); and secondly, to highlight what was being fought for.

Betjeman was now employing similar methods in his radio talks (at which he was becoming increasingly adept). In 'Some Comments in Wartime' (7 July 1940) he continued the theme of 'How to Like Everything', noting that he had 'become grateful for small things which [he] had not time to notice in that hurried turmoil we called civilisation before the war'.[65] This, and the idea that when his 'activity' was perforce 'slowed down' he 'started to see again and to feel', cleverly exhorted listeners to think not of destruction, but the beauty of their surroundings and to enjoy (if at all possible) the slower pace of life that war occasioned.[66] This at once acted as an emollient to fear and a catalyst to national pride:

> [n]ow the buildings stand out and I have time to see them – decent Georgian terraces [. . .] and often beautiful Victorian churches [. . .].

> [N]ow I am so forgiving I *like* suburbs: nothing is ugly.

> [T]hose ['sham Tudor'] houses: they are part of England.[67]

Near the end of the talk, the poet spelled out an important truth for his audience: 'what really does matter is people, not their possessions'.[68] Was this the stately home loving, aesthetic dandy of the 1930s? No, this was a *man*, whose love of England was nothing but heightened during his Irish "exile". As he wrote in *English Cities and Small Towns* (1943):

> [n]ot until you have been away from it, as has the author of this book for more than a year, do you realise how friendly, how beautiful is the meanest English town. [. . .] Even a town like Wolverhampton looks splendid through Memory's telescope.[69]

These ideas dominate the poet's first post-war volume of verse, *New Bats in Old Belfries* (1945). Despite its doubly humorous title – a play on *Old Lights for New Chancels*, as well as 'bats in the belfry' – it represents yet another advance. In fact it may be seen as *Old Lights for New Chancels*, only more so. Here we celebrate 'Bristol', 'Parliament Hill Fields', Surrey (again – in 'A Subaltern's Love Song'), and take a Hardyesque break 'In a Bath Teashop'. However the opener, 'Henley-on-Thames', also hints at the sense of impending loss which shrouded the country in the first five years of the decade:

When shall I see the Thames again?
The prow-promoted gems again,
          As beefy ATS
          Without their hats
Come shooting through the bridge?
                            ('HENLEY-ON-THAMES', LL. 19–23)

The 'beefy' girls may be typically Betjemanian, but as the poet wrote to John Sparrow, he also wanted to show 'the incongruity of A[uxilliary] T[erritorial] S[ervice] among the Edwardian baskets of geraniums' – beauty tainted by the unmistakeable hue of conflict, in other words.[70] Similar 'incongruity' may be found in 'Anticipation in Spring' – 'Still heavy with may, and the sky ready to fall, / Meadow buttercup high, shed and chicken and wire?' (l.1) – and 'Margate, 1940', in which Betjeman compares the wartime aspect of this seaside town with that of his childhood:

From out the Queen's Highcliffe for weeks at a stretch
I watched how the mower evaded the vetch,
So that over the putting-course rashes were seen
Of pink and of yellow among the burnt green.
:   :   :   :   :   :   :
Beside the Queen's Highcliffe now rank grows the vetch,
Now dark is the terrace, a storm-battered stretch;
And I think, as the fairy-lit sights I recall,
It is those we are fighting for, foremost of all.
                            ('MARGATE, 1940', LL. 1–4; 25–28)

General military references are also abundant in *New Bats*: note 'A Subaltern's Love Song' and '*Invasion Exercise* on the Poultry Farm', for example (my italics). The last poem in the book packs a harder punch, being an elegy for Betjeman's friend Basil Ava (that is, B. S. Blackwood, Earl of Ava, later Marquess of Dufferin and Ava), who was killed in Burma in 1945. It shows how the war, which had been an abstract political concept for many in its early months (as Waugh describes in *Put Out More Flags* (1942)), soon became an intensely, and painfully, personal matter:

Friend of my youth, you are dead!
          and the long peal pours from the steeple
Over this sunlit quad
          in our University city
And soaks in Headington stone.
:   :   :   :   :
Stop, oh many bells, stop
          pouring on roses and creeper
Your unremembering peel

> this hollow, unhallowed V.E. Day, –
> I am deaf to your notes and dead
> by a soldier's body in Burma.
> ('In Memory of Basil, Marquess of Dufferin and Ava', ll. 15–19; 37–42)[71]

Though the sheer volume of Betjeman's work in Ireland had a grave effect on the process of composition, he was able to continue to write – and write well. Indeed, it was in the February of 1941 that Cyril Connolly's *Horizon* had published 'A Subaltern's Love Song', one of the most enduring of all his poems.[72] Derek Stanford likened it to Frederick Locker Lampson's 'At Hurlingham' (1857), and though the connections – sport, romance and monologue – are there, Betjeman's quatrain is of a discernibly higher quality:

> Bang . . . bang . . . ! That's Willy! There's his bird,
>   Blithely it cleaves the skies above me!
> He's missed all ten! He's too absurd!
>   I hope he'll always, always love me!
>   (Lampson, 'At Hurlingham')

> Love-thirty, love-forty, oh! weakness of joy,
> The speed of a swallow, the grace of a boy,
> With carefullest carelessness, gaily you won,
> I am weak from your loveliness, Joan Hunter Dunn.
>   (Betjeman, 'A Subaltern's Love Song', ll. 5–8)[73]

It is of course the *narrator* who is inept in Betjeman's poem, but note how the rhyming couplets give a keener sense of verve in comparison with Lampson's. Indeed, the extracts show that 'A Subaltern's Love Song' is similar in only the loosest manner, and that Betjeman's mastery of language has given his poem a timeless quality, which Lampson's lacks.

By the close of 1941, Murray was encouraging Betjeman to send him more verses. Part of what he received, the poet referred to as his 'Epic', a large blank verse autobiographical piece which would undergo several changes before emerging as *Summoned by Bells* almost twenty years later. One extract of this became 'Sunday Afternoon Service in St Enodoc Church, Cornwall' (1944), a "Tennyson" piece about the place where Betjeman's body would eventually be buried.[74] Indeed, the parallels with Tennyson's work in this idiom show the weaknesses of those that Stanford drew between Betjeman and Lampson. Consider, for example, the following extract from 'Morte d'Arthur' (1842):

> The bold Sir Bedivere uplifted him,
> Sir Bedivere, the last of all his knights,
> And bore him to a chapel nigh the field,
> A broken chancel with a broken cross,
> That stood on a dark strait of barren land.

On one side lay the Ocean, and on one
Lay a great water, and the moon was full.
(TENNYSON, 'MORTE D'ARTHUR', LL. 6–12)[75]

The position of Tennyson's chapel is striking. Obviously, both poems are essentially set in Cornwall, but St Enodoc is also situated so that 'On one side lay the ocean' (albeit with a golf course on the other). The informality of Tennyson's Prologue and Epilogue are also reminiscent of Betjeman's conversational style, particularly in the early stages of 'Sunday Afternoon', where Betjeman adopts a relaxed but conservative iambic pentameter similar to his forebear's:

There's Enid with a silly parasol,
And Graham in gray flannel with a crease
Across the middle of his coat which lay
Pressed 'neath the box of his Meccano set,
Sunday to Sunday.
(BETJEMAN, 'SUNDAY AFTERNOON', LL. 16–20)

At Francis Allen's on the Christmas-eve, -
The game of forfeits done – all the girls kissed
Beneath the sacred bush and past away –
The parson Holmes, the poet Everard Hall,
The host, and I sat round the wassail-bowl,
(TENNYSON, 'THE EPIC', LL. 1–5)[76]

As one would expect in an early draft of autobiography, the social milieu of 'Sunday Afternoon' is all Betjeman's own. This, however, does not prevent Donald Davie from considering the piece in terms of Hardy. For him, it represents the best of Betjeman's verse in the sense that he is not consciously trying to "be" Hardy, rather allowing the *essence* of Hardy to colour his work.[77] Despite this, he does suggest a useful similarity with Hardy's 'Green Slates (Penpethy)' (1925):

It happened once, before the duller
Loomings of life defined them,
I searched for slates of greenish colour
A quarry where men mined them;
(HARDY, 'GREEN SLATES (PENPETHY)', LL. 1–4)[78]

Oh kindly slate of these unaltered cliffs,
Firm, barren substrate of our windy fields!
Oh lichened slate in walls, they knew your worth
Who raised you up to make this House of God
(BETJEMAN, 'SUNDAY AFTERNOON', LL. 102–105)

Betjeman avoids the literariness of Hardy's alliteration and double rhyme. But while it is the slates themselves that recall the woman the Penpethy narrator saw, and while Betjeman's slate too may be 'greenish' from lichen, the rock clearly has a greater theological significance in 'Sunday Afternoon'. Here, it is 'kindly' and altogether noble, offering 'shelter in this crevice dry' from the perils of the Atlantic: 'they knew your worth' indeed 'Who raised you up to make this House of God'. The implication is thus that the slate was instrumental in helping the Cornish saint to come to terms with the 'unfriendly shore' and the God who made it (and who, more significantly, fated seamen there 'to end their lives / Dashed on a rock' there). Furthermore, the sanctuary offered by St Enodoc seems to allow Betjeman to feel more pity for the 'large golfer, only four weeks dead', as if his death were more benign, more appropriate to the setting somehow (the links is, after all, just across the way). At the poem's close, the harmonium pipes up and Psalm 14 is announced as the service continues on into the 'sunlit and sea-distant' afternoon. Those who know the location will appreciate that the sea could not be described as 'distant' in any way, so it is clear that the slates help cocoon the narrator from some of death's horrors. Therefore, along with the 'cool silence' of the church's interior, they act as a barrier to doubt, although the reference to the Psalm betrays a certain irony:

> The fool hath said in his heart, *There is* no God.
>
> (PSALMS 14.1)

Such barriers are removed and such irony inverted in 'Before the Anaesthetic or A Real Fright' (1945). This poem, as Derek Stanford observes, is a 'dialectic between the affirming and rejecting spirit'.[79] It opens with a painterly description of 'the slanting summer rain' tapping the 'chestnut boughs' as St. Giles's bells fill the Oxford air with their 'Intolerably sad, profound' melody. Yet those bells quickly become inextricably linked with the fear of death, of nothingness, and the non-existence of God:

> Bells, ancient now as castle walls,
> Now hard and new as pitchpine stalls
> Now full with help from ages past
> Now dull with death and hell at last.
> Swing up! and give me hope of life,
> Swing down! and plunge the surgeon's knife.
> :   :   :   :   :   :
> Is it extinction when I die?
>
> (BETJEMAN, 'BEFORE THE ANAESTHETIC', LL. 15–20; 24)[80]

Despite the obvious Tennysonian reference in line 15, a similar emotional oscillation is hinted at in 'After', part of W. E. Henley's *In Hospital* sequence:

Like as a flamelet blanketed in smoke,
So through the anaesthetic shows my life;
So flashes and so fades my thought, at strife
With the strong stupor that I heave and choke
And sicken at, it is so foully sweet.

(HENLEY, 'AFTER', LL. 1–5)[81]

But, as the rhythm and mannered alliteration indicate, it is the quickness of mind that is moving in and out here. Henley's poem ends, after all, with a sense of 'immense, complacent dreamery'; in evocative, gasping, grasping eight-syllable lines, Betjeman's poem rather recalls the 'Christ is not risen' / 'Christ is yet risen' conundrum of Clough's 'Easter Day' poems. Similarly, the 'ebb and flow' of Arnold's 'Dover Beach' (1867), whose 'Sea of Faith' vanishes in a 'melancholy, long, withdrawing roar', seems to be in sympathy with the waves of sound coming from St. Giles's church tower. Betjeman also recognises that his fascination with 'church-crawling' may be more façade than faith:

I never knew the Lord at all.
Oh not in me your Saviour dwells
You ancient, rich St. Giles's bells.
Illuminated missals – spires –
Wide screens and decorated quires-
All these I loved, and on my knees
I thanked myself for knowing these
:   :   :   :   :
I, kneeling, thought the Lord was there.

('BEFORE THE ANAESTHETIC', LL. 36–42; 46)

In 'Sunday Afternoon', there is an understanding that a 'dispassionate and critic stare' is irrelevant to the church of St Enodoc, 'soaked in worship' and 'loved too well' as it was. During a BBC broadcast in 1948, Betjeman would also claim that the sight of St Mark's Church, Swindon taught him not to judge churches 'only by their architecture'.[82] In 'Before the Anaesthetic', however, there is a deep sense of terror, emphasised *in extremis*, that by seeking the Lord among the church furniture, salvation has been missed:

Now, lying in the gathering mist
I know that Lord did not exist
And lest this "I" should cease to be
Come, real Lord, come quick to me.

('BEFORE THE ANAESTHETIC', LL. 47–50)

There is a touch of Pascal's Wager about this, but Betjeman realises that, had he faith, 'There'd be no fight with kindly Death' (l. 60).[83] (There is also an outrageous (and very witty) pun on 'quick' – Betjeman wants the Lord to move with speed, yes, but also to be *alive*, as in the Anglo-Saxon 'cwic' – familiar from the prayerbook phrase 'the quick and the dead'.)

The beauty of Betjeman is that he never resolves this problem in his poetry. He writes verses and essays of great faith, notes about parish churches whose holiness brings one to one's knees – and then there are poems like 'Before the Anaesthetic', that come close to refuting all. But this is no less than just, for the question can only truly be answered after death – which takes us back to Pascal once more. Indeed the poem immediately after 'Before the Anaesthetic' deals with the other side of the argument, depicting as it does, the pervasive, belief-bolstering bells of another Swindon parish church:

> Your peal of ten ring over then this town,
> Ring on my men nor ever ring them down.
> :   :   :   :   :   :
> Now birth and death-reminding bells ring clear,
> Loud under 'planes and over changing gear.
> ('On Hearing the Full Peal of Ten Bells from
> CHRIST CHURCH, SWINDON, WILTS', LL. 1–2; 11–12)

This is a very clever piece of writing, there being ten syllables for ten bells, with the internal 'ten', 'then', 'men', 'planes [. . .] changing' motif adding a distinctly tintinnabulous chime to the rhyme – not to mention the pairing of 'over' and 'ever' as the only non-monosyllables in successive lines. The verse form is part of a poetic tradition as old as bell-founding and country churches alike. In industrialised Swindon, home to a great railway works until 1987, the bells have to fight to be heard (although heard they certainly are). Betjeman is topographically accurate here too, for Christ Church is situated both on a main road and under the flight path for RAF Lyneham. By contrast, in Bristol, an hour's train ride away to the west, the 'mathematic plain course' gives certainty as it 'cavern[s] out' the city's 'dying day'.[84]

Critically, *New Bats in Old Belfries* was a success. Rees again wrote a review for *The Spectator* and noted that the volume, while retaining certain 'obvious marks of eccentricity', conveyed 'an increasing mellowness and an increasing seriousness'.[85] G. W. Stonier (*New Statesman*) felt that, as an '*objet*', the book resembled something from the mid-nineteenth century, but went on to praise the vividness of the poetry which, he said, 'commands a liveliness and a depth rare in light verse'. The anonymous writer in *The Listener* was similarly enthusiastic and noted the mixture of 'easy running magazine poems' and 'the lyrical and more metrically elaborate' work, while the *TLS* called Betjeman 'the John Clare of suburbia'.[86] All well and good, and Betjeman doubtless revelled in the praise. Yet it seems that part of the point of the collection has been missed: for all the Victorianisms, the tennis-girls and ecclesiastical sketching, *New Bats in Old Belfries* is a defiant work that encapsulates some of what was best about Britain at the time. As such, it was the perfect complement to *Old Lights for New Chancels*, which, despite its pro-Britain, *Lyra Heroica* undercurrent included only one poem ('In Westminster Abbey') that referred to World War Two *specifically* (and that, being satirical, was contra to contemporary attitudes by and large). *New Bats in Old Belfries* was written chiefly *during* that conflict and is consequently of greater social relevance and purpose. That it was not available until after the declaration of peace is a mixture of post-war publishing austerity and Betjeman's other, more pressing, wartime commitments. His prose work fulfilled the necessary political role of showing how bright the home fires should be burning, but the reading public seems to have understood the ethos of *New Bats* even if the critics didn't, as the sales figures confirm. The first print run, at 2,020 copies, was back to the levels produced for *Continual Dew*, but this time sales were sufficiently high (1,749 copies between 19th and 31st December 1945) for a further run of 1,500 to be required. By the end of 1948, 3,404 had been sold (all but 19 of those printed). Betjeman's audience was still not huge, but it was expanding rapidly and would continue to do so.[87]

Flag Stones

Despite possible ambivalence about Pont Street, architecturally, Betjeman was on surer ground than he had been in the 1930s. In May 1940, for example, he produced another short piece on C. F. A. Voysey for the *Architectural Forum*. Voysey had recently won the RIBA's Royal Gold Medal, and the event allowed Betjeman to reiterate both the architect's influence on modern design, and how his work was based 'on the first principles of Gothic building'. No longer under the control of Hastings, however, he eschewed the concepts of 'individuality', 'necessity' and 'simplicity' that had been employed in the pages of the 'Archie Rev' (he also understood how 'puzzled' Voysey must have been 'to find himself associated with steel and glass and concrete buildings').[88]

This greater cohesion of attitude is exemplified in 'A Shropshire Lad', where the Victorian terraces act as a romantic backdrop to the figure of Captain Webb's ghost:

> The sun shone low on the railway line
> And over the bricks and stacks,
> And in at the upstairs windows
> Of the Dawley houses' backs,
>
> ('A SHROPSHIRE LAD', ll. 13–16)

Such portraiture is also employed in 'Blackfriars':

> By the shot tower near the chimneys,
> Off the road to Waterloo,

Stands the cottage of "The Ancient"
As in eighteen-forty-two.
('BLACKFRIARS', LL. 1–4)

Furthermore there are, in 'Myfanwy at Oxford' ('Tubular bells of tall St. Barnabas') and in 'St. Barnabas, Oxford' itself (which was included in *New Bats in Old Belfries*), allusions to Hardy's own architectural work of the period. Most strikingly, however, in 'Anticipation in Spring' (also from *New Bats*), the poet looks defiantly to the '*gallant* Victorian spire' (my italics).[89]

In prose, the message too had become clearer. In December 1940, the *Architectural Review* ran 'Nonconformist Architecture', a scholarly work that traced the history of these esoteric forms of preaching house. Nineteenth-century chapels, wrote Betjeman, were built as a result of the period's many religious revivals and built from contributions made by various local merchants: 'the local builder supplied the labour and the plan; the ironmonger the cast iron railings and the lamps' and so on.[90] Though some of these buildings were humble and had an unsophisticated feel, 'later Congregational churches' were Gothic.[91] Modern, post-1910, Nonconformist churches, however, lacked 'the individuality and strong character of those scrubbed conventicles of the seventeenth and eighteenth centuries or the gigantic preaching houses of the Victorian age'.[92]

While the hatred of nineteenth-century church vandalism would continue, and while he claimed no longer to judge a church by its architecture, by 1949 Betjeman decided that the time had come to "speak up" in favour of the Victorians. As he said in his BBC talk on St. Mark's Church, Swindon:

[w]hen they were restoring old buildings, even the greatest Victorian architects were often arrogant, heavy-handed and insensitive [. . .]. But when they were starting from scratch, Victorian church architects were often as original and creative and beautiful as any who've built before or since.[93]

Before returning to Gilbert Scott's St. Mark's, Betjeman gave examples of this excellence by naming G. E. Street's St. John's, Torquay (1867), the 'superb' church of Kingston, Dorset, and the 'splendid' nave of Bristol Cathedral. In his article on the capital's many examples, he also observed that '[t]he study of railway stations is something like the study of churches': '[f]or piscina, read cast-iron lamp bracket; for arcading, read girder construction; for transepts, read waiting rooms'.[94] These cathedrals of steam had always fascinated the poet, and as early as 1940 the Seeing Eye he wore in his BBC broadcast 'Back to the Railway Carriage' could see that the beauty of the railways lay in the very fact of their Victoriana.[95] There would be praise for Euston, praise for Newcastle Central and, in *Vintage London*, praise for the St. Pancras station hotel, that 'most ambitious' late Victorian edifice.[96] Indeed, the poet was conceivably more taken with it than its designer, Sir George Gilbert Scott (who felt it was 'possibly too good for its purpose'):

[t]he clock tower has always seemed to be a highly picturesque outline and the rows of middle-pointed windows along the whole curving sweep achieve an effect of unity with diversity. As a practical plan for an hotel, the building is appalling. But as an exercise in scale and the skilful use of brick and stone it is unsurpassed in railway architecture.[97]

But Betjeman was also aware of the sociological implications of Victorian industrial town planning, and, in *English Cities and Small Towns*, revealed once again his understanding that the needs of people did not necessarily centre round matters of piscinae and portico:

[w]e are inclined to blame the Victorians for the planlessness of industrial towns, for thin strips of two storey houses, that line either side of the railway line. But until trams and bicycles came into existence it was not practicable for people working in a factory to live in the outskirts of a mid-Victorian industrial town.[98]

Aside from a brief portrait of the artist (1944), Betjeman also joined forces with John Piper to co-edit two *Murray's Guides*: *Buckinghamshire* (1948) and *Berkshire* (1949). Timothy Mowl notes the disparity between Betjeman's text and Piper's photographs in the first volume and puts it down to the artist being a better time manager than the poet.[99] There may be something in this as, in a letter to Murray dated 27 August 1947, Betjeman wrote that he was suffering from a 'lack of inspiration, tiredness, dispiritedness and complete cessation'.[100] Indeed, the gazetteer of the Buckinghamshire guide is a mere sixteen pages long and may only be described as clinical in approach. Though there are *snatches* of prose-poetry – 'Chalfont-St-Giles' (p. 115 in the guide), for example, begins: '[f]ootpaths worn by weekend ramblers, lanes heavy with the cars of executives [. . .]' – much of the writing is perfunctory. However, there is an interesting point to note regarding the occasional references to obtrusive church electrics (such as at Hulcott, p. 120). This seems to have rankled, for an article Betjeman wrote for *Time and Tide* comments that all the hideous defacements, illustrated by John Piper, were taken from 'authentic examples in Buckinghamshire'.[101] He claimed to be enjoying the job, however, which, he said had 'taken up to two days a week for months now'. Murray replied that he thought his gazetteer 'stupendous work', but he may have been trying to buck his author up. It is possible that Betjeman was also sidetracked by the conversion of his wife to Roman Catholicism, Penelope having been received into that Church on 9 March 1948. (This matter had also been prevalent for most of the previous year, during which time Evelyn Waugh had tried to persuade Betjeman to take the same course.[102])

However, Mowl also draws attention to the fact that Betjeman gets the date of his own church (St. Mary's, Uffington, pp. 147–8) wrong in *Berkshire* (1150 instead of 1250, which implies a further error about the building of Salisbury Cathedral). This occurs twice, which seems to suggest an authorial, rather than a printing, error, though it is not perpetuated in the *Collins Guide to English Parish Churches* (1958).[103] But as Betjeman notes that St. Mary's is 'as complete an Early English parish church as exists' (p. 147), maybe it *was* a simple numeric aberration after all. Indeed, *Berkshire* is written with greater insouciance and bravery than its predecessor (only Betjeman could describe Reading (pp. 138–140) as a 'much-maligned town'!), which makes it hard to explain the inaccuracy in terms of a lack of interest. It is even possible that he felt a greater compulsion to throw himself into the work after recent developments at home.

At this time, Betjeman was also president of the Oxford Preservation Trust (1946–48). Hillier's account of this phase of his life shows a man bored once again with office life, just as he was at the British Council (1945) and even at *The Architectural Review* in the 1930s.[104] It seems that though Betjeman was perfectly sincere about the preservation of the nation's architectural heritage, his message had to be imparted on his own terms; that is, via the airwaves, articles, and poetry. 'The Planster's Vision' (from *New Bats* (originally *The New English Review*, June 1945)) is of this genre, showing as it does the blatant disregard for the past ('Remove those cottages, a huddled throng!') that Betjeman feared would taint post-war Britain. This 'vision of the future' is revisited in 'The Town Clerk's Views' (*Collected Poems*, 1958), where the Clerk himself would prefer to rename Devon '"South-West Area One"' and besmirch the landscape with 'concrete villas in the modern style'. (Note that both characters clearly have their roots in Mr Camshaft ('F.R.I.B.A.'), the architect of 'The Seeing Eye', who fantasised that England would become 'a place of soaring crystal towers'.[105])

A Poet For All?

The latter half of the 1940s was a significant time for Betjeman as poet. In America, his work was released under the title *Slick But Not Streamlined* (1947), while at home Murray's published *Selected Poems* on 5 October 1948, in time for the lucrative Christmas market. To be 'collected' in this way is something of a feather in the cap as such books are obviously more voluminous than those usually produced in the author's name. They also have a price to match: *Selected Poems* retailed at 8s 6d – 2/6 more than the standard edition of *New Bats in Old Belfries*. Murray clearly had faith that it would sell, though it is a little surprising that negotiations regarding its content began as early as June 1946.[106]

The poems in the American book were chosen by Auden, whose accompanying preface is perhaps not as pro-Betjeman as it at first appears. Though he claims that his friend's work made him 'violently jealous' and that certain sections (such as the last three lines of 'Calvinistic Evensong') made him feel annoyed because they were not by him, his tone soon changes. Later, he adds:

[e]ven if there was a real Betjeman once, I am afraid that he has been evicted and his place taken by the obstinate spirit of my favourite aunt Daisy.[107]

This is not a quaint li'l ol' English lady, concocted to endear Betjeman to a Stateside audience, this is a batty old fool – 'mentally retarded' (to use Auden's words), in fact. But he also notes that 'her brilliant skill at Happy Families belied her reputation for not being "quite all there"'. Indeed, the comparison is the only way Auden can find to explain how Betjeman could have versified the minute details of his childhood with such accuracy.[108]

Such arch jocundity was lost on John Sparrow, the Oxford bibliophile and Fellow (later Warden) of All Soul's, who had also become quasi-editor-in-chief of *Selected Poems*. He felt the preface was 'frightful – not just bad Auden, but bad with a badness of its own'.[109] Sparrow's essay was, as one would expect, more academic. Here, he likened the poet to Crabbe, noting that Betjeman too was a 'painter of the particular', though it was his portraits of the 'inhabited landscape' which had most appeal.[110] Betjeman disagreed and insisted that, unlike Crabbe, he wrote 'primarily with *people* in mind' and then related them 'to the background'.[111] This aside, Sparrow's piece is a useful, perceptive critique of the poet's work to date, although it can be slightly patronising in places, particularly with reference to those verses he felt to be 'juvenilia' (such as 'The Arrest of Oscar Wilde' and 'Death in Leamington'). Similarly, the blank verse 'Idyll' that Sparrow foresaw as being part of Betjeman's future development would be a masterpiece, yes, but '*in its own strange way*' (my italics).[112] This was an unfortunate way to close, but he did credit Betjeman with being a 'remarkable and original artist' and noted that even 'Tennyson himself' could not have written 'Sunday Afternoon Service' any better.[113]

The reviews of *Selected Poems* were very positive. Sean Rafferty, in *Time and Tide*, predicted Betjeman's poetic longevity, while H. A. L. Craig (*The Spectator*) wrote that he deserved the dedication that Auden had given him in *The Age of Anxiety* (1948). Frank O'Connor (*Evening News* – a friend from Dublin) claimed that he was 'the most interesting figure in English poetry today' and, in less negative terms than Sparrow, noted how his work had progressed since *Mount Zion*, citing 'St. Saviour's, Aberdeen Park, Highbury, London, N.', which, 'nobody,' he said, could 'mistake [. . .] for minor verse'.[114] But in heading his piece 'A POET FOR ALL', O'Connor was also both apposite and prophetic, for *Selected Poems* had sold a healthy 2,722 copies by the end of 1948, with the sum nearing 4,000 twelve months later. This is one of Betjeman's unsung achievements and Murray was clearly right to be optimistic: the company went on to shift an average of 511 copies a year between 1950 and 1965, with the total reaching over 12,000 before withdrawal.[115] When one compares this to earlier figures, the leap in popularity is astonishing. Why was this so? The Sparrow preface? The good reviews? Betjeman's increased presence on the airwaves? All these factors certainly played a part, but would they have helped to sustain such a *constant* stream of sales?

The truth is that Betjeman's verse really was becoming more and more relevant to his audience's lives. The rarefied posturing, about which Sparrow complained, and the desire always to amuse, against which Shand had warned, had now been tempered. As the decade progressed, he consolidated his ability to capture the minutiae of life that occupies most of us for most of our waking hours. Yet it went deeper than that: the exegeses, the contemplations of death – these are matters that matter and by 1948 Betjeman was writing verse which expressed, to use Dennis Brown's phrase, the 'social moment' prevalent in Britain at that time.[116]

This is shown most clearly in 'A Lincolnshire Church' (1948), where post-war Britain is portrayed with great precision. As one might expect, the church is a specific one – St. Mary's, Huttoft (near Sutton-on-Sea) – and Hillier notes that, while swampy fenland was certainly the predominant feature of this location, the reference to the 'green enormous marsh' might have been inspired by Tennyson's 'Ode to Memory' (V, 1830 – as in 'Stretch'd wide and wild the waste enormous marsh').[117] He also realises that Betjeman rhymes 'wold' and 'gold' (lines 2 and 4) as Housman had done in 'The Merry Guide' (A Shropshire Lad, 1896).[118] Though this shows Betjeman's ongoing interest with nineteenth-century poetry, it also indicates his decreasing reliance on it: he is no longer playing "Spot the Victorian"; instead, he allows his love and knowledge of the oeuvre to colour his work as he writes.

But the poem's 'usual woman in slacks [. . .] Regretting Americans' (ll. 12–14) has an important dual purpose. Brown is right to point out that the balance of world power had now passed from the UK to the US (Soviet Union excepted), but the lines also refer to the myriad broken relationships between English women and American G.I.s, spawned during the conflict. What is interesting is that the 'usual sprinkle of villas', like the woman, turn their backs on the Lincolnshire Middle Pointed in a manner that suggests it to be symbolic of the Church as a whole. Indeed, statistics show that between 1940 and 1950, Anglican membership fell from 3,911,000 to 3,444,000. While the war doubtless had an effect on this, as a percentage of the population, the total number of Christians (of whatever denomination) fell from 27 per cent to 25 per cent in this period. As history proves, there was a small upsurge in the 1950s, but the downward trend continued with a vengeance over the next twenty years.[119] Betjeman was clearly sensitive to this, and feared for 'bloody old England' with its paucity of souls to be won. Yet, as ever, he also sees hope:

> There where the white light flickers,
> Our Creator is with us yet,
> To be worshipped by you and the woman
> Of the slacks and the cigarette.
>
> ('A LINCOLNSHIRE CHURCH', LL. 45–48)

To quote Clough once more, 'Christ is yet risen'. Yet the poem has an unexpected conclusion. Brown notes Betjeman's post-colonialism in the reference to the 'Indian Christian priest' (l.60) at St. Mary's.[120] In literal terms, *post-*

colonial is correct: 'A Lincolnshire Church' was published the year after India regained its independence.[121] However, the crucial point is that Betjeman is both telling the truth (the vicar of St. Mary's from 1943 to 1959, the Rev Theophilus Caleb, *was* an Indian) and refusing to judge at a time when an Indian in Lincolnshire must have caused more than a few eyebrows to be raised:

> And why he was here in Lincolnshire
> I neither asked nor knew,
> Nor whether his flock was many
> Nor whether his flock was few
> ('A LINCOLNSHIRE CHURCH', LL. 61–64) [122]

Caleb is described at the poem's close as a 'friend' of God – as we *all* are – and in this Betjeman was indeed an 'early poet of multiculturalism'.[123] With the slacks, the radio, religion and race he thus gives us the micro and the macro here, and even suggests a tolerance which would not become general for many years (and to a great extent has yet to do so). As a result, this poem and the volume in which it appeared show that he really was becoming 'A POET FOR ALL'.[124]

CHAPTER FOUR

The 1950s

Love is Dead

It was during this first full post-war decade that Betjeman gained recognition as a popular writer. He also emerged as a pro-Victorian, anti-modern commentator. Critical credentials were retained, however, by continuing to teach the audience how to LOOK.

There was a false start in 1951, when Faber & Faber finally issued the Shell Guide to Shropshire. Research had begun before the war, the poet and John Piper travelling far and wide in search of the material that would make the volume, in Timothy Mowl's words, 'brilliant and idiosyncratic'.[1] The problem was that the first three books in Nikolaus Pevsner's *Buildings of England* series had also become available. Despite Betjeman's low opinion of them, they managed to capture the buying public's imagination. The Shropshire guide faltered and the vital impetus required to keep up with Pevsner was sadly lost.[2]

It was a setback, but only a minor one, for the following year would see the publication of Betjeman's 'manifesto' – *First and Last Loves* (1952), a collection of prose works interspersed with drawings by the increasingly omnipresent Piper. Its morbid introduction, 'Love is Dead', may have been the reflection of its author's 'depressed state of mind' that Hillier suggests – his marriage was still shaky, after all, and the family had endured a move to Wantage the previous year – but it clearly has a wider relevance and its meanings and nuances may be felt throughout Betjeman's work of this period.[3]

Although the 1950s suffered the Korean War (1950–53) and the Suez crisis (1956), along with rising property and retail prices, they have come to be epitomised by Harold Macmillan's famous comment that '[m]ost of our people have never had it so good'.[4] From Betjeman's point of view, it also marked the point at which post-war redevelopment started to make its presence felt more keenly. Much of the characteristic austerity associated with this era may have been dictated by the shortage of quality building materials, but, as Mowl agrees, 'Pevsner's years of greatest influence (1946–1970) were [. . .] the all-time low in national architecture'.[5]

Against this backdrop, 'Love is Dead' may be seen as an expansion of 'Slough', in which Betjeman realises that the stagnant, 'tinned' nation of which he had warned in 1937 was rapidly becoming a reality: 'England though not yet so ugly as Northern France and Belgium, is nearly so,' he lamented, and suburbs 'which once seemed so lovely [. . .] have spread so far in the wake of the motor car that there is little but suburb left.'[6] More disturbingly, the 'common man' ('better described as the suburban man') had, he felt, become a passive acceptor of the mediocre, whose indifference may be seen in the homogenous blandness of the burgeoning consumer age. He went on:

> [t]he well-known chromium and black gloss, Burton the Tailor of Taste, Hepworth, Halford, Stone, Woolworth & Co., [. . .] have transformed what was once a country town with the characteristics of its county into a home from home for the suburbanite [. . .]. When the suburbanite leaves Wembley for Wells he finds that the High Street there is just like home [. . .].[7]

The fear of passivity ('Too bored to think, too proud to pray, too timid to leave what we are used to doing') was heightened by the 'Herr-Professor-Doktors' (a scarcely veiled attack on Pevsner), who were 'writing everything down for us [. . .] so we need never bother to feel or think or see again'.[8]

There was now a sense of increasing urgency in Betjeman's writing and it is evident that he sensed action must be taken – and quickly. In 1953, he praised Evelyn Waugh's recently published novella *Love Among the Ruins* for having captured exactly the awfulness of contemporary urban initiatives – like Stevenage New Town, with its '[t]hree miles of Lionel Brett-style prefabs interrupted by Hugh Casson blocks of flats and two shopping arcades and concrete roads and lampposts throughout and no trees'.[9] Note the rhythm of this sentence – it has a palpable 'quick-march' call-to-arms about it. And yet the Seeing Eye was not wholly prejudiced, as his praise for Casson's 1851 Centenary Pavilion – which he described as 'the prettiest building' in the Festival of Britain – suggests.

This comment came in Betjeman's review of the event for *Time and Tide*. Though he doubtless appreciated its ethos – and the morale-boosting qualities it shared with the Great Exhibition – the poet's general mood makes the article's positive tone a little surprising. Nevertheless, the Festival left him 'exhausted but enchanted', while criticism was largely reserved for the angular kiosks and the Festival Hall itself, whose 'forbidding' exterior was not helped by a 'very ugly' roof outline.[10] As with *The Architectural Review* twenty years before, Betjeman was being paid to write within certain editorial limits. However, as before, there were ways around this, and the accompanying line drawings probably betray some of his true opinions. Did the Dome of Discovery *really* compare favourably to the Crystal Palace, for example? And what was the South Eastern & Chatham Railway bridge abutment doing there if not to jar against those kiosks and even the Skylon (which was humorously captioned 'Perpendicular' by *someone*).[11]

In spite of the agreement between the two men that *Love Among the Ruins* seemed to imply, Waugh felt *First and Last Loves* highlighted a certain hypocrisy in his friend. In typical ultra-montane Catholic fashion, he noted that Betjeman 'rants against state control, [despite being] a member of the Church of England'. The duplicity was also noted elsewhere:

> In January 1938 there was an architectural exhibition in London of all that
> Mr. Betjeman now deplores. The exhibitors called themselves the MARS
> group. [. . .] And in the group beside Arup, Gropius, Chermayeff, Lubetkin
> and Zweigenthal stands the name of Mr. Betjeman.[12]

This Betjeman, presumably, would have extolled the Festival without any reservation whatever. Remember that he joined the MARS Group when it was formed in 1933 – during his tenure at the *Architectural Review*, when it doubtless seemed like good manners and good work ethic to do so.[13] By 1938, his 'passion for Victorian Gothic' was gaining considerable momentum, so it is inaccurate to 'blame' him directly for MARS and all it stood for.[14]

First and Last Loves was collected and named by Myfanwy Piper. In 'The Text, the Poem, and the Problem of Historical Method' (1985), Jerome J. McGann discussed how Byron's *Don Juan* (1819–24, published, coincidentally, by Murray), exemplified the way a work becomes 'the product of a social engagement entered into [. . .] by author, printer, and publisher'.[15] To this list we add the friend, and the result of Mrs Piper's selection is that the essays, as Patrick Taylor-Martin astutely remarks, represent 'a plea for diversity'.[16] In this way, they are an enlargement of the introduction; many have been discussed in previous chapters, but one, 'Victorian Architecture' (from *World Review*, January 1951), is of especial interest (and at forty-six pages is also the most substantial work in the volume).

It is certainly no dewy-eyed eulogy: 'Victorian buildings,' the author asserts almost bluntly, 'will never become as smart as Georgian ones are today.'[17] Indeed, '[m]uch Victorian architecture is really bad and shoddy'. This is a clever device for preaching to the *un*converted: Betjeman begins his campaign by firing a few shots designed to tip the sceptics off balance by ostensibly *agreeing* with them. This allows him to build a useful platform from which to argue, hence his later comment that 'the chief objections to Victorian architecture are being overcome by time'; and when he writes that '[n]o one likes the architecture of his immediate predecessors, and most of the writers of architectural books are the children of Victorian parents', he may in fact have been showing a touch of the penitence that Waugh thought was absent.[18]

The poet develops his case with a summary of the accepted, and largely negative, contemporary view of Victorian architecture. The 'chief objections' of this faction included the misapprehension that nineteenth-century building practice stood mainly for 'back-to-back houses in Leeds', 'immoral' decoration (as on Tower Bridge) and a lack of planning (though Betjeman quickly refutes this last attack for its basis in 'ignorance'). Conversely, he goes on, it was acceptable to admire the Crystal Palace (for being 'the first prefab'), along with the engineering feats of Brunel, Stevenson [sic] and Barlow. This explains why Cubitt's King's Cross Station 'was preferred in all its stark simplicity to the romantic outlines of Gilbert Scott's St. Pancras Hotel'.[19] It is from here that the pro-Victorian argument begins, Betjeman noting that the way to appreciate the architecture of the period is 'to look at it in terms of architects'.

This characterises the rest of the text and so, after describing the Battle of the Styles, he praises Butterfield, Street and Shaw, who was 'the founder of modern English architecture as we know it at its domestic best'.[20] To emphasise the importance of the eye when viewing buildings, the last thirty-five pages of the article consist of illustrations with extensive captions written by the author. The overlapping that this brings about (for which he apologises) actually serves to re-focus attention on the text, and so, its point.[21] Betjeman may not have been an absolute pioneer by taking a pro-Victorian stance (Kenneth Clark's *The Gothic Revival: An Essay in the History of Taste* had been published back in 1928, for example); however, he was certainly walking close behind the standard-bearer: Clark's second edition was published just months before 'Victorian Architecture', note, while H. S. Goodhart-Rendel's *English Architecture Since the Regency* (1953) came a couple of years later.

Many of the other pieces in *First and Last Loves* are topographical. The Isle of Man, for instance, is painted as a haven of peace, the Isle of Wight praised for its bucolic railways and St. Endellion for its church. 'The Architecture of Entertainment', however, begins with the same sentiment that was present in the preface. Written in 1950 for *Diversion*, it brings Betjeman's concerns about post-war redevelopment fully to the fore: '[f]ire consumes and fashion changes,' he asserts, and 'new and more hideous structures arise on the sites of older and less hideous, as we continue to slide into deeper depths of barbarism.'[22] This had been given explicit poetic treatment in the two 'South London Sketch' poems in *New Bats in Old Belfries* (1945). Here, in the style of *Contrasts*, Betjeman gives us Pugin in verse:[23]

> Burst, good June, with a rush this morning,
> Bindweed weave me an emerald rope
> Sun, shine bright on the blossoming trellises,
> June and lavender, bring me hope.
> ('SOUTH LONDON SKETCH, 1844', LL. 9–12)

> Oh, in among the houses,
> The viaduct below,
> Stood the Coffee Essence Factory
> Of Robinson and Co.
> Burnt and brown and tumbled down
> And done with years ago
> Where the waters of the Wandle do
> Lugubriously flow.
> ('SOUTH LONDON SKETCH, 1944', LL. 9–16)

Note the lyrical ruralism of '1844' and the pert, almost advertisement-style rhythm of its modern counterpart.

But Betjeman did not only employ the 'Love is Dead' method for attacking 'barbarism'. In similar fashion to his patriotic wartime work – such as *English*

Cities and Small Towns, Vintage London and so on – he also strove to high-light the beauty of what remained (in buildings, customs or indeed anything else). The technique was used very successfully in the series of *Discovering Britain* films that he made for Shell in 1955. Though encouraging petrol sales may, like the slogans he coined for that company in the thirties, seem to jar with the ethos of his message, television did enable him to reach an ever-increasing number of people (something of a theme from this point on). Viewer of these 'shorts' were treated to such Victorian delights as Brunel's Clifton Suspension Bridge, William Burges's pseudo-medieval interior of Castell Coch (near Cardiff), Burton Agnes Hall, Bolsover Castle and Stourhead. At Stystead Mill (Essex), Betjeman quotes Tennyson's 'The Miller's Daughter' (1832) – 'I loved the brimming wave that swam [. . .]' – and at Wellingborough draws attention to Comper's St. Mary's Church (1906).

The films are brief – almost like the modern sound-bite – and each closes with Betjeman giving the road distances from the nearest city. Yet the camera angles also convey the impression of travel *on foot*: this is made more obvious in the film about Eastleach Martin (Wiltshire). Here, we are told that the way to look at a village is to 'get out of your motor-car and walk', and that Betjeman himself liked 'going slowly and stopping to stare'. Though it would be preposterous for Shell to have assumed that tourists would endeavour to see *all* the sights from the driver's seat, this almost borders on the subversive. 'If I have a mission,' the poet said at the time, '[. . .] it is to show people things which are beautiful so that they will very soon realise what is ugly. [. . .] [W]hen you look *at* things, instead of just looking through them, life starts absolutely crackling with interest and excitement.'[24]

Over-work and Under Pressure

In addition to his job on *Time and Tide*, Betjeman wrote weekly book reviews for the *Daily Telegraph* from 1951 and, from 1954 to 1958, contributed his famous 'City and Suburban' series to *The Spectator*.[25] The need to earn a living meant that such work continued to take up much of his time. As he wrote in 'The Weary Journalist' (1950):

> HERE, on this far North London height
> I sit and write and write and write;
> I pull the nothings from my head
> And weight them round with lumps of lead
> Then plonk them down upon the page
> In finely simulated rage.
>
> ('THE WEARY JOURNALIST', LL. 1–6)

This is only part of the story, for while the book reviewing was indeed arduous, with 'City and Suburban' Betjeman was able (amidst the humour, notes on accents, railways etc.) to promote the same idea of looking *at* a building rather than *through* it on a regular basis. He understood that what went unnoticed was often the first to go when the developers stepped in (and often the most widely mourned when it was too late). He reminded his readers that Paddington, for example, possessed 'the most impressive late-Georgian and early-Victorian stucco squares, crescents and terraces in London'.[26] Under the banner of 'A Spectator's Notebook', he also wrote angrily about the Bishop of Ripon's 'determination to pull down the beautiful eighteenth-century church of Holy Trinity, Leeds'. Following a reply from the City's Archdeacon to the effect that to keep a church open purely because of its architectural merit was to 'shirk reality', he also wrote an apposite poem, which ended:

> Its strange congregation was culled from afar,
> And you know how eclectic such worshippers are.
> The stipend was small but the site was worth more
> Than any old church I have sold before.
>
> ('NOT NECESSARILY LEEDS', LL. 13–16)

Thankfully, Betjeman's view triumphed and the demolition bid was abandoned.[27]

Instances such as this pepper the prose, particularly for *The Spectator*, but opinions were certainly not pulled in *Punch* either. In 'High Frecklesby', for instance, he outlined a ghastly 'vision of the future', just as his Planster and Town Clerk would have wished it to be.[28] Writing in character (as he did so well), he described Rutland as 'distressingly rural' and went on to suggest that the solution to Frecklesby's 'wasteful' use of land is to erect a tower in which such vital facilities as 'a cinema, greyhound track, clinic, youth parliament and amenity rockery' could be provided, along with housing and agricultural facilities, on one enclosed site. The walls of the town are glass and the ceilings 'of an opaque plastic material so as to ensure privacy between one flatlet and those above and below it'. Of course, in this clean, hygienic world, 'all hedges are to be uprooted [and], all traffic highways, major and minor, are to be straightened'.

Betjeman attacked from another angle in *Light and Lighting*, reiterating instead that 'England's beauty is in its variety' and that '[m]ore damage has been done since the war by lighting authorities to our landscape than ever was done by German bombs or greedy commercialism'.[29] This seems a trifle overdone, especially when one considers that he usually levelled this charge at the Plansters and Town Clerks, but by citing Launceston in Cornwall, he makes his point clear: 'the first thing one notices,' he wrote, 'is [the] skyline,' which 'is so much a feature of this town [that] it would obviously be a crime to dominate the place with the thick necks of sick concrete serpents'. Betjeman does not say it, but he doubtless knew that even Mr Pecksniff thought a lamppost ought to 'refine the mind' of an architect 'and give it a classical tendency'.[30] Sadly, this was not the case in Launceston. As an example of the surreptitiousness of change, the choice is also very poignant – lamp standards are at once everywhere and nowhere.

But how did such campaigning fit into Betjeman's poetic development? *A Few Late Chrysanthemums*, his fifth collection, was published by Murray in July 1954 – the same year that he joined the committee of the Society for the Protection of Ancient Buildings. The title, which came once again from Myfanwy Piper, prompted Evelyn Waugh to write that '[a]t first glance those mid-Victorian exotics, heavy and haunting in scent, rich in autumnal colours, might seem a happy epithet. But those ragged mops of petals? – no, in form Mr Betjeman's poems have the crisp precision of the iris'.[31] This is the collection that both John Press and Patrick Taylor-Martin consider to be the best of Betjeman. There is no preface (the poet felt it unnecessary to write one), but the book is split into three categories: 'Medium', 'Doom' and 'Light'.[32] The last includes such favourites as 'Hunter Trials' and 'How to Get on in Society', but the overall tone – even in the 'Medium' section – is most closely allied to 'Doom'. Those reviewers who were not Betjeman's friends pounced on the apparently groundless negativity. John Raymond (*The Observer*) felt that he had lost 'his magnificent knack of walking the sentimental-ironical tightrope', thanks to the general tone of 'disgust and misanthropy'.[33] Geoffrey Taylor, who wrote in *Time and Tide* that '[t]here is no poet a new poem of whose I, personally, approach with greater anticipation and pleasure,' nevertheless agreed: '[i]t is rather as though something friendly, familiar and furry and easily frightened had turned at bay and bitten one in the bathroom.'[34] While at odds with more recent critical views, in saying that Betjeman 'seems determined to sulk' because 'the world is not nearly so pleasant a place [. . .] as it was in 1924 or '34', it will become clear that Raymond has inadvertently hit the nail on the head.[35]

It is true to say that Betjeman was at as low an ebb now as he had been two years before when he wrote 'Love is Dead'. This was to continue, and on reaching 50 in 1956, he remarked: 'I thought of my many friends who are now dead, and terror of eternity made me want to scream. Fifty. Not much longer for this world, every day more precious.'[36] Despite Betjeman's frequently displayed sympathy for the elderly (see CHAPTER TWO), the thought of this worrying milestone is probably responsible for such poems as 'Late-Flowering Lust' (1950), 'Sun and Fun' (1952) and 'The Olympic Girl' (1954):

> My head is bald, my breath is bad,
> Unshaven is my chin,
> I have not now the joys I had
> When I was young in sin.
>
> ('LATE-FLOWERING LUST', LL. 1–4)

> But I'm dying now and done for,
> What on earth was all the fun for?
> For I'm old and ill and terrified and tight.
> ('SUN AND FUN – SONG OF A NIGHT-CLUB PROPRIETRESS', LL. 23–25)

> Fair tigress of the tennis courts,
> So short in sleeve and strong in shorts,
> Little, alas, to you I mean,
> For I am bald and old and green.
> ('THE OLYMPIC GIRL', LL. 25–28)[37]

Note the distance between 'Late-Flowering Lust' and 'Senex' (1947) in particular, the former resembling Hardy's 'I Look Into My Glass' (1898) even more than the latter (see CHAPTER THREE):

> I look into my glass,
> And view my wasting skin,
> And say, 'Would God it came to pass
> My heart had shrunk as thin!'
> (HARDY, 'I LOOK INTO MY GLASS', LL. 1–4)[38]

There is indeed a palpable yearning for the past in some of the new verses, though not always for the mid-1920s or 30s. In 'Essex' (1953), for instance, after looking at an early twentieth century book of colour plates, the poet laments that:

> Now yarrow chokes the railway track,
>   Brambles obliterate the stile,
> No motor coach can take me back
>   To that Edwardian "erstwhile".
> ('ESSEX', LL. 37–40)

There is a hint of Tennyson's pairing of 'barley and rye' ('The Lady of Shalott', l. 2) earlier on, but the influence of Housman is most apparent:

> Like streams the little by-roads run
>   Through oats and barley round a hill
> To where blue willows catch the sun
>   By some white weather-boarded mill.
> ('ESSEX', LL. 9–12)

> Into my heart an air that kills
>   From yon far country blows:
> What are those blue remembered hills,
>   What spires, what farms are those?
> (HOUSMAN, A SHROPSHIRE LAD, XL, LL. 1–4)[39]

In terms of form, the rhyme scheme matches, but the rhythm does not. More important, however, is the shared sense of landscape ('blue willows' for Betjeman, 'blue remembered hills' for Housman), along with the intoxicating notion of nostalgia itself.

This aside, the tone of 'Essex' indicates that the book is very much in tune with the way Betjeman saw Britain in the 1950s. And where it is negative or anti-modern, it is for a reason. In 'Harrow-on-the-Hill', for example, he begins with the plaintive 'When melancholy Autumn comes to Wembley', but then skilfully employs an anapaestic, Hardyesque rhythm to set a coastal idyll against the metropolitan present:

> And the constant click and kissing of the trolley buses hissing
>   Is the level to the Wealdstone turned to waves
>   And the rumble of the railway
>   Is the thunder of the rollers
> As they gather up for plunging
>   Into caves.
>
>   ('HARROW-ON-THE-HILL', LL. 11–16)

Betjeman has said that the poem echoes the way children 'try and find the sea again', in post-'Trebetherick' gloom, when they return home after a holiday.[40] It also expresses a yearning for the simple life. The images of trolley buses and trains are thus doubly pertinent as they convey both the constant noise of the city and the interest that they hold (or held) for young boys. On holiday, many children become subservient to the hypnotic lure of the sea – due in no small part to the fact that most of their toys are left at home. In an echo of some of his wartime prose, Betjeman reminds us here that material goods are not essential to happiness.

In 'Greenaway' (1954), conversely, the sea is portrayed as a source of terror. The first six stanzas are eulogistic, the 'the slowly dragging roar' evoking Arnold's 'Dover Beach', where the sea retreats with a similar 'melancholy, long, withdrawing roar' (l. 25). But then the tone changes and the breakers instead plunge 'Their weight of waters' over the narrator, who is eventually 'sucked [. . .] out of reach':

> Back into what a water-world
>   Of waving weed and waiting claws?
> Of writhing tentacles uncurled
>   To drag me to what dreadful jaws?
>
>   ('GREENAWAY', LL. 33–36)

Does this highlight the fragility of the benign dream portrayed in 'Harrow-on-the-Hill'? Or is it again related to Arnold's 'ebb and flow / Of human misery' ('Dover Beach', ll. 17–18)? For Dennis Brown, the use of the familiar Cornish backdrop is merely a 'trigger' for this depiction of horror.[41] However, Taylor-

Martin is right to note the 'absence of self-pity' and comments that 'the "dreadful jaws" of some sea-monster' act as a 'sort of Old Testament instrument of vengeance' (there is a hint of Lewis Carroll's 'Jabberwock' too).[42] From the evidence of the last stanza (quoted above), Betjeman could equally have based this monster on the imagery found in Tennyson's 'The Kraken' (1830):

> From many a wondrous grot and secret cell
> Unnumbered and enormous polypi
> Winnow with giant arms the slumbering green.
> (TENNYSON, 'THE KRAKEN', LL. 8–10)[43]

In addition to their shared connection with the sea (explored in the last chapter), Tennyson's influence may again be felt throughout *A Few Late Chrysanthemums*. 'Verses turned in aid of A Public Subscription' (1952), originally written for a pamphlet produced to aid the restoration of St. Katherine's Church, Chiselhampton, is an example of Betjeman putting his poetry in the campaigning front line. Its fourth stanza contains a familiar rhyme:

> How gracefully their shadow falls
> On bold pilasters down the walls.
> ('VERSES TURNED', LL. 19–20)

Clearly this is another reference to 'The splendour falls on castle walls' from *The Princess* (1847), which Betjeman repeats in 'Church of England Thoughts' ('I see its shapely shadow fall / On this enormous garden wall'). He thus confers a subliminal splendour on the church, lending it a cultural dignity that one might associate with some poetic dream. In his repetition, Betjeman was in good company, for Tennyson himself used the rhyme again in 'Maud' (1855):

> 'Tis a morning pure and sweet,
> And a dewy splendour falls
> On the little flower that clings
> To the turrets and the walls;
> (TENNYSON, 'MAUD', PART II.IV.VI, LL. 171–174)[44]

There are of course many other minor instances of the great Laureate's influence in the book, but in 'Christmas', which dates back to 1947, they are deliberate and of ideological importance. Press comments that this is 'one of [Betjeman's] most serene and unaffected expressions of Christian devotion'. However, it also belongs with 'A Lincolnshire Church' insomuch as it deals with a palpable decline in the power of Christian faith.[45] Brown makes a useful connection with *In Memoriam* too, noting that 'Christmas' has the same 'suggestive metonymy', with its bells, rain, holly, yew and villagers.[46]

Tennyson's 'pictorial method,' he goes on, 'is further made contemporary by virtually filmic technique'. An example of this may be found in the following lines:

> The holly in the windy hedge
>   And round the Manor House the yew
> Will soon be stripped to deck the ledge,
>   The altar, font and arch and pew,
> So that the villagers can say
> "The church looks nice" on Christmas Day.
>
> Provincial public houses blaze
>   And Corporation tramcars clang,
> On lighted tenements I gaze
>   Where paper decorations hang,
> And bunting in the red Town Hall
> Says "Merry Christmas to you all."
>
> ('CHRISTMAS', LL. 7–18)

The use of 'clang' is interesting (Betjeman had also used it in 'Exeter' (1937)), as it appears twice in *In Memoriam*:

> Above the wood which grides and clangs
> (TENNYSON, *IN MEMORIAM*, CVII. 11)[47]

> The names are signed, and overhead

> Begins the clash and clang that tells
>   The joy to every wandering breeze;
> (*IN MEMORIAM*, EPILOGUE, LL. 60–62)[48]

Note how Betjeman's use of the word is entirely urban, while Tennyson adheres to its rural nature (it being used originally to convey the sound of bird-song – as well as that of the trumpet). This aside, the Tennysonian overtones are evident: the first five stanzas of 'Christmas', for instance, are ostensibly full of happiness, yet even here there is an echo of the 'streets [. . .] fill'd with joyful sound' (XXXI. 10) and the 'merry merry bells of Yule' (XXVIII. 20) of *In Memoriam*'s first Noël. Consider too the yew in Betjeman's line 8: holly, thanks to the famous refrain, is more usually paired with ivy, but while yew is an evergreen not unknown at Christmas, in *In Memoriam* it is associated with death and churchyards:

> Old Yew, which graspest at the stones
>   That name the under-lying dead,
>   Thy fibres net the dreamless head,

> Thy roots are wrapt about the bones.
>
> :   :   :   :   :
>
> O not for thee the glow, the bloom,
>   Who changest not in any gale,
>   Nor branding summer suns avail
> To touch thy thousand years of gloom:
>   (IN MEMORIAM, II. 1–4; 9–12)[49]

This is conceivably a clue to the implied worthlessness of the season's 'fripperies' to which Betjeman draws our attention at the end of his poem, and to which nature plays second fiddle – the yew will be 'stripped', note, 'So that the villagers can say / "The church looks nice" on Christmas Day'; this image is clearly indicative of a rapacious desire for merely superficial pleasures.

When all these references are taken together, Betjeman's implication becomes apparent: in 1947, it is Christmas itself that is *in extremis*. As one might expect, a change in tone comes in the sixth stanza, which begins with the repeated question 'And is it true?'. Here the poet muses on the problem that Tennyson had outlined right at the beginning:

> Strong Son of God, immortal Love,
>   Whom we, that have not seen thy face,
> By faith, and faith alone, embrace,
>   Believing where we cannot prove;
>   (IN MEMORIAM, PROLOGUE, LL. 1–4)[50]

The 'girls in slacks', 'oafish louts' and 'sleepless children' are of course essential in showing what, to their author, Christmas had become: a time for 'Bath salts and inexpensive scent', 'hideous tie so kindly meant' *and little else*. Tennyson would have agreed: indeed, in 'The Epic' (1842), he is rather more scathing on this point:

> The host, and I sat round the wassail-bowl,
> Then half-way ebb'd: and there we held a talk,
> How all the old honour had from Christmas gone,
> Or gone, or dwindled down to some odd games
> In some odd nooks like this;
>   (TENNYSON, 'THE EPIC', LL. 5–9)[51]

When the tone does change in 'Christmas', the effect is not nearly as acute as elsewhere in Betjeman. The use of 'And' (which is almost a Biblical reference in itself) at the beginnings of no fewer than ten lines not only gives 'Christmas' a sense of breathless pace (perhaps to be associated with modern Yuletide), but also links the stanzas together so as to draw the debate in, almost making it a part of that modernity. Betjeman's questioning is therefore less a criticism than a suggestion, that 'most tremendous tale of all' being affirmed by the concluding expansion:

> And is it true? For if it is,
>   No loving fingers tying strings
> Around those tissued fripperies,
>   The sweet and silly Christmas things,
> Bath salts and inexpensive scent
> And hideous tie so kindly meant,
>
> No love that in a family dwells,
>   No carolling in frosty air,
> Nor all the steeple-shaking bells
>   Can with this single Truth compare –
> That God was Man in Palestine
> And lives to-day in Bread and Wine.
>
> ('CHRISTMAS', LL. 37–48)

This is clearly a very concise avowal of the poet's Anglo-Catholicism. Note the capital letter of 'Truth', and the grammar – if Betjeman were so very unsure, should not line 46 have read 'with *that* single Truth compare'? The use of 'this' implies that he has chosen Belief again and there is a build up to the valediction which offers further emphasis, for the 'sweet and silly' aspects of Christmas are succeeded by the more important yardsticks of family feeling and even the church bells themselves; and though each stanza ends with a rhyming couplet, the final one evokes a distinct sense of triumph – akin to Hamlet's 'The play's the thing / Wherein I'll catch the conscience of the King' (II. 2, ll. 602–603), or the similarly clinching close to a Shakespearian sonnet.

This theme is continued in 'Huxley Hall' (1953), although the hope that was present in 'Christmas' is conspicuous by its absence here. As Brown notes, the title is a nominal pastiche of the novelist Aldous Huxley (1894–1963) and Tennyson's 'Locksley Hall' (1842), with which it shares both rhythm and rhyme.[52] The sequel, 'Locksley Hall Sixty Years After' (1886), is equally vital, however, and while Brown also alludes to Huxley's *Brave New World* (1932), Waugh's *Love Among the Ruins* is more recognisable in the poem's 'bright, hygienic hell' – and probably more relevant, given Betjeman's noted view of it. The Tennyson connection is substantiated by the poet's annoyance that, for *A Few Late Chrysanthemums*, the piece had been set in four-line stanzas, and not couplets like the 'Locksley Hall' poems (an error that was corrected for its appearance in *Collected Poems* four years later).[53]

Betjeman's is a difficult verse that finds his narrator meditating on the Fall prior to a talk on 'Sex and Civics'. Brown feels he protests too much about his situation, calling this stance an 'unwonted Malvolio mood'.[54] But Derek Stanford, writing in 1961, drew a useful parallel with the sensations that East

End families, 'moved by their Councils to the raw new towns', must have felt having been uprooted and trans-located to Welwyn, Harlow – or Stevenage.[55] Britain's first designated New Towns came into being after the publication of the New Towns Act of 1946; by the time 'Huxley Hall' was published, eight had been established, and problems of higher costs, poorly developed leisure facilities and the prospect of living on a large, impersonal housing estate meant that, initially, crime, divorce and suicide rates tended to be worse than elsewhere.[56] So, although Hillier refers to the poem as a 'parody', it enables Betjeman once again to attack the New World of the New Town by using nineteenth-century poetics to critique the present.[57] There are a few obvious clues, other than the metre, which point to this:

> She that holds the diamond necklace dearer than the golden ring,
> (TENNYSON, 'LOCKSLEY HALL SIXTY YEARS AFTER' [1886], L. 21)[58]

> She who eats the greasy crumpets snugly in the inglenook
> (BETJEMAN, 'HUXLEY HALL', L. 7)

If the similarities of construction are clear, Tennyson's prophecies offer further correlation: he describes a 'Vision of the world' (l. 120) in which 'the heavens fill with commerce' (l. 121) and in which war ('the nations' airy navies grappling in the central blue', l. 124) results in a 'Parliament of man, the Federation of the world' (l. 128). Translate this to the twentieth century phenomena of World War Two and the inauguration of the United Nations (1945), and Betjeman's poem may be seen to paint a very bleak picture of what lies at *his* end of the 'grooves of change' (l. 182). The comrades that begin 'Locksley Hall' now plot against each other '"in the interests of the State"' ('Huxley Hall', l. 14), but that State is sterile, and this is indicated metaphorically by the lack of meat and alcohol in the narrator's repast, the murals in the café and the 'lightsome poplars' round the square, all of which hark back to that homogenous blandness derided in 'Love is Dead'. Even sex is sterilised by being made into the subject for a talk, while hope, if such it may be called, lies only in the inglenook of the 'birch-enshrouded homestead', where the butter dropped from the woman's 'greasy crumpets' connotes freedom from this uniformity. The 'stout', free-thinking husband carries this idea further, for though the notion of free-thought usually refers to the rejection of religious authority, here it clearly falls in with Betjeman's attack on what he saw as anathema to a fulfilling life.

We know from *In Memoriam* that Tennyson was aware of evolutionary theories (being derived from his readings of Charles Lyell's *Principles of Geology* (1830) and Robert Chambers's *Vestiges of Creation* (1844)).[59] In 'Locksley Hall Sixty Years After', he also asks: 'Have we risen from out the beast, then back into the beast again?' (l. 148) and laments that 'Evolution ever climbing after some ideal good', is constantly hampered by 'Reversion ever dragging Evolution in the mud' (ll. 199–200). For Peter Levi, there is no 'indictment of the Victorian age that is more terrible' than this poem, and it was clear that Tennyson 'did not like the England he was leaving':

> Is it well that while we range with Science, glorying in the Time,
> City children soak and blacken soul and sense in city slime?
>
> (TENNYSON, 'LOCKSLEY HALL SIXTY YEARS AFTER', LL. 217–218)[60]

Betjeman echoes this sentiment. He felt sin to be so intertwined with our decline that even 'the folk-museum's charting of man's Progress out of slime' is unable to offer any release. But is this primordial slime, or Tennyson's urban variety? Reading the poems back to back would suggest the latter. 'Huxley Hall' also conveys a sense of life's futility, and one could be forgiven for thinking that, to *this* Betjeman, even Tennyson's Evolution would not be an unattractive prospect.

Like 'Essex' before it, 'Middlesex' (1954) also contrasts the present with the past unfavourably; but, like 'Christmas', initially there is brightness:

> Gaily into Ruislip Gardens
> Runs the red electric train,
> With a thousand Ta's and Pardon's
> Daintily alights Elaine;
>
> ('MIDDLESEX', LL. 1–4)

The poem's first two stanzas concentrate on this young 'bobby-soxer' and her life, but the second was originally cut by *Punch* as, with its references to Windsmoor coats, Jacqmar scarves, Drene shampoo and Innoxa face cream, it was considered too close to advertisement.[61] In 'Myfanwy' (1940), the brand names help to set the scene and draw the reader in; here, the effect is the same initially, but as Mowl perceptively writes, '[w]ith audience empathy assured, Betjeman tilts the whole poem upward'.[62] And so the names become symbols for a 'Love is Dead' loss of individuality, Windsmoor, Jacqmar, Drene and Innoxa being available from Greenock to Greenwich by 1954 – as would the 'television screen'. A far cry from the 'lost Elysium' of the last two stanzas, with its 'Gentle Brent' and 'Low laburnum-leaned-on railings'; in fact, the only hint of this Past at the start of the poem is the garden ('father's hobby') to which Elaine returns. For Philip Larkin, it is only when Murray Posh and Lupin Pooter appear in the penultimate stanza that 'we see fair Elaine's function, to contrast with these "cockney anglers, cockney shooters" and represent, with her mindless consumption of branded products, those who now live in this built-over ex-paradise'.[63] Thus does 'her ironically Tennysonian name imply [...] the decline such a transformation has entailed'.[64] Yet, as Larkin recognised in an earlier article, the portrayal of 'fair Elaine' is by no means unattractive: in a different setting, and perhaps in tennis shorts, she could just as easily have become an object of Betjemanian desire. Press may feel that Messrs Posh and Pooter are no better than Elaine, but here they represent primarily a *fin-de-siècle* relish for individualism rather than their class or gender.[65]

'The Metropolitan Railway – BAKER STREET STATION BUFFET' (1953) – the last of this important quartet – is concerned with the median between the 'lost Elysium' summer of Middlesex and the winter world of Elaine and her generation (or rather, Betjeman's Now). Indeed, we are explicitly in '*autumn-scented Middlesex*' this time (my italics). Again, the beginning of the poem is infused with 'radiant hope', and the 'rich contrivance fill'd / Of copper' gives an impression of a world still interested in detail and beauty, the 'many-branched electrolier' having more than a touch of *art nouveau* splendour about it. This world is benign – the Baker Street Buffet, for example, with its 'fine woodwork and [. . .] smell of dinner', is comforting and even the Oxford Street store's hydraulic lift is described as 'safe'. 'Youth and Progress [are] in partnership' and home is 'far down the shining lines', 'set in murmuring pines'. These two images recall (almost paradoxically) the 'Surrey homestead' of 'Love in a Valley' (1937), but rather than carrying a 'Portable Lieutenant' to China and his girlfriend to 'lonely shopping in a brilliant arcade', the railway brings the 'Metropolitan' couple home together. The importance of this is emphasised by the capitalisation of the place names, which read like Metropolitan Railway guidebook:

> Smoothly from HARROW, passing PRESTON ROAD,
> They saw the last green fields and misty sky,
> At NEASDEN watched a workmen's train unload,
> :   :   :   :   :   :
> And all that day in murky London Wall
> The thought of RUISLIP kept him warm inside
> ('THE METROPOLITAN RAILWAY', LL. 13–15; 19–20)

In the final stanza, the narrative returns to the present and the effect is far colder and far harsher than that found even in 'Croydon' or 'On a Portrait of a Deaf Man':

> Cancer has killed him. Heart is killing her.
> The trees are down. An Odeon flashes fire
> Where stood their villa by the murmuring fir
> When "they would for their children's good conspire."
> Of their loves and hopes on hurrying feet
> Thou art the worn memorial, Baker Street.
> ('THE METROPOLITAN RAILWAY', LL. 31–36)

Note the power of those three curt sentences and the touch of Hopkins in the notion of the cinema flashing fire.[66] The pun on worn memorial/war memorial seems apt for Betjeman's 'Love is Dead' mood too, Baker Street having indeed become the 'worn memorial' to the couple's early optimism.

However, the poet did not limit himself to urban settings in order to show the decline he saw around him. In 'The Village Inn' (1950), for example, he takes a snapshot of a corporate brewery as it cuts a swathe through the countryside. The first thirty lines are written in tight rhyming couplets, the first four of which are the sales pitch of 'the brewer's P.R.O.', who gives a neat advertisement for 'the dear old inn, / So ancient, clean and free from sin' (ll. 1–2). Being made to feel 'a filthy swine / For loathing beer and liking wine' (ll. 21–22), the narrator takes a trip to his local and, in nine quatrains, questions the P.R.O. about what on earth has happened since his last visit:

> Ah, where's the inn that once I knew
> With brick and chalky wall
> Up which the knobbly pear-tree grew
> For fear the place would fall?
>
> *Oh, that old pot-house isn't there,*
> *It wasn't worth our while;*
> *You'll find we have rebuilt "The Bear"*
> *In Early Georgian style.*
>
> ('THE VILLAGE INN', LL. 31–38)

This carries echoes of Cowper's 'Where is the blessedness I knew / When first I saw the Lord?' (*Olney Hymns*, 1779), although Housman's music and idiom are also waiting to take us back to those 'blue remembered hills' again. In 'Love is Dead', Betjeman went into more detail, commenting wryly that

> [e]nterprising brewers, backing culture for all they are worth, have turned the old inns into "pubs" and "locals". They have made a virtue of the solemn drinking of their chemicals. They have had Izal and porcelain put in the gents, and made the bar similar to it, save that they have added little tables and a counter.[67]

The sanctuary of the poem's Inn, with its red walls, 'emerald tiles' and steel stools is reminiscent of the restored church in 'Hymn' (1928) – both types of building are equally at the centre of village life, after all. Such settlements are depicted in decidedly unflattering terms in 'The Dear Old Village' (1947), which appears as a companion piece in *A Few Late Chrysanthemums* (although it predates 'The Village Inn' by three years). While partly inspired by his uneasy relationship with his shady Uffington landlord Farmer John Wheeler (who appears as Farmer Whistle in the poem), the piece satirises modern values once again, this time by homing in on education and the working class:

> Civics, eurhythmics, economics, Marx,
> How-to-respect-wild-life-in-National-Parks;

Plastics, gymnastics – thus they learn to scorn
The old thatch'd cottages where they were born.
The girls, ambitious to begin their lives
Serving in WOOLWORTH'S, rather than as wives;
The boys, who cannot yet escape the land,
At driving tractors lend a clumsy hand.
An eight-hour day for all, and more than three
Of these are occupied in making tea
And talking over what we all agree–
Though "Music while you work" is now our wont,
It's not so nice as "Music while you don't."

('THE DEAR OLD VILLAGE', LL. 80–92)

Philip Larkin called the last five lines 'a pertinent summary of a subject no other present-day British poet has tried to deal with'.[68] Feminists will justly balk at the view of wifehood, though there is more than a suggestion that even *this* is preferable to working for Woolworth's! Larkin was no lover of the working class and his counterpart obviously aspired to the upper echelons, so it is easy to understand Taylor-Martin when he asks: '[w]hy should Betjeman, who loves the leisured life of the country house, patronize the workers for their laziness?'[69] Of course, this implies that the poet did not have to work for a living himself, but the references here, and in the preceding chapters, to journalism and its effect on his poetry negate this. Perhaps Betjeman's real target, then, is the way he felt education had veered away from the church, the place of one's birth and – most importantly of all – aspiration. For though the workers may tell themselves 'We are no longer slaves', they quite obviously are – their slave-master is simply no longer the squire, parson or schoolmaster, but commerce. '"Ah! This is England"' thinks 'The Mass-Observer with the Hillman Minx', '"Slow – yes. But sociologically sound"'. This is presumably a reference to the original Mass-Observation project of 1937–c.1949, but it is also a thumbnail sketch of the poet himself, who was nothing if not such a spectator.[70] Thus Betjeman is expressing two things: his annoyance that he did not see through his own landlord, and his continued anger that the Morrisian 'Earthly Paradise' has been lost. The latter is evident in his mirroring of Morris's rhythm and rhyme scheme:

Hear not the water lapsing down the rills,
Lift not your eyes to the surrounding hills,
While spring recalls the miracle of birth
Let us, for heaven's sake, keep down to earth.

(BETJEMAN, 'THE DEAR OLD VILLAGE', LL. 28–31)

Forget six counties overhung with smoke,
Forget the snorting steam and piston stroke,
Forget the spreading of the hideous town;

> Think rather of the pack-horse on the down,
>
> (WILLIAM MORRIS, *THE EARTHLY PARADISE*, 'INTRODUCTION', LL. 1–4)[71]

The old-versus-new pastoral is further emphasised by the Tennysonian 'lin-lan-lone' of that most English of pursuits, bell-ringing, which Betjeman quotes at the beginning of his poem:

> The dear old village! *Lin-lan-lone* the bells
> (Which should be six) ring over hills and dells,
> But now since the row about the ringers' tea
> It's *lin-lan-lone*. They're only ringing three.
>
> (BETJEMAN, 'THE DEAR OLD VILLAGE', LL. 1–4)[72]

Is this a sign that the village is not half the place it used to be? Betjeman wrote in the *Collins Guide to English Parish Churches* that 'the exercise' (as the practice is known) 'is a class-less folk art which has survived in the church despite all arguments about doctrine and the diminution of congregations'.[73] In 'Wantage Bells' (1954), he would assert that bell-ringing is perhaps our only loud and clear way of offering public thanks to God:

> Where are the words to express
>   Such a reckless bestowing?
> The voices of birds utter less
>   Than the thanks we are owing,
>   Bell notes alone
>   Ring praise of their own
> As clear as the weed-waving brook and as evenly flowing.
>
> ('WANTAGE BELLS', LL. 15–21)

The naturalism here is part of Betjeman's point, and the fact that the bells of 'The Dear Old Village' have been halved due to an argument about something as trivial as tea, says all that needs to be said, conceivably.

So was Betjeman sulking in *A Few Late Chrysanthemums* as John Raymond claimed? It is important to recall that the views it presents are by no means at odds with the thrust of his contemporaneous prose and that some of the despondency therein is balanced by the more positive arguments he offered in newsprint and on the television screen. I appreciate that this is the holistic view, and Raymond *et al.* were viewing the collection in isolation. Some writers, however, agreed with myself and Waugh. Significantly, the Cornish rural poet Charles Causley felt the book to be Betjeman's best, while Gerald Bullett wrote in the *Literary Guide* that 'Devonshire Street W.1' was 'one of the most simple and heartrending things' he had ever read.[74] But the idea that 'the world [was] not nearly as pleasant a place [. . .] as it was in 1924 or '34' is not as clear-cut as it appears. Of course, the General Strike and the Depression both fell into this decade, so it is beyond question that the 1950s were much better economically. Victory in the war added to the collective confidence, many people readily agreeing with Macmillan that they *had* never had it so good. Indeed, if consumerism is a measure of the Good Life, then statistics show that the Prime Minister was right: between 1950 and 1960, the number of motor-cars in Britain rose by nearly 145 per cent, the number of telephones by 52 per cent and the number of television licences from 344,000 to a staggering 10.5 million.[75] For some, however, there was a price to pay, and for all those who thought of Betjeman only in terms of conservatism (both with a large and a small 'c'), William D. Rubinstein notes in *Twentieth-Century Britain: A Political History* (2003) that '[i]n many respects, [the] Labour [Party] was far less ready to come to terms with the "affluent society" than were the Tories, especially with the hedonism seen as an inevitable conse-quence'. He adds that '[w]hile the Tories embraced the affluence brought about by the mixed system which had evolved since 1945, many traditional-ists of course were disturbed by the evidence it gave of a decline in moral and cultural standards'.[76]

This puts Betjeman's work of this period into perspective. He may or may not have been aware of the statistics, but he was certainly aware of the dangers of post-war redevelopment and inertia. As demonstrated, he was also very concerned about what he saw as the country's *spiritual* decline. Rubinstein shows that he was not alone in this. In *News from Nowhere* (1890), William Morris had explored the idea that the Middle Ages offered a greater sense of order than the nineteenth century; Betjeman's view that the age of *Morris* was better than his own may either be taken as ironic or a sad indictment of British society in the decades since.

Church Matters

In October 1954, Betjeman replied to his critics through the pages of *The Spectator*. Referring to his poems as his 'children', he admitted that he would 'gladly disown' three: 'Slough', 'In Westminster Abbey' and 'How To Get On In Society' (the last of which had featured in *A Few Late Chrysanthemums*). All were dismissed as 'merely comic verse', in a possible attempt to pre-empt further criticism. However, he goes on to say that his 'purest pleasure' in the 1930s was the 'exploration of the suburbs and provincial towns'. This allows him to set up an argument for later in this ostensibly apologetic essay, for Betjeman then reveals that '[w]hen most of the poems in my latest book were written, I was the self-pitying victim of remorse, guilt and terror of death'.[77] He adds that the advice to 'keep off satire and anger' is 'sound', but recog-nises that poetic criticism can only really be useful 'if it is written by poets'. They, after all, 'know the meaning of words like "technique" and "rhythm" as applied to poetry'. Most tellingly of all, he writes:

[i]nevitably there were a few people [who blamed the poems] for not

containing qualities they were never meant to have. I can only reply that I was not addressing myself to the *vieux jeu avant garde* [. . .] which still lingers on in the 'Critics' programmes of the BBC. Yet even to them I can express gratitude. A reaction was achieved and that by no means negative.

(Note the Wildean inflection at the close – there is indeed nothing worse than *not* being talked about!) But the sales figures for *A Few Late Chrysanthemums* belie the criticism. In fact, it was the fastest selling of Betjeman's single volumes to date, shifting 4,966 copies within the first six months of publication and a further 4,712 copies in the six months after that. Between 1954 and 1968, it sold a total of 16,004, but a staggering 14,123 of these came in the first five years, which indicates a marked increase in Betjeman's popularity during the 1950s and 60s – almost threefold in purely sales terms.[78] Unsurprisingly, the book was awarded the Foyle Poetry Prize in 1955.

It is interesting that, although Betjeman repeats his fear of death in the *Spectator* piece, his 'impatience with so-called "progress"' is added almost as an afterthought. He does himself a disservice here, but some of the emphasis on mortality both in the essay and the volume itself was the result not only of his age, but also of the death of his mother Bess, who passed away on 13 December 1952.[79] 'Devonshire Street W.1' (1953), 'House of Rest' (1953) and 'Variation on a Theme by T. W. Rolleston' (1954) were all published after this date. The first features another present-day scene presented against an Edwardian backdrop (in the 'faience adornments'), 'Variation' is based on Rolleston's 'The Dead at Clonmacnois', while 'House of Rest' has been likened by Dennis Brown to Wordsworth's 'We Are Seven' (1798).[80] 'Remorse' (1953), however, is specifically about the poet's own bereavement. It shares much with 'Death in Leamington' – the bedroom setting, the distant nurse – though there is also an echo of Hardy's 'The House of Hospitalities' (1909), which ends with the narrator seeing the 'forms of old time talking' (l.19).[81] Interestingly, both 'Remorse' and 'House of Rest' share a similar strand of clerical criticism too:

> Protestant claims and Catholic, the wrong and the right of them,
> Unimportant they seem in the face of death –
>
> ('REMORSE', ll. 9–10)

> I did not like to ask if he
>   Was "High" or "Low" or "Broad"
> Lest such a question seem to be
>   A mockery of Our Lord.
>
> ('HOUSE OF REST', ll. 17–20)

Stanford notes that in both cases these things only 'seem' to be.[82] However, remember 'Christmas': though it can be religious to be uncertain, Betjeman may be suggesting that these ecclesiastical 'fripperies' do not with that 'single Truth compare' either.

A Few Late Chrysanthemums was not Betjeman's only volume of verse to appear during 1954. The Society for Promoting Christian Knowledge (SPCK) also released *Poems in the Porch* (with drawings once again by John Piper) that October. As Betjeman wrote in his 'Author's Note', the works did not 'pretend to be poetry', because they 'were written for speaking on the wireless'. This places Betjeman firmly in the oral tradition and, as Marshall McLuhan noted, '[r]adio affects most people intimately, person-to-person, offering a world of unspoken communication between writer-speaker and listener'.[83]

All except 'The Friends of the Cathedral' canter along in jaunty rhyming couplets with eight-syllable, four-stress lines. But, as 'Not Necessarily Leeds' re-confirmed, Betjeman often employed comfortable, reassuring forms for satirical effect. He doubtless knew his critics' advice was not *that* sound, but neither is Patrick Taylor-Martin's assertion that these poems 'are loving celebrations' of the Church of England.[84] While there is *some* affection for 'the dear old C. of E.' ('Septuagesima', l. 12), bones of contention in fact appear in almost every poem. The benign 'Septuagesima' may lead the volume but, rather as Mowl said of 'Middlesex', once the readers are on the poet's side, the gloves are slightly slipped off. For example, 'Diary of a Church Mouse' is – beneath the jingle – a clever swipe at the hypocrisy of those who take from the church without giving. Thus the 'unfriendly rat' who thinks there is no God, still pilfers food from the Harvest Festival,

> While I, who starve the whole year through,
> Must share my food with rodents who
> Except at this time of the year
> Not once inside the church appear.
> ('DIARY OF A CHURCH MOUSE', LL. 47–50)

Of course, the whole point is to make the point that the humans do *not* 'only do / What their religion tells them to' (l. 54).

'Blame the Vicar' is a comic plea to treat incumbents as they would be treated and is, in effect, another dig at selfishness:

> For what's a Vicar really for
> Except to cheer us up?
> :   :   :   :
> The Vicar should be all pretence
> And never, never give offence.
> O preach on Sunday is his task
> And lend his mower when we ask
> ('BLAME THE VICAR', LL. 17–18; 23–26)

The other three pieces – 'Churchyards', 'The Friends of the Cathedral' and 'Electric Light and Heating' – deal with the aesthetics of modernisation, the last being a verse version of the article he wrote for *Time and Tide* ('Glories

of English Craftsmanship – Electricity and Old Churches') in 1953 (the poem
even uses the same illustration). 'The Friends of the Cathedral' lampoons tact-
less appendages assumed to be added by these benefactors. The 'modernistic
oak', 'The Children's Corner' and the notices hung 'Off old crusader's toes'
indicate a certain lack of respect, which recalls the 'restoration' work attacked
in 'Hymn' – are these Friends the new St. Aubyn?

> Those things that look like wireless sets
>   Suspended from each column,
> Which bellow out the Litany
>   Parsonically solemn –
>
> Are these a present from the Friends?
>   And if they are, how nice
> That aided by their echo
>   One can hear the service twice.
>   ('THE FRIENDS OF THE CATHEDRAL', LL. 17–24)

> He gave the brass for burnishing
>   He gave the thick red baize,
> He gave the new addition,
>   Pull'd down the dull old aisle,
>   – To pave the sweet transition
>   He gave th'encaustic tile.
>
>   ('HYMN', LL. 19–24)

'Churchyards', the title of which recalls Hardy in an instant, begins with a
description of beauty: 'How fresh the primrose clumps appear, / Those shining
pools of springtime flower / In our churchyard.' The poet praises Georgian
headstones, with their lettering 'Spaced like a noble title-page', but this image
is used to contrast with the present situation in recognisable style:

> I hate to see in old churchyards
> Tombstones stacked round like playing cards
> Along the wall which then encloses
> A trim new lawn and standard roses,
> Bird-baths and objects such as fill a
> Garden in some suburban villa.
>   ('CHURCHYARDS', LL. 54–59)

This 'garden of rest', which recalls Whispering Glades, the dreadful American
sham satirised by Waugh in *The Loved One* (1948), is conceivably too
'hygienic' for Betjeman. However, there is more than mere aesthetics here, for
'On the old tombstones of the past / We do not read "At peace at last" / But
simply "died" or plain "departed"'. As he says, 'It's no good being chicken-

hearted', yet given his back-catalogue to date, this is exactly what we might imagine him preferring. The answer lies in his faith:

> We die; that's that; our flesh decays
> Or disappears in other ways.
> But since we're Christians, we believe
> That we new bodies will receive
> To clothe our souls for us to meet
> Our Maker at his Judgement Seat.
> And this belief's a gift of faith
> And, if it's true, no end is death.
>
> ('CHURCHYARDS', LL. 70–77)

Though the Doubt is still there at the end of this extract ('if it's true'), Belief overwhelms it, rather as it does in 'Christmas', ultimately. And if the death of Betjeman's mother has affected him in terms of maturity, we can see it not only in 'Remorse', but here too.

Poems in the Porch was in many ways a prelude to the *Guide to English Parish Churches*, published by Collins in 1958. In the introduction to this volume, we find references to headstones and 'the lost ages of craftsmanship', Betjeman's dislike of euphemisms for death, and the inherent beauty of the church in Georgian times:[85]

> [o]ak posts and rails enclose the churchyard in which a horse, maybe the Reverend Dr. Syntax's mare Grizzel, is grazing. The stones are humble and few, and lean this way and that on the south side. They are painted black and grey and the lettering on some is picked out in gold. Two altar tombs, one with a sculptured urn above it, are enclosed in sturdy iron rails such as one sees above the basements of Georgian terrace houses. Beyond the church below a thunderous sky we see the elm and oak landscape of an England comparatively unenclosed.[86]

Betjeman had used this lyrical, painterly present tense to describe the past in vivid terms before (most notably in *Ghastly Good Taste*). Here, he urges us to '[s]ee now the outside of [the] church [. . .] in, let us say, 1805'; thus the reader is not informed of the past, but taken *to* the past – a quite different thing. Yet, as John Press remarks, the writing is 'glowing but unsentimental' and there are indeed a number of 'tartly satirical observations', which temper the romance.[87] Many – regarding electric lighting, 'children's corners' and so on – reflect the even tarter targets of *Poems in the Porch*, but some are familiar from other sources. One of the more subtle examples centres round a quotation from Thomas Hood's 'The Two Peacocks at Bedfont' (1827); Betjeman notes in particular how it 'describes with the colours of an aquatint the worshippers entering that then countrified Middlesex church'.[88] He also offers a critique of the suburb which not only ties in with 'Love is Dead', but also all the poetry right back to 'The Garden City' of 1931:

[w]e are in modern times, out of older and rich suburbs with their garden city atmosphere of guild craftsmen and Sarum Use, and into the big building estates. These large areas of semi-detached houses, built by private speculators or councils, have been eating up our agricultural land since 1920. They have been brought about by the change in transport from steam to motor-bus and electric train. People are moving out of the crowded early Victorian industrial lanes and terraces, into little houses of their own, each with its little patch of garden at the back and front, each isolated from its neighbour by social convention, in districts where miles of pavement enlivened by the squeak of perambulators lead to a far-off bus route and parade of chain stores, and a distant vita-glass school, used as a Community Centre in the evenings.[89]

The passage conveys a sense that these people have been let down by progress, progress that has created a poor replacement for the poor Victorian dwellings that the poet had witnessed in Leeds in 1933. This, in fact, is where 'tinned minds' are born.

Elsewhere, there are shades of 'Victorian Architecture', as well as tints of Betjeman's general 1940s work on nineteenth-century churches. Therefore he writes with enthusiasm that '[b]y 1850 began a great period of English church building, which is comparable with the 15th century'. Indeed, '[m]uch as we regret the Victorian architect's usual "restoration" of an old building, when he came to design a new one, he could produce work which was often original and awe-inspiring'.[90] Pugin is then praised for his writing, which, for Betjeman, was far greater than his churches, while Gilbert Scott, one of Pugin's 'chief Anglican equivalents', is noted as being 'at heart a copyist and not a thinker in Gothic'.[91] (Those who did think in Gothic were Butterfield, Street, J. L. Pearson and William Burges.[92])

The gazetteer is a reflection of Betjeman's intention that the book should be 'an aesthetic and atmospheric assessment' of its subject.[93] One must take care when viewing it, however, as not all the work was carried out by the poet himself. His main collaborator was Edward Long, who also helped compile the lists of churches to be visited.[94] These had to meet a set of five criteria: the first three centred around levels of Victorian restoration, the final one discounted all churches built after 1930, but the fourth admitted a building if it contained 'one object which, regardless of date, was aesthetically worth bicycling twelve miles against the wind to see'.[95] The connections between the introduction and Betjeman's earlier writing are all the more understandable when one considers that work began on the book as early as 1945.[96] But even without all the journalism, reviews and broadcasting work that he undertook between the end of the war and 1958, no one person could possibly have visited each church on the list. Thus an army of helpers was sought, and included Laurence King (Essex), Jack Simmons (Leicestershire) and Edward Long himself (Somerset). The poet took on Berkshire and London alone, while in some – Cornwall (with T. S. Attlee); Oxfordshire (John Piper); the Isle of Man (Basil Megaw) – he had assistance. Elsewhere (Devon, Essex, Hereford and Rutland, etc.) Betjeman wrote only the introductory section. This, despite his editorial stamp, gives the book a slightly irregular feel, a fact noted by Pevsner, who described the introduction as 'superb', but added that 'the gazetteer is done in an extraordinarily uneven way'. Nevertheless, he also generously noted that '[w]herever you have a paragraph of John Betjeman's own writing, it is worth reading'. Ian Nairn, reviewing the book in the *Architectural Review*, agreed, singling out the 'long, loving introduction on the five ages of the parish church' for special mention.[97] Modern critics also find the *Guide* to be of great significance; Taylor-Martin, for example, not only described it as some of Betjeman's 'best prose', but felt compelled to quote Sir Arthur Bryant's opinion that it was 'one of the finest pieces of historical reconstruction' ever written.[98]

Campaign and Caveats

In the last chapter, we saw how Betjeman linked the church and the railway architecturally. In 'Monody on the Death of Aldersgate Street Station' (1955), as with 'Distant View of a Provincial Town' (1935), he performs the same feat poetically. In the earlier piece, the churches are viewed from the train, while in the latter it is the impending closure of Aldersgate Street that leads him to muse on London's 'steepled forest' of Wren churches. As he had written in his 'City and Suburban' column,

> [n]o longer will we be able to ascend those dizzy heights of branching iron staircases to where the bombed refreshment room reminds us of how once there used to be written, in white china letters, on its plate-glass windows "Afternoon Teas a Speciality".[99]

Of the churches mentioned in the poem, Christ Church, Newgate Street had been gutted during the war so that only its tower remained, while St. Mildred's, Bread Street had been totally destroyed.[100] Therefore only St. Michael Paternoster (Wren, 1686–1713) appears in the *Collins Guide*, being described by Betjeman as having a steeple 'not unlike the western towers of St. Paul's'.[101] The sense of decay that this simple statement conveys is also present in the poem: snow falls in the buffet at Aldersgate Street because of an air-raid, so its loss, like the removal of the train shed a couple of years prior to closure, is man-made. The second and third stanzas portray the power of the church bells, with their 'ringing' and 'answering echoes'; this acts first as an emollient to the sad decline of the station, then as an evocative reminder of better times:

> Then would the years fall off and Thames run slowly;
> Out into marshy meadow-land flowed the Fleet:
> And the walled-in City of London, smelly and holy,
> Had a tinkling mass house in every cavernous street.
> ('MONODY ON THE DEATH OF ALDERSGATE STREET STATION', LL. 13–16)[102]

Despite the pungent atmosphere, Betjeman's poem represents another 'lost Elysium' in effect; the multiplicity of bells wash over the narrator and this, coupled with the enclosing walls of the City, creates a feeling of safety and familiarity. Sadly, the ringing lacks the power to stop the rot: in the penultimate stanza, we return to the present, and the decay of the 'broken arches', suffused with flowers ('rosebay, bracken and dock'), is reflected again in the last when the opening refrain is repeated:

> Snow falls in the buffet of Aldersgate station,
>   Toiling and doomed from Moorgate Street puffs the train,
> For us of the steam and the gas-light, the lost generation,
>   The new white cliffs of the City are built in vain.
> ('MONODY ON THE DEATH OF ALDERSGATE STREET STATION', LL. 25–28)

Shades of 'The Planster's Vision' (1945) abound in the last line and we see how cleverly Betjeman makes his point – the City, once almost avuncular in aspect, is now to be destroyed, just like the station, the steam trains which used it and the gas lamps which lit it. The use of 'white cliffs' is poignant too, this very English image (normally associated with Dover) implying that the station somehow represents the quintessence of these islands; thus its 'desecration' by German bombs is linked (as it was in the first stanza) to the 'next desecration', which will be at the hands of the poet's own countrymen. The parallel, as one will have realised, is quite deliberate.

It is significant that Betjeman referred to the work as a 'Monody'.[103] The form is associated with the remembrance of a creative mind, so his placing of a railway station into the genre is bold and challenging, rather than ironic, and represents an attempt to imbue the architecture with a respect for its beauty and all it represents. Indeed, the idea that post-war redevelopment was at least equal to, if not worse, than the Blitz is embodied in this single poem and offers one of the clearest explanations why Betjeman could not see that the Britain of the 1950s was superior to that of twenty or thirty years before.

As the decade moved on, he found himself increasingly at the front line when it came to matters of preservation. Candida Lycett Green notes that 'City and Suburban' had turned her father into the 'people's campaigner', a role aided by his becoming president of an increasing number of conservation groups.[104] This led to the formation of the Victorian Society in 1958, which the poet formed with his friend Anne Rosse, the noted gardening expert.[105] It was a timely move, as Hillier's picture of the way Victorian architecture was regarded in the 1950s demonstrates. In the second volume of his three-volume biography, he quotes from Agatha Christie's novel *They Do It With Mirrors* (1952), in which a nineteenth-century building is lambasted as being 'pretty ghastly' (a deliberate Betjemanism?), yet 'fun too, in a way'.[106] Indeed, John Summerson thought his friend 'mad' to defend St Pancras as forcefully as he did.[107] But Betjeman was no mad preservationist, as his considered letter to

Lionel Brett (later Lord Esher) of January 1957 reveals. Referring back to an earlier matter, he says he realised that:

> what was needed was to make people use their eyes and not just think all new things were ugly and all old ones lovely and all suburbs hideous, but make them see the good from the shoddy whatever its date [. . .].[108]

In the poem 'Pershore Station or A Liverish Journey First Class' (1958) he also hints at the desirability of *balance* between old and new:

> The train at Pershore station was waiting that Sunday night
> Gas light on the platform, in my carriage electric light,
> Gas light on frosty evergreens, electric on Empire wood,
> The Victorian world and the present in a moment's neighbourhood.
>
> ('PERSHORE STATION OR A LIVERISH JOURNEY FIRST CLASS', LL. 1–4)

Anne Rosse lived at 18 Stafford Terrace in London. Her grandparents, Marion and Linley Sambourne (the well-known Victorian illustrator and *Punch* artist) had bought the house in 1874 and decorated it in contemporary style. Thus it remained and Betjeman, who was also a friend of Anne's husband Michael Rosse, was virtually the only visitor who agreed with her that it should be saved and protected. (His own London abode in Cloth Fair had William Morris wallpaper, while the family home at The Mead, Wantage, enjoyed décor supplied by the church furnishers Watts and Co.[109]) The Society was founded on 28 February 1958, with Betjeman one of the two vice-chairmen – a post he was to hold for the rest of his life. Lord Esher was the first chairman proper, probably because he was both a peer and had connections with the National Trust – a situation not without irony, given Betjeman's contempt for 'Lionel Brett-style prefabs'.[110]

The Society's stated aim was 'to make sure that the best Victorian buildings and their contents do not disappear before their merits are more generally appreciated'.[111] More importantly, it was a statutory body with the legal right to be consulted when the redevelopment or demolition of a Victorian building was being mooted.[112] It was a timely move, for even Philip Morton Shand felt moved to write of his 'gnawing sense of guilt' that he might have helped bring about 'a monster neither [he nor Betjeman] could have foreseen'. 'Contemporary Architecture,' he added, '(= the piling up of gigantic children's toy bricks in utterly dehumanized and meaningless forms), "Art" and all that'. It was 'no longer funny; it [was] a frightening, all-invading menace'.[113]

Betjeman's campaign was starting to grow teeth, but there was a price to pay. The weekly production of his 'City and Suburban' column had become wearing; he was tired of the complaints it elicited, and felt that he was starting to look at the world purely in terms of a *Spectator* article.[114] Was he becoming a hack? Journalism had certainly held up the release of the *Collins Guide*, but he needed to make money and could not afford to sit back on his laurels and

wait for inspiration: he had a wife and two children to support, as well as rent
to find for 43 Cloth Fair and all the expense that goes with the ownership of
a large house in the country.

But the continual production line of prose could not last forever and, in
January 1958, Betjeman resigned from the *Spectator* and took up a monthly
column for the *Daily Telegraph* – 'Men and Buildings' – which he interspersed
with book reviews. This still allowed him to highlight what he thought was
important in architecture, whether good or bad: in 'Good Schools, Clinical
Homes, Dull Offices' (19 October 1959), for example, the title says it all, while
in 'Architecture for Entertainment' (16 November 1959), he revisited the
subject of Variety and outlined its decline since his 1950 article for *Diversion*.
He lamented that now 'we are beginning to get up from our chairs in front of
the television and go out in search of a play [. . .], most of our theatres have
disappeared'. Sometimes he was able to fire two shots at once. In the same
article, he wrote:

> [o]ne cannot divorce architecture from purpose and now that theatres,
> whether for the legitimate stage or variety, are becoming as rare as branch-
> line railways it is well to look at what we have left, to think of how much we
> may need them and how fast they are going and which are particularly worth
> preserving.[115]

(It should be remembered that British Railways started certain line closures
long before the infamous Beeching Report of 1963.)

'Variety versus Legitimate' (15 December 1958) highlights the contrast
between builders and architects by praising the work of the former. Betjeman
begins by recording the passing of Cannon Street Station's roof, which had
been built in 1865 by Hawkshaw and Wolfe Barry:

> The designers understood how important are light and shade, outline, depth
> and contrasting shapes in a country with a climate like ours which is usually
> grey and in which large slabs, flat roofs and cubes look heavy and dull.

This inspired him to consider 'how many of our most handsome buildings
have been the work of civil engineers'. Many were railway stations, such as
St. Pancras, King's Cross, York Central, Bristol Temple Meads and
Paddington, though he also delighted in nineteenth-century warehouses,
windmills, breweries and a plethora of other industrial buildings. The upshot
of this discussion was that, in Britain, not enough was being done in the way
of 'repair and adaptation'. As he said, '[w]e pull down rather than improve
and enlarge'. This sentiment was continued in his next column, 'Destruction
for Cash', which appeared on 12 January 1959. Here, Betjeman wrote that
'we have allowed the nibbling destruction of commercial speculators to
destroy whole districts of incomparably beautiful Georgian parts of towns like
Cheltenham, Leamington, Bath, Bristol, Liverpool, Birmingham, Newcastle

upon Tyne, Edinburgh, Margate, Brighton, Weymouth'. Many of these old buildings, he repeated, were reparable, and all were destroyed for 'cash reasons', being mainly in the centres of towns where land values would almost certainly increase. In an echo of his 'Love is Dead' essay (now some seven years old), Betjeman concluded thus:

> Baker Street, Edgware Road and Marylebone Road are London examples of what happens. They are no longer what we knew. They have become international commercial streets. They make remaining unbombed and planned Georgian London more precious if we are to preserve any individuality for London.[116]

A Star is Born

In her 1954 review of *A Few Late Chrysanthemums*, Renée Haynes suggested that a collected edition of Betjeman's verse should be produced.[117] John Murray quite understandably agreed and, after certain unavoidable delays, managed to publish one on 1 December 1958. The selection was made and prefaced by Lord Birkenhead, an old Oxford acquaintance of Betjeman's, who was probably put forward by his sister Lady Pamela Berry (the woman who had introduced the poet to his long-time companion, Elizabeth Cavendish).[118] As a body of work, this first edition was impressive. With an appropriately wider remit than John Sparrow had allowed himself with *Selected Poems*, Birkenhead omitted eleven pieces from *Mount Zion*, five from *Continual Dew*, but never above three from any subsequent volume. Some, like 'The Sandemanian Meeting House' (*Mount Zion*) and 'Variations on a Theme by T. W. Rolleston' (*A Few Late Chrysanthemums*) were welcome additions to later editions; less obvious choices, such as 'Public House Drunk' (*Continual Dew*), were to be granted longevity in the years ahead. After much to-ing and fro-ing between Betjeman and Murray regarding jacket design and illustration, *Collected Poems* was eventually issued with a plain cover of simple type on a pink background.[119]

Commenting on Anthony Powell's notice in *Punch*, Hillier observes that *Collected Poems* is a verse version of the novelist's sequence *A Dance to the Music of Time* (1951–1975) in the sense that both writers were 'using traditional forms to write about contemporary Britain'.[120] Powell had generously remarked that time had been kinder to Betjeman's 'pitch-pine and stucco' than it had to those who wrote of 'kestrels and pylons' in the 1930s. 'Crashing his way through the *zeitgeist* to the swelling notes of the church harmonium,' he added, 'John Betjeman has become, perhaps, the poet through whom the vagaries of our age will in the last resort be remembered.'

It is not a scholarly work like Sparrow's earlier effort, but Birkenhead's preface does instil in the reader the idea that Betjeman possessed that 'true poet's instinct of registering impressions wherever he finds himself'.[121] He said little that was new, but noted that Betjeman's satire was unsuccessful 'only because he is lacking in the cruelty and spite that are inseparable from that art'.[122] This is an early indication of the "teddy-bear" image that was, and continues, to dog the poet's reputation; yet Professor Bernard Bergonzi, reviewing the anthology in *The Twentieth Century* (February 1959), felt the failure was due to Betjeman's lack of 'clear convictions from which to direct his attacks'.[123] From our own twenty-first century viewpoint, it is plain that Betjeman's convictions centre round a fear that Britain was sinking into the mire. The critics of *A Few Late Chrysanthemums* could see this, even if they did not agree with it. On the whole, however, the poet's entire oeuvre to date failed to inspire the same opinions, even though 'Huxley Hall', 'The Dear Old Village' and 'The Village Inn' were all included in *Collected Poems*. Could it be that this new context had softened their blow? It would certainly explain the present critical attitude. With this in mind, it is somewhat ironic to note that Birkenhead chose to end his preface by saying that the satirical "Varsity Students' Rag' (1927) remained 'as fresh and witty to me now as [it] did [in the late 1920s]'.[124]

Of the seventeen poems that had not appeared in book form before, only 'The Heart of Thomas Hardy' belonged to an earlier era. The rest were collected under the heading 'Poems Written Since 1954', or to put it another way, poems written since Betjeman's answer to the critics of *A Few Late Chrysanthemums*.[125] Some of these poems *are* as light as his professed post-publication mood. Longfellow, a favourite Aunt Sally, is teased again in the form of 'Longfellow's Visit to Venice' (1955), for example, while even 'False Security' (1955) – a poem which looks towards *Summoned by Bells* (1960), and which deals with a humiliating childhood experience – ends with what can only be described as a punchline:

> Can I forget my delight at the conjuring show?
> And wasn't I proud that I was the last to go?
> Too overexcited and pleased with myself to know
> That the words I heard my hostess's mother employ
> To a guest departing, would ever diminish my joy,
> I WONDER WHERE JULIA FOUND THAT STRANGE,
>   RATHER COMMON LITTLE BOY?[126]
>
> ('FALSE SECURITY', LL. 29–34)

But as we saw with 'Monody on the Death of Aldersgate Street Station', it was by no means all joy and jingle. 'Variation on a Theme by Newbolt' (1956), for example, is a touching elegy for a businessman, while 'Inevitable' (1957) takes its inspiration from the weekly visits Betjeman made around this time to the patients of St Bartholomew's Hospital, London.[127] 'Felixstowe, or The Last of Her Order' (1958) is a poem in which the Arnoldian ebb and flow of the sea becomes entangled with the loneliness of the nun whose sisters are no more. Faith is her saviour ('my heart finds rest in Thee'); for 'Eunice' (1955), however, succour comes from the pastoral idyll of Kent:

> With her latest roses happily encumbered
>> Tunbridge Wells Central takes her from the night,
> Sweet second bloomings frost has faintly umbered
>> And some double dahlias waxy red and white.
>>>> ('EUNICE', LL. 1–4)

This poem portrays a strange sort of hibernation, in which Eunice spends each summer in 'her little hutment', only to return to Onslow Gardens and 'busy months of typing in the office'. It represents a different angle from Betjeman's usual argument, for here both rat race and retreat are in the present so that, this time, the countryside critiques the commercial.

Perhaps the two most interesting poems in this brief section are 'Thoughts on "The Diary of a Nobody"' (1955) and 'From the Great Western' (1957). The first deals with the Pooters' ill-fated lunch at Watney Lodge, which took place in the famous novel on Sunday, 28 April. Or rather it deals with the walk *to* the Lodge – in the *Diary* itself, the entry for that day merely begins: '[w]e found Watney Lodge farther off than we anticipated, and only arrived as the clock struck two, both feeling hot and uncomfortable'.[128] The poem, again like 'Middlesex', is in fact 'a paean to the vanishing semi-rural county':[129]

> The Pooters walked to Watney Lodge
>> One Sunday morning hot and still
> Where public footpaths used to dodge
>> Round elms and oaks to Muswell Hill
>
> That burning buttercuppy day
>> The local dogs were curled in sleep,
> The writhing trunks of flowery May
>> Were polished by the sides of sheep.
>>>> ('THOUGHTS ON "THE DIARY OF A NOBODY"', LL. 1–8)

The Lodge Betjeman seemed to see was 'gabled gothic hard and red', perhaps unsurprisingly, but the estate on which it lay 'Meant Morning Prayer and beef and wine / And Queen Victoria alive'. This is not intended to be whimsy, but indicates stability and the comfort of routine. The final stanza is most telling in this respect:

> Dear Charles and Carrie, I am sure,
>> Despite that awkward Sunday dinner,
> Your lives were good and more secure
>> Than ours at cocktail time in Pinner.
>>>> ('THOUGHTS ON "THE DIARY OF A NOBODY"', LL. 21–24)

Charles Pooter is a figure of fun. But while he is snobbish, prim and naïve, he is also a loyal, hard-working, honest man, and it is difficult not to like him.

At Watney Lodge he acts with characteristic gaucheness by commenting to a Mr Short that he hoped 'it would not be *long*' before he knew him – a joke he felt obliged to repeat. Having erred again prior to the meal by noting various facial facts about his host's recently demised relations, one can see why the afternoon was considered 'awkward'. Indeed, it is well that his old friend Teddy and he 'waxed rather eloquent' about their schooldays to the extent that the rest of the party fell asleep by the fire![130] Betjeman assumes that his readers know the details of the incident (which they probably did), though one could claim that the fire ('It being cold even for April') indicates a certain degree of idealism in the poem, which has the action take place on a day 'hot and still'. This was probably just a mistake – the Pooters are hot from an unexpectedly long walk, not because of the weather. What *is* significant, however, is that even this rather embarrassing party is seen as preferable to its modern equivalent. Given that the relationship between Betjeman and his own father places the poet (one would think) closer to *Lupin* Pooter than Charles, the future of those children being brought up to release their inhibitions 'in a hundred different ways' (cf. 'Huxley Hall') is decidedly bleak in comparison to the stability of Victorian middle-class life.[131]

'From the Great Western' gives some idea of that future. Like the wheels of the train, the work is cyclical, the opening refrain being repeated at the close, implying that progress is not teleological, but goes round and round and round, getting nowhere:

> These small West Country towns where year by year
> Newly elected mayors oppose reforms
> Their last year's Worships promised – down the roads
> Large detached houses, Croydons of the West,
> Blister in summer heat; striped awnings hang
> Over front doors, and those geraniums,
> Retired tradesmen love to cultivate,
> Blaze in the gravel.
>
> ('FROM THE GREAT WESTERN', LL. 1–8)

The tight rhythm captures that of the train to perfection, but note how this creates an impression of unstoppable inevitability. The 'Love is Dead'-style anti-standardisation stance is present in the reference to 'Croydons of the West', indicating that everywhere was starting to look the same (though this was partly due to the necessity of post-war mass housing).[132] The ephemeral nature of politics is also targeted: those mayors, like the political parties, think only in terms of terms of office – forward planning is impossible and each new incumbent feels a compulsion to put his own stamp on the district under his control. But the inevitability conveyed by the poem is that of the mess this situation produces. As it continues:

> From more furtive streets
> Unmarried mothers leave for London. Girls

Who had such promise suddenly lose their looks.
Small businesses go bankrupt. Corners once
Familiar for a shuttered toll gate house
Are smoothed away to make amenities.
('FROM THE GREAT WESTERN', LL. 8–13)

The town is *en route* to becoming a 'bright, hygienic hell', no doubt. Betjeman skilfully shows us what happened to places like Pooter's Holloway, but the fact that we are in the West Country and not London indicates that the situation is endemic.[133] Line 8 is the watershed, and after the fairly auspicious beginnings as the train passes through, we now see the town's decline through time. The church offers a certain protection, but when we reach the end of the piece, only to be carried back to the start again (where more newly elected mayors are in place to oppose reforms), the fatality of the situation becomes clear. 'From the Great Western' is as damning an indictment as any in *A Few Late Chrysanthemums*, but one which the critics of *Collected Poems* seemed to miss.

In fact, Professor Bergonzi's analysis aside, most of those critics agreed with Anthony Powell. Frank Kermode (*The Spectator*), Anthony Lejeune (*Time and Tide*) and W. G. Hoskins (*The Listener*) all praised the book unreservedly, Hoskins even going so far as to say that it was 'beyond question the best book to be published in 1958 about the landscapes and towns of England'.[134] In the *Manchester Guardian*, Philip Larkin wrote that the collection 'finally puts to flight the notion that Betjeman is no more than a dealer in a few preciosities such as Anglicanism or ghastly good taste'. He noted perceptively that the over-emphasis on lavish book production in the poet's early years had risked damage to his reputation, but that 'since 1940 [. . .], a succession of more chastely designed volumes has ousted the element of undergraduate hoax'. Here at least was one reviewer who came close to seeing what Betjeman was driving at. He was, after all, another poet:

Betjeman picks it all up: the decay of surviving nineteenth-century institutions, the decline of the Church, the altered countryside and ways of living, subtopia and socialism, and all the tiny vivid little manifestations of sadness and snobbery and silliness [. . .].

Recalling Wilde's axiom that only mediocrity develops, Larkin also commented that if his friend 'could hit the target so unerringly at 25 [with 'Death in Leamington'] he had clearly no need to change'. He concludes that, having 'knocked down the "No Through Road To Action" sign' and being a 'committed writer, whose poems spring from what he really feels about real life,' Betjeman was the only poet of the Auden, Thomas, Betjeman group (recently listed by Edmund Wilson) who was 'still a positive poetic force'.[135]

John Sparrow also wrote a very thoughtful piece for the *Times Literary Supplement*. After magnanimously referring to Lord Birkenhead's 'excellent preface' (which Larkin ignored), he went on to give a shrewd commentary on Betjeman's rising popularity, from the 'esoteric jokes' of the early volumes, to the problems that being considered amusing can bring:

> [i]t is upon the perverse element in his poetry that, in spite of his protests, his readers – and more recently his "listeners" and "viewers" – have fastened, and fastened with such enthusiasm that he must have been tempted to accept the role they have thrust upon him [. . .].[136]

He did not, and Sparrow felt that *Collected Poems* demonstrated 'the multiplicity of its author's talents', showing him to be 'a serious poet in two senses of the word'. '[I]n his own strange way,' he continued, Betjeman 'is often deeply moving, and by virtue of his solid and varied achievement he must be "taken seriously" by any critic who seeks to give an adequate account of English poetry in the twentieth century.' And (of course) he reiterated his earlier opinion that Betjeman was 'a master of that most difficult of mediums, blank verse'.

The public also agreed with Powell: the sales of *Collected Poems* were astonishing, the book soon being bought at a rate of just below 1,000 a day. It reached a total of 15,384 by the end of 1958, with a further 50,299 copies being sold by 31 December 1959.[137] It is difficult to explain why such an enormous increase should have taken place (compare the figures with the sales of *Selected Poems* or even *A Few Late Chrysanthemums*), but it is certainly not due to good notices alone. There was clearly something about Betjeman's work – *all* of it – that captured the public mood. But was there agreement that the world was not as pleasant as it had been twenty years before? Did people share his vision of Britain – and his fears for what it may become? Or was it the fact that all undercurrents could be ignored, leaving the verses to be enjoyed merely for their 'euphony'? One hopes that elements of all three ideas were involved.

In December 1958, Princess Margaret presented Betjeman with the Duff Cooper Prize (whose panel of judges included Maurice Bowra); the following year saw him receive a second Foyle Poetry Prize and an honorary D.Litt. from Reading University; in 1960, he was awarded the CBE and the prestigious Queen's Gold Medal for Poetry (*Collected Poems*).[138] Some distance had been travelled since *Mount Zion*, that 'precious, hyper-sophisticated' volume of 1931. Betjeman had reached his zenith but, sadly, soon after the 'golden glow' of his great success, a series of personal tragedies conspired to knock him back.[139] In a short space of time, 'Colonel' Kolkhorst, George Barnes, Jack Beddington (Shell) and Philip Morton Shand all passed away; Betjeman must have felt as though the carpet were being pulled from under him. Consolation came from his relationship with Elizabeth Cavendish – and *work*. Throughout that year, he would concentrate on his 'Epic' verse autobiography – *Summoned by Bells* was on its way and, as Sparrow had prophesied, it promised 'to be his masterpiece'.[140]

CHAPTER FIVE

The 1960s and 70s

The Euston Murder

Summoned by Bells (1960), Betjeman's autobiography in verse, was the next major publication to follow *Collected Poems*. Extracts were published in *The New Yorker* and the *Sunday Times* in August and November respectively, with the complete volume appearing soon after. It was not well received by the press and will be discussed in full in CHAPTER SEVEN. But as Britain started to swing, Betjeman's role as an architectural conservationist continued to grow, although it is important to realise that, while we might associate him with Victorian *Gothic*, nineteenth-century building styles were more diverse – as were his tastes. Indeed, one of his best-documented (albeit unsuccessful) campaigns concerned the proposed demolition of Philip Hardwick's great *Doric* arch (1837) at Euston Station. This was due to be razed to the ground when a new terminus was constructed as part of the British Transport Commission's West Coast Main Line electrification scheme.[1]

To rally support, Betjeman wrote 'Heritage of the Rail Age', a feature in his 'Men and Buildings' series for the *Daily Telegraph*. He could think of 'no worthier memorial to the fact that Britain built the first railways than to reconstruct [the] Arch, its lodges and railings on the Euston Road itself'.[2] Frustratingly, this had been the part of the original plan, but despite the efforts of the Georgian Group and the Victorian Society, it was soon revised, with formal notice of the intention to demolish being given the following January. The London County Council agreed to this, but stipulated that the structure be re-erected elsewhere 'in an appropriate, dignified and open setting'. An anonymous correspondent noted in the *Architectural Review* that this would cost £190,000; sadly it was not to be, and annihilation began at the end of 1961.[3]

The political historian William D. Rubinstein believes that the launch of Sputnik I (the first earth satellite) in October 1957, led to '[a] kind of panic [in the West regarding] the Soviet Union's technological advancements', which in turn led to 'greater investment in higher education and a determination to "modernise"'.[4] If so, one may speculate that Betjeman's deputational meeting with Macmillan in October 1961, at which John Summerson made a strong case in favour of the Arch, was never going to succeed.[5] However, it is more likely that, with an expensive upgrade under way, the nationalised Commission simply needed to save money, just as the Government doubtless had more pressing matters to deal with. Bernard Kaukas, then deputy to the chief architect of British Rail's London Midland Region, explains that so much time was wasted to-ing and fro-ing about the Arch that it was seen as endangering the completion of the whole scheme:

> I am sure that by that time Macmillan's advisers [. . .] were being told, 'We cannot wait any longer. We've got to have [Euston] station completed in time for the Queen to open it.' When you think that the Queen had to be booked a year ahead anyway – a minimum of a year – somebody was saying, 'If we go on like this we're never going to get anything done' and the London Midland manager, a powerful, good manager, said, 'Finish! Enough!'[6]

The Arch's fate was soon matched by that of Bunning's London Coal Exchange (1847–49), which had not only possessed a vast and very fine Victorian interior, but was also an example of the nineteenth-century 'engineering vision' that even the 'anti-Betjemanian' Pevsner admired.[7]

The poet had often discussed Euston during his journalistic life, but Timothy Mowl believes that his 1930s view, ostensibly at odds with that noted above, counted against him in later years with the Victorian Society (which chose to elect Pevsner as its second Chairman). To support this, he quotes a particular passage from the poet's 1933 article for the *Architectural Review*, 'Dictating to the Railways', in which he wrote that: '[i]f [in the proposed reorganisation of the site] the Great Hall must go, then that is that; and if the arch must be demolished then that is that too'.[8] Though fairly damning, this is not a true representation of the author's stance, which is clarified by the subsequent (and final) sentence (omitted by Mowl):

> [b]ut at least this splendid gateway should be re-erected in another place where it would be not only an excellent advertisement but also a permanent and impressive memorial of the once great architectural tradition of the railways.

This clarifies that Betjeman was *not* in favour of demolition. Furthermore, the 'that is that' fatalism was probably a reaction to the attitude of the London Midland and Scottish Railway (LMS), which owned Euston in the 1930s: when the company was working on plans for reconstruction in the latter part of that decade, a senior official was quoted in *Modern Transport* as saying '[w]e will make a present of the Arch to anyone who cares to take it away'.[9] Betjeman realistically perceived that the largest railway company in Britain was never going to allow itself to be thwarted by a fledgling journalist. Mowl may believe that the poet displayed 'no sign of anger or protest' in the article, but his true feelings about the Arch are evident from his choice of superlatives.[10]

Regarding the Great Hall (1849, by Hardwick and his son Philip C. Hardwick), "30s Betjeman" noted the 'general massiveness of the structure and [. . .] its powerful simplicity'. He surmised that the younger Hardwick had contributed the Roman details and concluded that, though unsuited to its Doric surroundings, the result was 'no less successful than his father's great arch'.[11] The problem comes with how the article continues, for the Hall, he then asserts, was 'belittled' by the son's later French extensions. This and the loathsome 'jazz-modern' kiosks added since led Betjeman to claim that he hoped the LMS 'will make a clean sweep of the building behind the Doric portico'. This seems to be at odds with his 1949 view that '[n]ever had there been and never has there been since in England so magnificent a piece of railway architecture' (though his hatred for the kiosks remained).[12] But the classic French Renaissance additions at Euston, while in keeping with what the LMS prescribed for its other stations, was *not* in keeping with what de Cronin Hastings prescribed for the pro-Modern Movement stance of the *Architectural Review*.[13] A key point: this was not so much a *volte face*, as another example of the need to follow editorial policy. Writing under such a regime required the display of a certain brashness, but the final sentence of 'Dictating to the Railways' does offer a tangible link to Betjeman's future writing as well as to his very public campaigning of the 1960s.

The new concrete Euston, opened by the Queen in 1968, did nothing to stir his passions. He described it tersely as '[n]o masterpiece' and commented that its lack of platform seating made it an 'inhuman structure, which seems to ignore passengers'.[14] British Rail's plan to make the building pay by adding multi-storey hotels and office blocks to the flat roof seemed to him 'a lame excuse for so inhospitable a building'.

These were dangerous times for lovers of nineteenth century architecture, or indeed any architecture, and in order to communicate his concerns as widely as possible, Betjeman wrote his first and only teleplay, *Pity About the Abbey*. Screened twice by the BBC (once on 29 July 1965 and again the following year), it was 'a very serious argument disguised as a comedy, against developers of an unscrupulous sort'.[15] Stuart Farrar, a professional television scriptwriter, added the film's romantic sub-plot but the main thrust belonged to Betjeman, who used the classic ploy of taking an extreme situation (or perhaps not so extreme) to ridicule reality and encourage debate. In brief, a group of planners decide that Westminster Abbey is 'in the way of a viable and comprehensive development'. They propose selling it to Texas in order to make way for traffic improvements and commercial buildings. As Betjeman later wrote: 'I imagined a situation in which it would be possible, on perfectly reasonable grounds and "in the public interest", to order the destruction' of the building.[16] 'The great thing to do in a matter like this,' he continued, 'is to keep the projected plan out of the newspapers, because once the public heard about it, there might be such serious opposition that even the developer and the Minister of Transport and the architects and engineers in charge might take fright.' When the story *is* leaked to the press, the fictional "Plansters" are let off as minds are swiftly changed and the Abbey is saved.

The play's clear message did not prevent the Royal Fine Art Commission from taking umbrage. Its members (despite Betjeman being one of them) believed that the body had been mocked: Farrar's 'bewitching lady from an amenity society' (as the poet described her) attracts the affections of one junior civil servant, who subsequently (or consequently) resigns in protest at the plan. This was seen as inappropriate behaviour, but the Commission's reaction amazed the author, who had intended to strike 'a blow in favour of preservation societies and a strong uncompromised equivalent [of that self-same group]'. However, by noting that the play admitted an irony 'so suavely gentle that its stings have a powerful delayed action effect', *The Times'* television critic highlighted something that is also an important trait of the poetry.[17] Such a delay is surely more valuable in the long run: a message that is obvious does not stimulate the viewer's mind – it is clear and so requires no effort. Something which seeps into the brain more slowly is appreciated in all its aspects more fully because the viewer has to do some *work*. Aside from this, Betjeman must have been delighted to learn that the *Times* correspondent felt the production 'tended to make the abbey itself the play's real hero'.

Betjeman's work of this period did not only feature venerable buildings, however, and (as we saw in the last chapter), his discerning tastes allowed him to retain a critical eye. In a 1969 broadcast for *Any Questions*, for example, he commented that he did not 'think everything old must necessarily be preserved', and that neither was 'everything Victorian [. . .] beautiful'.[18] He reasserted his view that people should 'use their eyes and not be prejudiced by dates'. This was advice he was prepared to take himself: in his 'Men and Buildings' feature on Sheffield ('The Best and Worst of an Era', 3 July 1961), for example, he praised the new block of flats at Park Hill (1956–1961, by J. L. Womersley) that had been erected on the site of older two-storey slums. One would expect such an edifice to be loathed by a man who, in his speech at the Annual Dinner of the Royal Academy of Arts in 1962, would refer to the 'rent-collecting slabs' by Hyde Park, and later still would write about the 'arid, monotonous new cubes with their garish mosaics [. . .] in post-war Gresham Street [London]'.[19] In 1953, he *had* conceded that there were some new 'cheerful and spaciously planned flats' which were 'comelier' than the office blocks that were starting to appear in London, but added that this was 'not saying much – to those who think that architecture should delight the man walking in the street and not make him feel like a crushed insect'.[20]

So why praise Park Hill? It must be said that there is a degree of ambivalence in the article: '[h]igh up here the living-room windows look out on to the magnificent moorland and if you cannot make out which dot in the area below is your child,' it states, 'you are at least centrally heated and with hot water and proper sanitation'.[21] Thus while Betjeman *is* initially horrified by the 'terrifying and inhuman' aspect with its 'tier on tier of concrete with ugly "contemprikit" detail', as with 'Leeds: A City of Contrasts' (see CHAPTER TWO), he finds himself 'acclimatised' when it becomes apparent how the improved facilities inside have fulfilled an important – and immediate – human need. This leads him to deem the planning of Park Hill 'thoughtful and ingenious', before noting that yet finer detail exists on the blocks rising on the city's outskirts (which he describes as 'well-proportioned and even noble').

Maybe the office of the *Daily Telegraph* had insisted, de Cronin-style, that Betjeman refrain from rocking the boat – to have a correspondent write disparagingly of a new building that it had been invited to visit might have led to great embarrassment (and unemployment for the correspondent). But Betjeman saw that the flats were 'kinder than the old streets', and no one could question the validity of *that* observation.[22] To say that they were 'super-human additions to a new landscape' does sound a little over-zealous, but he believed they suited 'the rugged hills of Sheffield and its people'. His reservation about the children shows that he recognised this was not the *best* solution, but it was certainly better than the modern suburb he found in the city, where there seemed to be no shops ('only houses, houses') and which seemed to be 'a wasteful use of Sheffield's countryside'. While policy may have dictated a certain slant to this piece, the poet was clearly able to see both the inhabitants of Sheffield and their problems. Besides, the block was already *in situ* (doubtless with a waiting list of tenants poised to take up residence), and had not replaced a Gothic delight like the St. Pancras Station Hotel – or Euston's Doric portico.

'The Best and Worst of an Era' also included an overview of Broomhill, 'where gabled black stone houses rise above the ponticums and holly and private cast-iron lamp-posts light the gravelled drives'. This was 'still the prettiest suburb in England', and Betjeman used it to contrast with his description of the 'worn little houses' that the poor were forced to live in. It also inspired him poetically:

> High dormers are rising
> So sharp and surprising,
> And ponticum edges
> The driveways of gravel;
> Stone houses from ledges
> Look down on ravines.
> The vision can travel
> From gable to gable,
> Italianate mansion
> And turretted stable,
> A sylvan expansion
> So varied and jolly
> Where laurel and holly
> Commingle their greens.

('An Edwardian Sunday, Broomhill, Sheffield', 1966, ll. 1–14)

It is interesting to note that the above scene is Edwardian and not Victorian: in a 1962 article for *The Spectator*, he was as complimentary of buildings erected in his own century as he was those of the previous one, pointing out that antipathy to Victorian *and* Edwardian architecture was due to the fact that 'the buildings of those periods are considered "too late" by those who set themselves up as experts'.[23] Of course, the Surrey-like Broomhill also contrasts with that twentieth-century Sheffield estate of no shops, but, as Dr. B. Burns wrote in response to 'The Best and Worst of an Era', it too was 'in the process of mutilation by a 13-storey students' hostel in the concrete crate style'.[24]

Live in Metroland

In an earlier 'Men and Buildings' piece, 'Suburbs Common or Garden', Betjeman had written that eighteenth-century thinking revolved around the 'extension of the town into the fields' (as in Birkenhead); subsequent builders, he went on, 'wanted to make country of towns' so that each dweller lived 'in a detached house in a garden of his own'. Newly enriched Victorians later extended the idea by building larger houses in areas like Streatham (London), Edgbaston (Birmingham) and Jesmond Dene (Newcastle-upon-Tyne):

> [g]as lamps and possibly a lodge at the entrance, laurels along the drive (in which Sherlock Holmes might be hiding with his bull's-eye lantern), red paper in the dining room and heavy mahogany chairs, green paper in the billiard room, pale silk on the drawing-room walls and armour in the hall, what are they now, these merchants' dreams of home? Clinics, branches of the pubic library, Ministry of Pensions offices, and their gardens filled with huts or new villas built in a feeble attempt to look like Frank Lloyd Wright.[25]

There is too much attention to detail here for this to be purely mocking (and is that reference to laurels – present also in the poem – a deliberate allusion to Pooter's house?). Indeed, the article was to become part of Betjeman's attempt to save the suburb of Bedford Park, Chiswick, which had been laid out by Norman Shaw in 1876. He described how its 'winding roads [had been] cut through by heavy traffic and [that] the fences so carefully designed as part of the whole composition [had become] dilapidated or altered'. Betjeman was evidently able to read the thoughts of councils and developers, for it was just two years later, in 1962, that the Acton Council demolished The Bramptons, a large house in Bedford Road, and built an old people's home of yellow brick in its stead. That Betjeman had called the estate '[t]he most significant suburb built in the last century, probably the most significant in the Western World', ensured that he became part of the struggle to stop further development.[26] Most of the credit for its success should, as Hillier rightly notes, go to the local campaigners, but with his writing and television appearances, Betjeman was instrumental in keeping the 'battle' in the public eye. After this, 'no letter of complaint to the press, about historic buildings, seemed valid without his signature'.[27]

This benign attitude towards The Suburb was to be the ostensible focus of the famous 1973 BBC film, *Metro-land*:

> Child of the First War,
> Forgotten by the Second,
> We called you Metro-land.
> We laid our schemes
> Lured by the lush brochure, down byways beckoned,
> To build at last the cottage of our dreams,
> A city clerk turned countryman again,
> And linked to the Metropolis by train.[28]

Of course, Betjeman would also have been aware of Sir Humphrey Maltravers, the ageing MP in Waugh's *Decline and Fall* (1928), who became Viscount Metroland (indicating perhaps that he was a Lord of sham mediocrity). However, it should be remembered that he had always been more ambivalent about suburbia than his friend. The argument was made earlier that 'Slough' (1937) was as concerned with compartmentalisation as bad architecture, and, as we saw in the last chapter, his verse criticism of such areas continued to focus on the loss of a pastoral idyll. Yet Timothy Mowl feels that *Metro-land* 'should be seen as a generous tribute to Pooterism, decentralization and all the unfashionable bourgeois values'.[29] According to Candida Lycett Green, her father had 'long harboured the desire to make a film about the beauties of suburbia'.[30] Indeed, Betjeman wrote to Robin Scott (controller of the BBC) in 1971 that such a programme would have 'a rich theme and could be full of praise and stimulation', adding that '[m]ost people are suburban and won't admit it'. 'What trim gardens we could show,' he gushed, 'what shopping arcades, front halls, churches, schools and human-scale paths and bicycle tracks and open spaces.' But the hint of teasing humour in the letter betrays the fact that the film is more complicated than Mowl and Lycett Green suggest. There are clues to this in his prose work on the same area: in 1963, for example, he wrote 'So Little Left of the Old Middlesex', a piece that was much harsher in tone than the poem about that county of ten years before. It included a description of an unnamed High Road: '[s]omewhere,' Betjeman lamented,

> if I dared to raise my eyes above the crowded pavement, there must have been sky, but between it and me were concrete lamp standards, the tops of buses and enormous lorries carrying mattresses, and bulk liquids, or dragging trailers full of chassis of motor-cars.[31]

The 'county that inspired Keats' was that place no longer: an old cottage 'with a glimpse of orchard behind' had been filled in by a huge chain store and the gardens of the Italianate villas 'are now full of second-hand motor-cars for sale and piles of tyres'. Who was to blame? The villains were clear: 'over-population, abetted by big business and "developers"'.[32] (Note how "developers" have inverted commas like the church "restorers" – his other *bêtes noires*.) The 'onslaught' began in the 1930s and 'gained pace' in the 1950s and 60s. In a reflection of his views on Slough, he saw how this process raped the county of 'the richest agricultural land near London'. Transport played a large part in the 'invasion', first by the mainline railway and then by the electrified Metropolitan: '[b]uses and motor-cars have filled [the] remaining gaps'.[33] As the situation is hardly likely to have improved by 1973, this 1963 article is pivotal for understanding the film.

Betjeman knew that a television audience would not look kindly on a programme that was over-critical of them, their homes and their way of life. No one could blame anyone for wanting to escape the grime and bustle of the city, and we already know that the poet's Seeing Eye allowed him to appreciate the humanity of such districts. Indeed, in 1970, he reiterated this: '"Live in Metroland", said the posters, and very charming Metroland was compared with the stock-brick and stucco of such congested suburbs of steam-railway days as Kilburn.'[34] But in print there is generally more leave to discuss the implications of urban residential areas with objectivity; on television, where a visual illustration must be provided, it is not so easy. This is not to say that the film is entirely disingenuous or sarcastic – Betjeman dispels such notions by drawing frequently on his own memories. As he says: 'I remember Marlborough Road Station, because it was the nearest station to the house where lived my future parents-in-law.'[35] Similarly, the Palace of Arts reminds him of how he 'used to wait while my father saw the living models in Pears' Palace of Beauty'.[36] However, the warnings are there to be found – could, for example, Betjeman's voice-over reference to 'early electric', as the footage shows a train leaving Baker Street, be anything other than a quotation from his poem about that locale?

> Early Electric! With what radiant hope
>   Men formed this many-branched electrolier,
> Twisted the flex around the iron rope
>   And let the dazzling vacuum globes hang clear,
> And then with hearts the rich contrivance fill'd
> Of copper, beaten by the Bromsgrove Guild.
> ('THE METROPOLITAN RAILWAY: BAKER STREET STATION BUFFET', LL. 1–6)

As discussed in CHAPTER FOUR, 'The Metropolitan Railway' centred on the same 'autumn-scented Middlesex' that he recalled in the *Daily Telegraph*, the Middlesex where 'Youth and Progress' were still (just about) in partnership. Yet the film's 'younger, brighter, homelier Metro-land' of Wembley is not *quite* a paradise: the house names for instance – 'Rusholme', 'Rustles', 'Rustlings', '*Rusty Tiles*', 'Rose Hatch', 'Rose Hill', 'Rose Lea', 'Rose Mount', '*Rose Roof*' (my italics) – are not recited by Betjeman (as Mowl suggests) to sell 'their charms to [the] viewers', and are certainly not intended to reverse a 'trite Wordsworthian' preconception. Rather, and despite each house being 'slightly different from the next', this gentle mocking implies a certain lack of imagination.[37] In *The City in History* (1961), Lewis Mumford was altogether less gentle on this same point:

> the mass movement into suburban areas [gave rise to] a multitude of uniform, unidentifiable houses, lined up inflexibly, at uniform distances, on uniform roads, in a treeless communal waste, inhabited by people of the same class, the same income, the same age-group [. . .].[38]

The picture was certainly not *this* bad, but when Betjeman notes that these Wembley residences are bastions 'of individual taste on fields that once were bright with buttercups', Mowl is wrong to claim that he is implying they are 'more aesthetically valuable' than the landscape.[39] If the fields had simply been *filled* with flowers, he may have been right, but the notion of their being *bright* with them is too poetic, too *Keatsian* (with all about truth and beauty that this infers), to convey anything other than regret. We are told, after all, that 'Bucks, Herts and Middlesex *yielded* to Metro-land' (my italics).[40]

More important, and more open to misinterpretation, is the section of the film concerning Harrow. Mowl asserts that 'Betjeman waved his arms to demand attention to rows of [the area's] suburban houses which no other commentator would have dreamt of including'. After showing a 'defiantly Ruskinian street of about 1880', we are treated, 'against shots of lawns being mown and cars washed', to views and vistas of what Betjeman calls this 'rising tide of Metro-land', with its later bow-fronted, two-storey semis – all half-timber and hydrangeas.[41] Mowl is right about the Ruskinian street of course, but there is some ambiguity about the poet's presentation, for that waving of arms is actually part of a comically over-acted intake of breath – '[t]he healthy air of Harrow in the 1920s and thirties' (which is when the villas in question were built).[42] Indeed, it would be difficult to prove that this was a style of architecture Betjeman favoured without reserve: in the *Shell Guide* to Devon (1936), for instance, he had written a sardonic caption to a Maurice Beck photograph that noted how Barnefield Crescent, Exeter (1798–1800) had been 'ingeniously ruined by [a] modern villa'.[43] But while those at Harrow enjoyed a much less distressing position contextually, consider how the film goes on:

> [y]ou paid a deposit and eventually we hope you had your own house with its garage and front garden and back garden. A verge in front of your house and grass and tree for the dog. Variety created in each façade of the houses – in the colouring of the trees. In fact, the country had come to the suburbs. Roses are blooming in Metro-land just as they do in the brochure.

The reference to the Metro-land brochure at the end surely suggests that this new Elysium is slightly forced and fake – remember that the poem 'Harrow-on-the-Hill' (1949) deals with the yearning for a simple life near the sea, and note that he had only recently attacked such housing developments in his architectural series for the *Daily Telegraph Magazine* – see CHAPTER TWO, re 'Slough' (the articles were later collected into a single volume, *A Pictorial History of English Architecture* [1972]).

The further along the line the film goes, however, the lighter its narrator's censure becomes. After praise for Norman Shaw's Grims Dyke (Harrow Weald) – once owned by W. S. Gilbert – and the eighteenth-century Venetian décor of the Moor Park Golf Club premises, Betjeman continues to Chorleywood (Herts.), which, he believes, is 'essential Metro-land'.[44] Here, the 'country quality' – the 'oak, hazel, hawthorn, [. . .] common and cricket pitch, Church School and Church' – had survived. Here, perhaps, it was still as rural as 'rural RAYNER'S LANE' ('The Metropolitan Railway', l.29). For Betjeman, Chorleywood also had the advantage of being the location of The Orchard, home of C. F. A. Voysey – an early hero, and a man whom he had met in the *Architectural Review* days. He thus describes the house in great detail, observing in particular

> [Voysey's] signature tune, the heart. It's there at the end of the hinge, it's here round the letterbox, it's also round the keyhole and it seems to be on the key. That's a Voysey key, and in the house he did everything down to the knives and forks. The plan of the house radiates out from this hall. Extreme simplicity is the keynote. No unnecessary decoration. The balusters here for the stairs, straight verticals, giving an impression of great height to this simple hall.[45]

The Orchard's simplicity and beauty certainly makes an interesting contrast with the oddly named High and Over, a *moderne*, Y-shaped concrete edifice by Connell, which 'scandalized' Buckinghamshire when it was built in 1931. Mowl is right to say that Betjeman is 'gently malicious' about it: '[a]nd one day, poor thing, it woke up and found developers in its back garden. Goodbye, *High* hopes and *Over* confidence – in fact, it's probably good-bye England'.[46] There was indeed 'not a note of regret in Betjeman's words', and though the poet had come a long way since his MARS membership days, the ghost of Hastings must have smiled at the unfaded contempt for jazz styling.[47]

After visiting Quainton Road station (circa 1890) and noting how the Metropolitan had intended it to be another Clapham Junction (with links to a possible Channel tunnel), Betjeman ends his journey at Verney. As all the company's elaborate schemes came to nothing, this rural outpost was left to become the outer limit of the network. Crucially, the houses 'never got as far' as the station: '[g]rass triumphs,' he concludes, '[a]nd I must say I'm rather glad.'[48]

To be fair to Mowl, *Metro-land* is NOT a diatribe and thus, if the viewer wishes, certainly can be taken as the 'generous tribute to Pooterism' that he suggests. However, amidst the education, the reminiscences, the Neasden

Nature Trail, the architecture and the people, the film is peppered with quiet criticism for what has been lost in the process. Like his ambivalence to 'fair Elaine', it is obvious that there are parts of Metro-land for which Betjeman has a penchant, yet it is equally obvious that not all is praiseworthy. The pill is sweetened with kindness for a mainstream television audience, though it is the image of the poet at Verney, and the sense that "enough is enough", which lingers.

TV Personality

Metro-land is widely regarded as being the best of Betjeman's television films, but he had made many equally enjoyable programmes in the decade leading up to it. They were similar in stance to his World War Two writing, and could take either of two paths (though often took both at once). Some, like his 1963 TWW postcards from Sidmouth and Weston-super-Mare, were effectively travelogue thumbnail sketches of British life, with much emphasis placed on local architecture and local people. Such films encouraged the viewers to use their eyes – an increasingly prevalent Betjemanian plea. Others were like the film on Bath (see CHAPTER TWO) and carried a more overt message. Two programmes in this mould were *Chippenham & Crewkerne* and *Swindon & North Lew* (both 1963). The former is a tirade against motor traffic and laments how, in Chippenham, old houses were being destroyed to make way for a car park, and how, in Crewkerne ('another traffic-murdered town'), the motor car was taking trade away from the traditional shops to larger towns. *Swindon & North Lew*, conversely, discusses the effect of the railway age. Though the London & South Western is charged with having taken away as much trade from North Lew as, presumably, the roads were starting to take from Crewkerne, Betjeman takes pleasure in the peace and tranquillity that has resulted. (He does, after all, note that '*some* people would say' that the railways had destroyed the village (my italics).) In Swindon, the place 'the railways made great', the focus is first on the former Great Western Railway Works, then on the Railway Village – 'what must be the first garden city in the world' – which the company had built for its new workforce in 1841. Discussing the expansion of the town (via 'private speculators', who 'spilt their ribbons of houses' further afield) enables Betjeman to criticise the post-war plans for accepting London overspill migrants. These estates are 'not haphazard growth' like the Swindon of old, but are 'sudden and deliberate, like a bomb'. 'You wouldn't know you were in Wiltshire,' he comments, as the camera pans round the new dwellings, 'you wouldn't even know you were in Swindon.' The only good he can see in all this is that the Old Town, high up on the hill, has become 'an oasis of quiet', much like North Lew. (Though he does not make this parallel himself, the film implies it.) The dangers of homogenisation that Betjeman had spoken out against in poems like 'Huxley Hall' (1953) and essays like 'Love is Dead' (1952) were given visual presence in these films. The new estates of Swindon could be 'anywhere', and even the portrait of the largely unspoiled Marlborough (1963) contains a warning about the 'coach load on coach load' of travellers who come not to enjoy the town's 'colonnaded shops', but to stop at a 'syndicated' dining hall before hurrying 'on to Bath and Bristol and the West' or 'back to London'. In this 'lonelier world of strangers', there was no time to stop and enjoy the surroundings.

Scenes and commentary such as these were not the only types of television work that the poet undertook, however. Occasionally, he could be seen conducting interviews, as in 1964, when he talked both to the music-hall star Randolph Sutton (then in his mid-seventies), and Philip Larkin. The two poets had admired each other's work for some time, Betjeman having included Larkin's poem 'Church Going' (1955) in his 1959 selection, *Altar and Pew*, Larkin having praised *Collected Poems* in the *Manchester Guardian* (see CHAPTER FOUR). They met for the first time in 1961, under circumstances which were odd to say the least: Larkin had just collapsed and been taken to hospital; Betjeman immediately went to visit him and offered to pay the specialist's fees as well as any general expenses.[49] The elder poet read the younger's 'The Whitsun Weddings' (1964) aloud so frequently that his daughter got to know it by heart. Writing about the collection of the same name, he lavished unstinting praise:

> [t]his unperturbed, unenvious, and compassionate poet of doubt, common experience, and the search for truth has a reverence for the vastness around us and stands on the brink of eternity wondering whether it will be day, twilight, or night when we are dead. He is the John Clare of the building estates, and as true to them as was Clare to the fields of Northamptonshire.[50]

This came towards the end of Betjeman's busiest period as a journalist, when he wrote an average of fifteen articles a year for various periodicals and newspapers. He failed to reach that height between 1964 and 1969, but this was partly due to his decision to cease the 'Men and Buildings' series, in order to release himself for more lucrative work. Thus in the last five years of the decade, he made yet more films (on such diverse topics as Isambard Kingdom Brunel (BBC, 1966), the Royal Mint (independent, 1967) and Tennyson (BBC, *Contrasts*, 1968)), while on the wireless could be heard talking about *British Cathedrals and Their Music* (BBC, 1966) and *Church & Collegiate Choirs* (BBC, 1967). In 1968, he also made a series called *Scenes That Are Brightest*, in which he brought the past to life by means of old recordings; this gave rise to pertinent pieces like 'London Before the Motor-Car'.[51]

Betjeman found that all this left him with an ever-decreasing amount of time for writing poetry. As he complained in *The Author* in 1967: '[t]he worst thing is the letters. [. . .] About thirty arrive every morning and they've all got to be answered. It's been bad for the last ten years but in the last two or three it's becoming hell'.[52] Fame was starting to cause problems, although it was a two-edged sword – the more people knew him, the greater chance his preservation bids had of success. But tempering the situation was becoming harder: at sixty years of age, he found he was working more slowly and had fewer places to hide: '[y]ou can go away to Cornwall,' he said, 'then they discover you and you have to go somewhere else. There just seem to be so many more literate people in the country, with more money to spend on stamps'. He had sent up something of this attitude in 'Reproof Deserved or After the Lecture' (1955):

> "Mr Betjeman, I grovel before critics of the novel,
>   Tell me, if I don't offend you, have you written one yourself?
> You haven't? Then the one I wrote is (not that I expect a notice)
>   Something I would like to send you, just for keeping on your shelf."
>   ('REPROOF DESERVED OR AFTER THE LECTURE', LL. 9–12)

Despite this, and an ever-*increasing* amount of time spent fighting preservation battles, further poetry *was* produced, Betjeman's most recent verses (including 'Reproof Deserved') being offered to the public in 1966 under the title *High and Low*. The book was divided into four sections – 'LANDSCAPES', 'PORTRAITS', 'LIGHT AND DARK' and 'PERSONAL' – but opened with a verse preface:

> MURRAY, you bid my plastic pen
> A preface write. Well, here's one then.
> Verse seems to me the shortest way
> Of saying what one has to say,
> A memorable means of dealing
> With mood or person, place or feeling.
>   ('PREFACE TO *HIGH AND LOW*', LL. 1–6)

The tone is almost flippant, the rhythm almost playful – and very much in the style of the *Poems in the Porch* verses. It is possible that Betjeman did not want to write a preface at all, and this piece was a mild form of protest, however the next two lines tally with later comment about the existence of inspiration: 'Anything extra that is given / Is taken as a gift from Heaven.' As the piece goes on, there is also a sense of a man setting out his stall, and of one skilled at pastiche. Statistically, it seems to run counter to Betjeman's Victorian stance: of the nine poets named, only Tennyson and Dowson really belong to the mid- to late nineteenth century. Yet some of the references are clearly derived from Betjeman's knowledge of Tennyson: the music of the English language may have 'organ power' with Milton, for example, but this is actually a reference to Tennyson's tribute to that poet, who is described as the 'God-gifted organ-voice of England' ('Milton: Alcaics' (1863), l. 3).[53] Likewise, the reference to Dowson's lamp 'burning low' probably alludes to stanza L of *In Memoriam*, which begins: 'Be near me when my light is low.'[54] Indeed, while language 'falls like winter crisp and light / On COWPER'S Buckinghamshire night' and can be as 'gentle as a lake' for Wordsworth, the notion that words 'rest with TENNYSON at ease / In sibilance of summer seas' plainly refers to 'The Revenge: A Ballad of the Fleet' (from *The Lover's Tale*, 1879), which contains the highly sibilant line 'and the sun smiled out far over the summer sea' (XI, l. 70).[55]

Betjeman's languorous lilies (l. 21) are more likely to derive from Swinburne's 'Dolores' (from *Poems and Ballads*, 1866 – as in 'The lilies and languors of virtue / For the raptures and roses of vice' (ll. 67–68)).[56] But the reference at the close to Byron, Crabbe, Moore and Campbell is not intended to offset the emphasis here, rather highlight Betjeman's own insecurities, the poet likening himself to a 'buzzing insubstantial fly' in comparison to those four earlier Murray men:

> Compare with them? I do not try,
> Pleased simply to be one who shares
> An imprint that was also theirs,
> And grateful to the people who
> Have bought my verses hitherto.
>
> ('PREFACE TO *HIGH AND LOW*', LL. 29–33)

The first five poems proper are set in Cornwall, and here Betjeman shows his ability to paint pictures with words once again:

> The sky widens to Cornwall. A sense of sea
>   Hangs in the lichenous branches and still there's light.
> The road from its tunnel of blackthorn rises free
>   To a final height
>
> ('OLD FRIENDS', LL. 1–4)

He had bought Treen House in Trebetherick in December 1959, and though his many pursuers soon shattered this haven of peace, it clearly provided much inspiration during the years running up to the publication of *High and Low*. Of the five, only 'Winter Seascape' first saw light of day in the book: 'Old Friends', 'Cornish Cliffs' and 'By the Ninth Green' were published initially in *The New Yorker* (in July 1962, May 1966 and October 1966 respectively), while 'Tregardock' first appeared in the February 1965 issue of *Atlantic Monthly*. The original audience of these poems (even one which might have purchased each magazine in question) would not have experienced the 'sameness' that Taylor-Martin did in 1983.[57] Yet while the grouping does create *cohesion*, it was perfectly logical for Murray's to organise the work in this way; more importantly, there was also a poetic precedent in that Hardy (curiously absent from the 'Preface') had included many pieces on the Duchy in the 'Poems of 1912–13' section of his *Satires of Circumstance* (1914) – in particular, the six that deal with the tragic death of his first wife, Emma Gifford: 'A Dream or No', 'After a Journey', 'A Death-Day Recalled', 'Beeny Cliff', 'At Castle Boterel' and 'Places'.

All but 'A Dream or No' and 'After a Journey' focus on Hardy's pilgrimage to Cornwall of March 1913, during which he visited many scenes of their courtship.[58] This month is referred to specifically in 'Beeny Cliff' and 'At Castle Boterel'. Ironically, Betjeman's 'By the Ninth Green, St. Enodoc', which captures a moment in time by the sea shore, is similarly dated:

> Hot life pulsating in this foreshore dry,
> Damp life upshooting from the reed-beds high,
> Under those barrows, dark against the sky,
>   The Iron Age dead –
>
> Why is it that a sunlit second sticks?
> What force collects all this and seeks to fix
> This fourth March morning nineteen sixty-six
>   Deep in my head?
> ('By the Ninth Green, St. Enodoc', ll. 17–24)

Whether Betjeman was aware of this parallel or not, Hardy's 'Primeval rocks' ('At Castle Boterel', l .21) are echoed in the younger poet's rather more startling 'primeval pine' ('By the Ninth Green', l. 1), while the 'pulsating' life (l. 17) in particular provides an interesting counterpoint with the melancholy air of Hardy's verses. (The barrows, 'dark against the sky' (l. 19), also recall the one at Egdon Heath in *The Return of the Native* (1878).[59])

Another Hardyism occurs in 'Autumn 1964' (1966), in which the 'sparkling flint' of line seven is paired with a 'darkling yew'. Though 'darkling' had been an established poeticism for the Romantics (and indeed Shakespeare), the poet is doubtless (consciously or subconsciously) referring to Hardy's 'The Darkling Thrush' (1900). Betjeman's verse, with its prodigal throwing of 'light and colour', is altogether more joyous than his predecessor's 'spectre-gray' vision, however; in fact, it is almost the polar opposite:

> The sparkling flint, the darkling yew,
>   The red brick, less intensely red
> Than hawthorn berries bright with dew
>   Or leaves of creeper still unshed,
> The watery sky washed clean and new,
>   Are all rejoicing with the dead.
>   (Betjeman, 'Autumn 1964', ll. 7–12)
>
> The land's sharp features seemed to be
>   The Century's corpse outleant,
> His crypt the cloudy canopy,
>   The wind his death-lament.
> The ancient pulse of germ and birth
>   Was shrunken hard and dry,

> And every spirit upon earth
> Seemed fervourless as I.
> (HARDY, 'THE DARKLING THRUSH', LL. 9–16)[60]

The rhythm of both poems is similar (8.8.8.8 for Betjeman against Hardy's 8.6.8.6), but note the perky internal rhyme of 'Autumn 1964' (in line 7 especially – see above) and the pert alliteration – as in 'The hawthorn berries bright with dew' (l. 9). Hardy's alliteration, conversely, creates a much more portentous tone ('His crypt the cloudy canopy'), although the shock of 'the dead' (l. 12) in the later poem recalls the classically Betjemanian turn that may be found in 'Croydon' (1931) and 'On a Portrait of a Deaf Man' (1940). However, the 'full-hearted evensong' of Hardy's aged thrush only heightens the feeling that there must be 'Some blessed Hope' *somewhere*, and it is significant that his narrator remains 'unaware' of it to the last. Betjeman, on the other hand, ends with a jubilant reaffirmation of the 'promise [. . .] / Of greater light where Love is found'. This echoes Goethe's last words, but is also part of the religious tradition (echoed too by Dante and Tennyson) of associating light, eternity and love.

But Hardy's is not the only spectre to touch 'Autumn 1964' (1966); the opening line – 'Red apples hang like globes of light' – is distinctly reminiscent of Christina Rossetti's 'Goblin Market' (1862), for example:

> She dropped a tear more rare than pearl,
> Then sucked their fruit globes fair or red'
> (ROSSETTI, 'GOBLIN MARKET', LL. 127–128)

Clearly, just as Betjeman was enthusiastic about more than Gothic architecture, he continued to be influenced by more than Tennyson and Hardy. Taylor-Martin adds that the metre of 'By the Ninth Green' derives from Campbell's 'Hohenlinden', while Hillier informs us that the 'Unmitigated England', with which 'Great Central Railway' (1962) begins, was noted by Betjeman as being Henry James's sobriquet for Warwickshire.[61] Thomas Moore (1779–1852) makes his pervasive presence felt in 'A Lament for Moira McCavendish' (1966), 'The Small Towns of Ireland' (1966) and 'Ireland's Own or The Burial of Thomas Moore' (1966). Indeed, Betjeman's love of the musicality of Irish verse is evident from his own, and he is particularly successful in interpreting Moore's characteristic anapaestic lilt and use of feminine rhymes (as in 'Sessions' / 'processions'). As Taylor-Martin remarks, 'The Small Towns of Ireland' also encapsulates a distinctly 'Irishman's view' of that country:

> I see thy grey granite, O grim House of Sessions!
> I think of the judges who sat there in state
> And my mind travels back to our monster processions
> To honour the heroes of brave Ninety-Eight.

The barracks are burned where the Redcoats oppressed us,
   The gaol is broke open, our people are free.
Though Cromwell once cursed us, Saint Patrick has blessed us–
   The merciless English have fled o'er the sea.
                    ('THE SMALL TOWNS OF IRELAND', LL. 25–32)[62]

But do all these references indicate that Betjeman was returning to his earlier, 'hyper-sophisticated' incarnation? Or was he going back into himself, effectively under siege in Cornwall?

In fact, the Tennysonian hand that may be detected in the 'Preface' was born out by the poetry. John Press, in his review of the volume for *Punch* (23 November 1966), for example, singled-out the penultimate stanza of 'Tregardock' as owing something to the great Laureate. Equally, 'Perp. Revival i' the North' (1966) may also derive from the 'Northern Farmer' poems ('Old Style', 1864; 'New Style', 1870) – as well as being reminiscent of Robert Burns (1759–96) and the dialect verses of William Barnes (1801–86):

   O, I wad gang tae Harrogate
      Tae a kirk by Temple Moore,
   Wi' a tall choir and a lang nave
      And rush mats on the floor;
            ('PERP. REVIVAL I' THE NORTH', LL. 1–4)[63]

As in 'The Small Towns of Ireland', here we see Betjeman's skill in becoming a character quite different from himself. This may also be distinguished in 'The Cockney Amorist' (1958), where he adopts the persona of a recent widower, even more recognisably Tennysonian in make-up:

   Oh when my love, my darling,
      You've left me here alone,
   I'll walk the streets of London
      Which once seemed all our own.

   The vast suburban churches
      Together we have found:
   The ones which smelt of gaslight
      The ones in incense drown'd;
   I'll use them now for praying in
      And not for looking round.
            (BETJEMAN, 'THE COCKNEY AMORIST', LL. 1–10)

Compare this with Tennyson's lyric 'Oh! that 'twere possible' (1837):

   Oh! that 'twere possible,
      After long grief and pain,

To find the arms of my true-love
Round me once again!

When I was wont to meet her
In the silent woody places
Of the land that gave me birth,
We stood tranced in long embraces,
Mixt with kisses sweeter, sweeter,
Than any thing on earth.

(TENNYSON, 'OH! THAT 'TWERE POSSIBLE', LL. 1–10)[64]

There is an obvious similarity in that both of the opening stanzas share a rhyme scheme (ABCB) and have three stresses per line (though in different places). The rhythm of the respective second stanzas is almost the same too (ABCBDB for Betjeman, ABCBAC for Tennyson). However, the point is that, like 'Love in a Valley', 'The Cockney Amorist' is not a precise model: while obviously inspired by 'Oh! that 'twere possible', it is equally obvious that it is only *loosely* based on it. So, while Tennyson does not adhere so rigidly to the form of the extract quoted above, Betjeman's verse continues in the manner of his second stanza until the final (fifth) one, when it returns to the form of the first. This creates a jauntier, more colloquial feel, though the idea at the close that churches will now be a place of worship and remembrance is again an unexpected valediction. Betjeman's mourner also laments his future absence from the 'Hackney Empire' and 'Finsbury Park' ('For these and all the other things / Were part of you and me'), while Tennyson's finds that it is the 'silent woody places / Of the land that gave me birth' which first recall his 'true-love'. Similarly, instead of the Cockney's once-beloved 'crowded High Road', Tennyson's protagonist steals through the 'hubbub of the market' (l. 42), loathing 'the square and streets, / And the faces that one meets' (ll. 58–59).

Past and Present

In *High and Low*, Betjeman again uses Victorian poetics to highlight the problems and injustices of the present. This is evident in 'Meditation on the A30' (1966), where 'A man on his own in a car' becomes so incensed at his 'pitiful life' and his impeded progress on the road that the two fatally become one. This shows, first, that 'road rage' is nothing new and, secondly, that the poem is just as relevant today as it was in 1966:

"You're barmy or plastered, I'll pass you, you bastard-
I *will* overtake you. I *will*!"
As he clenches his pipe, his moment is ripe
And the corner's accepting its kill.

('MEDITATION ON THE A30', LL. 17–20)

Although Betjeman read the piece aloud with differing speeds to suit the emotion, the rhythm is that of a modified limerick and this serves to increase the shock of the concluding death. The rhyme scheme also forces the reader from 'kill' back to 'will'; it is, after all, the will of the driver that leads directly to his demise.

Dennis Brown comments that here 'Tennyson's Lancelot and de la Mare's "traveller" combine in a postmodern scenario where masculinity loses its head and puts the blame on a nagging Eve'.[65] Miltonic undertones aside, the reference to the former presumably relates to 'Lancelot and Elaine' (from *Idylls of the King*, 1874 – to which Betjeman had also alluded in 'Middlesex'). This is a poem of misinterpretation: the two meet because of the knight's inaccurate reading of Guinevere's pained expression as he leaves for a tournament, while Elaine mistakes good manners for love and dies of unrequited passion. Yet perhaps Brown is being over-allusive – it is a very 'strange diagonal' indeed from here to Betjeman's narrator, who is actually one of the earliest examples of a bad-tempered, contemporary Everyman in modern verse: mark how he wields his car as if it were a weapon, unlike Lancelot, who, though vexed at having 'lied in vain' and annoyed that Guinevere's carefree love has been replaced by caution, accepts the hand he has been dealt and goes on. Furthermore, in Tennyson there is a build up of misfortune and fate (Elaine's death is almost inevitable), while in Betjeman the build up is of *anger*.

But 'Meditation' is modern in other ways, for though its internal dialogue style may be traced back to Browning, the language places it firmly in the 1960s. The Mini, for instance, is as iconic a car of that decade as the celebrated Jaguar E-Type and Mk.II models. It is also the first time that an expletive appears in a Betjeman poem. 'Bastard' may be very mild (though it was less so in 1966), but imagine it occurring in one of the poems from *Old Lights for New Chancels* or *Continual Dew*, say. As Brown writes, the poet's 'inherent sense of Englishness defines itself against such phenomena, and sees them as a violation of national decency'.[66]

Another poem in this mould is 'Harvest Hymn', where the Jaguar reappears as a status symbol, owned this time by a farmer who has lined his 'purse with pence'. Brown calls it 'a radical (rooted) attack on the raw exploitation of the wealth of Creation' and links it with *Silent Spring*, Rachel Carson's highly influential argument against the use of chemicals in the countryside (first published in Britain in 1963).[67] Indeed, although the poem remained unpublished until 1966, Betjeman quotes a draft of its first two stanzas in a letter he wrote to his friend Harry Jarvis in October 1963, adding that he may have heard it before (implying that conception could have come as early as the beginning of the year).[68] Either way, the probability of Betjeman having been influenced directly or indirectly by Carson is high; and while *Silent Spring* is largely based on American examples, Lord Shackleton wrote in its introduction that, despite a lower 'intensity of attack' in this country, the effects of insecticide use were becoming all-too-apparent in the fox and bird populations.[69] Carson herself commented that this was 'an era dominated by industry, in which the right to make a dollar at whatever cost is seldom chal-lenged'. And '[w]hen the public protests,' she went on, '[. . .] it is fed little tranquillizing pills of half truth'.[70] This is recognisably Betjemanian:

> We spray the fields and scatter
> The poison on the ground
> So that no wicked wild flowers
> Upon our farm be found.
> We like whatever helps us
> To line our purse with pence;
> The twenty-four-hour broiler-house
> And neat electric fence.
>
> ('HARVEST HYMN', LL. 1–8)

As with 'The Church's Restoration' (1928), Betjeman very skilfully adapts a relevant hymn (in this case the eighteenth-century German harvest hymn 'We Plough the Fields and Scatter' (translated 1861), of course) and inverts it to make a powerful point which, because of its irrevocable connection with a famous tune, tends to stay in the mind longer than it might have done other-wise. The message is hammered home all the more (again, as with the earlier 'Hymn') by the fact that, if sung, the highest note falls on the rapaciously capi-talistic 'line' (l. 6). But this peculiar use of form is not the only link with the poet's earlier work, for despite the seemingly obvious connection with Carson, Brown is right to claim that 'Harvest Hymn' in fact 'reflects Betjeman's emphasis since the 1930s'. The rape of the land was, after all, one of the central points of 'Slough'. It is also a poem that, like 'Meditation on the A30', seems just as pertinent today.[71]

Given the presence of such intelligent power, it is somewhat surprising to note yet another criticism of Betjeman's satiric poems in Graham Martin's review of *High and Low* (*The Listener*). For him, such verses represented little more than 'defeated sniping at the noise and ugliness of modern life'. '[G]ood targets,' he conceded, 'but a pop-gun isn't enough.'[72] This is an interesting idea and reminds us of the effect of *Pity About the Abbey*: Monty Python come-dian Terry Gilliam has recently written that '[it] has always been a concern with me as far as satire and comedy are concerned, in the sense that if people are laughing they're not getting angry enough to do what is needed to make a better world. It's a diversion as opposed to a means towards a solution'.[73] If the howitzer approach (more akin to *Private Eye* than Monty Python, admittedly) does not work any better than that of the 'pop-gun', maybe Betjeman's more subtle poetic suggestions penetrate the brain more stealthily and successfully than Martin supposed. Larkin had also said (and was to say again) that Betjeman was 'an acceptor, not a rejecter, of our time', but is even this a fair assessment?[74] Note 'In Willesden Churchyard' (1957), for instance, with its musings on the graves of 'many a Pooter and his Caroline':

Come walk with me, my love, to Neasden Lane.
The chemicals from various factories
Have bitten deep into the Portland stone
And streaked the white Carrara of the graves
Of many a Pooter and his Caroline,

('IN WILLESDEN CHURCHYARD', LL. 1–5)

For Peter Thomas, this poem (which he sees as a cross between Marvell's 'Coy Mistress' and Gray's 'Elegy') has a '*grimly* modern edge' (my italics).[75] Indeed, the modernism is heightened by the distance shown not only by the graves of the Pooter seniors, but also the next generation: Lupin Pooter himself has been 'lately gathered in', note, so is the chemical erosion – along with the 'telly-masts' of 'Cornish Cliffs', the whining motor-bike of 'Old Friends' and the 'broken glass' of 'A Bay in Anglesey' (1964) – simply a description of what is there (as Larkin seems to suggest), or is the very mention of such pollutants a criticism in itself? They certainly contrast with the timeless pastoral beauty of Eire in the volume's Irish verses – surely no coincidence. And do the 'comfortable', familiar forms that Betjeman prefers *bolster* such criticism? Are we surprised as readers by the unexpected presence of something nasty in the woodshed? One must remember that poetry, as we have seen throughout this book, was by no means Betjeman's only means of commenting on the world. It was a tactic that was set to continue.

In 1967, he contributed a foreword to Olive Cook's book *The Stansted Affair: A Case for the People*. Many were against the building of this third London airport, but the problem was not only environmental. Harold Wilson's government had ignored its own Public Inquiry, which had concluded that the site was not ideal. Having noted this, the fact that no adequate survey of the alternatives had been made, and that the people had been ignored, Betjeman went on to voice his fears for 'one of the few bits of remaining real country near London':

[a] visit to Bedfont, Feltham, Stanwell or Heston in the once glorious county of Middlesex will show you what these villages of the Essex and Hertfordshire borders could become.[. . .] Had this been deserted country, moorland or marsh there might be some excuse. Had it been sea there might be still more excuse. But it is a quiet, prosperous, agricultural area of old stone and flint churches, pargetted cottages with red tiled roofs, spreading farms and gabled manor houses, little hills, elms, oaks, willowy streams and twisty lanes leading to towns of such renowned beauty as Thaxted and Saffron Walden.

As Cook herself noted, '[t]he rapid growth of population, expanding industry and widespread car-ownership have made us intensely aware of the quality of our environment, intensely anxious about the receding regions of rural beauty and tranquillity in our tiny country'.[76]

One *High and Low* poem that encapsulates almost all the poet's concerns about this period is 'Inexpensive Progress'. It can hardly be called 'comfortable' either:

> Encase your legs in nylons,
> Bestride your hills with pylons
>   O age without a soul;
> Away with gentle willows
> And all the elmy billows
>   That through your valleys roll.
>
> ('INEXPENSIVE PROGRESS', LL. 1–6)

This first appeared in *Punch* in August 1955. Far from being a 'pop-gun' shot, it is (as Taylor-Martin rightly asserts) 'one of Betjeman's most savage poems'.[77] Many of the targets at which he had aimed in the 1950s (particularly in 'Love is Dead') are present: the 'Command, instruction, warning' of the road signs are attacked in stanza three (l. 16), as are the 'miles of black glass facia [sic]' of the faceless chain stores (l. 35) and the concrete lamp standards that hang 'like gallows overhead' (l. 45) elsewhere. The poem's reappearance in 1966 allowed Betjeman to keep up a sustained attack on these targets, although it should be noted that 'Inexpensive Progress' also looks forward in a manner not often noted by commentators, as in the second stanza, which begins: 'Let's say goodbye to hedges / and roads with grassy edges'. This predates both 'Harvest Hymn' *and* Carson. Moreover, stanza five shows that Betjeman was aware of the subject that would trouble Olive Cook a full twelve years later:

> Leave no old village standing
> Which could provide a landing
>   For aeroplanes to roar,
>
> ('INEXPENSIVE PROGRESS', LL. 25–27)

Betjeman's foresight, and in particular his ability to see issues which would continue to have import long after his death, is something that has been lost in the mists of time. Critics now seem too-often unable to see past the teddy bears and the *Collected Poems*.

The sense of a lost Elysium in 'Inexpensive Progress', of 'unpretentious greenery' versus Power Stations, also recalls the yearning for a pastoral idyll embodied by William Morris in *News From Nowhere* (1890). Morris's fleeting presence may be detected too in 'Narcissus' (as is a brief reference to 'Bedford Park'):

> Yes, it was Bedford Park the vision came from–
>   de Morgan lustre glowing round the hearth,
> And that sweet flower which self-love takes its name from

> Nodding among the lilies in the garth,
> ('NARCISSUS', LL. 1–4)

Note, however, that despite the mention of Morris's disciple William de Morgan (the pottery designer and novelist) and the fact that the archaic term 'garth' appears in *The Earthly Paradise*, the poem has little to do with Morris in an *ideological* sense.[78] Instead, it tells of two boys whose 'unwholesome' play leads to their separation by the narrator's mother, who is shocked by the 'evil thoughts' she saw in her son. Hillier confirms that the confession, with its shades of Browning's monologue style, is autobiographical and that the incident probably occurred when Betjeman was about ten.[79] Yet this topic is also apposite to the 1960s, as both the mother's horror and the references to Wilde critique the changing attitudes to homosexuality then prevalent. The effective legalisation of sexual acts between consenting males came in 1967, so Betjeman was clearly engaging with a debate which must have been heated at the time.

This subject recurs in 'Monody on the Death of a Platonist Bank Clerk', which first appeared in the *Sunday Times Weekly Review* on 30 October 1966.[80] It comes before 'Narcissus' in *High and Low*, but in many ways shows the upshot of the forced repression of that "unwholesome play", the clerk cutting a sad figure as he sits quietly reading Whitman at a bus-stop. The hint of the predatory Mr. Pedder (from 'Beside the Seaside', 1947) about the photographs of the 'Camp at Pevensey' and 'Scouts at Cleethorpes' (l. 11) is somewhat tempered by the clear impression one gets that desire never went further than 'serious talks' over tea and crumpets. This is no Wilde in the wings, and the closing 'punchline', though having the short-term effect of a joke, does little to lift the ultimate sense of loneliness:

> All the lot of them, how they came to him –
> Tea and chinwag – gay young lives!
> Somehow they were never the same to him
> When they married and brought their wives.
> ('MONODY ON THE DEATH OF A PLATONIST BANK CLERK', LL. 21–24)

The term 'Monody', discussed in the last chapter, has dignity enough for a Platonist, but not perhaps for a bank clerk. However, note how the rhythm has a Hardyesque plangency, reminiscent of 'The Voice' (from *Poems of 1912 – 1913*), as in 'Woman much missed, how you call to me, call to me' (l.1). (Note too that 'gay' was not a reference to homosexuality at the time of composition.)

Faith and Doubt

High and Low contains a number of poems about religion and mortality, embodying, as usual, much vacillation between Faith and Doubt. The first piece to deal with this is 'Old Friends', at the end of which (as Press later wrote) there is a sense of 'communion with the dead' inspired by the sea:

> Are they one with the Celtic saints and the years between?
>   Can they see the moonlit pools where ribbonweed drifts?
> As I reach our hill, I am part of a sea unseen-
>   And oppression lifts.[81]
>
> ('OLD FRIENDS', LL. 29–32)

Despite the Yeatsian touch at the beginning, the verse form follows a Hardy example once again, this time echoing 'The House of Hospitalities' (1909), with its almost Sapphic structure:

> Here we broached the Christmas barrel,
> Pushed up the charred log-ends;
> Here we sang the Christmas carol,
>   And called in friends.
>
> (HARDY, 'THE HOUSE OF HOSPITALITIES', LL. 1–4)[82]

The optimism of Betjeman's coda suggests that the answer to both his questions is yes. The conclusion of 'Autumn 1964' conveys a similar spirit: 'And in the bells the promise tells / Of greater light where love is found.' Yet in 'Matlock Bath' (1959), there is a sense of impending disaster, and though Faith suffuses the text by means of the hymns that Betjeman quotes with great skill throughout, it is shown as being inadequate for salvation.[83] For example, the sounds of Reginald Heber's (1783–1826) *By cool Siloam's shady rill* are described as being as 'sweet as strawberry jam' (l. 7). The lyric – 'How sweet the lily grows / How sweet the breath beneath the hill' – is certainly cloying, but the point is that words have no power, and Betjeman makes the reason for this clear:

> And from the whiteness, grey uprearing,
>   Huge cliffs hang sunless ere they fall,
> A tossed and stony ocean nearing
>   The moment to o'erwhelm us all:
> *Eternal Father, strong to save,*
> How long wilt thou suspend the wave?
>
> ('MATLOCK BATH', LL. 13–18)

What use would hymns be if God allowed 'the wave' to fall?

The poem's capitalised local place names ('HEIGHTS OF ABRAHAM', 'ROMANTIC ROCKS') are, as Taylor-Martin remarks, 'consciously archaic', though, like those of 'The Metropolitan Railway', they also help to create the impression of a guidebook. This serves to underline the particular, increasing the impression of fear even more. 'Deep in their Nonconformist setting / The shivering children wait their doom' (ll. 31–32), but any idea that this is merely an attack on creed is dispelled by the bleak image of the narrator 'high above the sliding river / And terraces of Matlock Bath' (ll. 39–40):

> A sense of doom, a dread to see
> The *Rock of Ages cleft for me*.
> ('Matlock Bath', ll. 41–42)

God's vengeance is inevitable.

'In Willesden Churchyard' also concludes with the idea that ageing flesh 'Frightens me, though the Blessed Sacrament / Not ten yards off in Willesden parish church / Glows with the present immanence of God' (ll. 33–35). This is akin to the 'strawberry jam' of the Matlock children's singing, in that the glow is not enough to dispel fear and uncertainty. 'Goodbye' (1966) reiterates this doubt with indecision, Betjeman imagining his own death throes when 'More worthless than ever / Will seem all the songs I have sung' (ll. 9–10). Ultimately, he is unsure as to whether it is 'Judgement or nothingness' (l. 19) that awaits him. This also heralds the 'lonely terror' (l. 16) at the end of 'Five o'Clock Shadow' (1966), which follows 'Goodbye', and is a poem that Hillier feels was inspired by Betjeman's frequent visits to Bart's Hospital in London.[84] 'Uffington', however, is more ambiguous:

> Tonight we feel the muffled peel
>   Hang on the village like a pall;
> It overwhelms the towering elms-
>   That death-reminding dying fall;
> The very sky no longer high
>   Comes down within the reach of all.
> Imprisoned in a cage of sound
> Even the trivial seems profound.
> ('Uffington')

Though the internal rhymes of lines 1, 3 and 5 give that chiming Tennysonian 'lin-lan-lone' to the piece, the effect is almost of oppression – note the 'pall', as though the whole village is entombed, the dying elms, as if nature is in sympathy with it, and the closeness of the dark sky, which presses down on that beneath. Betjeman's 30 January 1944 column for the *Daily Herald* began with a reference to an Uffington 'muffled peal' before explaining that an alternate loud (unpadded)/soft (padded) sequence was being rung out in remembrance for someone in the village.[85] This is too much of a coincidence and it is thus likely that the poem was written in wartime (or at least inspired by it). Brown feels that the final couplet might have been 'euphoniously self-mocking', but to most people the minutiae of everyday life *is* important and Betjeman's appreciation of this may partly explain the huge sales of *Collected Poems*.[86] In wartime, when "death-reminders" are all around, it is even more vital to cling to such supports; in this way the sensibility of 'Uffington' would seem to be completely at home with that of *English Cities and Small Towns* (1943) and indeed many of the other poems of that period.

Betjeman also returned to purely clerical haunts in *High and Low* (as the title suggests). For example, 'The Commander' (1966) – an elegy for his friend George Barnes – includes a reference to 'Quaker silence' (l. 7), showing that he had not entirely forgotten his brief spell as a Friend thirty years before. In 'Anglo-Catholic Congress' (1966), he recalls too the fun and faith of the 1920s, which for him was infinitely preferable to the 'bitter, terrifying theological earnestness' of the 1960s (a sentiment that echoes his earlier critiques of Calvinism – see CHAPTER TWO).[87] Betjeman had attended the third Congress in 1927 (at which the subject was the Holy Eucharist), and imagery like the 'blossoming May-time' (l. 6), the 'slapping of backs and the flapping of cassocks' (l. 8), reflects both the happy memory and the clear message that to believe is to enjoy.[88] However, though there may have been time for a game of 'Grandmother's Steps on the vicarage grass' (l. 9), faith was still 'taught and *fanned to a golden blaze*' (l. 20 – my italics). Here, unlike the sweet singing of Matlock and the glow of the Blessed Sacrament at Willesden, there is a sense of the *power* of belief and the fulfilment that can come from it. As he grew yet older – as death became increasingly a part of life – this grew in importance. To ease his fear and sorrow, some departed friends – like George Barnes, Anne Channel and Kathleen Stokes – were remembered in verse. Others, like Sir Ninian Comper (1864–1960), Philip Morton Shand (1888–1960) and Evelyn Waugh (1903–66) were celebrated in prose.[89]

Critically, *High and Low* was fairly well received. Notwithstanding his reservations (cited earlier), Graham Martin wrote in *The Listener* that both 'Uffington' and 'Five o'Clock Shadow' 'strike a successfully gloomy personal note which perhaps explains why [Betjeman] reads Larkin so well'.[90] In *The Spectator*, C. B. Cox was glad that 'the old gift for intimate nostalgia, [had] not been lost', but was grudging in his question as to 'how on earth these flat-footed rhymes, jingling rhythms and trite words achieve so much'. The answer, he concluded, was that 'the conventional verse forms are charged with passion for quiet English settings'; thankfully, he finished with the equally perceptive observation that Betjeman's oeuvre 'has always seemed about to slip into the past, touched by a hint of menace'.[91]

Almost in reply to Martin's 'pop-gun' theory, John Carey wrote in the *New Statesman* of 'the popular suspicion' that the poet, 'for all his tasteful delicacy, lacks power'. In fact, he went on, 'what his poetry constantly implies is raw passion'. Despite this, Carey felt it necessary to resurrect a thirty-year-old piece in order to finish his comments with a negative: '[i]n the end,' he wrote, 'one has misgivings about the poet of "Come, friendly bombs, and fall on Slough", however much passion bolsters his prejudices'.[92] Perhaps the knowledge that he was discussing *High and Low* between the latest volumes of Auden and Thom Gunn led Carey to play down what seemed to be a genuine interest in Betjeman's work: '[p]utting him next to Thom Gunn soon shows up Mr Betjeman's jaundiced patches,' he admitted, for 'Mr Gunn enters with firm understanding and clear sight the lives of people whom Mr Betjeman would shrink from or caricature'.

In addition to his praise for the Cornish poems (noted earlier), in *Punch* John Press appreciated Betjeman's 'metrical ingenuity, his gift for inventing delicious, idiosyncratic tunes, his delight in pastiche' and so on, but also asked the crucial question: 'how good a poet is he?' Press felt (as others had before him) that the feeblest pieces in *High and Low* were the satires, believing Betjeman was at his best when 'moved most sharply and deeply by the themes which have always haunted him: the sea; change and decay in human lives and the work of men's hands; above all, the terror of death [. . .]'. But he also praised 'Five O' Clock Shadow' and called Betjeman 'a serious artist who has portrayed with probing skill and unashamed emotional directness the way in which millions of his countrymen live and prepare to die'.[93] From this, we might see that the Laureateship was inevitable, though to his daughter Betjeman simply wrote: 'I'm so glad the critics didn't kill me.'[94] Perhaps the most rewarding comment, from a personal point of view, came from Maurice Bowra, who on receipt of his copy, wrote: '[w]hen I think of how few of our friends have fulfilled their first promise [. . .], your achievement in poetry stands up solid and splendid and encouraging and defiant'.[95] The public agreed, yet it is still somewhat staggering to note that in its first two months of publication (i.e. to 31 December 1966), *High and Low* sold a massive 25,987 copies, with another 5,519 being purchased by 30 June 1967.

These figures even rival the enormous sales of *Collected Poems* and is yet further evidence of Betjeman's growing popularity. The success of the anthology and the increasing amount of television and radio work clearly aroused the public's imagination as to what the poet would produce next, although the fact that sales exceeded 30,000 so quickly suggests that there was considerable substance behind the celebrity.[96]

Knight Bachelor

Betjeman's superior second edition of his *Shell Guide* to *Cornwall* (1964) was covered in CHAPTER TWO, but he and John Piper were still editing the series together at this stage. The poet, for his part, was finding the task increasingly difficult. There had been interference from the publishers, Faber & Faber, and a particular problem with James Lees-Milne's *Worcestershire* (1965), the author having accused Worcester's mayor and councillors of vandalizing their own town centre. (He had also, somewhat tactlessly, likened them to the Vikings and Oliver Cromwell.[97]) As Candida Lycett Green remembers, her father's enthusiasm for the project was starting to flag, and this sort of thing did not help. Knowing too that Piper was putting in many more hours' work, he 'picked a quarrel' with Shell in 1967 when they objected to a derogatory reference to the Northampton Norwich Union Society building that Juliet

Smith had made in her *Northamptonshire* volume. Betjeman was thus able to resign, leaving Piper in sole charge.[98]

The year of the Cornwall guide had also seen the publication of *English Churches*, on which Betjeman had worked with Basil Clarke. Though his colleague had been responsible for the majority of the text, it was Betjeman who selected most of the illustrations and wrote the captions. In his 'Preface to Pictures', he noted that '[i]f there seem to be too many Victorian churches, that is because there are more Victorian churches than churches of any other age'. He went on to say that '[m]uch as we may regret the over-enthusiastic "restoration" done to [churches] by Victorians, let us not forget that without such restoration many often would have fallen down [. . .]'.[99] This is undoubtedly true, but the inverted commas once again betray the aesthetic preference.

Elsewhere, previously held opinions are alluded to, if not repeated. Pugin's excellence as a 'witty and clever' writer is thus noted, and (in caption no. 208 – Leafield, Oxon, c. 1860), the work of Sir George Gilbert Scott is defamed as being neither over-original, nor 'interesting' in itself. Naturally, Sir Ninian Comper, '[t]he last Victorian', is praised for his substitution of a wooden screen and loft (in place of stone and iron 'restoration') at St. Elthelburga's, Bishopsgate, London; in line with his dim view of the new Euston station, Betjeman also commented tersely that 'it is only possible to distinguish a [modern] church from a public library, school, or small factory by a cross on its wall or above it'.

Betjeman's Pitkin Pictorial, *City of London Churches* (published in 1965), coupled his admiration for Wren with his sorrow at the poor treatment from which the master's work had started to suffer:

> Wren's cheerful genius pervades the whole City even today when his buildings have been dwarfed by boring office slabs and the famous skyline to which he gave such thought obliterated.[100]

Betjeman once again showed that he was not blinkered by the Victorians. It was they, he revealed, who launched a 'double assault' on the City's churches from the 1850s by dint of their 'serious medievalism', 'the craze for surpliced choirs in stalls in the chancel, and for stained glass giving a dim religious light'. 'Wren's Classical style,' he continued, 'was regarded as pagan and this furnished an excuse for destroying so many of his churches.' The use of stained glass ('unsuited to all Wren churches', p. 19) is a particular bugbear of this volume, and even Comper is criticised for painting the altarpiece of St. Clement, Eastcheap (Wren, 1683–1687) in gold and blue 'so that it no longer harmonises with the pulpit and woodwork'.[101] This was not such a heinous crime as occurred at St. Michael, Cornhill (1669–1672), however, where the work of Gilbert Scott ensured that '*nothing* [could] de-Victorianise this Wren church' (my italics).[102]

The three churches that appeared in 'Monody on the Death of Aldersgate Street Station' (1955) are all present, although St. Mildred's, Bread Street is only shown on the map in the book's centre-spread, being one of the many destroyed in World War Two. St. Michael Paternoster (Wren, 1686–94) is noted for its stone cherubs at the east end, while the remaining tower of Christ Church, Newgate Street (Wren, 1677–1691), we are reminded, was restored to its 'original splendour' by the late Lord Mottistone in 1960:[103]

> Sunday Silence! with every street a dead street,
>   Alley and courtyard empty and cobbled mews,
> Till "tingle tang" the bell of St. Mildred's Bread Street
>   Summoned the sermon taster to high box pews,
>
> :   :   :   :
>
> The bells rang down and St. Michael Paternoster
>   Would take me into its darkness from College Hill,
> Or Christ Church Newgate Street (with St. Leonard Foster)
>   Would be late for Mattins and ringing insistent still.
>
> ('MONODY ON THE DEATH OF ALDERSGATE STREET STATION', LL. 5–8; 17–20)

As discussed in CHAPTER FOUR, this poem shows the clear link between eccle-siastical architecture and that of those other cathedrals – railway stations. At the end of the following decade, Betjeman would train his eye on the termini of London once more by beginning a series on the subject for *Wheeler's Quarterly Review* (1968). These articles were later collected into the splendid Murray volume *London's Historic Railway Stations* (1972), referred to earlier.

Before this, in November 1966, came 'Temple to the Age of Steam', a feature on St. Pancras for the *Weekend Telegraph*. This followed his battle to thwart British Rail's intention to combine both it and King's Cross by demol-ishing all of the latter and most of the former (which had been announced that June). Recalling John Summerson's support for Euston, Betjeman sought his help again. 'Would you be prepared to write an appreciative article on it?' he asked. 'You count and I don't. It is no good my writing about Sir Gilbert and St Pancras in particular, because I have been so denigrated by Karl Marx [James Richards], and the Professor-Doktor [Pevsner] as a lightweight wax fruit merchant [. . .].'[104] Summerson replied that he 'couldn't put any heart into the idea of preserving it' and added that '[e]very time I look at the building I'm consumed with admiration in the cleverness of the detail and every time I leave it I wonder why as a whole it is so nauseating'. He did not feel that 'one could go to a Minister and say this is a great piece of architecture, a great national monument'.[105] For Mowl, this attitude 'deserves to be remembered as an indictment of the strange intolerance which characterized so many advo-cates of the Modern Movement'.[106] One cannot but agree. Betjeman, having escaped its prejudices, wrote the article himself and together with the Victorian Society (of which he was now vice-president), fiercely opposed the plan. A 1967 application for a Grade I listing for both the train shed at St. Pancras and the magnificent hotel was successful. The complex was safe and has recently been re-born (2007) as the new international terminus for Channel Tunnel rail traffic.[107] In his article for *Wheeler's Quarterly* (Winter 1969), doubtless with some relief, Betjeman continued his praise, commenting that '[t]oday we can appreciate Sir Gilbert's masterpiece. For grandeur of scale it compares with that best work of Sir Gilbert's grandson Sir Giles, Liverpool Cathedral'.[108] He also had a dig at the Modern Movement (perhaps as a result of Summerson's reluctance to assist):

> [p]uritans of the 'thirties were prepared to allow merit to Barlow's train shed, because it was simple and functional. Scott's hotel, however, filled them with horror, because its exterior was ornate and its style they considered sham mediaeval. If you look again at the hotel you will see it is not sham. It uses brick of the best quality and cast iron, and its proportions bear no resemblance to a mediaeval domestic building [. . .].[109]

At the close of the decade, Betjeman was awarded a knighthood in the Queen's Birthday Honours list. It is likely that this came at the suggestion of Mary Wilson, wife of the then Prime Minister Harold, whom the poet had met in 1967. Though pleased with the news, Lycett Green records that he was far from happy at this point in his life, and was even taking Valium. His friend, the Australian comedian Barry Humphries, has said that it was 'hard to say what the origins [of his depression] were *exactly*'.[110] Such melancholia was not new to Betjeman, as any reader of his verse can testify, but, unknown to both his doctor and himself – to say nothing of his friends – he was also suffering from the early stages of Parkinson's disease. The coming decade would see him receive the finest tribute that the State can bestow, but the ride was clearly not going to be a smooth one.

CHAPTER SIX

The 1970s and 80s

Royal Rhymester?

Sir John Betjeman was appointed Poet Laureate in Ordinary to Her Majesty Queen Elizabeth II on 10 October 1972, succeeding his friend Cecil Day-Lewis, who had died that May.[1] Depending on one's viewpoint, this was either the greatest accolade he could receive, or the biggest millstone that could be put about his neck.

In 1965, he had plumped for the latter, noting that the role would be 'too inhibiting': '[o]ne would feel,' he wrote, '[that] one was being watched by people with knives in their hands'.[2] But others saw him as the ideal choice, and when John Masefield died two years later, the poet Dan MacNabb told Betjeman that he should be next. While promising to accept the honour if offered ('[i]t would be arrogant not to'), the future recipient felt he was too 'unreliable' and 'eccentric' for this to occur.[3] Though his intuition proved to be right in some ways, initially he received many letters of congratulation, including one from Harold Acton, to whom the news gave 'the greatest pleasure in [what was] a blank and barren period'.[4] *The Times* also took a positive view and hoped Betjeman would 'help to put poetry on a rather higher pedestal among the arts'.[5] Indeed, as Larkin had written privately in 1967, the appointment 'would do more for poetry than all the Arts Co. grants put together'.[6]

From *Old Lights for New Chancels* onwards, the poetry had started to express recognisable truths about contemporary Britain; thus, as Larkin also wrote (publicly this time – in the *Daily Telegraph*): '[i]n a sense Betjeman was Poet Laureate already: he outsells the rest (without being required reading in the Universities), and his audience overflows the poetry reading public to take in the Housman-*Omar Khyyám* belt, people who, so to speak, like a rattling good poem'. This not only reflects Press's argument in his review of *High and Low* (see CHAPTER FIVE), but also Bowra's insightful mid-1960s comments:

> [y]our poetry is of course entirely your own (though you owe a bit to old Tom Hardy), but it is also the poetry of our times. It is these small corners of towns and villages, of the countryside and the suburbs that we have left to us out of the vast nature that was once there. Silly for us to go Wordsworthing about and you are the guide to secrets around the corner, which we should all have missed if you had not spotted them and given them just the right shape that keeps them real.[7]

When interviewed, Betjeman was characteristically self-effacing: 'I would never write state poetry,' he said, 'any more than Robert Bridges did.' For him, there was no question that he would be 'anything like as good' as Bridges – or Tennyson, whom he recognised as a 'superb' exponent of the art.[8] He joked that while he was as happy to succeed this pair as he was Wordsworth, he was 'not quite so pleased to be the successor of Alfred Austin', adding wryly: 'I am sure he wrote some good poetry. I have been reading his work looking for it.'[9] This may explain the touch of Austin that seems to be present in 'A Mind's Journey to Diss' (1974), a piece written for fellow versifier, Mary Wilson:

> Dear Mary,
> > Yes, it will be bliss
> To go with you by train to Diss
> Your walking shoes upon your feet;
> We'll meet, my sweet, at Liverpool Street.
>
> (BETJEMAN, 'A MIND'S JOURNEY TO DISS', LL. 1–4)

> > Shortly, shortly, we shall meet.
> Southern skies awhile are sweet;
> But in whatso land I roam,
> Half my heart remains at home.
>
> (AUSTIN, 'EXTRACT FROM "A LETTER FROM ITALY"', LL. 1–4)[10]

Both poems are of course epistles, sharing four stresses per line in the same tight AABB rhyme scheme. The difference in metre, however, is quite deliberate and implies that 'A Mind's Journey' is a colloquial spoof of Austen, whose trochaic solemnity is made fully iambic, and more natural, by the addition of an initial unaccented syllable. As if to underline his intent, Betjeman subtly includes his forebear's 'sweet'/'meet' as an internal rhyme and then takes it almost too far by adding 'Street' to create a triplet that must have amused his addressee.

Formally, the post (having had the associated duties of court historian dropped in 1860) was essentially that of Panegyricist Royal. Michael Hulse names Robert Southey (Laureate from 1813 to 1843) as the first of the modern incumbents, in that it was under him that the office began to steer away from its emphasis on the Monarchy and became more closely allied to national experience.[11] Yet Betjeman was no stranger to royal verse either – indeed, one could argue that his best work in this field preceded the Laureateship. Though he had written a light-hearted, extemporised piece on the birth of HRH Prince Andrew in February 1960, for example, his effort for the marriage of Princess Margaret later that year was more considered.[12] With its tight 8.8.8.8 metre and ABAB rhyme, it began with a greetings card-style bounce, but had developed a number of characteristic traits by the end:

> Within the hush before the vow
>   To love, to cherish and obey
> We place ourselves where they are now
>   As though it were our wedding day.
>
>   :   :   :   :   :
>
> And as throughout the steepled isle
>   The flood of our thanksgiving swells,
> The hills and lanes and valleys smile
>   And all the air is full of bells.
>
> ('A POEM FOR PRINCESS MARGARET'S WEDDING DAY', LL. 1–4; 13–16)[13]

However, Betjeman's *first* royal poem – 'Death of King George V' (originally entitled 'Daily Express') – dated back to 1937, and was a much finer, and shrewder, piece altogether:

> Spirits of well-shot woodcock, partridge, snipe
> Flutter and bear him up the Norfolk sky:
> In that red house in a red mahogany book-case
> The stamp collection waits with mounts long dry.
>
> ('DEATH OF KING GEORGE V', LL. 1–4)[14]

Here, the references to a well-documented love of philately and pheasant shoots capture the character of the Sailor King perfectly. The tone is manifestly sympathetic and also illustrates the watershed between the old world of men 'who never cheated, never doubted' and the new 'red suburb ruled by Lady Liner' (as it was in the original version – probably referring to Emerald, Lady Cunard).[15] John Langford (of The Betjeman Society) has noted the old/new, spiritual/mechanical symmetry of George V being borne skywards by birds, while (in the last line) his successor comes back to earth by aeroplane. He also comments that the 'hatlessness' of the young man provides a neat counterpoint with his father's insistence on correctness.[16] Of course, the abdication also ensured that Edward VIII remained ultimately *crownless*, and it is ironic – given his late father's hobby – that this is how he was portrayed (with the crown to the right of his head, rather than above it as usual) on his own short-lived issue of stamps.[17] In addition, Langford demonstrates the way in which Betjeman echoes Stanley Baldwin's words of condolence to the widowed Queen Mary at the close of his 'A Ballad of the Investiture, 1969' (1974):

> You knelt a boy, you rose a man.
> And thus your lonelier life began.
>
> ('A BALLAD OF THE INVESTITURE', LL. 67–68)[18]

It is possible that this couplet mirrors more closely the end of Hopkins's sonnet 'To seem the stranger lies my lot', which includes the refrain 'leaves me a lonely began'.[19] However, it is clear that Betjeman was much favoured by the poem's subject:

> Then, sir, you said what shook me through
>   So that my courage almost fails:
> "I want a poem out of you
>   On my investiture in Wales."[20]
>   ('A BALLAD OF THE INVESTITURE', LL. 10–13)

Prince Charles's request is jokingly referred to as a 'command', but Betjeman 'wondered what to do' for *several years* before settling down to the task. This suggests that the deferral was about more than simple awe: not wishing to tread on the toes of a friend was part of it (Cecil Day Lewis was still Poet Laureate at the time), while fear and doubt made up the rest. Nervousness of one sort or another is certainly imparted in the lines 'And now, at last, I've thought it better / To write a kind of rhyming letter' (ll. 17–18), although note how the regular octosyllabic lines and the sweep of the syntax (which minimises the pauses) create pace. This is particularly noticeable in the third and fourth stanzas, where Betjeman recounts his train journey from Euston to Caernarvon; however, it is checked in the final stanza proper, where the metre suddenly cuts to six syllables:

> You know those moments that there are
> When, lonely under moon and star,
>   You wait upon a beach?
> Suddenly all Creation's near
> And complicated things are clear,
>   Eternity in reach!
>   ('A BALLAD OF THE INVESTITURE', LL. 55–60)

This shift in tone underlines the reason behind the poem's success, for though public, it is addressed *privately* to the Prince (which is also suggested by the high number of first and second person pronouns). The alliteration is most effective here too, as is the way that 'Creation', 'complicated things' and 'Eternity', all in a kind of parallelism, resolve themselves into explanatory monosyllables – thus 'Creation's *near*', 'complicated things are *clear*', and Eternity is 'in *reach*' (my italics). Betjeman was in an ideal position to understand the implications of whirring cameras and the paraphernalia of the media, of course, but he also knew about the loneliness of fame and its effects on loved ones – hence the poem's final line: 'The Royal family waits alone' (l. 52).

He later cited Tennyson's 'The Charge of the Light Brigade' and 'Ode on the Death of the Duke of Wellington' (both 1855) as being among the best of any state verses written by a Laureate.[21] These are august models and Bevis Hillier sees a touch of the Tennysonian ability to set a scene (as in *The Princess*) in the opening of Betjeman's own first official piece, 'Hundreds of birds in the air' (1973), written to commemorate the marriage of HRH Princess Anne to Captain Mark Phillips on 14 November 1973:

> Hundreds of birds in the air
> And millions of leaves on the pavement.
> Then the bells pealing on
> Over palace and people outside,
> All for the words 'I will'
> To love's most holy enslavement.
> What can we do but rejoice
> With a triumphing bridegroom and bride?
>
> ('HUNDREDS OF BIRDS IN THE AIR')[22]

The poem in this form was published in both *Time* and *Newsweek* on 26 November. On completion, Betjeman wrote to Patrick Plunket, the Queen's private secretary, and told him that it had been 'composed last night on the Pullman [train] from Manchester to London after four double Scotches slowly consumed'. He added that '[p]erhaps in the cold light of tomorrow [the lines] will seem unworthy', but finished optimistically by saying he 'would like to think they are not too much like a Christmas card verse'.[23] Many people felt he was wrong: *Newsweek*, for one, found the work 'limpsy', while *Time* reported that a Labour MP had been so appalled by what he saw as '"turgid, unromantic and stamped with mediocrity"', that he called for Betjeman's resignation. Harold Acton's letter, had he re-read it, must then have seemed like a terrible joke.

The problem was that this was a 'duty' poem, and he had always equated poetry with freedom. Talking to Kingsley Amis for the BBC, he recalled how Masefield (in his view unsuccessfully) *compelled* himself to write royal verse, adding that 'you can't force something that has to be inspired'.[24] Auberon Waugh saw things a little differently, however, and with typical Waugh contrariness, acknowledged that though the poem was a failure, he was glad: '[Betjeman's] inability to produce anything but rubbish to commemorate a rubbishy event is a perfect commentary on the times and a perfect justification for the appointment.' Was he aware of the verse's alcoholic beginnings? If so, he would have doubtless surmised that the drink was vital; after all, 'Hundreds of birds' was hampered by the fact that 'very little is known about Princess Anne or about her bridegroom which is endearing or particularly likable [sic]'. In this context, the question posed at the end (ll. 7–8) is a reaction to the huge build-up the event was given by the media.

Waugh's suspicion that the poem was written in 'a state of profound melancholy', as if Betjeman had felt pushed into it, is entirely plausible given his comments to Amis. While the "Pot Pourri Pam" rhyming of 'pavement' and 'enslavement' was unlikely to win any literary prizes, Hillier also notes that it was 'recycled' from a verse Betjeman had written for Mary Shand. This gives the impression that he required some kind of poetic springboard to give impetus to the work. Such a need was to recur throughout this decade and into the next.[25]

Battling with Bulldozers

In terms of prose, Betjeman remained active in the early 1970s, contributing, among other things, a regular column to the *Sunday Express* at this time. It was similar to much of his previous output in that he either lambasted modern architectural abominations ('We Must Stop the March of the Concrete Monster', 28 February 1971), or discussed beauty both where it was never sought ('Why I Like to Have Holidays in the Industrial Cities', 13 December 1970), and where it often was ('The Island Tourism has not Spoilt' [The Isle of Man], 11 October 1970). The *Weekend* magazine of the *Daily Telegraph* also carried his major series on English building styles, which was later published by John Murray as *A Pictorial History of English Architecture* (1972). This was, as its title suggests, a lavishly illustrated volume, which the author hoped would 'communicate enthusiasm' and so disseminate the beauty of buildings to as wide an audience as possible.[26]

From the beginning, it imparted favour for the work of the nineteenth century and beyond: '[o]ne has the impression at the back of one's mind,' Betjeman wrote, 'that architecture stopped at the 18th century. This is a hangover from the Gothic Revival'. From standing stones and Saxon buildings, the ensuing chapters thus take the reader through the ages to the Norman era, the Early English, the Decorated and the Perpendicular. But though he had claimed that 'it is impossible to judge the present – we are of it', censure for mid-twentieth century architecture was not absent: '[i]t may well be that in reaction to the clinical glass boxes of the 1950s,' he added, the Elizabethan style 'may even come in for a revival'.[27] He also mourned the seeming absence of the artist-architect, whom, he felt, 'should be the only bar between us and the human anthill to which we may be reduced'.[28] In the post-war era, this hapless artisan 'became no longer an artist but a kind of public relations officer between local authorities and combines of developers, who employed him to give tone to their schemes for destroying old towns and creating new ones'.

This sentiment echoes Betjeman's first book on the subject, *Ghastly Good Taste* (1933), in which he had concluded that an architect needed to be both 'a town planner' and 'every sort of engineer', such were the pressures of the contemporary market place.[29] But he had also made the point that 'the finest tradition of architecture set by the Victorian age was in her commercial enterprises', listing the Crystal Palace, King's Cross and St. Pancras stations, along with 'engine sheds, [. . .] cast-iron bridges, [and even] gasometers'.[30] In the *Pictorial Guide*, Betjeman noted that, as the nineteenth century had progressed, architecture began to separate itself from civil engineering. His respect for men such as Telford, Brunel and Stephenson had clearly not diminished in the ensuing forty years, and he notes (with a side-swipe at John Summerson) that

> [architects] felt they were above the building trade and above men who constructed tunnels and bridges and enormous greenhouses like the Crystal Palace. They tried to forget that Leonardo was also an engineer.[31]

Candida Lycett Green has said that, in spite of his efforts, her father still felt 'the bulldozers were in full flood'.[32] In an attempt to increase pressure on developers and planners, he suggested to Richard Ingrams of *Private Eye* that he contribute a column which would allow modern monstrosities to be ridiculed by false praise. Ingrams accepted, and the result was a series called 'Nooks and Corners of the New Barbarism'. The first article featured Hillgate House, in London's Ludgate Hill, and was headed by a somewhat austere photograph of the same, along with Pevsner's view that it looked 'promising at the time of writing' (1962). 'To show that this is a modern building,' Betjeman teasingly wrote in the guise of the architect, 'we have deliberately off-centred the prominent features on an otherwise restrained façade. This has been skilfully done by the introduction of a concrete projection which, though affording no shelter, performs the function of drawing the eye down to the door and window which are themselves off centre with the projection.'[33] In a later column, Betjeman also implied that 6, Brunswick Square (WC1) was inspired by London University's Senate House building (1932), and commented caustically that the said institution should be thanked 'for destroying so many of the Georgian Squares and Terraces so long a notorious impediment to enlightened planning'.[34]

This was taken on at a time when Betjeman's doctor had ordered him to cut down on his many commitments, but while he had resigned from the Royal Fine Arts Commission (after eighteen years' service) in 1970, his output continued unabated.[35] As had been apparent in the previous decade, an increasing proportion of prose involved obituaries for old friends and heroes, such as Maurice Bowra, Frederick Etchells and W. H. Auden, whose passing was lamented in verse:[36]

> Without a doubt you towered high above us,
>   Reckless, generous, capable and kind.
> A great poet and loyal in your friendships
>   Despite the blessings of a 'First Class Mind'.

(Note that, although this is affectionate, the urge to dig at the intellectual set to which Auden had belonged was still impossible to resist – even though Auden himself only got a third!)

Betjeman had also spent three months Down Under during 1972, which resulted in a four-part BBC television series, *Betjeman in Australia* (1972). Here he was able to indulge his passion for Georgian-style architecture (which had continued right up to the 1890s) and even spiders (the second film contains the famous scene with the tarantula in the toilet).[37] He had enjoyed the trip, but the schedule had been arduous (and was almost certainly made more so by the symptoms of his Parkinson's disease).[38] But any pleasure he had taken is somewhat belied by the sonnet inspired by his return, 'Back from Australia' (1972), which includes one or two barbed remarks about homogenisation, speed and soulless modernity:

> Cocooned in Time, at this inhuman height,
>   The packaged food tastes neutrally of clay.
> We never seem to catch the running day
> But travel on in everlasting night
> With all the chic accoutrements of flight:
>   Lotions and essences in neat array
>   And yet another plastic cup and tray.
> "Thank you *so* much. Oh no, I'm quite all right."
>
>   ('BACK FROM AUSTRALIA', LL. 1–8)

Many readers must have recognised the characteristic blandness of 1970s air travel, just as they must the peculiarly British attribute (now in decline) of refusing to complain no matter what. Back in Cornwall at the poem's end, Betjeman shows his appreciation of the expanse of the autumn sky – in direct contrast to the claustrophobic environment of the aeroplane; this allows him to reflect on his own smallness, as 'the hills declare / How vast the sky is, looked at from the land' (ll. 13–14). This is after all the natural way to see the heavens. He had made a similar point in 'Old Friends' (1962), which begins 'The sky widens to Cornwall', but G. M. Harvey has also noted the juxtaposition of those 'inhuman' flight conditions (and their associated distortions of proportion), and the 'liberating sanity' of the (much more) human dimensions to be discerned from the earth.[39] However, to this one must add that it echoes precisely the views long held by Betjeman on the nature of high-rise flats: developers, as he wrote in 1958, 'forget that the higher you build a slab, the farther it must be from other slabs if sunlight is to reach the lower storeys'. In London, 'most of them are out of scale and out of texture with their surroundings'. They could not all be like Park Hill in Sheffield, alas (see CHAPTER FIVE).[40]

Autumn Chill

Like 'A Ballad of the Investiture, 1969' and the poem on Princess Anne's wedding, 'Back from Australia' was included in *A Nip in the Air* (1974), Betjeman's last collection of his most recent work. By this time, 'Hundreds of birds in the air' had both been renamed '14 November 1973' and altered thus:

Hundreds of birds in the air
  And millions of leaves on the pavement,
And Westminster bells ringing on
  To palace and people outside-
And all for the words 'I will'
  To love's most willing enslavement.
All of our people rejoice
  With venturous bridegroom and bride.

Trumpets blare at the entrance,
  Multitudes crane and sway.
Glow, white lily in London,
  You are high in our hearts today!
                                    ('14 NOVEMBER 1973')

Gone is the 'what can we do?' exasperation – now there can be no doubt that the people *are* rejoicing. Line 3 is another considerable improvement, though it could have been even better had 'pealing' not been replaced by 'ringing'. The near oxymoron of 'willing enslavement' (l. 6) is even more redolent of Pam than the original, and this is emphasised to an extent by the Swinburnian reference to the 'white lily' (l. 11), which recalls the decadent world of the 1890s once again (even though it originally comes from the iconography of the Annunciation).

Aside from these earlier efforts, two other 'public' verses were also included. 'In Memory of George Whitby, Architect' was delivered at St. Mary's, Woolnoth, on 29 March 1973, and Patrick Taylor-Martin is right to say that it is both 'dignified and solemn without being embarrassing'.[41] In fact, Betjeman speaks directly *to* his audience, rather than pontificating *at* them, and this gives the verse the same aural quality of one of his television commentaries:

Si monumentum requiris . . . the church in which we are sitting,
Its firm square ceiling supported by fluted Corinthian columns
In groups of three at the corners, its huge semi-circular windows
Lighting the elegant woodwork and plaster panels and gilding:
Look around you, behold the work of Nicholas Hawksmoor.
                    ('IN MEMORY OF GEORGE WHITBY, ARCHITECT', LL. 1–5)

The lines are loose, accentual hexameters, a grand classical metre perhaps suggested by the grave classical quotation, which, as it is from Wren's epitaph in St Paul's, dignifies Whitby yet further. Note also how the architectural points that Betjeman makes are emphasised by the alliteration, as in 'square ceiling supported' and 'fluted Corinthian columns' (l. 2), and that the invitation to 'Look around you', exactly translating *'circumspice'* (the last word of the epitaph) would already have been acted on by the poem's original audience.

In 'Inland Waterway', a poem declaimed at the opening of the Upper Avon at Stratford in 1974, Betjeman returned to the subtle policy of using a nine-teenth-century poetic model to comment on the present:

> He who by peaceful inland water steers
> Bestirs himself when a new lock appears.
> Slow swing the gates: slow sinks the water down;
> This lower Stratford seems another town.
> The meadows which the youthful Shakespeare knew
> Are left behind, and, sliding into view,
> Come reaches of the Avon, mile on mile,
>
> ('INLAND WATERWAY', LL. 1–7)

The pace is sedate, 'peaceful' and 'slow', and the poet is clearly relishing the scene, far removed as it is from the aeroplane of 'Back from Australia'. Such tranquillity is itself a criticism of the speed and greed of contemporary Britain, but the piece also ends with the notion that in this river (and so in all rivers and perhaps all similar idylls) lies 'the heart of England'. This is underscored by its construction, the rhyming couplets and decasyllabic metre obviously deriving (again!) from the 'Introduction' to William Morris's *The Earthly Paradise* (1868–1870):

> Forget six counties overhung with smoke,
> Forget the snorting steam and piston stroke,
> Forget the spreading of the hideous town;
> Think rather of the pack-horse on the down,
> And dream of London, small and white and clean,
>
> (WILLIAM MORRIS, *THE EARTHLY PARADISE*, 'INTRODUCTION', LL. 1–5)[42]

Betjeman's rhyming of 'town' and 'down' *à la* Morris provides further evidence of his intent. His 'homely Avon' and 'haughty Severn' are also at one with his forebear's 'clear Thames' (l. 6), which recalls the journey to Utopia undertaken in *News From Nowhere* (1890). That novel included the 'force-barges' that Morris hoped would replace the steam engine, yet he would surely have preferred the railway (steam or otherwise) to the automobile.[43] Perhaps believing this himself, Betjeman had cloaked himself in Morrisian garb for *Branch Line Railway*, a film made in Somerset in 1963. 'Forget motor-cars, get rid of anxiety,' he echoed, adding from his carriage that it was nice to see Glastonbury Tor 'without a foreground of villas and petrol stations.' As he had explored in 'Great Central Railway' (1962), the train was as good a means of seeing 'Unmitigated England' as the river, but his particular preference for steam is also revealed in the coda of 'Dilton Marsh Halt' (1968), the earliest of the poems in *A Nip in the Air*:

> And when all the horrible roads are finally done for,

And there's no more petrol left in the world to burn,
Here to the Halt from Salisbury and from Bristol
Steam trains will return.
('Dilton Marsh Halt', ll. 17–20)

Harvey believes that this 'mocks our allegiance to the illusory idea of progress', the halt providing, for him, a bridge to the 'realities of the natural world'.[44] The location, glimpsed through cedar trees (l. 3), is indeed delightfully bucolic, but the 1937–vintage wooden sleeper structure is also a last vestige of the pre-nationalised railway (emphasised by the fact that it retained its ageing lamps until the mid-1970s).[45] 'Dilton Marsh Halt' was first published in the official handbook of the 1968 Thomas Hardy Festival, Betjeman being at that time a vice-president of the Thomas Hardy Society. As one would expect, the work of the earlier poet is reflected here, there being an obvious connection with the 'shaded lamp' and 'waving blind' of Hardy's 'An August Midnight' (1899). But the reference to the future scarcity of petrol was another (and unexpected) example of Betjeman's poetic prescience, for though its reappearance in 1974 made it highly topical, the oil crisis of that period was still some way off when the poem was written.[46]

Both 'Dilton Marsh Halt' and 'Inland Waterway' repay repeated reading. This allows their understated criticisms of modernity to seep into the brain with great ease. However, Harvey believes Betjeman's later work is in fact characterised by the '*urgency*' of his 'social anger' (my italics).[47] It should be remembered that this flame was burning just as brightly in the 1950s, as a re-reading of 'Huxley Hall' will testify; yet Harvey is right to claim that 'The Newest Bath Guide' (1973) is suggestive of 'a fundamentally and powerfully reciprocal relation between people and their environment'.[48] As the header and second line make clear, it is based on Christopher Anstey's *The New Bath Guide* of 1766. As such, it is a splendid pastiche which romps through 'varied and human' (l. 17) scenes of eighteenth-century Bath before attacking the 'uniform nothingness' (l. 23) of modern architecture, and in particular the 'terrible "Tech" with its pointed behind' (l. 24). But for all the sallies at ugly municipal buildings, Patrick Taylor-Martin is also accurate in *his* judgement that the final couplet is more resigned than raging:

Goodbye to old Bath! We who loved you are sorry
They're carting you off by developer's lorry.
('The Newest Bath Guide', ll. 29–30)[49]

The poem was specially written for Adam Fergusson's *The Sack of Bath* (1973), which was aimed at halting the destruction – now! The situation countrywide was not improving, and the 'smell of deep-fry', 'wrappings of potato crisps' and 'broken plastic toys' were tarnishing even the beaches of Cornwall. These images are found in 'Delectable Duchy' (1974), which ends with a hope that 'One day a tidal wave will break / Before the breakfasters awake', sweeping the caravans and other carbuncles out into 'A waste of undulating ocean'. Here, the violence of the sea, which the poet had feared in 'Greenaway' (1954), has become the county's liberator.

Of course, such symbols of consumerism are promoted by a particular type of businessman, and it was on this breed, under the heading 'To the faceless ones "develop" means to "destroy"', that Betjeman had set his sights in the *Sunday Express* three years earlier (30 May 1971). The poem therein, re-titled 'Executive' for the book, captured perfectly the priorities of this modern money-grabber:

> I am a young executive. No cuffs than mine are cleaner;
> I have a Slimline brief-case and I use the firm's Cortina.
> In every roadside hostelry from here to Burgess Hill
> The *maîtres d'hôtel* all know me well and let me sign the bill.
>
> ('EXECUTIVE', LL. 1–4)

Though conceited, the protagonist veritably oozes charm for the first four stanzas, and it is only when he dons his 'other hat' that the façade slips:

> I do some mild developing. The sort of place I need
> Is a quiet country market town that's rather run to seed.
> A luncheon and a drink or two, a little *savoir faire*-
> I fix the Planning Officer, the Town Clerk and the Mayor.
>
> ('EXECUTIVE', LL. 17–20)

There, in line 20, we see the mask of urbanity turn into self-disclosed moral ruthlessness, as the Executive reveals himself to be another of Betjeman's twentieth-century versions of Browning's Duke ('My Last Duchess', 1842):

> Oh sir, she smiled, no doubt,
> Whene'er I passed her; but who passed without
> Much the same smile? This grew; I gave commands;
> Then all smiles stopped together.
>
> (BROWNING, 'MY LAST DUCHESS', LL. 43–46)[50]

The connection is just as deliberate as it was in 'Bristol and Clifton' (1940), though here there is also that sense of menace that the Duke possesses. Betjeman's protagonist could doubtless 'fix' whomever he wanted to get whatever he wanted just like his counterpart, who needs only give 'commands' to stop his wife's smiles forever. Indeed, the death of the Duchess and the impending doom of the small town are clearly synonymous, and this gives a clear indication of how Betjeman felt about developers and planners (remember that he had called Crewkerne a 'traffic-*murdered* town' in his 1963 film [my italics – see CHAPTER FIVE]).

This contempt is compounded by the fact that both Duke and developer are also loquacious, self-centred and obsessed with the ownership of goods: note how the former begins by drawing his audience's eye to the portrait and ends with his statue by the esteemed Claus of Innsbruck, while the latter starts with his 'Slimline brief-case' and goes on to his Aston Martin and fibreglass speedboat. And though the subject of that Innsbruck figurine – Neptune taming a sea horse – is just as apt to the younger man's aspirations, the poet's disdain for the shallowness of Executive's lifestyle is made clear by the revelation that his vessel has 'never touched the water' (l. 12) – an ironically impotent image in this context. It is called 'Mandy Jane', after 'a bird' he used to know, whose memory is clearly subordinate to that which her name adorns, just as the Duchess is now used merely to advertise the Duke's wealth and taste.[51]

Betjeman's brilliant observational skills are used again in 'The Costa Blanca' (1971), a pair of sonnets that deal with the English desire to seek sunnier climes. The first is narrated by a woman ('SHE'), while the second is in the persona of her husband ('HE') five years later. Their new home is called 'Casa Kenilworth', and while situated 'up a dusty lane', sits under pine trees in a setting which instantly recalls a typical Betjemanian Surrey homestead. The true concerns of the English abroad are thus neatly satirised: the couple are not interested in Spanish culture; they simply want the sun. This first sonnet ends with the presumably reassuring revelation that 'We have found / Delightful English people living round', although the 'Good-bye to democracy' swipe (General Franco was still in power at this time) hints in some small way at the crushing disappointment expressed by 'HIM' five years later:

> If you come out here put aside the fare
> To England. *I'd* run like a bloody hare
> If I'd a chance, and how we both have yearned
> To see our Esher lawn.
> ('THE COSTA BLANCA', LL. 18–21)

Their savings gone, conned by '[t]hat Dago', the couple live without piped water in a house 'with scorpions in the bath'.

Betjeman's mastery of the Browning technique serves a much darker purpose in 'Shattered Image', a poem which first appeared as 'The P.R.O.' in the *London Magazine* (July/August 1970). It evidently counts the sordid, Roman murder-story/verse-novel *The Ring and the Book* (1868–9) as one of its exemplars, but whereas Browning compels his readers to play the part of an alert magistrate, 'Shattered Image' deals with the psychology of the paedophile. In this extract, Rex, Betjeman's protagonist, wavers between denying that he has committed a crime at all and fearing that punishment is probably inevitable:

> I didn't touch-
> Well not in the way that Charlie used to do-
> :   :   :   :   :   :

> Look at it calmly. What can they really prove?
> What is the worst that Aleco could have said?
> And will they take his word against my own?
> I'm only charged-the case unproven still;
>   ('SHATTERED IMAGE', LL. 28–29; LL. 48–51)

Betjeman's skill here is that while Rex is talking candidly, and at times desperately (note the triplet of questions in lines 48 to 50), the reader feels no warmth for him at all. Indeed, although the inclusion of the official charge ('...and that you did with said intent procure / the aforesaid Sidney Alexander Green' (ll. 1–2)), and its later repetition, recalls the police presence in 'The Arrest of Oscar Wilde', Rex evokes no pathos – not even when he considers taking his own life:

> In bathrooms people often kill themselves.
> :   :   :   :   :
>   But I mustn't try,
> Especially now that I'm a Catholic.
>   ('SHATTERED IMAGE', L. 13; LL.32–33)

Note how the heavy iambic rhythm breaks down into a conversational flutter. Note too that while the thought of suicide comes to him early, it is only compounded when he remembers his friend Charlie being beaten up in prison:

> Of course they found out why he was inside–
> And that's a thing they will never forgive,
> Touching the little children, better pooves
> Or murderers, they said [. . .].
>   ('SHATTERED IMAGE', LL. 25–28)

Rex decides that Aleco must have fallen into a police trap, and his deduction of who was responsible finally betrays his underlying cynicism: it could not have been the boy's brother, after all, 'He came to Minehead with us in July' (l. 55); the father simply 'doesn't count' (l. 57), but the mother, more chillingly, could not have been involved because 'She's a pet' (l. 56). Yet despite the sly power over her that this implies, Rex decides that she must have been the one who alerted the authorities. He then rings around his friends for support, and this closes the first section of the poem, after which the narrative plots the shattering of his image via the words of three acquaintances: his solicitor friend George, his colleague Douglas, and his boss. Each behaves with guarded politeness, but with successively less empathy: George refuses to act on the grounds that he is a conveyancer and not a criminal lawyer; Douglas first thinks that Rex has slept with another man, but on realising Aleco's age, feels 'inclined to puke'; the boss, while sacking Rex, is perhaps politest of all, and were it not for the truth of the situation, the reader might feel some sort of sympathy instead of thinking that Rex gets what he deserves:

> Our business is – well simply what it's called,
> Public Relations. And our image counts
> Not with our clients only, but beyond
> In the hard world where men are selling things.
> And the sort of bloke we're dealing with,
> Frankly, we can't afford the sort of slur
> A case like yours brings with it.
>
> ('SHATTERED IMAGE', LL. 130–136)

Clearly, it is the image of the company that matters to the boss, not any moral question about the heinous nature of Rex's crime.[52]

Belief . . . and Unbelief

As with *High and Low*, death and its consorts, Faith and Doubt, continued to provide a nip in the air in 1974. Betjeman must have been acutely aware that his fears were now in danger of becoming reality – and not simply because of age: though 68 was closer to death's door then than it is now, he would have known that his Parkinson's disease was placing his hand on the handle sooner than the average man could reasonably expect. This led to musings like those found at the close of 'On Leaving Wantage 1972':

> borne along like twigs and bits of straw,
> We sink below the sliding stream of time.
>
> (LL. 28–29)

Amid the mood of doom, inevitability and helplessness, note that we sink, not swim, and that the bells 'clash out' (l. 18). This conveys a coldness that suggests Betjeman does not expect to dance to the music of time like Powell, but drown in its waters.

This theme is continued in 'Loneliness' (1971), where the bells sound an unsympathetic 'ordered metal clatter-clang' (l. 5), causing the poet to ask 'Is yours the song the angels sang?' They in fact open 'Our loneliness, so long and vast' (ll. 19–20) to the crematorium furnace, which is itself a metaphor for hell and damnation. This is preceded by, and therefore explains, both the ambivalence ('You fill my heart with joy and grief') *and* the ambience. Betjemanian narrators usually fit their settings like a foxglove, but here there is instead apathy and blunted sensitivity: twigs, note, are a deathly 'black', finches are 'indifferent' and even the rolling lorries are 'unheeding'. It is as though life were preparing to carry on as normal, without Betjeman, before his very eyes. In this, the undeniable influence is Clough:

> You fill my heart with joy and grief–
> Belief! Belief! And unbelief . . .
> And, though you tell me I shall die,
> You say not how or when or why.
>
> ('LONELINESS', LL. 7–10)

These lines reflect the 'Christ is not risen'/'Christ is yet risen' vacillation of the two 'Easter Day' poems (both 1865), the first of which focuses on the 'sinful streets' (I. 1) of Naples, later damned by the assertion that 'there is no Hell; / Save Earth' (I. 79–80). Clough's problem is in reconciling this scene with the existence of a just God, thus while his second poem is lighter in tone, the same 'sinful streets' are there to provide a backdrop of depravity. As the unctuous 'blear-eyed' (II.1) pimp lists his female wares, therefore, the narrator falls into musing with his 'secret self' (II.12), where a voice bids him to 'Weep not' (II. 17) for 'Christ is yet risen' (II. 21 *et al.*) . Clough's philosophising is based on intellectual conflict; though he would live for a further thirteen years, for Betjeman it is clearly based on infirmity and the imminence of death. The line 'Belief! Belief! And unbelief…' captures his religious dichotomy perfectly, but it would be a mistake to think that this was mere parody, or even pure admiration. By nodding to a specific poetic antecedent like this, Betjeman is deliberately opening out the debate: we may not need to know our Clough, but we are supposed to know that the poem refers to a particular Victorian religious quandary, and we are supposed to see that it is of much wider significance than its specific language might suggest.

Such connections between the personal and the general may be found elsewhere in Betjeman's work – particularly when his subject is mortality. In 'Aldershot Crematorium' (1971), for example, the precise location is used to show that our ultimate end is in fact omnipresent: it is no accident that the crematorium lies between two sporting venues – 'the swimming-pool and cricket-ground' (l. 1). What better way to illustrate the point? In this context, the straight driveway (l. 2) is almost a metaphor for life itself, while the 'little puffs of smoke without a sound' (l. 3) also hark back to the cold breezes that 'Carry the bells away on the air' in 'For Nineteenth-Century Burials' (1931). But however we try to 'dissipate our fears' (l. 10), 'doubt inserts the knife' (l. 12 – another reference to 'Before the Anaesthetic').

The cancer that was feared in 'Loneliness' is also implied in 'Fruit', an earlier lyric which first appeared in Roy Fuller's anthology, *Moments of Truth* (1965):

> Now with the threat growing still greater within me,
>   The Church dead that was hopelessly over-restored,
> The fruit picked from these yellowing Worcestershire orchards
>   What is left to me, Lord?
>
> To wait until next year's bloom at the end of the garden
>   Foams to the Malvern Hills, like an inland sea,

And to know that its fruit, dropping in autumn stillness,
    May have outlived me.

('FRUIT')

This is in the tradition of Victorian elegy, such as Arnold's 'Thyrsis' (1866) and Tennyson's *In Memoriam* (1850), and though 'Fruit' predates *A Nip in the Air* by nine years, its presence in it contributes significantly to the overriding sense of 'autumn stillness'.[53] And overriding it certainly is – even the tone of 'Lenten Thoughts of a High Anglican' (1973) – the only recognisably 'amatory' verse here – is tinged with death: its 'Mistress', whom Betjeman regularly saw on Sundays at a London church, may begin as a creature of wonder ('With her wide-apart grey-green eyes', l. 2), but she becomes at the end a symbol for the 'Unknown God' we all seek.[54] Similarly, the book closes with 'The Last Laugh' (1974), whose sense of finality makes it the perfect choice for this position:

I made hay while the sun shone.
    My work sold.
Now, if the harvest is over
    And the world cold,
Give me the bonus of laughter
    As I lose hold.

('THE LAST LAUGH')

Patrick Taylor-Martin is right to liken this to Tennyson's 'Crossing the Bar' (1889): both poems do indeed read like epitaphs.[55] The earlier piece is of course more defiant, but the idea of there being 'no sadness of farewell' (l. 11) is picked up by Betjeman, who had, after all, used humour as a weapon and a shield (against developers *and* depression) all his life. His pairing of 'sun' and 'cold' also recalls Hardy's 'Where the Picnic Was' (1914), in which a happy summer day is viewed from a lonely present ('Now a cold wind blows' (l. 10)). Betjeman makes significant use of the past tense too – as in 'the sun *shone*', 'my work *sold*' – and when he says '*if* the harvest is over', there can be no doubt that he thinks it is. Tennyson insisted that 'Crossing the Bar' be placed at the end of any volume in which it appeared; 'The Last Laugh' justly enjoyed equivalent status in *Collected Poems* until 2001, when *Uncollected Poems* (1982) and two additional pieces were added.

In *Books and Bookmen*, Betjeman's old friend Alan Pryce-Jones observed the characteristic 'deceptive air of innocence' inherent in *A Nip in the Air*, which, for him, echoed 'the tunes of Felicia Hemans and William Allingham'.[56] As we have seen, the content shows that the poet was continuing to read more widely than this suggests: aside from Morris, Tennyson, Browning, Hardy and even Austin, Housman also makes a brief reappearance in 'A Wembley Lad' (1971):

> To every ducal palace
>   When days were old and slow,
> Me and my sister Alice
>   By charabanc would go.
>
>   ('A WEMBLEY LAD', LL. 1–4)

Pryce-Jones's review is by no means awash with praise, a stance which reflects the general attitude of his colleagues. Though Philip Toynbee commented (*The Observer*) on the increasing savagery of the poet's satires, for example, he revealed himself to be another 'pop-gun' practitioner, seeing even 'Executive' as 'too direct and obvious'.[57] Similarly, Lyman Andrews (*Sunday Times*) said that 'a poor performance or two' made the book 'uneven'.[58] The John Murray Archive implies that 18,500 copies of *A Nip in the Air* were printed. This was a drop on the figures associated with its predecessor, although the third edition of *Collected Poems* was reprinted in February 1974 and both *A Few Late Chrysanthemums* and *High and Low* reappeared the following year. Clearly, Betjeman's popularity remained high, and, in spite of its notices, *A Nip in the Air* seems to have whetted the public's appetite for even more of his work.[59]

Jubilee Jingle

Candida Lycett Green records that the days when her father could write poetry with ease were over by the mid-1970s.[60] Producing Laureate verse was difficult at the best of times, but it was also seemingly thankless, many failing to appreciate the looming closure. The Queen celebrated her silver jubilee in 1977, and, in the May of the previous year, Prince Charles had contacted Betjeman to request one of his 'masterpieces of scansion': 'I would be enormously grateful,' he wrote, 'if you felt able to conjure up your muse!'[61] This appeal from on high must have compounded the sense of dread that Betjeman already felt. As he had said to Mary Wilson just days before: 'My God, I shall have to do a Pam Ayres about the Queen!'[62] In fact, the result had another touch of Austin about it:

> In days of disillusion
> However low we've been,
> To fire and to inspire us
> God gave to us our Queen.
>
> She acceded, young and dutiful
> To her much-loved father's throne;
> Serene and kind and beautiful,
> She holds us as her own.
>
>   :   :   :   :

> For Monarch and Her People
> United and yet free
> Let bells from every steeple
> Ring out the Jubilee.
>
> ('To the Queen', ll. 1–8; ll. 17–20)

The Prince was apparently so dissatisfied with the result that he contemplated asking Betjeman to try again, but as his mother had approved a modified version, which was to be set to music by Malcolm Williamson (the Master of the Queen's Musick), he decided against it.[63] Betjeman himself sensed the work was 'commonplace' and 'like a Christmas card', and though the verses did 'have to be comprehensible to the TUC and natives of Africa', to be fair, he knew that was 'all there [was] to be said for them'.

Jonathan Dimbleby finds 'To the Queen' 'lacklustre to the point of pastiche', but while it may be as a *poem*, printed cold on a page, one must remember that it was written to be sung.[64] In this, it *was* a 'masterpiece of scansion', each line having three clear stresses to carry it along with speed. Indeed, Williamson heartened the poet by telling him that the words were in fact exactly 'the sort he wanted as they left him the gaps he needed' for the arrangement.[65] As to the comment about pastiche, one needs only recall the tune of 'We plough the fields and scatter' to see where the metre came from, although the words may derive from Timothy Dudley-Smith's hymn 'Lord of the Years', to which Betjeman's opening in particular seems to owe something:

> Lord, for that Word, the Word of life which fires us,
>> speaks to our hearts and sets our souls ablaze,
> teaches and trains, rebukes us and inspires us:
>> Lord of the Word, receive your people's praise.

Other poetry produced at this time included 'Chelsea 1977', which appeared the following year in Penguin's *The Best of Betjeman* (1978). Its first stanza is a composite of two classic Betjeman lines bracketed by a pair of clearly Tennysonian fragrance. The Betjemanian ones (2 and 4) are beautifully elegiac in tone, but the rhyming of 'pink' with 'sink' and 'way' with 'day' skilfully mixes the poet's preoccupation with ordinary life in a manner that both focuses his disappointment and the brings the piece back to earth:

> The street is bathed in sunset pink,
> The air is redolent of kitchen sink,
> Between the dog-mess heaps I pick my way
> To watch the dying embers of the day.
>
> ('Chelsea 1977', ll. 1–4)

In the BBC television series, *Time With Betjeman* (1983), producer Jonathan Stedall quotes the poet's feeling that he lived in 'dog-mess walk'; but, with the

Chelsea day dying away, his thoughts become blackened by 'a sense of doom' (l. 7) as he trudges 'towards the tomb' (l. 8):

> The earth beneath my feet is hardly soil
> But outstretched chicken-netting coil on coil
> Covering cables, sewage-pipes and wires
> While underneath burn hell's eternal fires.
>
> ('CHELSEA 1977', LL. 9–12)

Lycett Green believes such 'vivid imaginings' were due in part to the drugs her father had been prescribed for Parkinson's disease.[66] Medical texts do confirm the likelihood of hallucinations, yet the tone and setting of the poem is very much in keeping with Betjeman's oeuvre, and in particular the work featured in *A Nip in the Air*.[67] The final couplet follows on from this and is also reminiscent of Betjeman's earlier work – particularly in its reference to a well-known children's breakfast cereal:

> Snap! crackle! pop! the kiddiz know the sound
> And Satan stokes his furnace underground.
>
> ('CHELSEA 1977', LL. 13–14)

We are never far from death, wherever we are or whatever our age; the reference to the 'kiddiz' makes this point suitably chillingly.

Though he may not have appreciated the effectiveness of his battles against the bulldozers, Betjeman was now beginning to attract an army of like-minded followers, such as the journalist Simon Jenkins and the historian Dan Cruickshank (for whose book, *The Rape of Britain*, he wrote a foreword in 1975).[68] This immediately refutes any criticism of Betjeman's satirical verses. And if he found the writing of patriotic *poetry* difficult, it was clear that the problem did not extend to his prose and media broadcasts. In 1974, for instance, he made *A Passion for Churches* for the BBC, which saw him visit Norfolk to celebrate the Anglican Church and its places of worship. Watching the film, one is never in doubt that it might equally have been called *A Passion for England*. In one memorable scene, Betjeman recalls childhood rowing trips across the Broads with his father, while pointing out such delights as Booton's 'haunting weird Victorian church' and (of course) Comper's genius at Wymondham Abbey, where the architect 'made the East Wall a lofty reredos of sculptured gold'. 'Scale is the secret of its majesty,' he goes on, and '[s]cale was Comper's secret – in 1914 they let him loose in [a] plain old country church [at Lound]. He turned it into a treasure house.'[69]

Similarly, *Vicar of this Parish* (1976) drew attention to the Reverend Francis Kilvert (1840–79), the Victorian diarist, whose musings had been edited into three volumes (1938–40) by Betjeman's friend William Plomer.[70] On radio, he also contributed to broadcasts on Byron (1971) and the Livesey Museum (1974), as well as appearing on *Desert Island Discs* (1975). From

1976 to 1978, he also recorded 23 programmes in a series on hymns and poetry called *Sweet Songs of Zion*. By now, his Parkinson's disease was official, but it was really due to this ongoing media work – coupled with the huge number of letters that he received each day – that his prose output dropped in this period. Nevertheless, he still found time to write reviews for *Books and Bookmen* and, in 1976, a piece for Margaret Drabble's *The Genius of Thomas Hardy*, in which he concentrated on his predecessor's architectural work:

> [a]nyone whose first introduction to Hardy was *Wessex Poems and Other Verses* (1898) might have supposed that the poet was an architect or architectural draughtsman by profession. The illustrations are distinctly architectural – a brick-built turret with a sundial on it and a conical tiled cap; a late fifteenth-century country church with square western tower; the cross-section of a church showing a Transitional Gothic arcade of two and a half bays furnished with box pews and at one end poppy-head bench-ends [. . .].

As the highly detailed list continues, it gives an idea of how irresistible Betjeman must have found Hardy, such was his unique blending of buildings and poetry. The Laureate's enthusiasm is clear and he goes on to give an inter-esting account of Hardy's early working life from his apprenticeship to the Dorchester architect John Hicks onwards. This enables him to toss in a comment about J. P. St Aubyn, whom, he recalled, restored the parish church at Lesnewth (Cornwall) 'far more violently' than the poet had that at St Juliot.[71] Despite writing that he much regretted 'having attacked certain people [in his youth], particularly people in architecture who were probably only trying to do their best', and despite this reference to St Aubyn being much kinder than those in 'Hymn' (1928), old bugbears clearly retained the power to rankle, and were still thought worthy of comment.[72]

Betjeman suffered a heart attack in 1978, but his recovery was sufficiently speedy to make that year's output hardly less than the one before.[73] However, his *poetic* Muse continued to pack her bags with some resolve. Indeed, the only new verse to appear was an eight-line ode to St. Bartholomew's Hospital, which was published in the *London Magazine* that December:

> The ghost of Rahere still walks in Bart's;
> It gives an impulse to generous hearts,
> It looks on pain with a pitying eye,
> It teaches us never to fear to die.
> ('St. Bartholomew's Hospital', ll. 1–4)[74]

Unfortunately the public nature of his office, in relation to both incumbent and event involved, magnified such scarcity. Betjeman's failure to produce a lament for the death of the popular Earl Mountbatten (murdered by the IRA in 1979) could not, therefore, go unnoticed. The wags at *Private Eye* were quick to act:

> In the bright September sunshine,
> See the sailors marching by.
> Here they come from Deal and Reading,
> Now the mighty crowd is heading
> Down the Mall towards the Abbey,
> Some are smart and some are shabby,
> Some are thin and some are flabby.
>
> (PRIVATE EYE, 'LINES WRITTEN BY THE POET LAUREATE ON LEARNING OF
> THE NEWS [SEVERAL WEEKS LATE] OF THE DEATH OF EARL MOUNTBATTEN
> OF BURMA', LL. 1–7)[75]

Though its target was obviously the poet, the subject makes this attack seem a touch tasteless. Furthermore, and unlike the same organ's parody of 'Lenten Thoughts of a High Anglican', these lines are simply not funny.

Somewhat incongruously, Lycett Green has written that the pressures of her father's post began to lift at this time as he 'sank back on to his laurels and began to enjoy life without quite such a disproportionately large dollop of guilt'.[76] Perhaps acknowledging the Muse's ebbing brought with it a sense of relief that he could no longer expect a performance, although in the case of the Mountbatten incident, Betjeman may also have been worried about measuring up to the high standard set by Tennyson in pieces like 'Ode on the Death of the Duke of Wellington' (1852). If the poem he composed for the 80th birthday of the Queen Mother (1980) is any measure, he may have been right to leave well alone – it is hard to read it without the feeling that it was written on autopilot:

> We are your people
> Millions of us greet you
> On this your birthday
> Mother of our Queen.
> Waves of good will go
> Racing out to meet you
> You who in peace and war
> Our faithful friend have been.
> You who have known the sadness of bereavement
> The joyfulness of family jokes
> And times when trust is tried.
> Great was the day for our United Kingdoms
> And God bless the Duke of York
> Who chose you as his bride.
>
> ('LINES WRITTEN TO COMMEMORATE THE 80TH BIRTHDAY OF
> HM QUEEN ELIZABETH, THE QUEEN MOTHER', LL. 1–14)

The imagery is lacklustre, the rhythm uneven, the logic at the end flawed (great, in fact, was the day *when* the Duke of York chose Lady Elizabeth

Bowes-Lyon as his bride). Yet the 'Lines' did retain the personal touch that the poet had employed in earlier work about the Royal Family. The Queen Mother would have been pleased by the reference to her late husband (l. 13), for example, and doubtless amused by the pun on her favourite sporting pastime of racing (l. 6). However, there is a touch of '14 November, 1973' here too: for 'millions of leaves on the pavement', read '[m]illions of us'; for "rejoicing", read 'joyfulness' (l. 10). These instances are admittedly minor, but they do give the impression that Betjeman might have scanned through his earlier work in hope of inspiration.

This idea is supported by a verse that appeared in *Church Poems* (1981), where the poet's efforts were reunited with the drawings of John Piper. 'Lines on the New Buildings, Magdalen College, Oxford' was an amalgam of those written by the Reverend James Hurdis (1763–1801), and those added by the Laureate (1980):

> How gracefully it rests upon its shadow
> In the deep quiet of this walled-in meadow,
> Grave, grey and classical and on its own
> A hymn by Addison in Oxford stone
> Magdalen New Buildings!
> :   :   :   :   :   :
> Let me go on in Hurdis's blank verse
> So very blank and to the point and terse;
>
> ('LINES ON THE NEW BUILDINGS', ll. 1–5; 9–10)

In his preface to the slender volume, Betjeman wrote that he hoped it would 'humanise churches a bit for those who think of them only in terms of architectural style or rateable value'.[77] Though he had softened his attitude towards Pevsner, this was a shot both at his type of academic rigour and at developers (recalling *Pity About the Abbey*). As he concluded: '[w]ithout a church I think a place lacks its heart and identity'.[78]

The technique of using someone else's words as a catalyst for his own was reprised when the Prince of Wales married in the summer of 1981. For the descriptively titled 'Ode on the Marriage of HRH Prince Charles to the Lady Diana Spencer in St Paul's Cathedral on 29 July 1981', assistance came by means of a four-line quotation from a Georgian 'ringer's rhyme' (l. 5) which adorns a board in the church at St. Endellion:

> *Let's all in love and friendship hither come*
> *Whilst the shrill Treble calls to thundering Tom,*
> *And since bells are for modest recreation*
> *Let's rise and ring and fall to admiration.*
>
> ('ODE ON THE MARRIAGE', ll. 1–4)

This tininnabulous pentameter gives Betjeman the means to continue and the result is in fact his best Laureate lyric for some years. Once again, this is partly due to the fact that he also addresses the couple (but especially the Prince) personally:

> Blackbirds in City churchyards hail the dawn,
> Charles and Diana, on your wedding morn.
> Come College youths, release your twelve-voiced power
> Concealed within the graceful belfry tower[.]
>
> ('ODE ON THE MARRIAGE', LL. 16–19)

In the final section, the tone changes in a manner which has since gained a certain irony. In neat quatrameters, Betjeman recalls his earlier 'Ballad of the Investiture', noting that the lonely life he had envisaged for Charles 'has disappeared'. 'And all of those assembled there,' he goes on, 'Are joyful in the love you share' (ll. 27–28). The Prince's marriage ended in divorce in 1996, and while the change in metre emphasises the poignancy of that outcome, it is really hindsight that suggests the minor key.

The 'Ode' turned out to be Betjeman's last poem of any magnitude. Printed on a decorated broadsheet, it was limited to 125 autographed copies. Sadly, he whose poor handwriting had long been the source of self-effacing humour now signed his name in an irregular, tortured scrawl. This both startlingly illustrates how his health had deteriorated, but also proves what resolve it must have taken to write the poem at all; that it is by no means a disgrace – and far finer than the 'Queen Mother' piece – is little short of a miracle. But the clinical observer would ignore these biographical matters and ask merely: was Betjeman any good as Poet Laureate?

It was (and remains) a difficult appointment: to some, those who receive it are a puppet of the Establishment; others, less radical in spirit, find themselves disappointed if the height they have set for the unhappy incumbent is not reached. Betjeman was indeed a Royalist: the 'Ode' refers to the 'human, friendly line that never fails' (l. 11), and he had stated in his earlier *Parkinson* television appearance that the monarchy gives continuity to life.[79] As to the work, it is evident that, thanks to infirmity, he increasingly needed a hook on which to hang his verses. The tactic only really worked for the 'Ode', but it was a question of getting the job done: for 'Hundreds of birds in the air', it had been whisky, for the Jubilee hymn, 'Lord of the Years'. When the subject itself was the hook, that is, when Betjeman found himself on more familiar territory (as in 'Inland Waterway' and 'In Memory of George Whitby, Architect'), he could clearly produce work that ranked with his best. Yet this only highlights the awkward nature of the Laureate Poem. The term itself is almost an oxymoron, for the difficulties of writing a piece that fits a time or event, that commemorates, celebrates, is understandable to all and yet remains quintessentially *of* its author, makes the task a chimera in the extreme. Consider again 'Hundreds of birds in the air', but at the same time consider the fact that of all the official pieces that Tennyson wrote, only 'Ode on the

Death of the Duke of Wellington' (1852) and 'The Charge of the Light Brigade' (1855) really stand close scrutiny today. Indeed, is his 'Opening of the Indian and Colonial Exhibition by the Queen' (1885) a poem from which the greatest Laureate's reputation may be *truly* divined?

> Welcome, welcome with one voice!
> In your welfare we rejoice,
> Sons and brothers that have sent,
> From isle and cape and continent,
> Produce of your field and flood,
> Mount and mine and primal wood;
>
> (TENNYSON, 'OPENING OF THE INDIAN AND COLONIAL EXHIBITION', ll. 1–6)[80]

(In a very strange diagonal indeed, this almost reads as if Tennyson were parodying Betjeman on a bad day!)

In his article, 'The Laureate Business or the Laureate in Englishness' (*Quadrant*, September 1985), Michael Hulse rightly commented that, like Masefield, 'Betjeman persuasively upheld a tradition of celebrating Englishness'. He was right too to add that this came less from the official poems than the 'body of work already written when [they] took office'.[81] However, as I have shown – and will continue to show – he is quite *wrong* to claim that Betjeman portrayed a 'sickly idyll' that adds up to a back catalogue that is 'almost all rubbish'.[82] In fact, there is a case to be made for claiming his argument to be unfairly loaded, including as it does quotations from 'Myfanwy' (1940), 'Youth and Age on Beaulieu River, Hants' (1945), 'St. Saviour's, Aberdeen Park, Highbury, London, N.' (1948) and 'I. M. Walter Ramsden' (1953). That is, two expressions of aestheticism, one of devotion and the London landscape, one of lament, but none more recent than 1954. How different the article could have been had he selected 'Shattered Image' (1970), 'Harvest Hymn' (1966), 'Inexpensive Progress' (1955) and 'Huxley Hall' (1953). Indeed, Hulse makes his intent clear from the outset by referring to a piece about the Wiltshire town of Highworth, which Betjeman had written in 1950. 'Ah, Highworth as a whole!', it begins, before revelling with glee in the '[i]vy-leafed toadflax with its little purple flowers', the 'sound of tea being cleared away', and the sudden 'burst of bells' from the church. 'That was Sunday evening in Highworth,' says Betjeman, '[t]hat was England.'[83] Except, says Hulse, it wasn't: '[s]omewhere in Birmingham a man was beating his wife, and in the next house another was sitting with his elbows on the table wondering how to pay the outstanding bills if he didn't come up with a job next week'. Betjeman's 'rhapsodic passage' must, therefore, be 'sentimental and fundamentally dishonest'.[84]

Crucially, this piece (despite appearing in *First and Last Loves* [1952]) was *not* an article, but the script of a radio broadcast. It formed one part of a series that saw Betjeman visit various places in the British Isles – Ventnor, Ilfracombe, Weymouth and so on – in order to comment on their situation, architecture and inherent beauty. It was thus a portrait of Highworth as viewed through the eyes of a poet on a particular day. But, yes, behind the door of any of the thatched cottages or inns a murder could have been taking place. Betjeman was content to leave such matters to the newspapers, the police and Agatha Christie: when they do not seek the news, people listen to the radio largely for pleasure, and this was clearly the ethos behind the series. It was also important that someone, in 1950, pointed out that beauty could still be found just up the road, so to speak. One has only to look at any contemporary comedy film (note, *comedy*) – *Passport to Pimlico* (1949), say – to see that, thanks to wartime bombing, large areas of many cities had become inhuman wastelands. Though the characters in those films act like they are used to the scars of destruction that lay about them, the real inhabitants of Pimlico, or Southampton, Bristol or Coventry might well have sought comfort in the affirmation that the Third Reich had not wiped the entire country off the planet.

Hulse's article implies that Betjeman's broadcast should have been relevant to everyone who might hear it, but the idea of a totalising grand narrative is unsustainable: we have to settle for an intertwining set of micro-histories, which coexist in some all-embracing Venn diagram of chronology. This point was clarified the year after Hulse's work was published when the translation of Jean-François Lyotard's *The Postmodern Condition* became available in Britain. In this influential text, Lyotard wrote that grand narrative (or meta-narrative) 'has lost its credibility, regardless of what mode of unification it uses, regardless of whether it is a speculative narrative or a narrative of emancipation'.[85] The decline, he continued, could be seen as 'an effect of the blossoming of techniques and technologies since the Second World War, which has shifted emphasis from the ends of action to its means'. The concept has continued to gain momentum in the ensuing years, although Anthony Powell pre-empted it in *A Dance to the Music of Time* (1951–1975), where the recurring reappearance of various characters throughout underlines the overlapping of life and life that exists in human relationships.

Coda

Following the discovery of a number of earlier works in the archive of the University of Victoria, Canada (which had bought some of Betjeman's papers when he moved from Cloth Fair in the 1970s), John Murray published *Uncollected Poems* in 1982. The best of its content has already been discussed, and it is not my intention to dwell on the rest now. Suffice it to say that it is not a fitting epitaph for the Laureate. Indeed, as Betjeman himself said when discussing proofs with Murray and John Sparrow, there may be 'a good line somewhere, [but] I think I was quite right to reject this or that'.[86] Yet *Time with Betjeman* – the series in which this sequence was shown – *was* a fitting epitaph. Produced for the BBC by Jonathan Stedall, it drew together clips of

Betjeman's best television broadcasts, interspersing them with contemporary interviews with the poet, and old friends like Osbert Lancaster, John Piper and Barry Humphries. The title was telling, as there is a very real sense throughout that the end is nigh. By now, Betjeman was wheelchair-bound and clearly very frail, but what is even clearer is that his mind had remained sharp: in the sixth programme, for example, he is not only seen reciting Tennyson's 'Northern Farmer, New Style' (1869) in a perfect North Country accent, but also Larkin's 'This Be The Verse' (1974), with eyes asparkle as he sounds the expletives (perhaps realising that the BBC will have to transmit the sequence after 9:00pm – or bleep them out – as a result).

In the final programme, Stedall takes Betjeman back to the North Cornish coast – the setting for several of his poems and the backdrop against which many of the happier interludes of his life were played out. Here, he reiterates that his success was due to no more than luck. He also reveals that his terror of dying was starting to diminish: 'I used to think death was some fearful jab of pain. I'm not so certain now that it's not with us all the time.' This explains the 'surgeon's knife' in 'Before the Anaesthetic' (1945), the spider's 'horrible poison blade' in 'The Cottage Hospital' (1948) and the 'painful deathbed' of 'Devonshire Street W.1' (1953). Stedall quotes the theologian H. A. Williams's view that death is simply 'letting go'. With this Betjeman agrees, but when asked if he has any regrets, he side steps by remarking famously: 'I haven't had enough sex.' Despite a couple of verses appearing in the autumn of 1983 – 'Honest Doubts' in *Orbis*, and 'Anniversary Comment' in *Outposts* – the harvest was almost over. In September, he suffered another heart attack and, the following month, another stroke. Friends would visit and read to him in his London home, including Gerard Irvine, who also gave communion. The room was usually so cluttered that he often had to arrange the wine on an ironing board.[87] This probably accounts for Betjeman's sudden uttering, during one such visit, of what Irvine believes to be his last poem:

> Of all the things within this house that are by me possessed
> I love, oh yes, I love by far, my *ironing* board the best.[88]

As the hay was gathered in and he 'lost hold', there remained 'the bonus of laughter'.

CHAPTER SEVEN

Summoned by Bells

Changing Horizons

In his preface to *Uncollected Poems* (1982), Bevis Hillier wrote that '[i]f you want to know what happened in the twentieth century, read A. J. P. Taylor's volume in the *Oxford History of England*; if you want to know what it was like to *live* in the twentieth century, read the poems of John Betjeman'.[1] This neat variation on Taylor's own comments about the French Revolution writings of Messrs. Thompson and Carlyle is challenged by Michael Hulse's colourful reminder that Betjeman did not mirror the lives of *everyone* in England at that time.[2] However, if we accept that history is comprised of a myriad micro-histories, then we must also accept that, to varying degrees, many of them intersect.

While discussing 'On Leaving Wantage 1972', G. M. Harvey noted Betjeman's skill in writing verses that focus on personal crises, but which then 'expand into a poignant general statement of the human condition'.[3] If such connection is evident in one of the shorter pieces, then it must be true of *Summoned by Bells* (1960), which, as an autobiography, *is* a micro-history. Indeed, at the end of the television version (1976), Betjeman hints that the poem's value is greatest where it overlaps with the lives of its readers: 'I think it's only when we're young that an autobiography is interesting [. . .],' he remarks, 'because it still has in it things we share in common: struggles at home; struggles at school; and then, struggles to get a job.'[4]

Of course, books that fail to do this do not cease to be important, as assimilating varying perspectives of time, place and circumstance helps create a more rounded view of society (and its history). Nevertheless, the tendency to impose our own socio-cultural viewpoint on a text is natural – and almost impossible to eradicate. Literature does not exist in a vacuum: readers bring with them an awareness of the past (both general and particular), an awareness of the author and an awareness of other texts. All of this can affect response; thus it is not only lives that intersect, but also reactions to discourse. These ideas were explored by the German theorist H. R. Jauss, whom we met in CHAPTER ONE. To recap, Jauss understood that the difference between what the reader anticipates from a work (the 'horizon of expectations') and what that work delivers is in some way quantifiable.[5] He defined this as the 'aesthetic distance', and found that the problem with much structuralist analysis was that it assumed a literary work to have a single meaning which required excavation; Jauss appreciated that discourse has a dynamism which leads to essential shifts in understanding, and that these shifts need to be explained.

As advance sales of *Summoned by Bells* were in the region of 35,000 copies, most purchasers had probably read 'Trebetherick' (1940), 'Parliament Hill Fields' (1940) and 'North Coast Recollections' (1947) and probably would have been aware of what they were going to get.[6] But the fact that an audience may know Betjeman's work well enough to make an informed guess about content does not necessarily mean it has any first-hand knowledge of all the experiences the book describes – in spite of its author's hopes. Though everyone endures the same 'struggles' that he listed, his life as an Oxford undergraduate, for example, is likely to have appeared elitist when the poem was first published, and even more so in 1985 when Hulse's article appeared in *Quadrant*. Such feelings have perhaps lessened in recent years as successful applications for university places have continued to rise. However, weighed against this is the absence of student grants, which forces many modern undergraduates to fund their studies by working. This is detrimental not only to intensive study, but also student solidarity, discussion and coterie humour – those 'private giggles of a private world' (p. 98) that Betjeman had enjoyed in the 1920s.

The aesthetic distance of *Summoned by Bells*, then, is in a constant state of flux, being affected by its author's fame, the time that has elapsed since his death and the fact that the world he describes has ceased to be. Yet its status as an autobiography makes it a social document that is just as worthy of study historically as it is in terms of any literary contribution; it also represents Betjeman's most sustained attempt at establishing an identity – and, in this, recalls Tennyson's 'Supposed Confessions of a Second-Rate Sensitive Mind' (1830). Furthermore, if its nuances are present elsewhere in Betjeman's back catalogue, it clearly represents a microcosm of his work as a whole.

The Epic

It was probably *My Apologia* (1940), a long verse-autobiography by his old Oxford tutor, J. M. Thompson (1878–1956), which gave Betjeman the idea for the poem.[7] Thompson's title was undoubtedly a reference to Cardinal Newman's *Apologia Pro Vita Sua* (1864) and *An Agnostic's Apology* (1893) by Sir Leslie Stephen. In calling the preface to the 1970 edition of *Ghastly Good Taste* 'An Aesthete's Apologia', it is evident that Betjeman too identified with these Victorian thinkers. But, as Hillier notes, the 'ultimate model' for *Summoned by Bells* (in terms of poetry) was obviously Wordsworth's *The Prelude* (1850).[8]

While both Laureates employed regular decasyllabic blank verse, there are certain differences between these two works which should be noted. *The Prelude*, for instance, begins in classical epic fashion, *in medias res*, during Wordsworth's walk to 'the Vale that I had chosen' (I. 100). There is veritable delight in his escape 'From the vast city, where I long had pined / A discontented sojourner' (I. 7–8). Betjeman, conversely, is *not* discontented, and by opening his story instead from a remembered beginning at suburban 31 West Hill *as a child*, he asserts his distance not only from Wordsworth, but also the epic tradition. (One can also assume, therefore, that his early working title of 'The Epic' was laced with irony):

> Here on the southern slope of Highgate Hill
> Red squirrels leap the hornbeams. Still I see
> Twigs and serrated leaves against the sky.
> The sunny silence was of Middlesex.
> (BETJEMAN, *SUMMONED BY BELLS*, I [P. 3])[9]

That this suburbia is leafy seems to subvert Wordsworth's pastoral idyll further, though it also explains why the post-war rape of the Middlesex landscape became such an important part of Betjeman's writing (see CHAPTER FOUR). It was also, as Maurice Bowra would later write, '[s]illy [. . .] to go Wordsworthing about' when it simply wasn't necessary.[10]

In terms of tone, the elder statesman is also much grander than the younger. Indeed, the radio broadcast of *Summoned by Bells* conveys a conversational intimacy that would be hard to reproduce for any reading of *The Prelude*. The main difference between the poems, however, is in the poets' estimations of themselves. The Lord of the Lakes means to show us the growth of his own mind, to convey the development of a 'transitory Being'.[11] But he also aligns himself quite explicitly with Milton very early on:

> The earth is all before me. With a heart
> Joyous, nor scared at its own liberty,
> I look about; and should the chosen guide
> Be nothing better than a wandering cloud,
> I cannot miss my way.
> (WORDSWORTH, *THE PRELUDE*, I. 14–18)[12]

Compare this with the conclusion of *Paradise Lost* (1667, revised 1674):

> The world was all before them, where to choose
> Thir place of rest, and Providence thir guide:
> They hand in hand with wandering steps and slow,
> Through *Eden* took their solitarie way.
> (MILTON, *PARADISE LOST*, XII. 646–649)[13]

Milton was the poet against whom Wordsworth measured himself, and Milton's was the torch he wanted to take forward. This is self-evident here, but there is also a sense that he sees himself as an Adam-like pioneer. It is telling that he foresees 'poetic numbers' coming 'Spontaneously to clothe in priestly robe / A renovated spirit singled out' (I. 51–53). Though such ecclesiastical terms refer to the nature of poetry, they betray the fact that Wordsworth sees himself as a preacher too. Later, he writes:

> In the familiar circuit of my home,
> Here might I pause, and bend in reverence
> To Nature, and the power of human minds,
> To men as they are men within themselves.
> How oft high service is performed within,
> When all the external man is rude in show,-
> Not like a temple rich with pomp and gold,
> But a mere mountain chapel, that protects
> Its simple worshippers from sun and shower.
> Of these, said I, shall be my song; of these,
> If future years mature me for the task,
> Will I record the praises, making verse
> Deal boldly with substantial things; in truth
> And sanctity of passion, speak of these,
> That justice may be done, obeisance paid
> Where it is due: thus haply I shall teach,
> Inspire, through unadulterated ears
>
> Pour rapture, tenderness, and hope, – my theme
> No other than the very heart of man [. . .].
> (WORDSWORTH, *THE PRELUDE*, XIII. 223–241)[14]

Betjeman's aim was rather more humble:

> My urge was to encase in rhythm and rhyme
> The things I saw and felt (I could not *think*).
> (*SUMMONED BY BELLS*, II [P. 17])

This is an honest claim, for it is not Betjeman's goal to mock his predecessor, rather to assert his 'otherness'. Dennis Brown makes an interesting point regarding the use of the word 'encase' here, suggesting that it may be an allusion to Wordsworth's own 'Cased in the unfeeling armour of old time' (in 'Elegiac Stanzas Suggested by a Picture of Peele Castle, in a Storm, Painted by Sir George Beaumont', 1807, l. 51).[15] However, he is probably correct to conclude that it is more a reflection of the 'artisan skills of the family firm the poet rejected'. This was certainly expected of him: soon into the second chapter, we learn that '"Following in Father's footsteps" was the theme / Of all my early childhood' (pp. 14–15). Similarly, 'Fourth generation – yes, this is the boy' is a phrase which recurs throughout the poem from hereon, serving as fanfare now and reproach later when it becomes clear to Betjeman Senior that his dream is never going to be realised:

I was a poet. That was why I failed.
My faith in this chimera brought an end
To all my father's hopes. In later years,
Now old and ill, he asked me once again
To carry on the firm, I still refused.
And now when I behold, fresh-published, new,
A further volume of my verse, I see
His kind grey eyes look woundedly at mine,
I see his workmen seeking other jobs,
And that red granite obelisk that marks
The family grave in Highgate Cemetery
Points an accusing finger to the sky.

(*SUMMONED BY BELLS*, II [p. 21])

Brown is (to date) the only commentator to try to understand *Summoned by Bells* without criticising its author for failing to come up to some arbitrary standard. He agrees that one of the central themes of the poem is guilt, and adds masculinity – but masculinity on Betjeman's own terms, the poet being ever aware of this 'otherness' of his.[16] He is also aware that to be different is not always a good thing. Such becomes clear just two pages into the poem when, as the opening chapter's title page reveals, 'the author is told he is an alien':

"Your name is German, John"–
But I had always thought that it was Dutch . . .

(*SUMMONED BY BELLS*, II [p. 4])

This, in those grim days of the early twentieth century, leads to bullying taunts:

"Betjeman's a German spy–
Shoot him down and let him die:
Betjeman's a German spy,
A German spy, a German spy."

(*SUMMONED BY BELLS*, II [p. 28])

It is also around this time that Betjeman first learns about hell, being told of its horrors by Maud, the 'sadist and puritan' nanny of 'N.W.5 & N.6' (1958). This exposes an important dichotomy about *Summoned by Bells*: despite the safety of 'those evenings of the pre-war world' (p. 4) – that 'world of trains and buttered toast' – it is apparent that the poet's childhood was *not* intrinsically happy, after all. Darkness always seems to be lurking and the aforementioned bullying leads into a passage about the 'art' of walking home from school unattacked; this is soon joined by the 'Doom! Shivering Doom!' (p. 66) of Marlborough College, where 'Big Fire' (a group of captains and their friends who ran the Upper School) dished out humiliating punishments, the fear of which kept Betjeman in check for his first term under their jurisdiction – 'And three terms afterwards' (p. 71).[17]

Perhaps, then, the poet's emphasis on childhood throughout his work reflects the fact that its innocent joys did not seem to last for long. Even on those carefree Cornish holidays, and despite the statement to the contrary, the list of frustrations that he gives is too long to dispel this idea:

> Bright as the morning sea those early days!
> Though there were tears, and sand thrown in my eyes,
> And punishments and smells of mackintosh,
> Long barefoot climbs to fetch the morning milk,
> Terrors from hissing geese and angry shouts,
> Slammed doors and waitings and a sense of dread,
> Still warm as shallow sea-pools in the sun
> And welcoming to me the girls and boys.
>
> (*SUMMONED BY BELLS*, IV [P. 35])

The warmth of the welcome is intended to negate the negativity that preceded it, but greater brevity would have been more effective, as the following abridgement indicates:

> Though there were punishments and angry shouts,
> Still warm and shallow sea-pools in the sun
> And welcoming to me the girls and boys.

In spite of the upbeat close, the memory clearly retained the things that caused discomfort and distress.

Ironically, had Betjeman played out the role his parents had written for him, it could have distanced him even further from the world in which he lived. The problem was that the family's lower social position already set him apart from the other Highgate residents. Indeed, the pain of being spurned by the parents of Peggy Purey-Cust, his childhood sweetheart, is explained almost too fully in 'False Security' (1955), where he is branded (in block capitals) a 'COMMON LITTLE BOY'. The exact same charge is levelled by the Misses Tunstall and Usher, swarthy (and ghastly) holiday helpers, in chapter IV. It is small wonder that in trying to disprove such accusations, Betjeman – in childhood – became a snob himself; and while this does *not* explain the yearning for words over woodwork, it probably did not help matters, as his father seems to have been aware:

> "– now I look at you –
> Bone-lazy, like my eldest brother Jack,
> A rotten, low, deceitful little snob.
> Yes, I'm in trade and proud of it, I am!"
>
> (*SUMMONED BY BELLS*, VIII [P. 84])

(Note how the poet gives his father his due here – at his own expense.)

Betjeman looks to have got what he wanted as far as Brown is concerned, who ends his assessment with the notion that the product of *Summoned by Bells* is 'a Betjeman, and a *gentleman*'.[18] Underpinning both, but especially the former, is the journey that takes this self-proclaimed 'middle-class youth' from boy to poet.[19] And whereas Wordsworth might refer to himself merely as 'a youth undisciplined in verse' (VI. 670), Betjeman is candid about his early efforts, allowing us to see what the 'magic of [his] Highgate pen' (p. 18) could (or rather, *could not*) produce:

> When the moors are pink with heather
>   When the sky's as blue as the sea,
> Marching all together
>   Come fairy folk so wee.
> :   :   :   :   :
> Some in green and some in red
>   And some with a violet plume,
> And a little cap on each tiny head
>   Watching the bright white moon.
>
>   (*SUMMONED BY BELLS*, II [P. 18])

'My goodness me! It seemed perfection then,' he tells us with mild embarrassment before recalling how he later 'falsified the date' below to make it seem as though he were only seven, not eight, when these 'weak stanzas' were written. 'Atlantic rollers [. . .] pealing church bells and the puff of trains' were calling out for expression, but Betjeman found himself unable to translate what he saw and felt into words: 'I caught at them and missed and missed again' (p. 20), as he says. This is a nod to Book I of *The Prelude*, where the young Wordsworth flounders in a stolen rowing boat: 'I struck and struck again' (I.380). One can imagine his successor seeing the words drip like water through his fingers, never to be held on the page.

Pocketfuls of rhyme continue to highlight this growth, but the lyrics also create a degree of rhythmic variation that *The Prelude* lacks. Indeed, they are, as Patrick Taylor-Martin remarks, very much 'in the manner of Tennyson's *The Princess*', though they do more than simply 'diversify the tone'.[20] John Wain, in his otherwise scathing review, realised that they come into play at 'most of the poem's more intense moments'.[21] However, he was attempting to argue with the preface, where Betjeman tells us that his use of rhyme is limited to 'the more hilarious' incidents in the narrative. For Wain, this suggests that the reader is supposed 'to take the whole performance as a joke'.[22] Examples of undergraduate drollery, such as this parody of 'John Peel', perhaps lend weight to the charge:

> D'ye ken Kolkhorst in his artful parlour,
>   Handing out the drink at his Sunday morning gala?

Some get sherry and some Marsala –
With his arts and his crafts in the morning!
(*SUMMONED BY BELLS*, IX [P. 96])[23]

However, like 'The Fairies' (which Wain may have taken to be fake), this is a *quotation* from Betjeman's earlier incarnation.[24] The lyrics, conversely, are written by the contemporaneous Betjeman *in the manner of that earlier self.* Of course, it is possible that he was also attempting to diffuse future humiliation by giving himself a means of saving face should his inner thoughts be mocked after publication. The sensitivity he felt on this point is evident in 'Tregardock', which first appeared in *Atlantic Monthly* in February 1965:

Only the shore and cliffs are clear.
   Gigantic slithering shelves of slate
In waiting awfulness appear
   Like journalism full of hate.
   :   :   :   :
And I on my volcano edge
   Exposed to ridicule and hate
Still do not dare to leap the ledge
   And smash to pieces on the slate.
('TREGARDOCK', LL. 5–8; 25–28)

The brittle fragility of the poet is unmistakable, his nakedness obvious and his awareness of critical contempt acute.

It is with some significance that the first lyric proper comes at the end of chapter V, for this moment sees Betjeman start to become the person that Brown describes.[25] Here, at the Dragon School (1917–20), his acting capabilities began to grow and his talent for oration started to flourish.[26] In the context of the whole poem, it is also evident that this was where Betjeman was first treated with respect by an adult: his father encourages his writing at first, but only as a hobby; his nanny, as we know, is a terrifying sadist; the Misses Usher and Tunstall dismiss him and his mother is still largely absent at this stage. Against these there stands the 'formidable' Gerald Haynes ('(Harrow and Keble)'), who is introduced, ironically, when he gives the young poet a beating for admitting to talking. Though innocent, Betjeman saw that this act made him a 'schoolboy hero to the dorm at last' (p .48); the important difference is that Haynes seems to have agreed:

"I liked the way you took that beating, John.
Reckon yourself henceforth a gentleman."
(*SUMMONED BY BELLS*, V [P. 49])

Despite the almost Biblical simplicity of the question 'Were those the words that made me follow him [. . .]?', the poet admits that they were not: Haynes's vital ingredients were in fact his 'kindness and his power to share / Joys of his own, churches and botany' (p. 49). The former cemented the bond for it was also at the Dragon School that Betjeman's penchant for church-crawling started to grow: 'Can words express,' he enquires, 'the unexampled thrill / I first enjoyed in Norm., E.E. and Dec?' (p. 48).[27] For him, Haynes 'was the giver: ours it was to take' (p. 49) and it is at this precise instant that the lyric appears, beginning with an almost Wordsworthian pastoral idyll:

> The bindweed hung in leafy loops
> O'er half a hundred hawthorn caves,
> For Godstow bound, the white road wound
> In swirls of dust and narrow shaves,
> And we were biking, Red Sea troops,
> Between the high cow-parsley waves.
> (SUMMONED BY BELLS, LYRIC I, P. 49, LL. 1–6)

From Godstow, the pupils take a boat, and Betjeman muses on the 'world of water weed' beneath:

> Deep forests of the bladed reed
> Whose wolves are rats of slimy coat,
> Whose yellow lily-blossoms need
> Broad leaves to keep themselves afloat.
> (SUMMONED BY BELLS, LYRIC I, P. 50, LL. 21–24)

Note how he likens the cow-parsley to the parted Red Sea in Exodus 14, and thus the children of the Dragon School's flight to the children of Israel's escape from bondage in Egypt. Indeed, the lyric (and so the chapter) ends with the regret that the escapees must, as 'sad returning slaves', go back to 'bell and rule and smell of school' (ll. 40–41).[28] Such makes this a taste of freedom, palpable and pure, and freedom – as will become apparent – is an essential theme in *Summoned by Bells*. Thus it can be no coincidence that a change in tone comes first with the guidance that Haynes offered and, secondly, with the discovery of nineteenth-century aesthetics:

> One lucky afternoon in Chaundy's shop
> I bought a book with tipped-in colour plates-
> 'City of Dreaming Spires' or some such name-
> Soft late-Victorian water-colours framed
> Against brown paper pages. Thus it was
> 'Sunset in Worcester Gardens' meant for me
> Such beauty in that black and shallow pool
> That even today, when from the ilex tree
> I see its shining length, I fail to hear
> The all-too-near and omnipresent train.
> (SUMMONED BY BELLS, V [P. 47])

The Journey Begins

With the trio of books, churches and Victoriana in place, here indeed was the start of Betjeman *as* Betjeman – the public Betjeman that the world would come to know. But it can be no coincidence either that the chapter opens with a description of 'Percival Mandeville, the perfect boy' (p. 43).[29] As an example of masculinity, the 'Upright and honourable, good at games, / Well-built, blue-eyed' youngster is a parody of an English stereotype. By placing Lyric I at the *end* of the chapter, the future Laureate is thus showing himself to be the polar opposite of Mandeville and his perceived flawlessness. This is underlined by the fact that, like its author, the lyric itself is not perfect.[30] Amidst nature's beauty, for instance, is this rather jarring metaphor:

> The hideous larva from the mud
> Clung to a reed with patient hold,
> Waiting to break its sheath and make
> An aeroplane of green and gold.
> (*SUMMONED BY BELLS*, LYRIC I, P. 50, LL. 27–30)

While an earlier reference to a bicycle, with its 'Sturmey-Archer gear' (l. 9), carries a nostalgia that works well in this setting, the aeroplane is decidedly out of place. As a description of a dragonfly, it is an amusing variation on Hopkins's 'As kingfishers catch fire, dragonflies draw flame' (1881). However, like the reference to the 'belly-floppers' (l. 33), it is quite deliberate.

In chapter III, Betjeman recounts his poetic progress and reveals how he felt himself 'as good as Campbell [. . .] / And very nearly up to Longfellow' (p. 29); earlier still, we learn that 'Internal rhyming, as in Shelley's "Cloud", / Seemed [. . .] perfection' and that poeticisms such as '"O'er" and "ere" and "e'en" / Were words [he] liked to use' (p. 17). Both these elements, which are rare in Betjeman, are present in the first stanza of Lyric I:

> O*'er* half a hundred hawthorn caves,
> For Godstow *bound*, the white road *wound*
> (*SUMMONED BY BELLS*, LYRIC I, P. 49, LL. 2–3 – MY ITALICS)

Taken with all the other evidence, it becomes clear that youthful inability is present by design and that the piece is a pastiche of his early attempts to reach the goal he set himself. Thus poetic clumsiness is reflected in the physical clumsiness displayed in the boat ('I boarded one and made her rock – / "Shut up, you fool," a master cried.' (ll. 15–16)), which is reflected in turn by the metre: though there are four stresses to each line, three different rhyme schemes are at play (the first stanza is ABCBAB, the fourth ABABAB, the rest ABABCB). Such lack of symmetry prevents this from merely mirroring the oscillations of the water (which could have been achieved if the final stanza had been ABCBAB like the first). But though the 'gap from feeling to accomplishment' was '[i]n Highgate days [. . .] yawning wide' (p. 18), for all its imperfections, Lyric I indicates that it was starting to close by the dawn of the 1920s.

The point that many critics seem unable to appreciate Betjeman's ability to become a character has been raised before. In *Summoned by Bells*, it is evident that the character presented is not *himself* so much as his *younger self*. Sadly, this self-dramatising skill has led to some confusion. Patrick Taylor-Martin, for one, feels compelled to berate the poet for the following:

> Poor Mother, walking bravely on the lawn,
> Her body one huge toothache! Would she die?
> And if she died could I forgive myself?
>
> (*SUMMONED BY BELLS*, VIII [P. 80])

This is out of context and actually comes after a long list of ailments that Mother claims are troubling her:

> "Dr. Macmillan, who's so good and cheap,
> Says I will tire my kidneys if I stoop[.]
> :   :   :   :   :   :
> He says my teeth are what is wrong, the roots
> Have been attacked by dangerous bacilli
> Which breed impurities through all my blood[.]
> :   :   :   :   Mrs. Bent
> Had just the same (but not, of course, so bad);
> She nearly died, poor thing, till Captain Bent
> Insisted she should have them out at once.
> But mine are ossified into my gums – [. . .]"
>
> (*SUMMONED BY BELLS*, VIII [P. 80])

Having already drawn attention to his apparently artless record of the 'artless things' his mother used to say (p. 80), Betjeman – with proto-Alan Bennett precision – is obviously mocking her hypochondria. This makes the image of her body being 'one huge toothache' almost cruel, but note that, as usual, it is tempered by the poet's omnipresent sense of guilt.

A second lyric is introduced prior to this cameo, depicting the end of the poet's time at Marlborough School. A thumbnail sketch of adolescence, it also demonstrates an improvement in ability since those Dragon days:

> The smell of trodden leaves beside the Kennet,
>   On Sunday walks, with Swinburne in my brain,
> November showers upon the chalk dust, when it
>   Would turn to streaming milk in Manton Lane
> And coming back to feel one's footsteps drag
> At smells of burning toast and cries of "Fag!"
>
> (*SUMMONED BY BELLS*, LYRIC II, P. 71, LL. 1–6)

Unlike Lyric I, Lyric II is completely even: neither its iambic pentameters, nor its rhyme scheme (ABABCC) waver from their bounds. The teenage Betjeman's affinity for Swinburne is also obvious from the reference to him, but is heightened by the pairing of 'Kennet' (l. 1) and 'when it' (l. 3), which appropriately recalls the 'roses' / 'snow's is' rhyming in that poet's 'A Ballad of Dreamland' (1878). However, on the radio broadcast of *Summoned by Bells*, Betjeman pronounces 'when it' with stress on the final hard 't'. By suggesting it to be a single word in this way, he emphasises the humour of ineptitude and so informs the reader that the level of verse-making competence he sought still eluded him a little.

The second stanza is also awash with suitably romantic images of Marlborough. In fact, it almost drowns in them:

> The after-light that hangs along the hedges,
>   On sunward sides of them when sun is down,
> The sprinkled lights about the borough's edges,
>   The pale green gas-lamps winking in the town,
> The waiting elm-boughs black against the blue
> Which still to westward held a silver hue-
>
> (SUMMONED BY BELLS, LYRIC II, P. 71, LL. 7–12)

Though Tennyson, Hardy or even Morris's *The Earthly Paradise* could have inspired the imagery, here is that 'rollicking alliteration' that Betjeman admired in Swinburne, and later noted as a particular feature of the chorus in *Atalanta in Calydon* (1865) – as in 'The mother of months in meadow or plain' (l. 66).[31] (One laments that Betjeman did not update Swinburne by writing 'Atalanta in Croydon'.)

As Betjeman would later assert, 'when one's in love, what other way can you express yourself really effectively but in poetry?'[32] This is the emotional crux of the third stanza, where the focus shifts to the school fives-courts. Having returned here, after waiting for 'God knows what' (l. 14), he then somewhat theatrically invokes the heavens: 'O stars above! / Perhaps what I was waiting for was love!' (ll. 14–15). This is teenage angst in a nutshell; the final couplet is similarly revealing:

> And what is love? And wherefore is its shape
> To do with legs and arms and waist and nape?
>
> (SUMMONED BY BELLS, LYRIC II, P. 72, LL. 17–18)

The references to body parts are Swinburnian yes, but they are also adolescent – note how the stresses in the last line fall on the 'legs and arms and waist and nape', accentuating lustful preoccupation exactly as it exists at that impressionable age. These 'tremulous desires' (l. 19) are spoken by Betjeman in a soft, almost breathless voice, and it therefore seems inappropriate that the 'delightful illness' (l. 21) is described as putting him off his *'stroke'* (l. 22, my italics); inappropriate, that is, until one realises that it heralds the object of this yearning – the unnamed, motor-car mad, bicycling boy with whom the chapter closes.[33] In light of this, the shift from lyric back to blank verse is worth considering:

> Here, 'twixt the church tower and the chapel spire
> Rang sad and deep the bells of my desire.
>
> Desire for what? I think I can explain.
> The boys I worshipped did not notice me:
> The boys who noticed me I did not like . . .
> And life was easier in terms of jokes
> And gossip, chattered with contemporaries-
> (SUMMONED BY BELLS, VII [P. 72])

The explanation of course comes from the adult Betjeman. On radio, he underlines this by going from that whisper to a sturdy (and much louder) enunciation, which takes the listener from waves of young love back to the pseudo-objectivity of reminiscence. This form of role-playing reappears in the brief third lyric:

> How proud beneath the swelling dome
> I sang Lord Ullin's daughter
> At Mrs. Dugdale's grand At Home
> To Lady Horsbrugh-Porter.
> (SUMMONED BY BELLS, LYRIC III, P. 100, LL. 1–4)

The 'swelling dome' is that of Sezincote House in Gloucestershire, where Betjeman spent many happy hours as an undergraduate. Note that he uses the same rhythm and rhyme as the *real* 'Lord Ullin's Daughter' (1875), written by his early role model Thomas Campbell. This implies the enjoyment of extemporised showing-off, and thus the lyric comes to symbolise the tremendous sense of freedom that we shall see he experienced at Oxford. Such newfound privacy and dignity is contra to the world of chapter VIII, which portrays the (by now) stifling Cornish holidays that marked the nadir of Betjeman's relationship with his father:

> "Just down for breakfast, sir? You're good enough
> To honour us by coming down at ten!
> Don't fidget, boy. Attention when I speak!
>   :   :   :   :   :   :
> "My boy, it's no good sulking. Listen here.
> You'll go to Bates and order me the car,
> You'll caddy for me on the morning round,
> This afternoon you'll help me dig for bait,

You'll weed the lawn and, when you've finished that,
I'll find another job for you to do.
I'll keep you at it as I've kept myself-
I'll have obedience! Yes, by God, I will!"
(*SUMMONED BY BELLS*, VIII [P. 84])

'"You damn well won't!"' retorts the young Betjeman, with what must have been shocking language for the time. Making for the door, slamming it against his father's weight he 'ran like mad and ran like mad and ran...': '"I'm free! I'm free!"' (p. 85). Free to do what? It is telling that Betjeman's rebellion was not against the establishment *per se*, but against his father's regimen. Indeed, after escaping this 'bogey-man' (p. 81), he goes church-crawling, and it is during one such trip that he finds the church of St. Ervan, whose priest lends him a copy of Arthur Machen's *The Secret Glory* (1922). The book clearly reflected his own life and needs, portraying as it does a callow, aesthetically minded youth with an interest in architecture. As Machen himself wrote, the story was essentially about a 'wretched, exiled, homesick boy comforted marvellously [. . .] with the theoria'.[34] Betjeman added that there were also:

[. . .] laughs
At public schools, at chapel services,
At masters who were still 'big boys at heart'–
While all the time the author's hero knew
A Secret Glory in the hills of Wales.
(*SUMMONED BY BELLS*, IX [P. 87])

Prior to this meeting, Betjeman is religiously unfulfilled: 'Give me a God whom I can touch and see' (VII, p. 67), as he pleads from the chapel at Marlborough. The institutionalised portrayals of God that may have been found in public schools gave him nothing, and this lack is pivotal to both man and poem. Machen's schoolboy novel, coupled with earlier experiences at the Dragon School, gave him a taste of something that was missing. And while he fails to find religious experience on the grand scale when he visits such sites as the Holy Well near St. Enodoc (p. 87),

somewhere, somewhere underneath the dunes,
Somewhere among the cairns or in the caves
The Celtic saints would come to me, the ledge

Of time we walk on, like a thin cliff-path
High in the mist, would show the precipice.
(*SUMMONED BY BELLS*, VIII [P. 88])

What he needs is near, but remains always just out of reach. This explains the continuation of church-crawling, the acquisition of extensive knowledge re

High and Low, and the flirtation with Quakerism and the Countess of Huntingdon's Connection. It was a search for contentment and a means of allying his fears of the afterlife, but it was also about seeking acceptance: Betjeman, though a rebel in search of freedom (on his own terms), needed to *belong*. Hence his jokes, but hence his social aspiration too. This stemmed first from the fear of rejection ignited by the revelation about his 'German' name (p. 4), was compounded by the children who taunted him, and augmented by the mothers and others who rejected him as a Common Little Boy. No wonder he adored the peers at Oxford. No wonder he became famous. But do we blame these parents, maids, minders, captains, masters and tutors, as Larkin suggests we ought, or do we thank them?

Such angst contrasts with the liberty of the next chapter, the main title of which is 'The Opening World'. As the poet writes in its early stages –

> Too pleased with life, swept in the social round,
> :   :   :   :   :   :
> I cut tutorials with wild excuse,
> For life was luncheons, luncheons all the way–
> (SUMMONED BY BELLS, IX [P. 93])

(Note how the last line echoes Browning's 'The Patriot' (1855), which begins 'It was roses, roses, all the way'.) It was during this period that Betjeman became a regular attendee of G. A. Kolkhorst's Sunday morning salons, where sherry and humour were seen as the key ingredients of life. He was also a regular member of the set led by Maurice Bowra, the inimitable Dean (later Warden) of Wadham.

It was Bowra who imbued the poet with the idea that wisdom was 'Not memory-tests [. . .] / Not "first-class brains" and swotting for exams, / But humble love for what we sought and knew' (p. 103). This apparent authorization of 'otherness' leads straight into Lyric IV, essentially a suite in three parts, opening with the casting of a panoramic eye around undergraduate life. With its erratic rhyme scheme, it captures well the insouciance of those youthful undergraduate days:

> Come, Michael Arthur Stratford Dugdale, rise,
>   And Lionel Geoffrey Perry. It is ten.
> Binsey to Cowley, Oxford open lies.
>   They breakfasted at eight, the college men
> In college blazers clad and college ties
>   Who will be pouring out of lectures when
>   Eleven strikes,
> For morning coffee at 'The Super' bound,
>   And stack their bikes
> St. Mary Mag's Tractarian walls around.
> (SUMMONED BY BELLS, LYRIC IV, P. 103, LL. 1–10)

Betjeman and his set 'are pledged to drink with Ben' at the Liberal Club, and in these ten lines, the distance between the poet's 'open' Oxford of possibility, and the 'closed' Oxford of the (literally) uniform 'college men', is even more clear, the allegiances of the latter being skilfully underlined by both repetition ('college' appears three times) and alliteration (as in 'breakfasted' / 'blazers', 'college' / 'clad').

The roll call of full names would always be a particularly Betjemanian characteristic, but those here recall Claude in Clough's *Amours de Voyage* (1858), who begins the first letter to his friend Eustace with the salutation 'Dear Eustatio', thus immediately betraying his (rather less amusing) self-absorbed intellectuality. The same trait is apparent at the end of chapter VIII, when Betjeman explains to 'Aunt Elsie' that borrowing her car would help him get close enough to Biddy Walsham for his love to 'race along to her / On the electron principle' when they held hands. It is to Elsie's credit that she sees through this rubbish: '"So surely, John, it's sensible to walk?"' (p. 90).

The remainder of the first part of Lyric IV takes the form of a tour of Oxford. Thus after the Liberal Club we visit New College ('with her Wykehamists'), where the regularity of form is more obvious and reflects that quarter's academic rigour. It is perhaps no coincidence that we meet John Sparrow here, upon whose rigour Betjeman frequently called for proofreading purposes (not least for *Summoned by Bells* itself). We then find ourselves passing Balliol – where the Dean (F. F. 'Sligger' Urquhart) presides over "clever satyrs" and "well-bred fauns" (p. 104) – on our way to the Oxford University Dramatic Society. After the scenes of work in progress here, the narrative changes from its usual pentameter to lines of three and four stresses as the key simultaneously drops to the minor:

> And does an unimportant don
> In Pembroke College linger on,
>   With sported oak, alone?
> Do nearby bells of low St. Ebbe's
>   Ring all unnoticed there?
> (*SUMMONED BY BELLS*, LYRIC IV, P. 105, LL. 58–62)

Thus in the midst of all this life, we have death (and an indication of how it would preoccupy Betjeman until the end of his days).

In the final stanza, the key changes once again in yet another illustration of vacillation and caprice. In Wordsworthian style, he bids his 'Friends' to join him at his final port of call: Christ Church – 'The place they call The House / That shelters A. L. Rowse'. Here the tempo rises to the speed of

> my friend Auden and the clever men,
> Running like mad to miss the upper ten
> Who burst from 'Peck' in Bullingdonian brawl,
>   Jostling some pale-faced victim, you or me.
> (*SUMMONED BY BELLS*, LYRIC IV, P. 106, LL. 86–89)

As at Marlborough, Betjeman's aestheticism and 'otherness' in comparison to the hearties is plain:

> I tell you, Brian Howard,
> 'Fore God, I am no coward –
> But the triumphant philistines I see,
> And hear a helpless body splash in muddy Mercury.[35]
>
> (SUMMONED BY BELLS, LYRIC IV, P. 106, LL. 90–93)

Up to this point, the lyric is almost exclusively written in the present tense. This creates the impression of it having been composed contemporaneously, off the cuff, as it were – in similar fashion to the pastiche of 'Lord Ullin's Daughter'. The effect is compounded both by Betjeman's use of rhyme, which is erratic to say the least, and his use of metre, which, though hovering round the pentameter with some adhesion, deviates here and there for stress. Clearly, the tour is not only of Oxford, but also his own versifying skill. Such variety indicates that, while on course *to* himself, the essence *of* that self continued to elude him:

> With sports Bugattis roaring in my ears,
>   With 'Blackbirds' bursting from my gramophone,
> Lunching with poets, dining late with peers,
>   I felt that I had come into my own.
>
> What *was* my own? Large parts of it were jest.
>   :   :   :   :   :   :
> What was 'my own'? I partly liked to shock-
>   But strawberry-coloured trousers soon made way
> For shirts by Hawes and Curtis, hats by Lock,
>   And suits for which my father had to pay.
>
> What was my own? Week after sunny week
>   I climbed, still keeping in, I thought, with God,
> Until I reached what seemed to me the peak-
>   The leisured set in Canterbury Quad.
>
> (SUMMONED BY BELLS, LYRIC IV, PP. 106-7, LL. 94–98; 106-113)

With a perfect five-stressed rhythm, we have returned to Betjeman's present, looking back with him on his own past. The now constant ABAB rhyme keeps the momentum going and helps to break away from the carefree mood of the previous seven stanzas. The poet was becoming more discerning, and the eschewing of garish dress for quality garments is a metaphor for his burgeoning sophistication (although the fact that his father was still footing the bill is a reminder that he was not yet a man).

Separated by a break in the typesetting, the final section sheds light on the pinnacle Betjeman felt he had reached. Christ Church's Canterbury Quad was home to Edward James, godson of Edward VII, and patron to the Surrealist art movement.[36] But while James was a 'good catch' socially, this extract shows a much more powerful and enduring bond between the two:

> The sun that shines on Edward James
>   Shines also down on me:
> It's strange that two such simple names
>   Should spell such mystery.
> The air he breathes, I breathe it too–
> But where's he now? What does he do?
>   (*SUMMONED BY BELLS*, LYRIC IV, P. 107, LL. 114–119)

Notice the reference to Matthew 5: 45 – 'he maketh his sun to rise on the evil and on the good, and sendeth rain on the just and on the unjust'. There is both mockery and reverence here, Betjeman affording himself the former, James both! Yet there is also a sense that the poet is telling us that, to do what he eventually did, one needs a hero of *some* sort. The affinity he thus felt for James is indicated by way that the rhyme and metre pair 'me' with 'mystery' (both lines 115 and 117 being the only trimeters in the whole section). They were indeed two of a kind, and in the stanzas that follow we see them in their 1890s-style artistic reverie, discussing Eliot and Wilde as they drink champagne for breakfast in a silver-panelled room. Around those walls, according to the verse, were the words 'ARS LONGA VITA BREVIS EST' (l. 124). Hillier reveals that the full version (in James's translation) read 'art is long, life is short, but you can make life seem longer if you know how to use it'.[37] Very *Dorian Grey* is the sense of this 'own' that Betjeman had discovered, and very apart from the world of those 'contemporaries', with their 'tests and teams and toughs and games" (l. 133). But James was also phenomenally rich: he could afford to be at one with nature, tender as the Sensitive Plant in the Botanic Gardens (ll. 150–155). For Betjeman, reality was about to step in:

> But in the end they sent me down
>   From that sweet hothouse world of bells
> And crumbling walls of golden-brown
>   And dotty peers and incense-smells
> And dinners at the George and hock
> And Wytham Woods and Godstow Lock.
>   (*SUMMONED BY BELLS*, LYRIC IV, P. 108, LL. 156–161)

The abundance of those other riches, at once linked and underlined by the conjunctions, shows the regret Betjeman felt at losing them. Yet while art may be long, undergraduate life is certainly short and for many its end means the end of dreaming about what might be. Thenceforth the need for money becomes the overriding motivation of existence.

> Failed in Divinity! Oh count the hours
> Spent on my knees in Cowley, Pusey House,
> St. Barnabas', St. Mary Mag's, St. Paul's,
> Revering chasubles and copes and albs!
> Consider what I knew of 'High' and 'Low' . . .
>
> (*SUMMONED BY BELLS*, IX [P. 108])

We now know that Betjeman did, in fact, pass his 'Divvers'.[38] So why lie about it?

Betjeman may not have left Oxford 'as a Byronic figure', but he certainly didn't get what he wanted, which was to become 'a don, / Reading old poets in the library, / Attending chapel in an MA gown' (p. 109). As Dr. Judith Priestman of the Bodleian put it, the pass degree that Betjeman would have landed 'is a degree designed for rugby players'. I have no doubt that, to an aesthete, there can be no greater ignominy than to be awarded a prize meant for a hearty. Thus, in his eyes, *he might as well have failed*. Hence the pain that all Oxford – even 'The lean acacia tree in Trinity' – 'Stood strong and confident, outlasting me' (p. 109).[39] As Betjeman sips at his friend Ava's Amontillado, this self-inflicted failure allows guilt to rear its head once more, as his father's Biblically inflected words ring loud in his ear:

> "My boy, henceforward your allowance stops:
> You'll copy me, who with my strong right arm
> Alone have got myself the victory."
>
> (*SUMMONED BY BELLS*, VII [P. 110])[40]

The fear of going from Canterbury Quad to talking of 'samples, invoices and stock' makes the sight of the door to Gabbitas, Thring & Co., the scholastic agency in Sackville Street, a very welcome one. Yet the young poet is treated brusquely, the company being interested only in his commission-earning potential. To the reader, this awakening is a rude one:

> "The Principal will see you." "No degree?
> There is, perhaps, a temporary post
> As cricket master for the coming term
> At Gerrard's Cross. Fill in this form and give
> Qualifications – testimonials
> Will help – and if you are accepted, please
> Pay our commission promptly. Well, good day!"
>
> (*SUMMONED BY BELLS*, VII [P. 110])

The blank verse ends here, with Betjeman poised to go off like Paul Pennyfeather in Waugh's *Decline and Fall* (1928), although the poem continues, going on with a reprise of the final section of Lyric IV (by now in the past tense):

> The sun that shone on Edward James
>> Shone also down on me –
> A prep-school master teaching Games,
>> Maths, French, Divinity.
> Harsh hand-bells harried me from sleep
> For thirty pounds a term and keep.
>> (*SUMMONED BY BELLS*, LYRIC V, P. 110, LL. 1–6) [41]

(Note that the shorter second and fourth lines now pair – surely with deliberate irony – 'me' with 'Divinity'.) Edward James was not unceremoniously whisked away to the drudgery of the dorm; he continued to write poems, publishing them 'in volumes rare / Of hand-made paper bound up fine', which again recall that volume of corruption in Wilde's *The Picture of Dorian Gray* (1890). However, where the preface to that novel declares all art to be 'quite useless', James sees the worth of his friend's work and does something about it. Betjeman, for his part, seems somewhat surprised: 'And then, by Jove, he published mine!' (l. 12):

> They tell me he's in Mexico,
>> They will not give me his address;
> But if he sees this book he'll know
>> I do not value him the less.
> For Art is long and Life must end,
> My earlier publisher and friend.
>> (*SUMMONED BY BELLS*, LYRIC V, P. 111, LL. 13–18)

James may have been 'lost', but he is paid this tribute at the poem's close. The significance of the position is deserved, as it is because of him that Betjeman's art has enjoyed such great longevity. James was also the first man truly to believe in the future Laureate's poetry and, in so doing, offered him a way of realising his dream. And Betjeman, if not *quite* Betjeman at this point, was well on the road that would get him there in subsequent decades.

CHAPTER EIGHT

Conclusion

The Identity of Betjeman

Summoned by Bells has been described as 'the blank verse mini-epic of a sensitive and clever man, who invented himself in the teeth of parental, educational, and commercial pressure'.[1] Betjeman's fight against the rules is indeed central to the poem, and also explains his blasé attitude towards most of the paid employment he undertook, from Plunkett and Heddon Court onwards.

In his short treatise on the poet, Dennis Brown quotes Jean-François Lyotard's definition of postmodernism, and notes that 'Death in Leamington' (1930) is an example of the '*petit récit*' that the philosopher saw as 'the quintessential form of imaginative invention', vital in expressing mistrust of the hitherto prevalent metanarrative.[2] Similar examples may be found throughout Betjeman's work (even the 'Highworth' broadcast loathed by Hulse is a '*récit*' of a kind), but many pieces, like 'On Leaving Wantage, 1972', seem to connect with the world outside his immediate cultural sphere.

Summoned by Bells is certainly no metanarrative, but if the socio-cultural milieu of the 'struggles' therein has changed, the essence of them has not. Movements in the Jaussian aesthetic distance do not mean that a text ceases to be relevant and, as Lyotard reminds us, though a '*self* does not amount to much, [. . .] no self is an island; each exists in a fabric of relations that is now more complex and mobile than ever before. Young or old, man or woman, rich or poor, a person is always located at "nodal points" of specific communication circuits, however tiny these may be'.[3] The idea that Betjeman might be postmodern, then, is not as bizarre as it may first appear.

Marshall McLuhan differentiated between what he called the 'Gutenberg Galaxy' (that is, a culture of the printed word) and the 'electric age'. 'We are today as far into the electric age as the Elizabethans had advanced into the typographical and mechanical age,' he wrote. But '[w]hereas the Elizabethans were poised between medieval corporate experience and modern individualism, we reverse their pattern by confronting an electric technology which would seem to render individualism obsolete and the corporate interdependence mandatory'.[4] Thus for McLuhan, television 'symbolised a new era of global intercommunication which could not merely be subsumed within metanarratives about the progress of Western knowledge'.[5] Betjeman, we should recall, was one of the very first television personalities in the world, making his inaugural appearance for the BBC in September 1937.[6] He was also unquestionably the first television *poet*. At the conclusion of *The Poetry of*

Postmodernity (1994), Brown comments that the importance of this 'electronic age' has led to a situation in which songs like Bob Dylan's 'The Times They Are a-Changin'' now seem 'more relevant' than Larkin's 'Annus Mirabilis' (1967) or Tony Harrison's 'A Kumquat for John Keats' (1981); he cites the television version of Harrison's *v* (poem, 1985; film, 1987) as an acknowledgement of the 'cultural shift brought about by the possibilities of postmodern media'.[7] However, this came some 11 years after Betjeman's televised *Summoned by Bells*, which further begs the question of whether, as both an 'electronic' poem and a '*petit récit*', it might truly be called a postmodern *Prelude*.

Brown also states that postmodernism embodies a 'conjunction of textual and oral modes', linked to a 'comprehensive electronic culture'.[8] He cites Allen Ginsberg's 'America' (1956) as an example but, in addition to *Summoned by Bells*, one also thinks of the many radio (and television) broadcasts of Betjeman reading his own verse. One thinks too of all the hymn and song rhythms that had always been an inherent part of his compositional process. Indeed, it was on radio that he commented on the essential need to 'say [a poem] over to yourself time after time to see whether it fits right and sounds naturally'.[9] This oral tradition goes back centuries of course, but its resurgence is not exclusive to postmodern verse. In Betjeman, one must say that it is more likely to relate to the following note by Hopkins, cited (somewhat ironically) by McLuhan:

> [o]f ['Spelt from Sybil's Leaves'] above all remember what applies to all my verse, that it is, as living art should be, made for performance and that its performance is not reading with the eye but loud, leisurely, poetical (not rhetorical) recitation, with long rests, long dwells on the rhyme and other marked syllables, and so on.[10]

But what of the growing sales figures noted throughout this book? Are they a sign that Betjeman straddled the 'Gutenberg' *and* 'electronic' ages? Does this make him the ultimate postmodern pioneer? And what of the 'enormously complicated' issue of architecture?[11] For Betjeman, there was the important difference between the truly modern architecture of the 1930s (all 'pure and simple and Scandinavian'), and the *moderne* (or 'jazz-modern', or art deco – as in the contemporary Odeon cinema style).[12] As a journalist on the *Architectural Review*, he was permitted to like the former (it was practically compulsory), but not the latter. But was his adherence to this dictum, and his membership of the MARS Group, symptomatic of a conscious embrace of modernism? Subsequent emphasis on the merits of Georgian and Victorian architecture would, as I have suggested, indicate that he was merely trying to earn a living by following the editorial line laid down before him.

Also crucial to a postmodern stance is a sense of universality. Auden, for example, may be said to have achieved this by 'internationalising' himself when he went to America.[13] Peter Porter's comment that 'Englishness is not a barrier to people that are not English' (because 'Englishness' has been a successful export) is not sufficient to help Betjeman, though. His work – regardless of Harvey's assertion – attains universality in only brief glimpses – as in 'Harvest Hymn' (1966), with its attack on the use of pesticides, and 'Back From Australia' (1972), with its notions of time and space. This means that, despite all the *'petit récits'*, the multi-media dissemination and the references to brand names, Betjeman's love of traditional forms ensures that he remains more parochial than postmodern.[14] Indeed, Philip Larkin realised that '[t]hroughout the work of the writer, broadcaster, propagandist and poet John Betjeman can be traced the same insistent pattern, a *rejection* of modernism' (my italics).[15]

So what exactly *is* Betjeman? Larkin posed this very question in 'Betjeman en bloc' (1959), the article from which the above quotation was taken. As we saw in CHAPTER TWO, the references to Victorian poetry begin almost as "buttresses", but there can be no doubt that this was due to a love of such verse, as well as a desire to differ from the new style of writing that was starting to emerge. As his work progressed, this was replaced by a sense of connoisseurship, where his interest in the oeuvre began to colour his verse with more subtle tones. In later years, the emphasis changes again when the poetics of the past are used to critique the present. In this light, the title *New Bats in Old Belfries* describes exactly what Betjeman came to do – put new ideas in old verse forms. We need only add all those radio and television programmes, articles, letters and personal appeals to save beleaguered Victorian buildings (older ones too) to see that Larkin was absolutely right.

But what of the 'propagandist' label? Was this Poet Laureate and former Press Attaché perhaps part of the Ideological State Apparatus (in an Althusserian sense)?[16] Betjeman's Laureate verses certainly smiled unstintingly on the monarchy – that 'human, friendly line that never fails', as he wrote in his ode on the Prince of Wales's marriage (1981), for example. His work during the Second World War also promoted a view of his homeland that can be seen as striving to perpetuate the *status quo*. Yet – in poems such as 'The Dear Old Village' (1947), 'Huxley Hall' (1953) and 'Middlesex' (1954), to say nothing of his prose output – he was far too critical of post-War government policy, building practices and social trends to be part of any great machine of oppression. As Brown reminds us, Lyotard saw those *'petit récits'* as 'politically subversive', an idea that immediately refutes the charge levelled by many critics that the satires are weak.[17] Though he had his admirers, Betjeman was never a critical darling; however, the sales figures show that he was certainly a *public* one. The disparity between readers and reviewers, coupled with the foregoing analysis, suggests that it is the latter who are 'lightweight': Jaussian depths are there to be plunged into if one takes trouble to look for the diving board. Though one might cite the example of 'On a Portrait of a Deaf Man' (1940), even in such a seemingly superficial piece as 'In a Bath Teashop' (1945), the theologian H. A. Williams could see 'the divine Charity'.[18]

This approach brings post-colonialism into the frame: as discussed in CHAPTER FOUR, 'A Lincolnshire Church', with its reference to the Indian Christian incumbent thereof, does make Betjeman an 'early poet of multiculturalism' in that he accepts the man rather than objects to him.[19] Although it was at this time that the retreat from Empire began (India gained independence in 1947), issues of race would not come fully to the fore in Britain until the 1960s. This is therefore another example of Betjeman's prescience – and his benignity. Obviously, the poem is an isolated example, and to be post-colonial *per se* requires something more. A similar connection may be made with feminism.

At first, this sounds even more ridiculous: could there really be a sense in which this lover of tennis-playing blonds is *feminist*? Recall, however, that virtually all Betjeman's women have Amazonian might: 'See the strength of her arm, as firm and hairy as Hendren's', as he wrote of Pam in 'Pot Pourri from a Surrey Garden' (1938); recall too the assistance that Myfanwy Piper had given in choosing articles for *First and Last Loves* (1952), and how her *intellect* as well her beauty was celebrated in 'Myfanwy at Oxford' (1938):

> Tentative brush of a cheek in a cocoa crush,
>   Coffee and Ulysses, Tennyson, Joyce,
> Alpha-minded and other dimensional,
>   Freud or Calvary? Take your choice.
>
> ('MYFANWY AT OXFORD', LL. 27–30)

In the end, of course, this is not quite enough either: there is far too much emphasis on sexuality and aesthetics throughout the work, and though the 'freckled undergraduettes appear' in *Summoned by Bells*, with their 'Handlebar baskets heavy with the load / Of books on Middle English', they do not feature with sufficient frequency in this male-dominated world for a feminist to smile on Betjeman's portraits of women.

The fact is that Betjeman never quite fits in anywhere. His identity depends on contrariness; hence he is always a square peg in a round hole or a round peg in a square hole – often for the sheer enjoyment, one feels, of so being. It is, as Donald Davie understood, 'infernally difficult to get any sort of critical callipers' on him – except perhaps to dismiss him as a cuddly, stuffed bruin.[20] In a sense, his desire to be as non-conformist as a Quaker meeting house makes him a *radical*, rather than the reactionary that his interests make him seem. He was a champion of beauty, a champion of the British Isles, and clearly did more than anyone to make us see the worth of that which our Victorian forebears achieved. Such was against the poetic grain in his earliest days, and against the cultural variety engendered by the post-war period of urban "development". This drags one back inexorably to that wise observation of Maurice Bowra: 'Betjeman has a mind of extraordinary originality; there is no one else remotely like him'.[21] Never was – nor will there ever be – a truer word written about the man.

Appendix

Glossary of nineteenth-century poets listed by Betjeman in the preface to *Old Lights for New Chancels* (1940)

Crabbe*: George Crabbe (1754–1832), poet, author of *The Village* (1783) and *The Parish Register* (1807).

Praed: Winthrop Mackworth Praed (1802–1839), poet and politician, author of 'Good Night to the Season' (1827).

Hood: Thomas Hood (1799–1845), writer of humorous verse, now chiefly remembered for more serious pieces such as 'The Bridge of Sighs' (1844).

Clare*: John Clare (1793–1864), author of *Poems Descriptive of Rural Life and Scenery* (1820) and *The Shepherd's Calendar* (1827).

Ebenezer Elliott*: Ebenezer Elliott (1781–1849), poet, referred to as 'the Corn Law Rhymer' in Betjeman's *Collins Guide to English Parish Churches* (1958), p. 64.

Capt. Kennish: William Kennish R. N. (1799–1862), Manx explorer, engineer, inventor and poet, whose principal work was *Mona's Isle and Other Poems* (1844).

Neale: John Mason Neale (1818–1866), church historian and hymn writer, whose *A History of the Holy Eastern Church* (1847–1850) includes 'O Happy Band of Pilgrims' and 'Good King Wencleslaus'.

Charles Tennyson Turner*: (1808–1879), elder brother of Alfred Tennyson, whose early collection of fifty sonnets (1830) caught the attention of many, including Samuel Taylor Coleridge.

Poets marked '*' are among those selected for *English Scottish and Welsh Landscape 1700 – c.1860* (London: Frederick Muller Ltd., 1944) by Betjeman and Geoffrey Taylor.

Clough: Arthur Hugh Clough (1819–1861), great friend of Matthew Arnold and author of *Amours de Voyage* (1858) and *Dipsychus and the Spirit* (1865).

William Barnes*: (1801–1886), schoolteacher who specialised in writing verse in the Dorset dialect. Admired by Allingham, Patmore, Tennyson, Hopkins and Hardy.

Meredith: George Meredith (1828–1909), author of 'Love in the Valley' (1851), a poem which influenced Betjeman in the 1930s, along with several novels, such as *The Egoist* (1879).

William Morris: (1834–1896), the author-socialist-craftsman-painter, who wrote *The Earthly Paradise* (1868–1870) and several romances, including the Utopian vision, *News from Nowhere* (1890).

Notes

CHAPTER ONE **Introduction**

1 Alan Bell, 'The Times Profile: Sir John Betjeman – By Appointment: Teddy Bear to the Nation', *The Times*, 20 September 1982, p. 5.

2 Humphrey Carpenter notes that the bear was 'an implicit comment on the immaturity of the English upper classes', adding that it was also a way of attracting attention and 'subverting paternalistic authority'. Humphrey Carpenter, *The Brideshead Generation: Evelyn Waugh and his Friends* (London: George Weidenfeld & Nicolson Ltd., 1989), p. 102. Paulin's views are quoted from 'New Views on Betjeman: The Teddy Bear and His Critics', *The Listener*, 23 May 1985, pp. 20–1. The article was based on a BBC Radio 3 discussion, chaired by Anthony Thwaite.

3 Quoted in YB, p. 141.

4 *The Reader's Guide to Twentieth Century Writers*, for example, observes that the 'underlying melancholia' in Betjeman's work 'prevents it from ever being merely cosy'. *The Reader's Guide to Twentieth Century Writers*, ed. by Peter Parker, consultant ed. Frank Kermode (Helicon: Oxford, 1995), p. 78; Geoffrey Grigson, *Recollections – mainly of writers and artists* (London: The Hogarth Press, 1984), p. 167.

5 Andrew Sanders, *The Short Oxford History of English Literature* (Oxford: Oxford University Press, 1996), pp. 603–4.

6 H. R. Jauss, 'Literary History as a Challenge to Literary Theory', tr. Elizabeth Benzinger, *New Literary History*, vol. 2 (1967), pp. 7–37 (15); ibid., pp. 11–19.

7 'New Views on Betjeman: The Teddy Bear and His Critics', *The Listener*, 23 May 1985, pp. 20–1 (and ibid.).

8 John Betjeman, *Slick But Not Streamlined*, ed. by W. H. Auden (New York: The Country Life Press, 1947), pp. 9–16 (p. 9). See also Greg Morse, 'Betjeman and Auden: Strange Bedfellows?', *The Betjemanian*, vol. 19 (2007/08), pp. 52–62.

9 Bill Ruddick, '"Some ruin-bibber, randy for antique": Philip Larkin's response to the poetry of John Betjeman', *Critical Quarterly*, 28/4 (Winter 1986), 63–9 (p. 69).

10 BTBOL, pp. 713–14 (and ibid.).

11 Ibid., pp. 605–6.

12 T. S. Eliot, 'Tradition and the Individual Talent', in *T. S. Eliot: Selected Essays*, ed. by T. S. Eliot, 3rd edn (London: Faber & Faber, 1966), pp. 13–22. Reproduced with the kind permission of Faber & Faber.

13 Harold Bloom, *The Anxiety of Influence* (1973), pp. 87–92, in Rice and Waugh, pp. 95–7; Terry Eagleton, *Literary Theory: An Introduction*, 2nd edn (Oxford: Blackwell Publishers, 1996), p. 159.

14 The evocative phrase 'steam and gaslight' was used by Derek Stanford. It is derived from Betjeman's poem 'Monody on the Death of Aldersgate Street Station' (1955,

l. 27). Derek Stanford, *John Betjeman: A Study* (London: Neville Spearman, 1961), p. 155.

15 'Executive' was originally published (under the heading 'To the faceless ones "develop" means "destroy"') in the *Sunday Express* (no. 2729, 30 May 1971, p. 3).

16 See *The Real John Betjeman*. Dir. Marion Milne, Channel 4 (2000).

17 John Press, *Writers and Their Work: John Betjeman* (Harlow: Longman, 1974), p. 40; Stanford, p. 130.

18 Dennis Brown, *Writers and Their Work: John Betjeman* (Plymouth: Northcote House, 1999), p. 35.

CHAPTER TWO The 1930s

1 This sub-heading is taken from Chapter IX of Betjeman's verse-autobiography, *Summoned by Bells* (1960).

2 Malcolm Muggeridge, *The Thirties: 1930–1940 in Great Britain*, 2nd edn (London: Collins, 1967), p. 12.

3 Valentine Cunningham, *British Writers of the Thirties* (Oxford: Oxford University Press, 1989), pp. 14–16.

4 L1, p. xxi.

5 Copies of *Idylls* were given as prizes at within about ten years of Betjeman's schooling at Highgate (1915–1917). Unpublished letter to author from David Tabraham-Palmer, archivist of Highgate School, 14 February 2002 (and ibid.); for the Dragon school reference, see YB, p. 40.

6 Two editions were by Macmillan (1886 and 1952), two by the Oxford University Press (1912 and 1924). See Hamish Riley-Smith, *The Betjeman Library* (Swanton Abbot, Hamish Riley-Smith, 1996), entries 677–80. Details of the *Desert Island Discs* appearance (12 April 1975) may be found on *John Betjeman: Recollections from the BBC Archives* (selected and introduced by Candida Lycett Green, BBC, 1998), side 1.

7 YB, pp. 69–70.

8 From *Ghastly Good Taste* by John Betjeman, published by Century Hutchinson. Reprinted by permission of The Random House Group Ltd. John Betjeman, *Ghastly Good Taste*, 3rd edn (London: Century Hutchinson, 1986), p. xvii.

9 JBNFNL, p. 409 (and ibid.).

10 YB, pp. 116–17 (and ibid.).

11 John Betjeman, *An Oxford University Chest*, 2nd edn (Oxford: Oxford University Press, 1979), p. 27.

12 Letter to C. S. Lewis, 13 December 1939. L1, pp. 250–3.

13 Humphrey Carpenter, *The Brideshead Generation: Evelyn Waugh and his Friends* (London: George Weidenfeld & Nicolson Ltd., 1989), p. 471.

14 YB, p. 353; Edward James, *Swans Reflecting Elephants: My Early Years*, ed. by George Melly (London: Weidenfeld & Nicolson, 1982), p. 62.

15 Letter to Betjeman from Edward James, 11 May 1931. Courtesy of The McPherson Library, University of Victoria, Canada (and ibid.).

16 Alan Pryce-Jones, 'Chronicles: Poetry' (review of *Mount Zion*), *The London Mercury*, December 1931, pp. 202–3 (203).

17 Julian Symons, *The Thirties – A Dream Revolved* (London: Faber & Faber, 1975), p. 20.

18 Pryce-Jones, p.202. The paper was by Brock's, which did indeed manufacture fire-works. YB, p. 354.

19 Letter to Mary St. Clair-Erskine, 17 April 1929. L1, p. 57.

20 YB, p. 353.

21 'New Views on Betjeman: The Teddy Bear and His Critics', *The Listener*, 23 May 1985, pp. 20–1 (21).

22 Hamish Riley-Smith, entry 1746.

23 Ibid., entry 2117.

24 YB, p. 212.

25 Dante Gabriel Rossetti, *Collected Poetry and Plays*, ed. by Jerome McGann (New Haven and London: Yale University Press, 2003), pp. 72–4 (72). © Yale University Press. Reproduced with kind permission.

26 Derek Stanford, *John Betjeman: A Study* (London: Neville Spearman, 1961), p. 110.

27 Joan Rees, *The Poetry of Dante Gabriel Rossetti: modes of self-expression* (Cambridge: Cambridge University Press, 1981), p. 77.

28 Dante Gabriel Rossetti, *Collected Poetry and Plays*, ed. by Jerome McGann (New Haven and London: Yale University Press, 2003), pp. 72–4 (73).

29 Cunningham, *British Writers*, p. 106.

30 Geoffrey Grigson, *Recollections – mainly of writers and artists* (London: The Hogarth Press, 1984), p. 167.

31 Letter to Frank Rutherford, 25 May 1954. L2, pp. 66–7.

32 J. R. Watson, *The English Hymn: A Critical and Historical Study* (Oxford: Clarendon Press, 1999), p. 1.

33 John Betjeman, 'Marginalia: The Church's Restoration', *The Architectural Review*, vol. LXVII, no. 399 (February 1930), pp. 107–8.

34 *Ghastly Good Taste*, p. 96.

35 Watson, *The English Hymn*, p. 393.

36 Ibid., p. 344. For more on Colenso, see Owen Chadwick, *The Victorian Church – Part II*, 2nd edn (London: Adam & Charles Black, 1972), pp. 468–9.

37 YB, p. 70; p. 421 (note 18).

38 L1, p. 37 (and ibid.).

39 John Betjeman, 'R. S. Thomas: Introduction to *Song at the Year's Turning* by R. S. Thomas (Hart-Davis, 1955)', in CH, pp. 322–5 (p. 324).

40 Carpenter, *Brideshead*, p. 253.

41 Dennis Brown, *Writers and Their Work: John Betjeman* (Plymouth: Northcote House, 1999), p. 8.

42 Patrick Taylor-Martin, *John Betjeman: His Life and Work* (Harmondsworth: Penguin Books, 1983), pp. 59–60.

43 Pryce-Jones, p. 202.

44 Francis Mahony (aka Father Prout), *The Reliques of Father Prout* (London: Bell, 1875), pp. 159–60 (160).

45 C. S. Calverley, *The English Poems of Charles Stuart Calverley*, ed. by Hilda D. Spear (Leicester: Leicester University Press, 1974), p. 79.

46 Randolph Churchill, 'Arts and Crafts' (review of *Mount Zion*), *The Architectural Review*, LXX/421 (December 1931), pp. 39–41.

47 *Times Literary Supplement*, 'Looking Backward' (includes review of *Mount Zion or In Touch with the Infinite*), *Times Literary Supplement*, 26 November 1931, p. 944.

48 Letter to Tom Driberg, 10 November 1931, L1, p. 85. This may be illustrated by an anecdote from Edward James, who wrote: 'Lady Chetwode was very upset [at the prospect of her daughter becoming Mrs. Betjeman]. One day Aunt Venetia said to me, "That Dutch friend of yours [. . .] wants to marry Star Chetwode's daughter. I find that the father has quite a lot of money." [. . .] "One can know people like that," she added, "but one doesn't marry them!" I repeated this to Betjeman. It was the sort of joke he would make about himself, but he was deeply offended.' James, p. 67.

49 *John Betjeman: The Last Laugh*. Dir. Edward Mirzoeff, BBC (2001).

50 Cunningham, *British Writers*, p. 140.

51 Carpenter, *Brideshead*, p. 211.

52 JBNFNL, pp. 109–12. See also letter to Jock Murray, 28 September 1936. L1, pp. 159–60.

53 JBNFNL, p. 117.

54 Symons, *The Thirties*, p. 21.

55 Ibid., p. 33. (Prices of Auden's 1930s volumes are courtesy of John Bodley of Faber & Faber (Unpublished letter to author, 11 September 2002).)

56 Figures obtained from 'Copies Ledger K1' (folios 39 and 40), the John Murray Archive.

57 JBNFNL, p. 114.

58 Even as late as 1961, Stanford felt that 'Clash Went the Billiard Balls' – not Betjeman's finest hour – could be described merely as a 'little bit of fun [. . .] at the expense of working-class characters'. Stanford, p. 67, note 1.

59 Peter Quennell, 'Flowers of Mediocrity' (review of *Continual Dew*), *The New Statesman and Nation*, 13 November 1937 (and ibid.). It is possible that Quennell was also making a reference to T. S. Eliot's 1930 article on Baudelaire. See *T. S. Eliot: Selected Essays*, 4th edn, ed. by T. S. Eliot (London: Faber & Faber, 1999), pp. 419–30.

60 Evelyn Waugh, 'A Parnassian on Mount Zion' (review of Continual Dew), *Night and Day*, 25 November 1937, pp. 24–5 (and ibid.).

61 J. B. Morton, 'English Humour' (includes review of *Continual Dew*), *The Listener*, 8 December 1937 (and ibid.).

62 'Competition', along with 'The 'Varsity Students' Rag', 'A Seventeenth-Century Love Lyric', 'Mother and I', 'For Nineteenth Century Burials', 'School Song', 'Camberley', 'Arts and Crafts' and 'St. Aloysius Church, Oxford' were the *Mount Zion* poems which Betjeman felt could be omitted from *Continual Dew* ('and any others you would like to remove'). Letter to Jock Murray, 28 September 1936, L1, pp. 159–60.

63 Stanford also believed that 'the genuine evangelistic note' of 'Undenominational' harks back to Masefield's *The Everlasting Mercy* (1910). Stanford, p. 127.

64 This is somewhat ironic when one considers the disagreement between Betjeman and Evelyn Waugh on this subject. It was Waugh's hand in Penelope Betjeman's conversion to Catholicism which led to the ultimate decline of his friend's marriage.

65 Whether Betjeman had wanted the whole volume to be this way only to be prevented by cost, or whether this "insert" was always the intention is not known (although he was certainly happy with the result). Letter to Jock Murray, 23 October 1937. L1, pp. 180–1.

66 Edward Wilson, 'Betjeman's *Riddel Posts*: An Echo of Ninian Comper', *Review*

of English Studies (November 1991), pp. 541–50 (545). Wilson also notes the more overt reference to 'Comper tracery' in 'Myfanwy at Oxford' (1938). 'STAN-FORD in A', mentioned in the last lines of the second and fifth verses of 'Exeter', is an evening service, commissioned in 1880. As such, it is one of the great late-Victorian musical settings.

67 Donald Davie, *Thomas Hardy and British Poetry* (London: Routledge and Kegan Paul, 1973), p. 108.

68 Thomas Hardy, *Selected Poems*, ed. by Tim Armstrong (Harlow: Longman, 1993), pp. 63–5 (63). Reproduced throughout with kind permission of Pearson Education Ltd.

69 Ibid., p. 109 (and ibid.).

70 Taylor-Martin, p. 65.

71 Ryme Intrinseca lies about three miles south of Yeovil (just inside the Dorset border). The village was known as 'Ryme Intrinsica' circa 1611, while 'Rime' seems to date from the thirteenth century. Unpublished letter to author from Deborah Stevenson, Archivist, Dorset Record Office, 27 September 2002. Betjeman thus muddled the correct spellings somewhat, although selecting 'Rime' may have been a semi-conscious reference to Coleridge.

72 Ibid., p. 191.

73 Grigson, *Recollections*, p. 7.

74 In his foreword to Theodore Wratislaw's *Oscar Wilde: A Memoir* (1979), Betjeman describes the Wilde portrayed therein as 'confident, benevolent and witty, still writing *An Ideal Husband*'. He concludes by proclaiming Wratislaw's book to show 'a last streak on [sic] sunlight' and urges the reader to 'bask in it'. Theodore Wratislaw, *Oscar Wilde: A Memoir* (London: The Eighteen Nineties Society, 1979), p. 2.

75 Stanford, pp. 87–8 (and ibid.).

76 Richard Ellmann, *Oscar Wilde* (London: Hamish Hamilton, 1987), p. 429 (and ibid.).

77 It was a matter of geography too – the Cadogan *does* overlook Pont Street. Carpenter alsoquoted Osbert Lancaster's concept of 'Pont Street Dutch' (*Here, of All Places* (1959)). Carpenter, *Brideshead*, p. 298. For more on Betjeman's more complicated view, see page 60–1.

78 Confirmed in an unpublished letter to author from Kenneth Hillier, Hon. Sec. of the John Buchan Society, 16 August 2005.

79 YB, p. 116.

80 Ellmann's own *Oscar Wilde: A Collection of Critical Essays* was published in 1969 (London: Prentice Hall). Other volumes released during the decade include: *The Letters of Oscar Wilde*, ed. by Rupert Hart-Davis (London: Hart-Davis, 1962) and P. Jullian, *Oscar Wilde* (Paris: Perrin, 1967).

81 Ellmann, *Wilde*, pp. 8–10.

82 Alfred Lord Tennyson, *The Poems of Tennyson in Three Volumes*, ed. by Christopher Ricks (Harlow: Longman Group, 1987), II, pp. 118–30 (130). Reproduced throughout with kind permission of Pearson Education Ltd.

83 Hallam Tennyson, *Tennyson: A Memoir by his Son, Vol. I* (London: Macmillan & Co. Ltd., 1897), p. 195.

84 John Betjeman, 'City and Suburban (4)', cited from *The Spectator*, 19 October 1956, in CH, pp. 338–43 (339).

85 David Williams, *George Meredith: His Life and Lost Love* (London: Hamish

Hamilton, 1977), p. 104. N. B. Betjeman's poem is based on the 1878 version of 'Love in the Valley'.

86 Later versions (such as that in *Collected Poems* (1958)) read simply: 'Portable Lieutenant! they carry you to China'.

87 George Meredith, *The Poetical Works of George Meredith*, ed. by G. M. Trevelyan (London: Constable & Co. Ltd., 1912), pp. 230–6 (231); ibid., p. 232; p. 234. Reproduced by kind permission of Meredith's great-granddaughter, Mrs. Patricia Sedgwick.

88 Ibid., p. 235.

89 Cunningham, *British Writers*, p. 279.

90 Carpenter, *Brideshead*, pp. 301–2.

91 John Betjeman and John Piper, eds, *Murray's Buckinghamshire Guide* (London: John Murray (Publishers) Ltd., 1948), pp. 124–5 (125).

92 Letter to a Mr Percival, 9 January 1967. L2, pp. 326–7 (327).

93 William Morris, *The Earthly Paradise: A Poem by William Morris*, 4 vols (London: Longmans Green, 1905), I, p. 3. Reproduced throughout with kind permission of Pearson Education Ltd.

94 John Betjeman, *A Pictorial History of English Architecture*, 2nd edn (Harmondsworth: Penguin Books Ltd., 1974), p. 98.

95 Ibid., pp. 98–100.

96 Timothy Mowl, *Stylistic Cold Wars: Betjeman Versus Pevsner* (London: John Murray (Publishers) Ltd. 2000), p. 90.

97 According to Betjeman, this is what the architect Baillie Scott used to call *The Architectural Review*. YB, pp. 260–1.

98 L1, pp. 39–40.

99 Letter to Malcolm Brereton, 19 January 1929. Ibid., p. 50.

100 YB, p. 268. The MARS Group was founded by Wells Coates and Philip Morton Shand in 1933 to support and promote Modernist architects in Britain.

101 Mowl, *Stylistic Cold Wars*, p. 22 (and ibid.).

102 John Betjeman, 'Architecture', *The London Mercury*, vol. XXIX, 169 (November 1933), pp. 65–7, quoted in YB, p. 274. One of Betjeman's pseudonyms, 'Lionel Cuffe' (of whom more later), was discovered by Horace Liberty, who speculates (with good reason!) that the rather splendid-sounding 'Rockingham Newbolt' may have been another. Horace Liberty, 'Hidden Under the Wallpaper', *The Betjemanian*, vol. 14 (2002/2003), pp. 28–31. Sadly, confirmation may be impossible as the records of the *Architectural Review* for this period were destroyed many years ago. Unpublished letter to author from Lynne Jackson, *The Architectural Review*, 14 October 2004.

103 John Betjeman, 'The Electrification of Lambourne End – A Poem in the Manner of the Rev. George Crabbe', *The Architectural Review*, vol. LXXIV, 444 (November 1933), pp. 209–10.

104 Mowl, *Stylistic Cold Wars*, pp. 15–34.

105 Ibid., p. 18.

106 YB, pp. 162–3. More recently, Hillier has noted that Betjeman read the Rev Francis Harton's *Elements of the Spiritual Life* in 1937 and 'felt his faith renewed by it'. JBNFNL, p. 84.

107 YB, p. 213.

108 The Diary of Sir Horace Plunkett (unpublished), 17 February 1929, p. 48. (Held by The Plunkett Foundation.) See also YB, p. 214.

109 The Diary of Sir Horace Plunkett (unpublished), 10 February 1929, p. 41. See also YB, p. 212. No other references to Betjeman's religious beliefs were found in Plunkett's diary between 1 January and 30 April 1929 (visit by author to The Plunkett Foundation, 22 November 2002).

110 The Diary of John Betjeman, 12 October 1935. Notebook MC7, held by the McPherson Library, University of Victoria, Canada. See also JBNFNL, p. 62; p. 65.

111 YB, p. 378; L1, p. 96.

112 Unpublished letter to author from Peter Daniels, Assistant Librarian, the Religious Society of Friends, 14 August 2002.

113 Letter to Alan Pryce-Jones, 12 February 1929. L1, p. 53.

114 Notes from Westminster and Longford Monthly Meeting minutes, 1931 gleaned from the Library of the Religious Society of Friends in Britain.

115 YB, p. 299; p. 401. Note that, according to the current Clerk to Old Jordans Trust, Betjeman does not appear in the Visitor's books for the period April 1932 to July 1933. Unpublished letter to author from Valerie McFarlane, Clerk to Old Jordans Trust, 4 February 2005.

116 Ibid., p. 299. See also L1, pp. 103–20.

117 'Preparative Meeting Minute Book' (Jordans) (AR56/2004) and 'Jordans Monthly Meeting Minute Book' (NQ5/1/1), courtesy of the Centre for Buckinghamshire Studies, Aylesbury. (Visited by author, 7 December 2004.)

118 Letter to Betjeman from Mildred Alston, 24 March 1937. Courtesy of The McPherson Library, University of Victoria, Canada.

119 According to the *Dictionary of National Biography*, the Sandemanians evolved from John Glas's (1695–1773) group, founded in 1728. Glas's principles have been described as 'akin to Brownism', but were closer to 'the type of independent presbyterianism set forth by early English puritans' (such as Bradshaw). See Vol. VII (1937/8), p. 1296. Glas's son-in-law, Robert Sandeman (1718–71), added nothing to the sect's theological principles, but 'his advocacy gave them vogue'. See Vol. VII (1937/8), p. 745.

120 *Ghastly Good Taste*, p.7.

121 Ibid., p. 98.

122 Ibid., p. 60; pp. 103–4.

123 John Betjeman, '1837–1937', in John Betjeman, *First and Last Loves*, 2nd edn (London: John Murray (Publishers) Ltd., 1969), pp. 120–31 (122).

124 Ibid., p. 127.

125 Ibid., p. 129.

126 *Ghastly Good Taste*, pp. 110–12.

127 Quoted in Paul Thompson, *The Work of William Morris*, 2nd edn (London: Quartet Books Ltd., 1977), p. 64 (and ibid.).

128 John Betjeman (as Lionel Cuffe), 'William Morris', *The Architectural Review*, vol. LXIX, 414 (May 1931), p. 151.

129 John Betjeman, 'Nonconformist Architecture', in John Betjeman, *First and Last Loves*, 2nd edn (London: John Murray (Publishers) Ltd., 1969), pp. 90–119 (92).

130 Ibid., p. 93.

131 Mowl, *Stylistic Cold Wars*, p. 25.

132 YB, p. 259.

133 John Betjeman, '1830–1930 – Still Going Strong: A Guide to the Recent History of Interior Design', *The Architectural Review*, vol. LXVII, 402 (May 1930), pp. 230–72 (231).

134 Ibid., p. 240.
135 YB, p. 261.
136 C. F. Annesley Voysey, '1874 & After (Foreword by Sir Edwin Lutyens)', *The Architectural Review*, vol. LXX, 419 (October 1931), pp. 91–2 (92).
137 Ibid.
138 Ibid., p. 91.
139 Thompson, p. 75; John Ruskin, *The Stones of Venice*, part II, chapter VI, in *John Ruskin: Selected Writings*, ed. by Philip Davis (London: J. M. Dent, 1995), p. 210.
140 John Betjeman, 'Charles Francis Annesley Voysey: The Architect of Individualism', *The Architectural Review*, vol. LXX, 419 (October 1931), pp. 93–6 (96).
141 John Betjeman, 'The Death of Modernism: *The Architectural Review*, December 1931', in CH, pp. 21–3 (22).
142 Mowl, *Stylistic Cold Wars*, p. 42.
143 John Betjeman, *Trains and Buttered Toast*, ed. by Stephen Games (London: John Murray (Publishers), 2006), p. 53 (and ibid.).
144 CH, 'The Death of Modernism', p. 21.
145 Ibid.
146 YB, p. 276. Hillier reports that, by 1947, pylons had become eyesores for Betjeman and that, in the April of that year, he also campaigned against a Post Office proposal to site a television relay station on White Horse Hill. JBNFNL, pp. 417–18.
147 L1, p. 93.
148 *Ghastly Good Taste*, p. xvii.
149 Ibid., p. xix.
150 Ibid., p. xxiv.
151 Ibid., p. 13; p. 19.
152 Ibid., pp. 19–20.
153 Ibid.
154 Ibid., p. 92.
155 Ibid., p. 98.
156 Ibid., pp. 99–100. By 1951, Betjeman's attitude had altered to the extent that he now felt Street's Law Courts 'will impress everyone for its many-vista-ed thoughtfulness'. John Betjeman, 'Victorian Architecture', in John Betjeman, *First and Last Loves*, 2nd edn (London: John Murray (Publishers) Ltd., 1969), pp. 132–78 (138).
157 Ibid., pp. 101–2.
158 'Charles Francis Annesley Voysey: The Architect of Individualism', p. 95.
159 *Ghastly Good Taste*, pp. 11–12.
160 Ibid., pp. 20–1.
161 Carpenter, *Brideshead*, p. 212; Mowl, *Stylistic Cold Wars*, p. 151.
162 John Betjeman, 'Antiquarian Prejudice', in John Betjeman, *First and Last Loves*, 2nd edn (London: John Murray (Publishers) Ltd., 1969), pp. 48–66 (48).
163 JBNFNL, p. 417.
164 *First and Last Loves*, 'Antiquarian Prejudice', p. 57.
165 John Betjeman, *An Oxford University Chest* (London: John Miles, 1938), p. 169.
166 *Ghastly Good Taste*, p. 58.
167 William Morris, *Works* XXII, p.392. Quoted by Thompson, p. 64.
168 *An Oxford University Chest*, p. 169.
169 Carpenter, *Brideshead*, p. 212 (and ibid.).

170 *An Oxford University Chest*, pp. 144–5.

171 This comment was made at an 'Evening of Bad Taste' given by the United Arts Society on 7 March 1935. Betjeman did not appear in person (having his column for the *Evening Standard* to write), but sent a gramophone recording of his speech instead. JBNFNL, p. 48.

172 Ibid., p. 72.

173 John Betjeman, *Cornwall, Illustrated in a Series of Views* [. . .] (London: The Architectural Press, 1934), p. 6.

174 That is, Nickolaus Pevsner (1902–83), architectural historian and author of the *Buildings of England* series.

175 Ibid., p. 24.

176 Betjeman seems to have got this idea from Arthur Machen's *The Secret Glory* (1922): a mere two pages in, a comment is made about a church that had been 'completely "restored"' in the early 'forties'. Arthur Machen, *The Secret Glory*, 3rd edn (London: Tartarus Press, 1991), p. 2.

177 John Betjeman, *Cornwall: A Shell Guide*, 2nd edn (London: Faber & Faber, 1964), p. 58; p. 55.

178 JBNFNL, p. 73.

179 *Cornwall* (1964), p. 26.

180 This parallel is asserted, and discussed at length, by Mowl (pp. 70–2).

181 Ibid., p. 66.

182 John Betjeman, *Devon, compiled with illustrations and information of every sort by* (London: The Architectural Press, 1936), pp. 24–5.

183 Ibid.

184 L1, p. 170; Mowl, *Stylistic Cold Wars*, p. 58 (and ibid.).

185 John Betjeman, 'The Seeing Eye or How to Like Everything', *The Architectural Review*, vol. LXXXVI, 516 (November 1939), pp. 201–4 (202).

186 Ibid. (and passim).

187 Mowl, *Stylistic Cold Wars*, p. 105.

188 *First and Last Loves*, 'Antiquarian Prejudice', p. 59.

189 In Jonathan Stedall's 1983 BBC television series *Time With Betjeman* (part 5), the (then) Greater London Council's Surveyor of Historic Buildings, Ashley Barker, in fact credited the poet with making one 'unafraid to believe one's own eyes' in *Ghastly Good Taste*.

190 Note the Puginesque resonance of 'contrasts': Betjeman owned a copy of the architect's book of that name – A. Welby Pugin, *Contrasts: or a Parallel between the Noble Edifices of the Middle Ages and Corresponding Buildings of the Present Day; Shewing the Present Decay of Taste*, 2nd edn (London: Charles Dolman, 1841). Riley-Smith, entry 3658.

191 John Betjeman, 'Leeds – A City of Contrasts', in John Betjeman, *First and Last Loves*, 2nd edn (London: John Murray (Publishers) Ltd., 1969), pp. 30–8 (30).

192 Ibid., pp. 31–2.

193 Ibid., pp. 34–5.

194 Ibid., p. 36.

195 From *The Uses of Literacy* by Richard Hoggart, published by Chatto & Windus. Reprinted by permission of The Random House Group Ltd. Richard Hoggart, *The Uses of Literacy*, 2nd edn (Harmondsworth: Penguin Books Ltd., 1966), pp. 58–9.

196 *First and Last Loves*, 'Leeds – A City of Contrasts', p. 36.

197 Ibid., p. 38.
198 John Betjeman, 'A Note on J. N. Comper – Heir to Butterfield and Bodley', *The Architectural Review*, vol. LXXXV, 507 (February 1939), pp. 79–82 (79).
199 YB, pp.86 and 266.
200 L1, p. 383.
201 Mowl, *Stylistic Cold Wars*, p.126; the quotation on Comper comes from a 1948 broadcast on the Church of St. Protus and St. Hyacinth, at Blisland, Cornwall. *First and Last Loves*, 'Three Churches', pp. 179–88 (180).
202 'A Note on J. N. Comper', p. 79.
203 Ibid., p. 79.
204 L1, p. 200; *First and Last Loves*, 'Antiquarian Prejudice', p. 65.
205 JBNFNL, p. 415.
206 Unpublished letter from Tim Bennett to Jack Pritchard, 6 October 1941. Courtesy of the University of East Anglia Library (Archives Department).
207 YB, p. 141.
208 Letter to Frederick Booker, 31 January 1948. L1, p. 438.
209 YB, p. 233.
210 Sigmund Freud, *Jokes and Their Relation to the Unconscious* (Harmondsworth: Penguin Books, 1960), p. 147.
211 Ibid., p.194; YB, p. 238.
212 In his biography of John Cleese, Jonathan Margolis offers Bergson's theory as a possible explanation of why we laugh at Basil Fawlty. Jonathan Margolis, *Cleese Encounters* (London: Chapmans Publishers Ltd., 1992), pp. 125-7.
213 YB, p. 395.

CHAPTER THREE   The 1940s

1 JBNFNL, p. 143.
2 Ibid., pp. 158–81.
3 Letter to Jock Murray, 20 October 1939. L1, p. 245.
4 A deluxe edition of 29 copies, printed on blue-laid paper, lavishly bound and signed by the author was sold for 10s 6d. JBNFNL, p. 189.
5 Betjeman remarks that the master had accused him of 'preciosity, unkindness, snobbishness'. A footnote records that the same man had 'translated Homer into Esperanto'! John Betjeman, *Old Lights for New Chancels* (London: John Murray (Publishers) Ltd., 1940), p. xi.
6 Ibid.
7 Ibid., p. xii; p. xiii.
8 Ibid., p. xvi.
9 Ibid., pp. xvi–xvii.
10 Ibid., p. xvii.
11 JBNFNL, p. 185. (See also Chapter 1.)
12 Letter to Jock Murray, 11 July 1945. L1, p. 356.
13 John Betjeman, *Vintage London* (London: William Collins, 1942), p. 16.
14 JBNFNL, p. 185.
15 The title *Old Lights for New Chancels* may have been suggested by Ford Madox Hueffer's 1911 volume, *Ancient Lights and Certain New Reflections*, a copy of which Betjeman owned. Hamish Riley-Smith, *The Betjeman Library* (Swanton Abbot: Hamish Riley-Smith, 1996), entry 1630; letters to Jock Murray, 23

November 1939 and 10 January 1940. L1, p. 248; p. 254.

16 JBNFNL, pp. 186–9.

17 Old Lights, p.xvi. A number of these poets also appeared in English Scottish and Welsh Landscape (1944), which Betjeman selected with Geoffrey Taylor. See Appendix A for Glossary.

18 T. S. Eliot wrote that '[n]o poet, no artist of any art, has his complete meaning alone [. . .]. You cannot value him alone; you must set him, for contrast and comparison, among the dead'. T. S. Eliot, 'Tradition and the Individual Talent' (1919), in T. S. Eliot: Selected Essays, 3rd edn, ed. by T. S. Eliot (London: Faber & Faber, 1966), pp. 13–22.

19 Old Lights, p. xvi.

20 W. E. Henley ed., Lyra Heroica: A Book of Verse for Boys, 6th edn (London: David Nutt, 1900), p. vii.

21 Riley-Smith, entry 423.

22 Patrick Taylor-Martin, John Betjeman: His Life and Work (Harmondsworth: Penguin Books, 1983), p. 78.

23 JBNFNL, p. 107.

24 Goronwy Rees, 'An Original Poet' (review of Old Lights for New Chancels), The Spectator, no. 5836, 3 May 1940, pp. 636–8 (636).

25 Ibid., p. 638.

26 John Ruskin, Selected Writings, ed. by Philip Davis (London: J. M. Dent, 1995), pp. x–xx.

27 Isobel Armstrong described the 'double poem' as embodying 'systematically ambiguous language, out of which expressive and phenomenal readings emerge'. Isobel Armstrong, Victorian Poetry: Poetry, Poetics and Politics (London: Routledge, 1993), pp. 13–17.

28 Rees wrote that 'if Mr. Betjeman is one of the most original of modern poets, he is also, in his mock-innocent way, one of the most perverted'. Rees, Spectator, p. 638.

29 J. S. Mill, 'Thoughts on Poetry and Its Varieties', in The Victorian Poet: Poetics and Persona ed. by Joseph Bristow (Beckenham: Croom Helm, 1987).

30 Armstrong, Victorian Poetry, p. 37.

31 See Arthur Hallam in Victorian Scrutinies: Reviews of Poetry 1830–1870, ed. by Isobel Armstrong (London: The Athlone Press, 1972), p. 85.

32 Betjeman sent a copy of 'Myfanwy at Oxford' to the Pipers afraid, as Lycett Green remarks, 'that it was going too far'. He needn't have worried, for in a note dispatched the following week, he wrote: 'I am so glad you like the verses. It is most odd how you have undone an unpublishable gush of verse in me'. Letter to Myfanwy Piper, 28 January 1938. L1, pp. 204–5.

33 YB, pp. 176–7.

34 YB, pp. 320–1.

35 Ibid., p. 77. According to John Press, the title derives from a late-Victorian work by Mrs C. W. Earle, which took the form of a diary with cooking and gardening sections. John Press, Writers and Their Work: John Betjeman (Harlow: Longman Group, 1974), p. 32.

36 Alfred Lord Tennyson, The Poems of Tennyson in Three Volumes, ed. by Christopher Ricks (Harlow: Longman Group, 1987), II, pp. 185–296 (240).

37 A. H. Clough, A. H., Selected Poems, ed. by J. P. Phelan (Harlow: Longman Group, 1995), pp. 75–154 (85). Reproduced throughout with kind permission of Pearson Education Ltd.

38 Ibid., p. 76.

39 As well as recognising the audacious rhyming, Press notes that 'Pot Pourri' shares certain similarities with A. J. Munby's *Dorothy: A Country Story* (1880). Press, p. 33.

40 C. S. Calverley, *The English Poems of Charles Stuart Calverley*, ed. by Hilda D. Spear (Leicester: Leicester University Press, 1974), pp. 58–9 (59).

41 Ovid, *Metamorphoses* III; YB, pp. 64–6.

42 Interestingly, the first edition of *Old Lights* includes this third stanza, omitted from later versions:

> To love her for her mind alone,
>   Her tiny little mind,
> To curve and colour blind alone
>   But to the fact resigned alone
> That oh! she is refined.

It may have been that its lack of concord with the rest of the poem spelled its demise. However, as the verse was missing by the time the piece appeared in *Selected Poems* (1948), it is likely that it was the noted academic John Sparrow who insisted on its removal. For the severe strictures Sparrow placed on this volume (for which he also wrote the preface), see JBNFNL, pp. 392–401.

43 Ibid., p. 2.

44 Thomas Hardy, *Selected Poetry*, ed. by David Wright (London: Penguin Books Ltd., 1978), p. 57.

45 Thomas Hardy, *Selected Poems*, ed. by Tim Armstrong (Harlow: Longman Group, 1993), pp. 121–6 (123).

46 Press, p. 40.

47 Dennis Brown writes that 'Olney Hymns', with its 'slopes of clay' and so on, 'give[s] expression to the organic, fluvial, and grounded characteristics of the Olney Poets' work'. Given the somewhat critical eye that Betjeman cast over Calvinist doctrine in his earlier poetry, this would seem to be yet more proof of religious doubt allayed. Dennis Brown, *Writers and Their Work: John Betjeman* (Plymouth: Northcote House, 1999), pp. 54–5.

48 Note that line 35 is probably a reference to 'The Cell Beside the Sea' (1840), a poem by the Rev R. S. Hawker of Morwenstow, included by Betjeman in his 1959 selection *Altar and Pew*.

49 L1, p. 245; Donald Davie, *Thomas Hardy and British Poetry* (London: Routledge and Kegan Paul, 1973), pp. 109–11 (and ibid.).

50 Philip Larkin, 'It Could Only Happen in England', *Cornhill Magazine* (Autumn 1971), 1069, pp. 21–36 (27).

51 Note that 'In Westminster Abbey' also shares its title with a piece by Francis Beaumont (1586–1616) – another *Lyra Heroica* poet.

52 Betjeman's left-wing friend Mervyn Stockwood (later Bishop of Southwark) had a very public row with the right-wing Bristol alderman, Sir John Hampden Inskip. See JBNFNL, pp. 281–2.

53 Robert Browning, *Poetical Works 1833–1864*, ed. by Ian Jack (London: Oxford University Press, 1970), pp. 367–9 (369).

54 Betjeman's story 'Lord Mount Prospect' featured 'The Society for the Discovery of Obscure Peers', which endeavoured to find said Lord in the backwaters of Eire. See John Betjeman, 'Lord Mount Prospect: *London Mercury*, December 1929', in CH, pp. 10–20.

55 The idea that both Tennyson and Betjeman 'find in the sea and in their childhood an immensely rich source of emotional power and resonance' was noted by John Press. Press, p. 20.

56 Alfred Lord Tennyson, *The Poems of Tennyson in Three Volumes*, ed. by Christopher Ricks (Harlow: Longman Group, 1987), II, p. 24.

57 "Senex", 'Neo-Romantic' (a review of *Old Lights for New Chancels*), *The New Statesman an Nation*, 30 March 1940, pp. 439–40 (439) and ibid.; *The Times Literary Supplement*, 'Some Modern Poets' (includes a review of *Old Lights for New Chancels*), *The Times Literary Supplement*, 23 March 1940, p. 148 and ibid.

58 Figures obtained from 'Copies Ledger K1' (folio 389), the John Murray Archive. Of the 1,417 printed, 1,327 of the 5s edition were available for sale after deductions for the press and so on. In addition, there was one "over", also sold, and 29 copies of a deluxe edition (priced at 10s 6d), which had all been dispatched by the end of June 1940.

59 JBNFNL, p. 236.

60 Unpublished letter to the author from Christopher Hunt of the Imperial War Museum, 27 December 2002.

61 *The Real John Betjeman*. Dir. Marion Milne, Channel 4 (2000).

62 Olivier's companion on the Ireland trip, Dallas Bower, felt that '[w]ithout John Betjeman, we could not have made that sequence there'. JBNFNL, pp. 221–4 (222).

63 *Vintage London*, pp. 3–4 (and ibid.).

64 Letter to the Editor, *Times Literary Supplement*, 21 November 1942. L1, p. 307.

65 John Betjeman, 'Some Comments in Wartime' (talk given on the BBC Home Service, 7 July 1940), in CH, pp. 106–10 (106).

66 Ibid., p. 107.

67 Ibid., p. 108.

68 Ibid., p. 109.

69 John Betjeman, *English Cities and Small Towns* (London: William Collins, 1943), p. 7.

70 Letter to John Sparrow, 25 December 1947. L1, p. 426.

71 Note that Tennyson's 'To the Marquis of Dufferin and Ava' (1889) was an expression of grief for the loss of his son Lionel, who had died while en route to England after staying with the Viceroy of India. There is no poetic connection between the verses – the Laureate's has the same rhythm and metre as *In Memoriam* – and one may assume that, as each knew the Dufferin and Ava of his day, their existence is purely coincidental. See Peter Levi, *Tennyson* (London: Macmillan, 1993), pp. 308–11.

72 Betjeman lamented to John Piper in March 1941 that he had 'not written a line'. Letter to John Piper, 17 March 1941. L1, pp. 282–4, p. 283. He also explained to Oliver Stonor the following month that, quite apart from poetry, there was not even time to 'think at all or feel'. Letter to Oliver Stonor, 19 April 1941. Ibid., pp. 285–6, p. 285.

73 See Derek Stanford, *John Betjeman: A Study* (London: Neville Spearman, 1961), pp. 134–7.

74 Letter to John and Myfanwy Piper, 12 July 1941. L1, pp. 291–2, p. 291.

75 Alfred Lord Tennyson, *The Poems of Tennyson in Three Volumes*, ed. by Christopher Ricks (Harlow: Longman Group, 1987), II, pp. 1–19 (5).

76 Ibid., p. 1.

77 Davie, *Hardy*, pp .106–7; pp. 111–12.

78 Thomas Hardy, *Selected Poetry*, ed. by David Wright (London: Penguin Books Ltd., 1978), p. 334.

79 Stanford, p. 130.

80 Note the reference to *The Princess* – 'The splendour falls on castle walls' – in the first line of the extract. There is also a nod to Dr. Watts in line 17 ('O God our help in ages past') and to the hymn 'Guide me O great Jehovah', whose line 'death of death and hell's destruction' is reflected in Betjeman's line 18 ('Now dull with death and hell at last').

81 W. E. Henley, *The Works of W. E. Henley*, 7 vols, vol. 1, *Poems* (London: David Nutt, 1908), p. 10.

82 The text of the broadcast was later published as 'St. Mark's, Swindon', in John Betjeman, *First and Last Loves*, 2nd edn (London: John Murray (Publishers) Ltd., 1969), pp. 185–8 (188).

83 In brief, Pascal's wager (from *Pensées*, 1670) is as follows: '"God is or he is not." But to which side shall we incline? [. . .] Let us weigh the gain and the loss in wagering that God is. Let us estimate the two chances. If you gain, you gain all; if you lose, you lose nothing. Wager then without hesitation that he is.'

84 'Bristol' first appeared as 'A Plain Course on the Bells' in *Horizon*'s February 1945 issue.

85 Goronwy Rees, 'Clever and Good' (review of *New Bats in Old Belfries*), *The Spectator*, 15 February 1946, p. 176

86 Extracts from reviews in *The New Statesman* (19 January 1946), *The Listener* (14 February 1946) and the *Times Literary Supplement* (5 January 1946) are quoted from JBNFNL, pp. 335–9.

87 Figures obtained from 'Copies Ledger N1' (folio 25), the John Murray Archive.

88 John Betjeman, 'C. F. A. Voysey', *The Architectural Forum*, vol. 72 (May 1940), pp. 348–9 (349).

89 'Anticipation in Spring' was re-titled 'Before Invasion, 1940' in 1958, when it appeared in *Collected Poems*.

90 John Betjeman, 'Nonconformist Architecture', in John Betjeman, *First and Last Loves*, 2nd edn (London: John Murray (Publishers) Ltd., 1969), pp. 90–119 (104).

91 Ibid., p. 113.

92 Ibid., p. 119.

93 This passage was not part of that anthologised in *First and Last Loves*, but is included in the full broadcast available on *John Betjeman: Recollections from the BBC Archives* (selected and introduced by Candida Lycett Green, BBC, 1998), side 2. It also appeared, in abridged form, in *The Church Observer* (no. 21, 2 September 1949, p. 2).

94 John Betjeman, 'London Railway Stations', in John Betjeman, *First and Last Loves*, 2nd edn (London: John Murray (Publishers) Ltd., 1969), pp. 75–89 (75). This article had initially appeared in *Flower of Cities: A Book of London* (1949).

95 John Betjeman, 'Back to the Railway Carriage' (talk given on the BBC Home Service, 10 March 1940), in CH, pp. 111–14.

96 *Vintage London*, p. 16.

97 *First and Last Loves*, 'London Railway Stations', pp. 82–3.

98 *English Cities and Small Towns*, p. 40.

99 Timothy Mowl, *Stylistic Cold Wars: Betjeman Versus Pevsner* (London: John Murray (Publishers) Ltd. 2000), p. 111.

100 JBNFNL, p. 396 (and ibid.).
101 John Betjeman, 'Glories of English Craftsmanship – Electricity and Old Churches', vol. 34, no. 49, 5 December 1953, pp.1582–1583. See also ibid., pp. 437–9.
102 Ibid., pp. 302–11. See also L1, pp. 373–5; 408; 460–462 and passim. The poet's pain was expressed in a sonnet called 'The Empty Pew', which remained unpublished until 2001, when it appeared in the Betjeman Society's journal (*The Betjemanian*, vol. 12):

> I, present with our Church of England few
> At the dear words of Consecration see
> The chalice lifted, hear the sanctus chime
> And glance across to that deserted empty pew.
> In the Perspective of Eternity
> The pain is nothing – but, ah God, in Time.
> ('The Empty Pew', ll. 9–14)

103 Mowl, p. 120. In the Collins guide, Betjeman is more explicit; here, the church is 'almost wholly Early English (13th century)'. John Betjeman, *Collins Guide to English Parish Churches* (London: Collins, 1958), pp. 94–5.
104 There are many stories of Betjeman's hi-jinks in the workplace, from Heddon Court School onwards. See YB, pp. 221–48 (Heddon Court); JBNFNL, pp. 340–58 (British Council) and pp. 368–82 (Oxford Preservation Trust).
105 John Betjeman, 'The Seeing Eye or How to Like Everything', *The Architectural Review*, vol. LXXXVI, 516 (November 1939), pp. 201–4 (202).
106 JBNFNL, p. 392.
107 John Betjeman, *Slick but not Streamlined*, ed. by W. H. Auden (New York: The Country Life Press, 1947), pp. 9–16 (10).
108 See Greg Morse, 'Betjeman and Auden: Strange Bedfellows?', *The Betjemanian*, vol. 19 (2007/08), pp. 52–62.
109 Ibid., p. 396.
110 John Sparrow, Preface to John Betjeman, *Selected Poems* (London: John Murray (Publishers) Ltd., 1948), pp. ix and xi.
111 Letter to Jock Murray, 25 December 1947. JBNFNL, p. 399.
112 John Sparrow, Preface to John Betjeman, *Selected Poems*, p. xxii.
113 Ibid., p. xxi.
114 JBNFNL, pp. 402–5.
115 Figures obtained from 'Copies Ledger N1' (folio 247), the John Murray Archive.
116 Brown, p. 36 (and ibid.).
117 JBNFNL, p. 366.
118 YB, p. 450, note 53.
119 *The UK Christian Handbook 2000/01*, ed. by Heather Wraight and Dr Peter Brierley (London: HarperCollins Religious, 1999), p. 25.
120 Brown, p. 36.
121 C. P. Hill, *British Economic and Social History 1700–1982*, 5th edn (London: Hodder & Stoughton, 1985), p. 282.
122 For information on Theophilus Caleb, see JBNFNL, pp. 365–6 and the following: Kit Lawrie, 'Theophilus Caleb – the "Indian Christian priest"', *The Betjeman Society Newsletter*, Rev. Michael Wright, 'Betjeman's Lincolnshire Church', 45 (April 2001), p. 6.
   Rev. Michael Wright, 'Betjeman's Lincolnshire Church', *The Betjemanian*, vol. 12 (2000/01), pp. 19–22.

123 Brown, p. 37.

124 Per Frank O'Connor's review of *Selected Poems*. JBNFNL, pp. 402–5.

CHAPTER FOUR   The 1950s

1   Timothy Mowl, *Stylistic Cold Wars: Betjeman Versus Pevsner* (London: John Murray (Publishers) Ltd. 2000), p. 122.

2   Ibid., p. 75.

3   JBNFNL, p. 479.

4   C. P. Hill, *British Economic and Social History 1700–1982*, 5th edn (London: Hodder & Stoughton, 1985), pp. 292–3.

5   Timothy Mowl, letter to *The Times*, Saturday, 30 November 2002.

6   John Betjeman, 'Love is Dead', in John Betjeman, *First and Last Loves*, 2nd edn (London: John Murray (Publishers) Ltd., 1969), pp. 1–5 (1) and ibid.

7   Ibid., p. 2; p. 3. Ironically, the origins of uniformity may be traced back to the invention of moveable type, a technology that tended 'to process experience homogeneously' by translating 'the dialogue of shared discourse into packaged information'. Marshall McLuhan, *The Gutenberg Galaxy* (London: Routledge & Kegan Paul Ltd., 1962), p. 165; p. 164.

8   Ibid., p. 5.

9   Letter to Evelyn Waugh, 24 May 1953. L2, p. 42. Waugh's fictional Satellite City boasted a Festival-esque 'Dome of Security', albeit obscured 'for ever among the roofs and butting shoulders of the ancillary wings'. But, '[t]here were no workers' flats, no officials' garden suburb, no parks, no playgrounds yet. These were all on the drawing-boards in the surveyor's office [. . .]'. Evelyn Waugh, *Love Among the Ruins* (London: Chapman and Hall, 1953), pp. 15–16.

10 John Betjeman, 'The Festival Buildings: *Time and Tide*, 5 May 1951', in CH, pp. 277–81.

11 Ibid.

12 Reproduced from 'Mr. Betjeman Despairs' (review of *First and Last Loves*), *The Month*, vol. 8, no. 6 (December 1952, pp. 372–5 (374)), by Evelyn Waugh (Copyright © The Estate of Evelyn Waugh 1952) by permission of PFD on behalf of the Estate of Evelyn Waugh.

13 Mowl, p. 46; YB, p. 268; pp. 276–7.

14 JBNFNL, p. 415.

15 Jerome J. McGann, 'The Text, the Poem, and the Problem of Historical Method', from The Beauty of Inflexions (1985), pp. 111–32, taken from *Modern Literary Theory: A Reader* ed. by Phillip Rice and Patricia Waugh, 3rd edn (London: Arnold, 1996), pp. 251–68.

16 JBNFNL, p. 479 (Betjeman also notes Myfanwy Piper's involvement in his original acknowledgements); Patrick Taylor-Martin, *John Betjeman: His Life and Work* (Harmondsworth: Penguin Books, 1983), p. 173.

17 John Betjeman, 'Victorian Architecture', in John Betjeman, *First and Last Loves*, 2nd edn (London: John Murray (Publishers) Ltd., 1969), pp. 132–78 (132) and ibid.

18 Ibid., p. 133.

19 Ibid., pp. 133–4 (and ibid.).

20 Ibid., p. 140.

21 *First and Last Loves*, 'Victorian Architecture', p. 142.

22 John Betjeman, 'The Architecture of Entertainment', in John Betjeman, *First and*

Last Loves, 2nd edn (London: John Murray (Publishers) Ltd., 1969), pp. 67–74 (67).

23 In 1836, Pugin had published *Contrasts, A Parallel between the Noble Edifices of the 14th and 15th centuries and Similar buildings of the Present Day. Showing a Decay of Taste*. He was making a case for Gothic purity.

24 From a 1955 interview with Betjeman in the *Illustrated London News*, quoted in L2, p. 55.

25 L2, p. xxi.

26 John Betjeman, '"City and Suburban", *The Spectator*, 21 January 1955', in CH, p. 267.

27 JBNFNL, pp. 531–2.

28 John Betjeman, '"High Frecklesby has a Plan", *Punch*, 27 May 1953', in CH, pp. 246–9 (and ibid.).

29 John Betjeman, '"Lamp Posts and Landscape", *Light and Lighting*, November 1953', in CH, pp. 307–10 (and ibid.).

30 Charles Dickens, Martin Chuzzlewit, 4th edn (Harmondsworth: Penguin Books Ltd., 1994), p. 143.

31 JBNFNL, p. 489; 495.

32 Press wrote that the book 'dispelled any lingering suspicions that [he] was not a serious artist'. John Press, *Writers and Their Work: John Betjeman* (Harlow: Longman Group, 1974), p. 36. Taylor-Martin called it his 'finest achievement'. Taylor-Martin, p. 53. For the poet's disinclination to write a preface, see JBNFNL, pp. 488–9.

33 Ibid., p. 494.

34 Geoffrey Taylor, 'New Notes in Old Numbers' (review of *A Few Late Chrysanthemums*), *Time and Tide*, 17 July 1954, p. 971. See also ibid., p. 495.

35 Ibid., p. 494.

36 John Betjeman, '"City and Suburban: At Fifty", *The Spectator*, 31 August 1956', in CH, p. 338.

37 In the poem 'Archibald', even his bear 'seem[ed] to say [. . .] "You're half a century nearer Hell"'. Though this was not published until *Uncollected Poems* in 1982, the reference to being fifty means that it must have been composed circa 1956.

38 Thomas Hardy, *Selected Poems*, ed. by Tim Armstrong (Harlow: Longman Group, 1993), pp. 70–1 (70).

39 Housman, A. E., *The Poems of A. E. Housman*, ed. by Archie Burnett (Oxford: Clarendon Press, 1997), pp. 1–66 (40).

40 John Betjeman: Poetry from the BBC Archives (BBC, 1994), side 1.

41 Dennis Brown, *Writers and Their Work: John Betjeman* (Plymouth: Northcote House, 1999), p. 14.

42 Taylor-Martin, p. 122.

43 Alfred Lord Tennyson, *The Poems of Tennyson in Three Volumes*, ed. by Christopher Ricks (Harlow: Longman Group, 1987), I, pp. 269–70 (270).

44 Alfred Lord Tennyson, *The Poems of Tennyson in Three Volumes*, ed. by Christopher Ricks (Harlow: Longman Group, 1987), II, pp. 513–84 (573).

45 Press, p. 40.

46 Brown, pp. 56–7 (and ibid.).

47 Alfred Lord Tennyson, *The Poems of Tennyson in Three Volumes*, ed. by Christopher Ricks (Harlow: Longman Group, 1987), II, pp. 304–459 (429).

48 Ibid., p. 454.

49 Ibid., p. 319; p. 320.
50 Ibid., p. 315.
51 Ibid., pp. 1–19 (1).
52 Brown, p. 47.
53 JBNFNL, p. 493.
54 Brown, p. 48.
55 Derek Stanford, *John Betjeman: A Study* (London: Neville Spearman, 1961), pp. 66–7.
56 Punnett, Neil and Peter Webber, *The British Isles* (Oxford: Basil Blackwell Ltd., 1984), pp. 110–1.
57 JBNFNL, p. 493.
58 Alfred Lord Tennyson, *The Poems of Tennyson in Three Volumes*, ed. by Christopher Ricks (Harlow: Longman Group, 1987), III, pp. 148–59 (150).
59 D. L. Olroyd notes that the famous quotation 'Nature, red in tooth and claw' (*In Memoriam*, LVI.15) is a presentiment of Darwin. D. L. Olroyd, *Darwinian Impacts: An Introduction to the Darwinian Revolution* (Milton Keynes: Open University Press, 1980), p. 312. See also *English Verse: 1830–1890*, ed. by Bernard Richards (London: Longman Group, 1980), p. 116, note 55.
60 Alfred Lord Tennyson, *The Poems of Tennyson in Three Volumes*, ed. by Christopher Ricks (Harlow: Longman Group, 1987), III, pp. 148–59 (157); Peter Levi, *Tennyson* (London: Macmillan, 1993), pp. 308–9.
61 L2, p. 61.
62 Mowl, *Stylistic Cold Wars*, p. 153.
63 Murray Posh and Lupin Pooter are two would-be aesthetes from George and Weedon Grossmith's *The Diary of A Nobody* (1892).
64 Larkin was presumably referring to Tennyson's 'Lancelot and Elaine' (*Idylls of the King*, 1859–1885), which begins: 'Elaine the fair, Elaine the loveable' and includes many other references to that quality. Philip Larkin, 'It Could Only Happen in England', *Cornhill Magazine* (Autumn 1971), 1069, 21–36 (p. 28).
65 In 'Betjeman En Bloc' (first published in *Listen*, Spring 1959), Larkin wrote that Elaine's 'frown of concentration and Friday ritual are too endearing to suggest that Betjeman wants to do away with her'. Philip Larkin, *Philip Larkin 1922–1985: A Tribute*, ed. by George Hartley (London: The Marvell Press, 1988), pp. 55–67 (58). Press, p. 38. *The Diary of a Nobody* is, as Stanford notes, likely to be responsible for the line 'Taverns for the *bona fide*'. Pooter's entry for Sunday 15 April records a walk over Hampstead and Finchley. Until 1914, only those who had travelled more than three miles were permitted to drink out of hours on a Sunday. Thus by claiming to be '*bona-fide* travellers' (from Blackheath), Stillbrook, Cummings and Gowing are able to obtain alcohol at The Cow and Hedge. Pooter, being honest about his Holloway abode, was less fortunate. George and Weedon Grossmith, *The Diary of a Nobody*, ed. by Ed Glinert, (Harmondsworth: Penguin Books Ltd., 1999) pp. 22–4; p. 212, note 5; Stanford, p. 84.
66 See 'As kingfishers catch fire, dragonflies draw flame' by G. M. Hopkins (composed circa 1881).
67 *First and Last Loves*, 'Love is Dead', pp. 3–4.
68 Larkin, p. 31. For more on Wheeler, see JBNFNL, pp. 23–6.
69 Taylor-Martin, p. 127.
70 This was created by the anthropologist Tom Harrisson and the poet-journalist

Charles Madge, who endeavoured to collect information about the minutiae of everyday life. The Mass-Observation Archive is held by the University of Sussex. See *Poets and Polymaths: Special Collections at the University of Sussex*, ed. by Neil Parkinson (Brighton: University of Sussex, 2002), pp. 62–9.

71 William Morris, *The Earthly Paradise: A Poem by William Morris*, 4 vols (London: Longmans Green, 1905), I, p. 3.

72 Peter Levi notes that Tennyson first used this refrain in 'New Year's Eve' (c.1830–1842), which appeared in *Unpublished Early Poems*, edited by Charles Tennyson, 1931. Levi, p. 326, note 8.

73 John Betjeman, *Collins Guide to English Parish Churches* (London: Collins, 1958), pp. 28–9.

74 JBNFNL, p. 496.

75 William D. Rubinstein, *Twentieth-Century Britain: A Political History* (Basingstoke: Palgrave Macmillan, 2003), p. 255.

76 Ibid., p. 256.

77 John Betjeman, 'John Betjeman Replies', *The Spectator*, no. 6589 (8 October 1954), pp. 443–4 (and ibid.).

78 Figures obtained from 'Copies Ledger R1' (folios 285, 286 and 287) and 'Copies Ledger 4', from the John Murray Archive. For the reference to the Foyle Prize, see L2, p. xxi.

79 JBNFNL, pp. 442–3.

80 On 'Variations', see Taylor-Martin, p. 115; on 'House of Rest', see Brown, p. 59. Rolleston (1857–1920) was a translator and poet known to Yeats; he was a late-Victorian Celtic revivalist.

81 For the parallel with 'Death in Leamington', see Brown, p. 60.

82 Stanford, p. 128.

83 Marshall McLuhan, *Understanding Media*, 2nd edn (London: Routledge, 2001), p. 327.

84 Taylor-Martin, pp. 124–5 (and ibid.). Unfortunately, SPCK does not hold sales figures dating back to 1954 in its archive. Unpublished letter to author from Kay Kershaw, Editorial Assistant, SPCK, 13 August 2003.

85 *Collins Guide*, pp. 18–21.

86 Ibid., pp. 33–4 (and ibid.). Syntax was the comic creation of William Combe (1741–1823). He made three 'tours' *In Search of*: *The Picturesque* (1809), *Consolation* (1820) and *A Wife* (1821). Betjeman owned copies of the first two of these poetic odysseys. See Hamish Riley-Smith, *The Betjeman Library* (Swanton Abbot: Hamish Riley-Smith, 1996), entries 222–4.

87 Press, pp. 16–17 (and ibid.).

88 *Collins Guide*, p. 43.

89 Ibid., p. 82.

90 Ibid., p. 67.

91 Ibid., pp. 69–73.

92 Ibid., pp. 73–6; *First and Last Loves*, 'Victorian Architecture', pp. 137–8 (Betjeman was quoting Professor Lethaby). Other architects named as 'hard' in this article are: James Brooks, E. G. Paley, J. P. Seddon, S. S. Teulon, William White and Henry Woodyer. Ibid., p. 138.

93 *Collins Guide*, p. 15.

94 L2, p. 7.

95 *Collins Guide*, pp. 13–14.

96 L1, p. 341.
97 Cited by Mowl, *Stylistic Cold Wars*, p. 134 (for Pevsner); Ian Nairn, 'Intermittent Enthusiasm' (includes review of the *Collins Guide to English Parish Churches*), *The Architectural Review*, vol. CXXVIII, no. 765 (November 1960), p. 323.
98 Taylor-Martin, pp. 174–5.
99 John Betjeman, 'City and Suburban', *The Spectator*, no. 6592 (29 October 1954). Cited in JBNFNL, p. 542.
100 The Metropolitan Railway's station at Aldersgate Street was opened on 23 December 1865. It was renamed Aldersgate in 1910, Aldersgate & Barbican in 1923 and became merely Barbican on 1 December 1968. The overall roof was demolished in 1955. See Desmond F. Croome, *The Circle Line* (Capital Transport, 2003).
101 *Collins Guide*, p. 254.
102 The first line of this extract possibly refers to Eliot's *The Waste Land* (1922), which includes the line 'Sweet Thames, run softly, till I end my song' (Section III ('The Fire Sermon'), l. 176), although Betjeman's most likely source is Spenser's *Prothalamion* (1596 – see I. 18).
103 Coleridge published his 'Monody on the Death of Chatterton' in 1796, and Arnold subtitled 'Thyrsis' (1866) with the note that it was 'A MONODY, / to commemorate the author's friend, / ARTHUR HUGH CLOUGH, / who died at Florence, 1861'.
104 CH, pp. 319–20.
105 L2, p. 100.
106 JBNFNL, p. 567.
107 CH, p. 320.
108 Letter to Lionel Brett, 25 January 1957, L2, pp. 120–1, p. 120.
109 Ibid., p. 56; pp. 3–4.
110 Mowl, *Stylistic Cold Wars*, p .148.
111 L2, pp. 127–8.
112 Mowl, *Stylistic Cold Wars*, p. 147.
113 Letter to Betjeman from P. Morton Shand, 21 October 1958. YB, pp. 277–8.
114 CH, p. 321.
115 John Betjeman, 'Men and Buildings: Architecture for Entertainment', *Daily Telegraph and Morning Post*, 16 November 1959, p. 13.
116 John Betjeman, 'Men and Buildings: Variety versus Legitimate', *Daily Telegraph and Morning Post*, 15 December 1958, p. 9; John Betjeman, 'Men and Buildings: Destruction for Cash', *Daily Telegraph and Morning Post*, 12 January 1959, p. 11.
117 JBNFNL, p. 601 (and ibid.).
118 Ibid., p. 602.
119 Ibid., pp. 604–5.
120 Powell's review, 'The Swan of Wantage', appeared in *Punch* (17 December 1958). Ibid., p. 606 (and ibid.).
121 John Betjeman, *Collected Poems*, complied and selected by the Earl of Birkenhead, 6th edn (London: John Murray (Publishers) Ltd., 2001), xiv–xxiv (xiv).
122 Ibid., p. xxiii.
123 Bergonzi's review is quoted by Derek Stanford. Stanford, pp. 65–6.
124 *Collected Poems*, p. xxiv.
125 John Betjeman, 'John Betjeman Replies', *The Spectator*, no. 6589 (8 October 1954), pp. 443–4 (and ibid.).

126 Hillier notes that this 'social slight' rankled with Betjeman and that he was able to write it out of his system thus. YB, p. 20.
127 JBNFNL, pp. 505–10.
128 George and Weedon Grossmith, *The Diary of a Nobody*, ed. by Ed Glinert (Harmondsworth: Penguin Books Ltd., 1999), pp. 165–8. Derek Stanford notes that Betjeman 'lovingly fills in the background of time and place' in this poem. Stanford, p. 54.
129 Ibid., p. xx.
130 Pooter comments that the expression of a portrait was 'not quite pleasing', which is hardly surprising, given that the picture, which shows his host's late sister-in-law, was completed after the subject's death. After moving on to a picture of 'a jolly-looking middle-aged gentleman', he tries to make amends by claiming that '[l]ife doesn't seem to trouble him much'. It didn't, for he, the host's brother, was dead too. Ibid., pp. 165–8.
131 One must also note some development of thought here – in 'Love is Dead', Pooter is seen as merely the least offensive face of the average man and average lifestyle against whom the piece is directed ('At his best [the average man] is as loveable as Mr. Pooter, but he is no leader'). *First and Last Loves*, 'Love is Dead', p. 1.
132 In 1950, the Conservative government pledged to build 300,000 houses a year through the private and public sector. In 1953, they built 327,000, with 354,000 following in 1954. Rubinstein, p. 255.
133 Glinert notes that in the twentieth century, 'Holloway continued to be developed, so that now almost no parkland or greenery, let alone a bean field, remains [. . .]. The area is also no longer classed as suburban, but inner-city.' *The Diary of a Nobody*, p. xxi.
134 JBNFNL, p. 607.
135 Philip Larkin, 'Poetry Beyond a Joke' (review of *Collected Poems*), *The Manchester Guardian*, 19 December 1958. Reproduced by kind permission of the Society of Authors as the Literary Representative of the Estate of Philip Larkin.
136 John Sparrow, 'A Serious Poet' (review of *Collected Poems*), *Times Literary Supplement*, 12 December 1958, p. 720 (and ibid.).
137 JBNFNL, p. 605; p. 706, note 44. Specific figures were gleaned from 'Copies Ledger T1' (folios 385 and 386), the John Murray Archive.
138 Ibid, p. 609; L2, p. xxii.
139 L2, pp. 154–9 (and ibid.).
140 Sparrow, 'A Serious Poet', p. 720.

CHAPTER FIVE   The 1960s–70s

1   L2, p. 181.
2   John Betjeman, 'Men and Buildings – Heritage of the Rail Age', from *The Daily Telegraph*, 8 February 1960' (as 'The Demolition of Euston Arch') in CH, pp. 412–15.
3   Anonymous, 'The Euston Murder', *The Architectural Review*, vol. CXXXI, 782 (April 1962), 235–9 (p. 236). Given the detail in this article, and the fact that Betjeman had described Crewkerne as a 'traffic-*murdered* town' (my italics – see p. 119), it is possible that it was he who wrote it. Alas *The Architectural Review* has 'no way of knowing' if this is the case. Unpublished letter to author from Lynne Jackson, *The Architectural Review*, 14 April 2005. The same is true of the

Victorian Society, which has no reference to the piece in its archives. Unpublished letter to author from Dr. Ian Dungavell, Director, The Victorian Society, 25 May 2005.

4 William D. Rubinstein, *Twentieth-Century Britain: A Political History* (Basingstoke: Palgrave Macmillan, 2003), p. 265.

5 L2, p. 218.

6 BTBOL, p. 140.

7 Timothy Mowl, *Stylistic Cold Wars: Betjeman Versus Pevsner* (London: John Murray (Publishers) Ltd. 2000), p. 158.

8 Ibid., p. 52; John Betjeman, 'Dictating to the Railways', *The Architectural Review*, vol. LXXIV, 442 (September 1933), pp. 83–4 (84) (and ibid.).

9 *The London Midland & Scottish Railway: A Century and a Half of Progress – LMS 150*, ed. by Patrick Whitehouse and David St. John Thomas (Newton Abbot: David & Charles (Publishers) Ltd., 1987), p. 69.

10 Mowl, *Stylistic Cold Wars*, p. 52.

11 'Dictating to the Railways', p. 84 (and ibid.).

12 John Betjeman, 'London Railway Stations' [from *Flower of Cities: A Book of London*, 1949], in John Betjeman, *First and Last Loves*, 2nd edn (London: John Murray (Publishers) Ltd., 1969), pp. 75–89 (80).

13 Betjeman notes 'French' detail at Charing Cross, Cannon Street, Broad Street and many other stations. Ibid. For de Cronin's editorial policy see CHAPTER TWO and YB, pp. 259–60.

14 John Betjeman, *London's Historic Railway Stations* (London: John Murray (Publishers) Ltd., 1972), pp. 124–6.

15 Letter to Lionel Esher, 17 May 1966. L2, pp. 317–18 (and ibid.). Esher served on the Royal Fine Art Commission from 1951 to 1969.

16 John Betjeman, 'A Pity About the Abbey', in *The Twelfth Man: A book of original contributions brought together by The Lord's Taverners in honour of HRH The Prince Philip, Duke of Edinburgh KG, KT*, ed. by Martin Boddey (London: Cassell, 1971), pp. 207–10 (and ibid.).

17 *The Times* Television Correspondent, Review of *A Pity About the Abbey*, *The Times*, Friday, 30 July 1965, p. 13 (and ibid.).

18 *Any Questions*, BBC Radio, 23 May 1969. *John Betjeman: Recollections from the BBC Archives* (selected and introduced by Candida Lycett Green, BBC, 1998), side 4 (and ibid.).

19 Extracts from Betjeman's speech at the Annual Dinner of the Royal Academy of Arts, 1 May 1962, *John Betjeman: Recollections from the BBC Archives* (selected and introduced by Candida Lycett Green, BBC, 1998), side 1; John Betjeman, 'Men and Buildings – What a Town Ought to Be', from *The Daily Telegraph*, 24 February 1964 (as 'The Ideal Town') in CH, pp. 406–9 (408).

20 John Betjeman, 'Men and Buildings – Size Without Greatness', *Daily Telegraph*, 10 March 1958, p. 11.

21 John Betjeman, 'Men and Buildings – The Best and Worst of an Era', from *The Daily Telegraph*, 3 July 1961 (as 'Sheffield') in CH, pp. 398–401 (400) (and ibid.).

22 'Men and Buildings – The Best and Worst of an Era', pp. 398–400 (and ibid.).

23 John Betjeman, 'A Century of English Architecture', *The Spectator*, no. 7000 (24 August 1962), pp. 252–4 (252).

24 Burns sent Betjeman a copy of the letter he submitted to the *Telegraph*, believing that the paper would fail to print it. Unpublished letter to Betjeman from Dr. B.

Burns (10 July 1961), courtesy of The McPherson Library, University of Victoria, Canada. The poem, like the prose, also made reference to the 'Corn Law Rhymer', Ebenezer Elliott (1781–1849); Betjeman's quoting of Elliott in the article elicited a delighted response from T. Rigby Taylor, great-grandson of the poet, who wrote that his forebear's work allegedly 'had more influence in the repeal of the Corn Laws than Cobden & Bright'. Unpublished letter to Betjeman from T. Rigby Taylor, CBE, JP (6 July 1961), courtesy of The McPherson Library, University of Victoria, Canada.

25 John Betjeman, 'Men and Buildings – Suburbs Common or Garden', from *The Daily Telegraph*, 22 August 1960 (as 'Garden Suburbs') in CH, pp. 409–12 (and ibid.).

26 For more on 'The Battle of Bedford Park', see BTBOL, pp. 219–35.

27 Ibid., p. 235.

28 An abridged script is included in Guest's anthology. See John Betjeman, *The Best of Betjeman*, ed. by John Guest (Harmondsworth: Penguin Books Ltd., 1978), pp. 215–36. The term 'Metro-land' was coined by James Garland, a copywriter for the Metropolitan Railway, who told a colleague how, during a spell of sick leave in 1915, he had leapt from his bed with excitement when the word came to him. The company's guidebooks, which used it as a title, are featured in the film and may well have been Betjeman's own, for he owned copies of the 1931 and 1932 editions. See Alan A. Jackson, *London's Metropolitan Railway* (Newton Abbot: David and Charles (Publishers) Ltd., 1986), p. 238. For Betjeman's ownership of the Metro-land guides see Hamish Riley-Smith, *The Betjeman Library* (Swanton Abbot: Hamish Riley-Smith, 1996), entries 3924–5.

29 Mowl, *Stylistic Cold Wars*, p. 164.

30 L2, p. 447 (and ibid.).

31 John Betjeman, 'Men and Buildings – So Little Left of the Old Middlesex', from *The Daily Telegraph*, 12 August 1963 (as 'Middlesex') in *The Best of Betjeman*, pp. 191–3 (191) (and Ibid.).

32 Ibid., p. 192.

33 Ibid., p. 193.

34 The article on Marylebone and Baker Street Stations, from which this quotation comes, originally appeared in *Wheeler's Quarterly Review* (Summer 1970). It was subsequently reproduced in *London's Historic Railway Stations* (pp. 114–23, p. 119).

35 *The Best of Betjeman*, pp. 215–36 (p. 218). *Metro-land* was first broadcast on BBC2 at 10.10 p.m. on Monday, 26 February 1973 (Swindon *Evening Advertiser*, TV listing, p. 3).

36 Ibid., p. 222.

37 Ibid., p. 223–4; Mowl, *Stylistic Cold Wars*, p. 165; *The Best of Betjeman*, p. 224.

38 From *The City in History* by Lewis Mumford, published by Secker & Warburg. Reprinted by permission of The Random House Group Ltd. Excepts copyright © 1961 and renewed 1989 by Lewis Mumford, reprinted in the USA by permission of Harcourt Inc. Lewis Mumford, *The City in History* (London: Secker and Warburg, 1961), p. 486, cited in David C. Thorns, *Suburbia* (London: MacGibbon and Kee Ltd., 1972), p. 60.

39 *The Best of Betjeman*, p. 224; Mowl, p. 165.

40 *The Best of Betjeman*, p. 217.

41 Mowl, p. 165; *The Best of Betjeman*, p. 225.

42 *The Best of Betjeman*, p. 225 (and ibid.).

43 The photograph shows the sweeping, elegant line of the crescent, with a villa seemingly slapped at the end of it. John Betjeman, *Devon, compiled with illustrations and information of every sort by* (London: The Architectural Press, 1936), p. 24.

44 *The Best of Betjeman*, p. 231 (and ibid.).

45 Ibid., pp. 231–3.

46 Mowl, *Stylistic Cold Wars*, pp. 165–6; *The Best of Betjeman*, p. 235.

47 Mowl, *Stylistic Cold Wars*, p. 166.

48 *The Best of Betjeman*, pp. 235–6.

49 L2, p. 201 (and ibid.).

50 John Betjeman, 'Common Experiences' (review of Philip Larkin's *The Whitsun Weddings*), from *The Listener*, 19 March 1964 (as 'Philip Larkin: "The Whitsun Weddings"') in CH, pp. 394–7 (396–7).

51 Selections from *Scenes that are Brightest* (including 'London Before the Motorcar') are available on *John Betjeman: Recollections from the BBC Archives* (selected and introduced by Candida Lycett Green, BBC, 1998).

52 John Betjeman, 'Penalties of Success', *The Author*, Spring 1967, cited in L2, p. 310 (and ibid.).

53 Alfred Lord Tennyson, *The Poems of Tennyson in Three Volumes*, ed. by Christopher Ricks (Harlow: Longman Group, 1987), II, pp. 651–2 (652).

54 Ibid., pp. 304–459 (366).

55 Alfred Lord Tennyson, *The Poems of Tennyson in Three Volumes*, ed. by Christopher Ricks (Harlow: Longman Group, 1987), III, pp. 25–9 (28).

56 A. C. Swinburne, *Swinburne: Selected Poems*, ed. by L. M. Findlay (Manchester: Carcanet New Press Ltd., 1982), pp. 63–75 (65).

57 Taylor-Martin, p. 141.

58 Hardy's second wife noted in her biography of her husband that this trip commenced on 6 March 1913, 'almost to a day, forty-three years after his first journey to Cornwall'. Florence Emily Hardy, *The Life of Thomas Hardy: Volume II – 1892–1928*, 2nd edn (London: Macmillan and Co. Ltd., 1933), p. 156. See also Michael Millgate, *Thomas Hardy: A Biography* (Oxford: Oxford University Press, 1982), pp. 486–8.

59 'Tregardock' is easily the most important of this sequence. However, as it is clearly a reaction to the bad reviews that *Summoned by Bells* (1960) received, it will be discussed in the chapter on that volume. The barrow in *The Return of the Native* is described as a 'bossy projection of earth above its natural level', occupying 'the loftiest ground of the loneliest height that the heath contained'. Thomas Hardy, *The Return of the Native*, ed. by Tony Slade (London: Penguin Books Ltd., 1999), p. 17.

60 Thomas Hardy, *Selected Poems*, ed. by Tim Armstrong (Harlow: Longman Group, 1993), pp. 88–91 (89–90).

61 Patrick Taylor-Martin, *John Betjeman: His Life and Work* (Harmondsworth: Penguin Books, 1983), p. 144; JBNFNL, p. 543.

62 Ibid.

63 For Press's views on the Cornish poems, see John Press, 'Change and Decay' (review of *High and Low*), *Punch*, 23 November 1966, p. 789.

64 Alfred Lord Tennyson, *The Poems of Tennyson in Three Volumes*, ed. by Christopher Ricks (Harlow: Longman Group, 1987), II, pp. 20–4 (21).

65 Dennis Brown, *Writers and Their Work: John Betjeman* (Plymouth: Northcote House, 1999), p. 45.

66 Ibid.

67 Ibid., p. 44.

68 Letter to Harry Jarvis, 13 October 1963. L2, pp. 261–2.

69 Rachel Carson, *Silent Spring* (Harmondsworth: Penguin Books Ltd., 1999), pp. 12–17.

70 Ibid., p. 29.

71 This continued relevance is discussed by Brown (p.44) and also the present author (who refers to GM crops – politically topical at the time of writing). See Greg Morse, 'Betjeman Lives?', *The Betjemanian*, vol. 12 (2000/01), pp. 23–5 (24).

72 Graham Martin, 'New Poetry' (includes review of *High and Low*), *The Listener*, 26 January 1967, pp. 140–1 (140).

73 Graham Chapman, John Cleese, Terry Gilliam, Eric Idle, Terry Jones and Michael Palin (with Bob McCabe), *The Pythons – Autobiography by the Pythons* (London: Orion Publishing Group Ltd., 2003), p. 351.

74 Philip Larkin, 'The Blending of Betjeman' (review of *Summoned By Bells*), *The Spectator*, 2 December 1960, p. 913.

75 Peter Thomas, 'John Bull Speaks: Reflections on the Collected Poems of John Betjeman', *Western Humanities Review*, vol. 27, 1973, pp. 289–94 (292). In fact, the opening of 'In Willesden Churchyard' owes more to Christopher Marlowe's 'The Passionate Shepherd to his Love' (1600), which begins: 'Come live with me, and be my love, / And we will all the pleasures prove.' Thus Betjeman's poem deliberately emphasises the 'anti-pastoral' mid-twentieth century.

76 Olive Cook, *The Stansted Affair: A Case for the People* (with a foreword by John Betjeman) (London: Pan Books Ltd., 1967), pp. 9–10; pp. 11–12. Quoted with kind permission of Pan Macmillan. Copyright © Olive Cook, 1967.

77 Taylor-Martin, p. 149 (and ibid.).

78 This discovery was made by Hillier. See YB, p. 323.

79 Ibid., p. 18.

80 Hillier has discovered that it actually dates from the period of *New Bats in Old Belfries* (circa 1945). JBNFNL, p. 327

81 John Press, *Writers and Their Work: John Betjeman* (Harlow: Longman Group, 1974) p. 42.

82 Thomas Hardy, *Selected Poetry*, ed. by David Wright (London: Penguin Books Ltd., 1978), p. 72.

83 See also Taylor-Martin, p. 147 (and ibid.).

84 JBNFNL, p. 509.

85 This was discovered by Hillier. Ibid., p. 259.

86 Brown, p. 21.

87 Betjeman made this comment before a contemporary reading of 'Anglo-Catholic Congress'. *John Betjeman: Poetry from the BBC Archives* (BBC, 1994), side 3.

88 YB, p. 164.

89 See John Betjeman, 'P. Morton Shand: A Personal Memoir', *The Architectural Review*, vol. CXXVIII, 765 (November 1960), 325–8, John Betjeman, 'Obituary: Sir Ninian Comper: 1864–1960', *The Architectural Review*, vol. CXXIX, 769 (March 1961), pp.153–4 and John Betjeman, 'Evelyn Waugh: A Brief Life', *The Listener*, vol. 78, no. 2004 (24 August 1967), p. 226.

90 Graham Martin, 'New Poetry' (includes review of *High and Low*), *The Listener*, 26 January 1967, pp. 140–1 (140).

91 C. B. Cox, 'Betjeman Land' (review of *High and Low*), *The Spectator*, 9 December 1966, p. 763.

92 John Carey, 'Unpolitical Auden' (includes review of *High and Low*), *New Statesman*, 23 December 1966, pp. 941–2 (942).

93 John Press, 'Change and Decay' (review of *High and Low*), *Punch*, 23 November 1966, p. 789.

94 Letter to Candida Lycett Green, 11 November 1966. L2, p. 325.

95 Letter to Betjeman from Maurice Bowra, 29 October 1966, quoted by Lycett Green. Ibid., p. 309.

96 Figures obtained from 'Copies Ledger 4', the John Murray Archive. Sales of *High and Low* continued to sell until stocks ran out in 1985 (though these were augmented by a reprint of unspecified magnitude in 1975).

97 L2, p. 256; Mowl, *Stylistic Cold Wars*, p. 137.

98 L2, p. 256; ibid., p. 312.

99 John Betjeman and Basil Clarke, *English Churches* (London: Vista Books, 1964), p. 55.

100 John Betjeman, *City of London Churches*, 3rd edn (London: Pitkin Guides Ltd., 1997), p. 3; ibid., p. 4.

101 Ibid., p. 12.

102 Ibid., p. 23.

103 Ibid., p. 15; p. 24; p. 28.

104 Letter to John Summerson, 14 June 1966. L2, p. 319.

105 Letter from John Summerson to Betjeman, 15 June 1966, quoted in L2, pp. 319–20.

106 Mowl, *Stylistic Cold Wars*, p. 149.

107 L2, p. 319.

108 *London's Historic Railway Stations*, p. 15.

109 Ibid.

110 L2, p. 370.

CHAPTER SIX   The 1970s–80s

1   L2, p. 437.

2   Letter to Mark Ogilvie-Grant, 2 May 1965. Ibid., p. 290.

3   Letter to Dan MacNabb, 3 June 1967. Ibid., p. 333.

4   Ibid., p. 438.

5   John Winder, 'Sir John Betjeman: Poet Laureate in Ordinary, who felt humbled', *The Times*, 11 October 1972, p. 1.

6   Letter from Larkin to Judy Egerton, 17 May 1967, *Selected Letters of Philip Larkin: 1940 to 1985*, ed. by Anthony Thwaite (London: Faber & Faber, 1992), p. 375. He added (dryly quoting George Bernard Shaw) that 'England doesn't deserve great men'. For his part, Betjeman wrote that Larkin himself ('and failing you, Charles Causley') would have been his choice in 1972. Letter to Larkin, 17 October 1972. L2, pp. 454–5.

7   Letter to Betjeman from Maurice Bowra, 29 October 1966, quoted by Lycett Green. L2, p. 309.

8   Tim Devlin, 'Summoned by Success', *The Times*, 11 October 1972, p. 16.

9   *The Times*, 11 October 1972, p. 1.

10 Alfred Austin, *English Lyrics*, ed. by William Watson, 4th edn (London: Macmillan and Co. Ltd., 1896), pp. 100–1 (100). Reproduced by permission of Palgrave Macmillan.

11   Michael Hulse, 'The Laureate Business or the Laureate in Englishness', *Quadrant*, September 1985, pp. 45–9 (47).

12   'William Hickey' reported in the *Daily Express* on 17 February 1960 how he had telephoned a bathing Betjeman, who came up with the following at very short notice indeed:

> You might have thought the world absurd
> That could so advertise a birth
> With louder trumpets than that stable heard
> When our Creator came to earth
> But if you did, then you were wrong
> To let those brazen voices smother
> A deeper, universal song –
> Such as is sung by every mother.
>   ('THE POEM HE WROTE IN THE BATH', ll. 1–8)

See BTBOL, p. 363.

13   This was probably requested either by the 'Beautiful daughter of a king' (l. 11) herself, or by Betjeman's mistress, Lady Elizabeth Cavendish, who was one of the princess's Ladies in Waiting. John Betjeman, 'A Poem for Princess Margaret's Wedding Day', *Harper's Bazaar*, vol. LXII, no. 2, May 1960, pp. 62–3. For Betjeman's relationship with Elizabeth Cavendish, see JBNFNL, pp. 462–3 (and passim).

14   The game birds in the first line may have been suggested by William Morris's 'Woodcock and snipe when swallows go'. William Morris, *Works* III, p. 26 – cited in Paul Thompson, *The Work of William Morris*, 2nd edn (London: Quartet Book Ltd., 1977), p. 196.

15   Interestingly, Lady Cunard had a brief conversation with Evelyn Waugh about Betjeman at a party in December 1931. Having established that she disliked religion, and satires thereon, Waugh mentioned that Betjeman was a Quaker. 'Oh,' she replied, 'they're much the worst.' YB, pp. 357–8. In a letter to Edward James (1 January 1937), the poet included a draft which shows that the original line had read (more inflammatorily): 'At a red suburb ruled by Mrs Simpson.' The piece was, as the poet realised, 'strongly prophetic'. L1, pp. 164–5 (165).

16   John Langford, 'The Stamp Collection Waits . . . ', The Betjeman Society Newsletter, 49 (April 2002), p. 4.

17   *Stanley Gibbons GB Stamp Album*, 2nd edn (London: Stanley Gibbons Publications Ltd., 1981), p. 7.

18   Langford, 'Stamp Collection', p. 6

19   JBNFNL, p. 258.

20   See also L2, pp. 474–5.

21   *Parkinson*, 17 February 1973, *John Betjeman: Recollections from the BBC Archives* (selected and introduced by Candida Lycett Green, BBC, 1998), side 4.

22   YB, p. 77.

23   L2, p. 442.

24   *Newsweek* Correspondent, 'Mrs. Phillips the Princess', *Newsweek*, 26 November 1973, pp. 20–1 (20); *Time* Correspondent, 'Anne's Day: Simply Splendid', *Time*, 26 November 1973, pp. 14–5 (14). Betjeman was interviewed by Kingsley Amis for BBC TV's *Omnibus* series, 5 November 1972. See also Auberon Waugh, 'Royal Rhymester', *New York Times Magazine*, 6 January 1974, pp. 18–26.

25   BTBOL, pp. 379–80. For the Mary Shand poem, see JBNFNL, p. 278.

26 John Betjeman, *A Pictorial History of English Architecture*, 2nd edn (Harmondsworth: Penguin Books Ltd., 1974), p. 7.

27 Ibid., p. 7; p. 49.

28 Ibid., p. 102; ibid., p. 101.

29 John Betjeman, *Ghastly Good Taste*, 3rd edn (London: Century Hutchinson, 1986), p. 110.

30 Ibid., p. 97; ibid., p. 98.

31 *Pictorial History*, p. 81. In *Victorian Architecture: Four Studies in Evaluation* (1970), Summerson had written that '[. . .] Crystal Palace architecture, while undoubtedly suitable for a great exhibition, a palm house, or a railway shed, was suitable for little else'. John Summerson, *Victorian Architecture: Four Studies in Evaluation* (London and New York: Columbia University Press, 1970), p. 8.

32 CH, p. 437.

33 John Betjeman, 'Nooks and Corners of the New Barbarism: 1 – Hillgate House, Ludgate Hill', *Private Eye*, no. 246 (21 May 1971), p. 7.

34 John Betjeman, 'Nooks and Corners of the New Barbarism: 6 – Brunswick Square, WC1', *Private Eye*, no. 260 (13 August 1971), p. 7.

35 L2, p. 373.

36 John Betjeman, 'A Formative Friend', from *Maurice Bowra: A Celebration*, ed. by Hugh Lloyd-Jones (London: Duckworth, 1974), (as 'Maurice Bowra: A Formative Friend') in CH, pp. 488–91 (488–489); John Betjeman, Obituary of Frederick Etchells, from *The Architectural Review*, October 1973 (as 'Frederick Etchells'), ibid., pp. 466–8 (467–8); John Betjeman, 'Oxford', from *W. H. Auden: A Tribute*, ed. by Stephen Spender (London: Weidenfeld and Nicolson, 1974), (as 'W. H. Auden at Oxford'), ibid., pp. 483–5 (484–5); John Betjeman, 'Without a doubt you towered high above us', *New Statesman*, 5 October 1973, p. 478.

37 For more on *Betjeman in Australia*, see BTBOL, pp. 289–305.

38 L2, p. 378.

39 G. M. Harvey, 'Poetry of Commitment: John Betjeman's Later Writing', *Dalhousie Review*, 56 (1976), pp. 112–24 (114).

40 John Betjeman, 'Men and Buildings – Size Without Greatness', *Daily Telegraph*, 10 March 1958, p. 11.

41 Patrick Taylor-Martin, *John Betjeman: His Life and Work* (Harmondsworth: Penguin Books, 1983), p. 153.

42 William Morris, *The Earthly Paradise: A Poem by William Morris*, 4 vols (London: Longmans Green, 1905), I, p. 3.

43 William Morris, *News from Nowhere and Other Writings*, ed. by Clive Wilmer (Harmondsworth: Penguin Books Ltd., 1993), pp. 185–6.

44 Harvey, p. 113 (and ibid.). Betjeman had also described the 'precision and beauty', and indeed the 'beautiful rhythmic motion', of the Crofton Beam Engine (near Marlborough, Wiltshire) in his 1955 film for Shell.

45 Duncan Harper, *Wilts & Somerset: A Railway Landscape* (Bath: Millstream Books, 1987), pp. 101–6.

46 Oil prices rose dramatically in October 1973 as a result of the Yom Kippur war between Israel and the Arab nations. William D. Rubinstein, *Twentieth-Century Britain: A Political History* (Basingstoke: Palgrave Macmillan, 2003), p. 305.

47 Harvey, p. 113.

48 Ibid., pp. 114–15 (and ibid.).

49 Taylor-Martin, p. 150.

50 Robert Browning, *Poetical Works 1833–1864*, ed. by Ian Jack (London: Oxford University Press, 1970), pp. 367–9 (368).

51 Developed more fully in Greg Morse, 'Betjeman Lives?', *The Betjemanian*, vol. 12 (2000/01), pp. 23–5 (23–4).

52 In a letter to Mary Wilson (27 June 1969), Betjeman referred to this 'queer poem' (as he described it) and added that he was going to rewrite it so as to 'hint more at the crime'. He added: '[t]he point is that it should be an unacceptable crime'. L2, pp. 383–4.

53 Taylor-Martin notes that this is reminiscent of Arnold's 'The bloom is gone, and with the bloom go I!' of 'Thyrsis' (l. 60). Taylor-Martin, p. 157.

54 John Press likened 'Lenten Thoughts' to D. H. Lawrence's 'mystical' view of sex, while Harvey found the poem 'subtly and powerfully subversive'. But on seeing 'Betjers in the Express today', Philip Larkin wrote to Anthony Thwaite (13 May 1973) that 'sometimes I'm ashamed of liking him. I hope he pulls himself together'. In similar vein, *Private Eye* ran an amusing parody which began: 'Lovely lady in the pew, / Goodness, what a scorcher – phew!' See John Press, *Writers and Their Work: John Betjeman* (Harlow: Longman Group, 1974), p. 44; Harvey, p. 117; Larkin, *Selected Letters*, p. 480; L2, p. 443.

55 Taylor-Martin, p. 158.

56 Alan Pryce-Jones, 'Bonus of Laughter' (review of *A Nip in the Air*), *Books and Bookmen*, April 1975, p. 45. Pryce-Jones also used 'The Bonus of Laughter' as the title for his autobiography. L2, p. 594.

57 Philip Toynbee, 'Summoned by knells' (review of *A Nip in the Air*), *The Observer Review*, 24 November 1974.

58 Lyman Andrews, 'Autumn Collection' (review of *A Nip in the Air*), *The Sunday Times*, 24 November 1974 (and ibid.).

59 Unpublished letter to author from Virginia Murray of the John Murray Archive, 9 August 2005.

60 L2, p. 444.

61 Letter from HRH Prince Charles to Betjeman, 13 May 1976, cited in Jonathan Dimbleby, *The Prince of Wales: A Biography* (London: Little, Brown and Co., 1994), p. 233.

62 Letter to Mary Wilson, 5 May 1976, L2, pp. 498–9. Pam Ayres wrote humorous lyrics on country life, which Betjeman liked but knew were not poetry (as, presumably, did she). Her huge sales at the time put her into the same place as the Laureate in many people's minds.

63 Dimbleby, *Prince of Wales*, p. 234.

64 Ibid., p. 234.

65 Letter to Tom Driberg from Betjeman, 21 July 1976. L2, p. 504.

66 Ibid., p. 495.

67 Abraham N. Lieberman and Frank Williams *et al.*, *Parkinson's Disease – The Complete Guide for Patients and Carers* (London: HarperCollins*Publishers*, 1995), p. 148.

68 L2, p. 446 (Jenkins).

69 John Betjeman, 'A Passion for Churches', in CH, pp. 498–521 (498; 513; 514).

70 An abridged version was published not long after Betjeman's film was transmitted, which itself came soon after Plomer's death in 1973. See Francis Kilvert, *Kilvert's Diary*, ed. by William Plomer (Harmondsworth: Penguin Books Ltd., 1977).

71 John Betjeman, 'Hardy and Architecture', from *The Genius of Thomas Hardy*,

ed. by Margaret Drabble (London: Weidenfeld & Nicolson, 1976), in CH, pp. 469–73 (469; 470–1; 472).

72 John Betjeman, 'The Lonely Laureate', cited in L2, p. 511.

73 Ibid., p. 517; p. 549.

74 Rahere, a clergyman of Frankish descent, founded the hospital, construction of which began in 1123.

75 *Private Eye*, 'Poetry Corner', issue 464, p. 17. Reproduced by kind permission of *Private Eye*.

76 L2, p. 516.

77 John Betjeman, *Church Poems* (London: John Murray (Publishers) Ltd., 1981), p. 11.

78 Lycett Green notes that by the mid-1970s her father had 'come to like and recognise' Pevsner. L2, p. 470; *Church Poems*, p. 11.

79 *Parkinson*, 17 February 1973, *John Betjeman: Recollections from the BBC Archives* (selected and introduced by Candida Lycett Green, BBC, 1998), side 4.

80 Alfred Lord Tennyson, *The Poems of Tennyson in Three Volumes*, ed. by Christopher Ricks (Harlow: Longman Group, 1987), III, pp. 147–8 (147).

81 Hulse, p. 48.

82 Ibid., p. 46.

83 John Betjeman, 'Highworth' [from *Coast and Country*, BBC Radio, 29 September 1950], in John Betjeman, *First and Last Loves*, 2nd edn (London: John Murray (Publishers) Ltd., 1969), pp. 231–2 (232).

84 Hulse, p. 45.

85 Jean-François Lyotard, *The Postmodern Condition: A Report on Knowledge*, translated by Geoff Bennington and Brian Massumi (Manchester: Manchester University Press, 1986), p. 37 (and ibid.).

86 *Time with Betjeman*, produced by Jonathan Stedall for BBC Television, 1983 (Show 6).

87 This story was relayed by Irvine to John Heald, Chairman of The Betjeman Society, who in turn passed it on to the author in an unpublished letter, dated 1 August 2005.

88 L2, pp. 556–7.

CHAPTER SEVEN   Summoned by Bells

1 John Betjeman, *Uncollected Poems*, with a foreword by Bevis Hillier (London: John Murray (Publishers) Ltd., 1982), pp. 1–14 (14). Like Betjeman, Thompson and Taylor had both been Magdalen men.

2 J. M. Thompson, *The French Revolution* (Oxford: Blackwell, 1943); Thomas Carlyle, *The French Revolution: A History* (London: Chapman-Hall, 1837).

3 G. M. Harvey, 'Poetry of Commitment: John Betjeman's Later Writing', *Dalhousie Review*, 56 (1976), pp. 112–24 (120).

4 *Summoned by Bells*, produced by Jonathan Stedall for BBC Television, 1976.

5 H. R. Jauss, 'Literary History as a Challenge to Literary Theory', tr. Elizabeth Benzinger, *New Literary History*, vol. 2 (1967), pp. 7–37 (11–19).

6 This figure is revealed in an unpublished letter from Jock Murray to Lovell Thompson (of Houghton Mifflin and Co.), 29 November 1960 (*Summoned by Bells* correspondence file). Courtesy of the John Murray Archive.

7 YB, p. 77.

8 Ibid.

9 He wrote to his wife that he had finished the 'Epic' in February 1960. See L2, p. 156.

10 Letter to Betjeman from Maurice Bowra, 29 October 1966, quoted by Lycett Green. L2, p. 309. (See Chapter 6.)

11 M. H. Abrams, 'The Design of *The Prelude*: Wordsworth's Long Journey Home', in M. H. Abrams, *Natural Supernaturalism: Tradition and Revolution in Romantic Literature* (New York: W. W. Norton & Co., 1971), taken from William Wordsworth, *The Prelude: 1799, 1805 and 1850*, ed. by Jonathan Wordsworth, M. H. Abrams and Stephen Gill (London: W. W. Norton & Co., 1979), pp. 585–98 (586). Abrams was quoting from Wordsworth's *The Recluse*, the unpublished precursor to *The Prelude*.

12 Ibid., p. 29.

13 The Milton references are noted in the Norton edition of *The Prelude*. Ibid., p. 28, note 3.

14 Ibid., p. 449.

15 Dennis Brown, *Writers and Their Work: John Betjeman* (Plymouth: Northcote House, 1999), pp. 5–6 (and ibid.).

16 Ibid., pp. 24–7.

17 The worst form of punishment 'Big Fire' could administer involved partially stripping a victim, throwing him into a huge waste-paper basket, dousing him in treacle and ink and then hoisting the ensemble into the rafters of the Upper School building. In disgrace, the boy usually left Marlborough soon after. In *Summoned by Bells*, such an incident is described on pages 68 to 70.

18 Brown, p. 35.

19 In his Preface, Betjeman describes the poem as an 'account of some moments in the sheltered life of a middle-class youth'. John Betjeman, *Summoned by Bells* (London: John Murray (Publishers) Ltd., 1960), Preface (page not numbered).

20 Patrick Taylor-Martin, *John Betjeman: His Life and Work* (Harmondsworth: Penguin Books, 1983), p. 138.

21 John Wain, 'A Substitute for Poetry' (review of *Summoned by Bells*), *The Observer*, 27 November 1960. Notes on all reviews of *Summoned by Bells* were made from press cuttings held at the John Murray Archive. Page numbers will therefore not be cited.

22 Ibid.

23 This was a reference to G. A. Kolkhorst (1898–1958), the Oxford University Reader in Spanish, who, like Maurice Bowra, was a great influence on the young Betjeman. L1, p. 560 (etc.).

24 Hillier discovered 'The Fairies' in a notebook entitled *Versatile Verse*, held by the Betjeman Archive of the University of Victoria, Canada. YB, p. 29.

25 Whilst at the Dragon, Betjeman came a creditable third place (behind the future Labour politicians Per Mallalieu and Hugh Gaitskell) in a speaking competition. Ibid., pp. 33–50.

26 Ibid., pp. 43–4; p. 42.

27 Hillier writes that other pupils at the Dragon School 'collected butterflies or postage stamps; John collected churches'. Ibid., p. 48. Regarding the architectural terminology, 'Norm' relates to the Norman style of the post-Conquest era, 'E. E.' stands for the Early English that succeeded it (13th century), while 'Dec' is for the Decorated style, which lasted roughly from 1272 to 1377. See (for example) John

Betjeman, *A Pictorial History of English Architecture*, 2nd edn (Harmondsworth: Penguin Books Ltd., 1974), pp. 16–39.

28 This is a toned-down version of the enduring hostility Betjeman had for Marlborough College: in the 1962 film for TWW, he referred to the 'shades of my prison house'. The director, Jonathan Stedall, also recalled in a documentary on the film's video release (1994) how he had had trouble getting the poet through the front gates.

29 Hillier reveals that Mandeville was Per Mallalieu (1908–80). YB, pp. 41–2.

30 Taylor-Martin quotes Betjeman as saying that he read both *The Prelude* and Tennyson's idylls before starting work on *Summoned by Bells*. Taylor-Martin, p. 133.

31 John Betjeman, 'The Rhyme and Reason of Verse', from *The Daily Telegraph Magazine*, 8 January 1971, in CH, pp. 382–6 (384).

32 This was during a radio interview conducted by four teenagers. The poet correctly guessed that they had all written as much as he in this respect. Extracts from *Let's Find Out*, 10 August 1962, *John Betjeman: Recollections from the BBC Archives* (selected and introduced by Candida Lycett Green, BBC, 1998), side 3.

33 Betjeman's biographer reveals that this was one Donovan Chance, who in fact opened a garage in the 1930s. YB, p. 118.

34 Arthur Machen, *The Secret Glory* (London: Tartarus Press, 1991), p. vii. Hillier also notes that the poet's affinity for the book's protagonist, Ambrose Meyrick, was probably heightened by the fact that his relatives included the family of Merrick. YB, pp. 5–6; p. 122.

35 The Mercury is a fountain in the middle of Tom Quad, Christ Church.

36 L1, p. 559.

37 YB, p. 172.

38 Jack Malvern, 'Betjeman's guilty secret – he passed his divinity', *The Times*, 28 August 2006, p. 13 (and ibid.).

39 In Stedall's film, Betjeman removes the reference to the tree, altering the line to: 'the locked and double gates of Trinity'. Although this is a colder image than the original, admirably conveying the poet's sense of his own banishment, it does lose the feeling of powerlessness as measured against the slender acacia.

40 This is a reference to Psalm 98:1: 'O sing unto the LORD a new song: for he hath done marvellous things: his right hand, and his holy arm, hath gotten him the victory'.

41 Evelyn Waugh told him: '[y]ou will remember these school days as the happiest time of your life'. YB, p. 221. The poet in fact had a brief stint working for Sir Horace Plunkett first – see Chapter 2. He started teaching at Heddon Court the following April (1929).

CHAPTER EIGHT   Conclusion

1 Dennis Brown, *Writers and Their Work: John Betjeman* (Plymouth: Northcote House, 1999), p. 35.

2 Jean-François Lyotard, *The Postmodern Condition: A Report on Knowledge*, tr. by Geoff Bennington and Brian Massumi (Manchester: Manchester University Press, 1986), p. 60. Note that this is 'postmodern' in the philosophical sense; in the *architectural* sense, 'postmodern' can mean a neo-traditionalism (which of course circumvents modernism).

3　Ibid., p. 15.
4　Marshall McLuhan, *The Gutenberg Galaxy* (London: Routledge & Kegan Paul Ltd., 1962), p. 1.
5　Dennis Brown, *The Poetry of Postmodernity* (London: The Macmillan Press Ltd., 1994), p. 3.
6　JBNFNL, pp. 551–6.
7　Brown, *Postmodernity*, p. 135.
8　Ibid., p. 31 (and ibid.).
9　From *Let's Find Out*, 10 August 1962, *John Betjeman: Recollections from the BBC Archives* (selected and introduced by Candida Lycett Green, BBC, 1998), side 3.
10　From *A Gerard Manley Hopkins Reader*, ed. by John Pick (London: Oxford University Press Ltd., 1953), p. xxii, cited in McLuhan, p. 83.
11　Brown, *Postmodernity*, p. 4.
12　For the description of modern architecture see John Betjeman, 'Mackay Hugh Baillie Scott', *The Journal of the Manx Museum*, vol. VII, 84 (1968), quoted in YB, p. 260.
13　Brown, *Postmodernity*, p. 15.
14　Porter's comments were quoted in 'New Views on Betjeman: The Teddy Bear and His Critics', *The Listener*, 23 May 1985, pp. 20–1. The article was based on a BBC Radio 3 discussion, chaired by Anthony Thwaite.
15　Philip Larkin, 'Betjeman En Bloc' (first published in *Listen*, Spring 1959), in *Philip Larkin 1922–1985: A Tribute*, ed. by George Hartley (London: The Marvell Press, 1988), pp. 55–67 (55).
16　Althusser was talking from a Marxist perspective. See, for example, Louis Althusser, 'Ideology and the State', in B. Brewster, tr. *Lenin and Philosophy and Other Essays* (1969), pp. 136–8; 152–3; 154–5; 155–6; 160–2; 162–4; 168–9, taken from *Modern Literary Theory: A Reader* ed. by Phillip Rice and Patricia Waugh, 3rd edn (London: Arnold, 1996), pp. 53–69.
17　Brown, *Postmodernity*, p. 58, note 21.
18　H. A. Williams, *The True Wilderness*, 2nd edn (Harmondsworth: Penguin Books Ltd., 1968), p. 97. For the relationship between Williams's text and Betjeman's verse, see Greg Morse, 'John Betjeman: Out of the Wilderness', *The Betjemanian*, vol. 16 (2004/05), pp. 47–50.
19　Brown, *John Betjeman*, p. 37.
20　Thwaite, *The Listener*, 23 May 1985, pp. 20–1.
21　John Betjeman, *Collected Poems*, complied and selected by the Earl of Birkenhead, 6th edn (London: John Murray (Publishers) Ltd., 2001), xiv–xxiv (xiv).

Bibliography

I   Primary Sources (Unpublished)

I.I   *Unpublished Letters to the Author*

From David Tabraham-Palmer, archivist of Highgate School, 14 February 2002.

From Peter Cowley, Trustee, The Telephone Museum, Milton Keynes, 27 May 2002.

From Peter Daniels, Assistant Librarian, the Religious Society of Friends, 14 August 2002.

From John Bodley, Faber & Faber, 11 September 2002.

From Deborah Stevenson, Archivist, Dorset Record Office, 27 September 2002.

From Christopher Hunt, the Imperial War Museum, 27 December 2002.

From Kay Kershaw, Editorial Assistant, SPCK, 13 August 2003.

From Lynne Jackson, *The Architectural Review*, 14 October 2004.

From Valerie McFarlane, Clerk to Old Jordans Trust, 4 February 2005.

From Virginia Murray, the John Murray Archive, 16 March 2005.

From Lynne Jackson, *The Architectural Review*, 14 April 2005.

From Dr. Ian Dungavell, Director, The Victorian Society, 25 May 2005.

From John Heald, Chairman of The Betjeman Society, 1 August 2005.

From Virginia Murray, the John Murray Archive, 9 August 2005.

From Kenneth Hillier, Hon. Sec. of the John Buchan Society, 16 August 2005.

I.II   *Unpublished Letters to Betjeman*

From Edward James, 11 May 1931 (courtesy of The McPherson Library, University of Victoria, Canada) – also quoted (briefly) in L1 (p. 48).

From Mildred Alston, 24 March 1937 (courtesy of The McPherson Library, University of Victoria, Canada).

From Dr. B. Burns, 10 July 1961 (courtesy of The McPherson Library, University of Victoria, Canada).

From T. Rigby Taylor, CBE, JP, 6 July 1961 (courtesy of The McPherson Library, University of Victoria, Canada).

I.III   *Other Unpublished Letters*

From Tim Bennett to Jack Pritchard, 6 October 1941 (courtesy of the University of East Anglia Library (Archives Department)).

From Jock Murray to Lovell Thompson (of Houghton Mifflin and Co.), 29 November 1960, *Summoned by Bells* correspondence file (courtesy of the John Murray Archive).

I.IV   *Archive Documents*

'Copies Ledger K1' (folios 39, 40 and 389), from the John Murray Archive.

'Copies Ledger N1' (folios 25 and 247), from the John Murray Archive .

'Copies Ledger R1' (folios 285, 286 and 287), from the John Murray Archive.
'Copies Ledger 4', from the John Murray Archive.
The Diary of Sir Horace Plunkett (unpublished), held by The Plunkett Foundation –
also quoted in YB (pp. 212–14).
The Diary of John Betjeman, 12 October 1935. Notebook MC7, held by the
McPherson Library, University of Victoria, Canada – also referred to and quoted in
JBNFNL (pp. 60–5).
'Preparative Meeting Minute Book' (Jordans) (AR56/2004) and 'Jordans Monthly
Meeting Minute Book' (NQ5/1/1), courtesy of the Centre for Buckinghamshire
Studies, Aylesbury.

.

II   Primary Sources (Published)

*(Note: these are listed chronologically, in order to remain in keeping with the approach
to Betjeman's oeuvre taken throughout this book; multiple editions are, however,
grouped together for convenience.)*

Betjeman, John, 'Marginalia: The Church's Restoration', *The Architectural Review*,
vol. LXVII, no. 399 (February 1930), pp. 107–8.
Betjeman, John, '1830–1930 – Still Going Strong: A Guide to the Recent History of
Interior Design', *The Architectural Review*, vol. LXVII, no. 402 (May 1930), pp.
230–272.
Betjeman, John (as Lionel Cuffe), 'William Morris', *The Architectural Review*, vol.
LXIX, no. 414 (May 1931), p. 151.
Betjeman, John, 'Charles Francis Annesley Voysey: The Architect of Individualism',
The Architectural Review, vol. LXX, no. 419 (October 1931), pp. 93–6.
Betjeman, John, *Mount Zion or In Touch with the Infinite* (London: The James Press,
1931).
Betjeman, John, 'The Death of Modernism', *The Architectural Review*, vol. LXX, 421
(December 1931), p.161 (later collected in CH, pp. 21–3).
Betjeman, John, 'The Passing of the Village', *The Architectural Review*, vol. LXXII,
no. 430 (September 1932), pp. 89–93.
Betjeman, John, 'Dictating to the Railways', *The Architectural Review*, vol. LXXIV,
442 (September 1933), pp. 83–4.
Betjeman, John, 'Leeds – A City of Contrasts', *The Architectural Review*, vol. LXXIV,
443 (October 1933), pp. 129–38 (later collected in *First and Last Loves*, pp. 30–8).
Betjeman, John, 'The Electrification of Lambourne End – A Poem in the Manner of
the Rev. George Crabbe', *The Architectural Review*, vol. LXXIV, 444 (November
1933), pp. 209–10.
Betjeman, John, *Cornwall Illustrated in a Series of Views* [. . .] (London: The
Architectural Press, 1934).
Betjeman, John, *Devon, compiled with illustrations of every sort by* (London: The
Architectural Press, 1936).
Betjeman, John, '1837 – 1937', *The Studio*, vol. CXIII, 527 (February 1937), pp.
56–73 (later collected in *First and Last Loves*, pp. 120–31).
Betjeman, John, *Continual Dew: A Little Book of Bourgeois Verse* (London: John
Murray (Publishers) Ltd., 1937).
Betjeman, John, *Continual Dew: A Little Book of Bourgeois Verse*, facsimile reissue
(London: John Murray (Publishers) Ltd., 1977).
Betjeman, John, 'A Shell Guide to Typography', *Typography*, no. 2 (Spring 1937), pp.
2–3.

Betjeman, John, *An Oxford University Chest*, 2nd edn (Oxford: Oxford University Press, 1979).

Betjeman, John, 'A Note on J. N. Comper – Heir to Butterfield and Bodley', *The Architectural Review*, vol. LXXXV, no. 507 (February 1939), pp. 79–82.

Betjeman, John, *Antiquarian Prejudice* (London: Hogarth Press Ltd., 1939) (later collected in *First and Last Loves*, pp. 48–66).

Betjeman, John, 'The Seeing Eye or How to Like Everything, *The Architectural Review*, vol. LXXXVI, no. 516 (November 1939), pp. 201–4.

Betjeman, John, 'C. F. A. Voysey', *The Architectural Forum*, vol. 72 (May 1940), pp. 348–9.

Betjeman, John, 'Nonconformist Architecture', *The Architectural Review*, vol. LXXXVIII, 529 (December 1940), pp. 161–74 (later collected in *First and Last Loves*, pp. 90–119).

Betjeman, John, *John Piper* (Harmondsworth: Penguin Books Ltd., 1944).

Betjeman, John, *Ghastly Good Taste, or a depressing story of the rise and fall of English architecture*, 2nd edn (London: Anthony Blond Ltd., 1970).

Betjeman, John, *Ghastly Good Taste, or a depressing story of the rise and fall of English architecture*, 3rd edn (London: Century Hutchinson, 1986).

Betjeman, John, *Old Lights for New Chancels* (London: John Murray (Publishers) Ltd., 1940).

Betjeman, John, *Vintage London* (London: William Collins, 1942).

Betjeman, John, *English Cities and Small Towns* (London: William Collins, 1943).

Betjeman, John and Geoffrey Taylor, eds., *English Scottish and Welsh Landscape 1700 – c.1860* (London: Frederick Muller Ltd., 1944).

Betjeman, John, *New Bats in Old Belfries* (London: John Murray (Publishers) Ltd., 1945).

Betjeman, John, *Slick but not Streamlined*, ed. by W. H. Auden (New York: The Country Life Press, 1947).

Betjeman, John and John Piper, *Murray's Buckinghamshire Guide* (London: John Murray (Publishers) Ltd., 1948).

Betjeman, John, 'West Country Churches III: In Praise of the Victorians', *The Church Observer*, no. 21 (2 September 1949), p. 2.

Betjeman, John and John Piper, *Murray's Berkshire Architectural Guide* (London: John Murray (Publishers) Ltd., 1949).

Betjeman, John, 'Victorian Architecture', *World Review*, New Series, 23 (January 1951), pp.46–52 (later collected in *First and Last Loves*, pp. 132–78).

Betjeman, John and John Piper, *Shropshire: A Shell Guide* (London: Faber & Faber, 1951).

Betjeman, John, *First and Last Loves*, 2nd edn (London: John Murray (Publishers) Ltd., 1969).

Betjeman, John, 'High Frecklesby has a Plan', *Punch*, vol. CCXXIV, 5877 (27 May 1953), pp. 624–5 (later collected in CH, pp. 246–9).

Betjeman, John, 'Lamp Posts and Landscape', *Light and Lighting*, November 1953, pp. 409–12 (late collected in CH, pp. 307–10).

Betjeman, John, *A Few Late Chrysanthemums* (London: John Murray (Publishers) Ltd., 1954).

Betjeman, John, 'John Betjeman Replies', *The Spectator*, no. 6589 (8 October 1954), pp. 443–4.

Betjeman, John, *Poems in the Porch* (London: S.P.C.K, 1954).

Betjeman, John, 'City and Suburban', *The Spectator*, no. 6604 (21 January 1955), p. 67 (later collected in CH, p. 267).

Betjeman, John, 'City and Suburban', *The Spectator*, no. 6688 (31 August 1956), p. 284 (later collected in CH, p. 338).

Betjeman, John, 'City and Suburban', *The Spectator*, no. 6695 (19 October 1956), p. 535 (later collected in CH, pp. 338–43).

Betjeman, John, *Collected Poems*, 4th edn (London: John Murray (Publishers) Ltd., 1993).

Betjeman, John, *Collected Poems*, 5th edn (London: John Murray (Publishers) Ltd., 2001).

Betjeman, John, 'Men and Buildings – Size Without Greatness', *Daily Telegraph and Morning Post*, 10 March 1958, p. 11.

Betjeman, John, ed., *Collins Guide to English Parish Churches*, 2nd edn (London: Wm. Collins Sons and Co. Ltd., 1959).

Betjeman, John, ed., *Altar and Pew: Church of England Verses*, The Pocket Poets Series (London: Edward Hulton and Co. Ltd., 1959).

Betjeman, John, 'Men and Buildings: Variety versus Legitimate', *Daily Telegraph and Morning Post*, 15 December 1958, p. 9.

Betjeman, John, 'Men and Buildings: Destruction for Cash', *Daily Telegraph and Morning Post*, 12 January 1959, p. 11.

Betjeman, John, 'Men and Buildings: Architecture for Entertainment', *Daily Telegraph and Morning Post*, 16 November 1959, p. 13.

Betjeman, John, 'Men and Buildings – Heritage of the Rail Age', *Daily Telegraph and Morning Post*, 8 February 1960, p. 15 (later collected in CH (as 'The Demolition of Euston Arch'), pp. 412–5).

Betjeman, John, 'A Poem for Princess Margaret's Wedding Day', *Harper's Bazaar*, vol. LXII, no. 2, May 1960, pp. 62–3 .

Betjeman, John, 'Men and Buildings – Suburbs Common or Garden', *Daily Telegraph and Morning Post*, 22 August 1960, p. 11 (later collected in CH (as 'Garden Suburbs'), pp. 409–12).

Betjeman, John Betjeman, 'P. Morton Shand: A Personal Memoir', *The Architectural Review*, vol. CXXVIII, 765 (November 1960), pp. 325–8.

Betjeman, John, 'Men and Buildings – The Best and Worst of an Era', *Daily Telegraph and Morning Post*, 3 July 1961, p. 15 (later collected in CH (as 'Sheffield'), pp. 398–401)..

Betjeman, John, *Summoned by Bells*, 2nd edn (London: John Murray (Publishers) Ltd., 1976).

Betjeman, John, 'Obituary: Sir Ninian Comper: 1864–1960', *The Architectural Review*, vol. CXXIX, 769 (March 1961), pp. 153–4.

Betjeman, John, 'A Century of English Architecture', *The Spectator*, no. 7000 (24 August 1962), pp. 252–4.

Betjeman, John, 'Men and Buildings – So Little Left of the Old Middlesex', *Daily Telegraph and Morning Post*, 12 August 1963, p. 13 (later collected in The Best of Betjeman (as 'Middlesex'), pp. 191–3).

Betjeman, John, 'Men and Buildings – What a Town Ought to Be', *Daily Telegraph and Morning Post*, 24 February 1964, p. 15 (later collected in CH (as 'The Ideal Town') pp. 406–9.

Betjeman, John, 'Common Experiences' (review of Philip Larkin's *The Whitsun Weddings*), *The Listener*, vol. LXXI, 1825 (19 March 1964), p. 483 (later collected in CH (as 'Philip Larkin: "The Whitsun Weddings"'), pp. 394–7).

Betjeman, John and Basil Clarke, *English Churches* (London: Vista Books, 1964).

Betjeman, John, *High and Low* (London: John Murray (Publishers) Ltd., 1966).

Betjeman, John, 'The Rhyme and Reason of Verse', *The Daily Telegraph Magazine*, 8 January 1971, p. 30 (later collected in CH, pp. 382–6) .

Betjeman, John, 'Nooks and Corners of the New Barbarism: 1 – Hillgate House, Ludgate Hill', *Private Eye*, no. 246 (21 May 1971), p. 7.

Betjeman, John, 'Nooks and Corners of the New Barbarism: 6 – Brunswick Square, WC1', *Private Eye*, no. 260 (13 August 1971), p. 7.

Betjeman, John, 'A Pity About the Abbey', in *The Twelfth Man: A book of original contributions brought together by The Lord's Taverners in honour of HRH The Prince Philip, Duke of Edinburgh KG, KT*, ed. by Martin Boddey (London: Cassell, 1971), pp. 207–10.

Betjeman, John, *London's Historic Railway Stations* (London: John Murray (Publishers) Ltd., 1972).

Betjeman, John, Obituary of Frederick Etchells, *The Architectural Review*, October 1973, pp. 271–3 (later collected in CH (as 'Frederick Etchells'), pp. 466–8.

Betjeman, John, 'Without a doubt you towered high above us', *New Statesman*, 5 October 1973, p. 478.

Betjeman, John, *A Pictorial History of English Architecture*, 2nd edn (Harmondsworth: Penguin Books Ltd., 1974).

Betjeman, John, *A Nip in the Air* (London: John Murray (Publishers) Ltd., 1974).

Betjeman, John, *Jubilee Hymn, Written for the Occasion of the Silver Jubilee of Her Majesty the Queen in 1977* (London, Joseph Weinberger, 1977).

Betjeman, John, *The Best of Betjeman*, ed. by John Guest (Harmondsworth: Penguin Books Ltd., 1978).

Betjeman, John, 'We are your people . . . ' (lines written to celebrate the 80th birthday of HM Queen Elizabeth, the Queen Mother), *The Times*, 4 August 1980, p. 2.

Betjeman, John, *Ode on the Marriage of HRH Prince Charles to the Lady Diana Spencer in St Paul's Cathedral on 29 July 1981* (London: Warren Editions, 1981).

Betjeman, John, *Church Poems* (John Murray (Publishers) Ltd., 1981).

Betjeman, John, *City of London Churches*, 3rd edn (London: Pitkin Guides Ltd., 1997).

Betjeman, John, *Trains and Buttered Toast*, ed. by Stephen Games (London: John Murray (Publishers), 2006).

Lycett Green, Candida, ed., *John Betjeman – Letters Volume One: 1926–1951*, 2nd edn (London: Reed International Books Ltd., 1995).

Lycett Green, Candida, ed., *John Betjeman – Letters Volume Two: 1951–1984*, 2nd edn (London: Reed International Books Ltd., 1995).

Lycett Green, Candida, ed., *John Betjeman: Coming Home – An Anthology of Prose*, 2nd edn (London: Vintage, 1998).

Maugham, Robin, *The Barrier: A Novel* (including five sonnets by John Betjeman) (London: W. H. Allen, 1973).

Thomas, R. S., *Song at the Year's Turning: Poems 1942–1954* (London: Rupert Hart-Davis, 1955) – introduction by John Betjeman, pp. 11–14 (later collected in CH (as 'R. S. Thomas'), pp. 322–5).

Various, *Flower of Cities: A Book of London* (London: Max Parrish, 1949) – includes Betjeman, John, 'London Railway Stations', pp. 13–30 (later collected in *First and Last Loves*, pp. 75–89).

Various, *Diversion: Twenty-Two Authors on the Lively Arts* (London: Max Parrish, 1950) – includes Betjeman, John, 'The Architecture of Entertainment' (as 'Pleasures and Palaces), pp. 17–24 (later collected in *First and Last Loves*, pp. 67–74).

Various, *Maurice Bowra: A Celebration*, ed. by Hugh Lloyd-Jones (London: Duckworth, 1974) – includes Betjeman, John, 'A Formative Friend', pp. 86–90 (later collected in CH (as 'Maurice Bowra: A Formative Friend'), pp. 488–91.

Various, *W. H. Auden: A Tribute*, ed. by Stephen Spender (London: Weidenfeld and Nicolson, 1974) – includes Betjeman, John, 'Oxford', pp. 43–5 (later collected in CH (as 'W. H. Auden at Oxford'), pp. 483–5).

Various, *The Genius of Thomas Hardy*, ed. by Margaret Drabble (London: Weidenfeld and Nicolson, 1976) – includes Betjeman, John, 'Hardy and Architecture', pp. 150–3 (later collected in CH, pp. 469–73).

Wratislaw, Theodore, *Oscar Wilde: A Memoir (foreword by John Betjeman)* (London: The Eighteen Nineties Society, 1979).

III   Secondary Sources (About Betjeman)

Andrews, Lyman, 'Autumn Collection' (review of *A Nip in the Air*), *The Sunday Times*, 24 November 1974.

Anon (review of *Mount Zion*), *Times Literary Supplement*, 26 November 1931, 944.

Bell, Alan, 'The Times Profile: Sir John Betjeman – By Appointment: Teddy Bear to the Nation', *The Times*, 20 September 1982, p. 5.

Brown, Dennis, *Writers and Their Work: John Betjeman* (Plymouth: Northcote House, 1999).

Carey, John, 'Unpolitical Auden' (includes review of *High and Low*), *New Statesman*, 23 December 1966, 941–942 (p. 942).

Cox, C. B., 'Betjeman Land' (review of *High and Low*), *The Spectator*, 9 December 1966, p. 763.

Churchill, Randolph, 'Arts and Crafts' (review of *Mount Zion*), *The Architectural Review*, LXX/421 (December 1931), pp. 39–41.

Devlin, Tim, 'Summoned by Success', *The Times*, 11 October 1972, p. 16.

Gammond, Peter (with John Heald), *A Bibliographical Companion to Betjeman* (Guildford: The Betjeman Society, 1997).

Harvey, G., 'Poetry of Commitment: John Betjeman's Later Writing', *Dalhousie Review*, 56 (1976), pp. 112–24.

Hillier, Bevis, *Young Betjeman* (London: John Murray (Publishers) Ltd., 1988).

Hillier, Bevis, *John Betjeman: New Fame, New Love* (London: John Murray (Publishers) Ltd., 2002).

Hillier, Bevis, *Betjeman: The Bonus of Laughter* (London: John Murray (Publishers) Ltd., 2004).

Horder, Mervyn, 'Setting John Betjeman to Music', *Contemporary Review*, 265/1542 (July 1994), pp. 39–41.

Hulse, Michael, 'The Laureate Business or the Laureateship in Englishness', *Quadrant*, 29/2 (September 1985), pp. 46–9.

Langford, John, 'The Stamp Collection Waits . . . ', *The Betjeman Society Newsletter*, 49 (April 2002), p. 4.

Larkin, Philip, 'Poetry Beyond a Joke' (review of *Collected Poems*), *The Manchester Guardian*, 19 December 1958.

Larkin, Philip, 'The Blending of Betjeman' (review of *Summoned By Bells*), *The Spectator*, 2 December 1960, p. 913.

Larkin, Philip, 'It Could Only Happen in England', *Cornhill Magazine* (Autumn 1971), p. 1069.

Lawrie, Kit, 'Theophilus Caleb – the 'Indian Christian priest'', *The Betjeman Society Newsletter*, 45 (April 2001), p. 6.

Liberty, Horace, 'Hidden Under the Wallpaper', *The Betjemanian* vol. 14 (2002/2003), pp. 28–31.

Martin, Graham, 'New Poetry' (includes review of *High and Low*), *The Listener*, 26 January 1967, pp. 140–1.

Morton, J. B., 'English Humour' (includes review of *Continual Dew*), *The Listener*, 8 December 1937.

Morse, Greg, 'Betjeman Lives?', *The Betjemanian*, vol. 12 (2000/01), pp. 23–5.

Morse, Greg, 'John Betjeman: Out of the Wilderness', *The Betjemanian*, vol. 16 (2004/05), pp. 47–50.

Morse, Greg, 'Betjeman and Auden: Strange Bedfellows?', *The Betjemanian*, vol. 19 (2007/08), pp. 52–62.

Mowl, Timothy, *Stylistic Cold Wars: Betjeman Versus Pevsner* (London: John Murray (Publishers) Ltd. 2000).

Nairn, Ian, 'Intermittent Enthusiasm' (includes review of the *Collins Guide to English Parish Churches*), *The Architectural Review*, vol. CXXVIII, no. 765 (November 1960), p. 323.

Newsweek Correspondent, 'Mrs. Phillips the Princess' (includes Betjeman's verse 'Hundreds of birds in the air'), *Newsweek*, 26 November 1973, pp. 20–1.

Powers, Alan, 'Guides to Betjeman Country', *Country Life*, 30 August 1984, pp. 542–4.

Press, John, 'Change and Decay' (review of *High and Low*), *Punch*, 23 November 1966, p. 789.

Press, John, *Writers and Their Work: John Betjeman* (Harlow: Longman Group, 1974).

Pryce-Jones, Alan, 'Chronicles: Poetry' (review of *Mount Zion*), *The London Mercury*, December 1931, pp. 202–3.

Pryce-Jones, Alan, 'Bonus of Laughter' (review of *A Nip in the Air*), *Books and Bookmen*, April 1975, p. 45 .

Quennell, Peter, 'Flowers of Mediocrity' (review of *Continual Dew*), *The New Statesman and Nation*, 13 November 1937.

Rees, Goronwy, 'An Original Poet' (review of *Old Lights for New Chancels*), *The Spectator*, no. 5836, 3 May 1940.

Rees, Goronwy, 'Clever and Good' (review of *New Bats in Old Belfries*), *The Spectator*, 15 February 1946, p. 176.

Riley-Smith, Hamish, *The Betjeman Library* (Swanton Abbot: Hamish Riley-Smith, 1996).

Ruddick, Bill, '"Some Ruin-Bibber, Randy for Antique": Philip Larkin's Response to the Poetry of John Betjeman', *Critical Quarterly*, 84/4 (Winter 1986), pp. 63–9.

Schröder, Leena Kore, 'Heterotopian Constructions of Englishness in the Work of John Betjeman', *Critical Survey*, 10/2 (1998), pp. 15–34.

"Senex", 'Neo-Romantic' (review of *Old Lights for New Chancels*), *The New Statesman and Nation*, 30 March 1940.

Sparrow, John, 'A Serious Poet' (review of *Collected Poems*), *Times Literary Supplement*, 12 December 1958, p. 720.

Stanford, Derek, *John Betjeman: A Study* (London: Neville Spearman, 1961).

Taylor, Geoffrey, 'New Notes in Old Numbers' (review of *A Few Late Chrysanthemums*), *Time and Tide*, 17 July 1954, p. 971.

Taylor-Martin, Patrick, *John Betjeman: His Life and Work* (Harmondsworth: Penguin Books, 1983).

Thomas, Peter, 'Reflections on the Collected Poems of John Betjeman', *Western Humanities Review*, 27 (1973), pp. 289–94.

Thwaite, Anthony, ed., *Selected Letters of Philip Larkin: 1940 to 1985* (London: Faber & Faber, 1992).

Time Correspondent, 'Anne's Day: Simply Splendid' (includes Betjeman's verse 'Hundreds of birds in the air'), *Time*, 26 November 1973, pp. 14–15 .

Times Literary Supplement, 'Looking Backward' (includes review of *Mount Zion or In Touch with the Infinite*), *Times Literary Supplement*, 26 November 1931, p. 944.

Times Literary Supplement, 'Some Modern Poets' (includes review of *Old Lights for New Chancels*), *Times Literary Supplement*, 23 March 1940.

Toynbee, Philip, 'Summoned by Knells' (review of *A Nip in the Air*), *The Observer Review*, 24 November 1974.

Wain, John, 'A Substitute for Poetry' (review of *Summoned by Bells*), *The Observer*, 27 November 1960.

Waugh, Auberon, 'Royal Rhymester', *New York Times Magazine*, 6 January 1974, pp. 18–26.

Waugh, Evelyn, 'A Parnassian on Mount Zion' (review of *Continual Dew*), *Night and Day*, 25 November 1937, p. 24.

Wilson, Edward, 'Betjeman's Riddel Posts: An Echo of Ninian Comper', *Review of English Studies*, 42/168 (November 1991), pp. 541–50.

Winder, John, 'Sir John Betjeman: Poet Laureate in Ordinary, who felt humbled', *The Times*, 11 October 1972, p. 1.

Wright, the Rev. Michael, 'Betjeman's Lincolnshire Church', *The Betjemanian*, vol. 12 (2000/01), pp. 19–22.

IV Primary Printed Sources by Other Authors

Acton, Harold, *Memoirs of an Aesthete* (London: Methuen and Co. Ltd., 1948).

Amory, Mark, ed., *The Letters of Evelyn Waugh* (London: Orion Books Ltd., 1995).

Arnold, Matthew, *The Poems of Matthew Arnold*, ed. by Kenneth Allott, 2nd edn ed. by Miriam Allott (London: Longman Group, 1979).

Auden, W. H., *Collected Poems*, ed. by Edward Mendelson (London: Faber & Faber, 1976).

Auden, W. H., *As I Walked Out One Evening – Songs, ballads, lullabies, limericks and other light verse*, ed. by Edward Mendelson (London: Faber & Faber, 1995).

Austin, Alfred, *English Lyrics*, ed. by William Watson, 4th edn (London: Macmillan and Co. Ltd., 1896).

Bradley, Simon, *St. Pancras Station* (London: Profile Books Ltd, 2007).

British Broadcasting Corporation, The, *The BBC Hymn Book (with music)*, 6th impression (Ely House, London: Oxford University Press, 1966).

Browning, Robert, *Poetical Works 1833–1864*, ed. by Ian Jack (London: Oxford University Press, 1970).

Browning, Robert, *The Poems of Browning*, ed. by John Woolford and Daniel Karlin (London: Longman Group, 1991).

Calverley, C. S., *The English Poems of Charles Stuart Calverley*, ed. by Hilda D. Spear (Leicester: Leicester University Press, 1974).

Carlyle, Thomas, *Past and Present*, ed. by Richard D. Altick (New York: New York University Press, 1965).

Clough, A. H., *Selected Poems*, ed. by J. P. Phelan (Harlow: Longman Group, 1995).

Combe, William, *The Three Tours of Doctor Syntax* (London: Alex Murray & Son, 1871).

Davie, Michael, ed., *The Diaries of Evelyn Waugh* (London: George Weidenfeld & Nicolson Ltd., 1976).

Davis, Philip, ed., *John Ruskin: Selected Writings* (London: Everyman, 1995).

Dickens, Charles, *Martin Chuzzlewit*, 4th edn (Harmondsworth: Penguin Books Ltd., 1994).

Eliot, T. S., *Collected Poems 1909–1962* (London: Faber & Faber, 1963).

Eliot, T. S., ed., *T. S. Eliot: Selected Essays*, 3rd edn (London: Faber & Faber, 1966).

Eliot, T. S., ed., *T. S. Eliot: Selected Essays*, 4th edn (London: Faber & Faber, 1999).

Farrar, Frederic W., *St. Winifred's or the World of School*, 5th edn (London: Adam and Charles Black, 1912).

Grigson, Geoffrey, *Recollections – Mainly of Writers and Artists* (London: The Hogarth Press, 1984).

Grossmith, George and Weedon Grossmith, *The Diary of a Nobody*, ed. by Ed Glinert, 3rd edn (Harmondsworth: Penguin Books Ltd., 1999).

Hardy, Thomas, *The Return of the Native*, ed. by Tony Slade, 2nd edn (London: Penguin Books Ltd., 1999).

Hardy, Thomas, *Selected Poetry*, ed. by David Wright (London: Penguin Books Ltd., 1978).

Hardy, Thomas, *Selected Poems*, ed. by Tim Armstrong (Harlow: Longman Group, 1993).

Hardy, Thomas, *Thomas Hardy: The Complete Poems*, ed. by James Gibson (Basingstoke: Palgrave, 2001).

Henley, W. E., *The Works of W. E. Henley*, 7 vols, vol. 1, *Poems* (London: David Nutt, 1908).

Henley, W. E., ed., *Lyra Heroica – A Book of Verse for Boys*, 6th edn (London: David Nutt, 1900).

Housman, A. E., *The Poems of A. E. Housman*, ed. by Archie Burnett (Oxford: Clarendon Press, 1997).

James, Edward, *Swans Reflecting Elephants – My Early Years*, ed. by George Melly (London: George Weidenfeld & Nicolson Ltd., 1982).

Kilvert, Francis, *Kilvert's Diary*, ed. by William Plomer (Harmondsworth: Penguin Books Ltd., 1977).

Larkin, Philip, *Philip Larkin 1922–1985: A Tribute*, ed. by George Hartley (London: The Marvell Press, 1988).

Larkin, Philip, *The Whitsun Weddings*, 3rd edn (London: Faber & Faber, 2001).

Machen, Arthur, *The Secret Glory*, 3rd edn (London: Tartarus Press, 1991)

Mahony Francis, *The Reliques of Father Prout* (London: Bell, 1875).

Marlowe, Christopher, *Complete Plays and Poems*, ed. by E. D. Pendry with J. C. Maxwell, 2nd edn (London: J. M. Dent & Sons Ltd., 1983).

Masefield, John, *Selected Poems* (with a preface by John Betjeman) (London: Book Club Associates, 1978).

Meredith, George, *The Poetical Works of George Meredith*, ed. by G. M. Trevelyan (London: Constable & Co. Ltd., 1912).

Milton, John, *The Complete Poems*, ed. by Gordon Campbell (London: J. M. Dent & Sons Ltd., 1980).

Morris, William, *The Earthly Paradise: A Poem by William Morris*, 4 vols (London: Longmans Green, 1905).

Morris, William, *News From Nowhere and Other Writings*, ed. by Clive Wilmer (Harmondsworth: Penguin Books Ltd., 1993).

Richards, Bernard, ed., *English Verse: 1830 – 1890* (London: Longman Group, 1980).

Rees, Joan, *The Poetry of Dante Gabriel Rossetti: modes of self-expression* (Cambridge: Cambridge University Press, 1981).

Rossetti, Dante Gabriel, *Collected Poetry and Plays*, ed. by Jerome McGann (New Haven and London: Yale University Press, 2003).

Ruskin, John, *Selected Writings*, ed. by Philip Davis (London: J. M. Dent, 1995).

Spenser, Edmund, *Selected Shorter Poems*, ed. by Douglas Brooks-Davies (London: Longman Group, 1995).

Swinburne, A. G., *The Poems of Algernon Charles Swinburne: Vol I – Poems and Ballads* (London: Chatto and Windus, 1905).

Swinburne, A. G., *Swinburne: Selected Poems*, ed. by L. M. Findlay (Manchester: Carcanet New Press Ltd., 1982).

Tennyson, Alfred Lord, *The Poems of Tennyson in Three Volumes*, ed. by Christopher Ricks (Harlow: Longman Group, 1987).

Tennyson, Alfred Lord, *Selected Poems*, ed. by Aidan Day (Harmondsworth: Penguin Books Ltd., 1991).

Tennyson, Alfred Lord, *Alfred Tennyson*, ed. by Adam Roberts (Oxford: Oxford University Press, 2000).

Voysey, C. F. Annesley, '1874 & After (Foreword by Sir Edwin Lutyens)', *The Architectural Review*, vol. LXX, no. 419 (October 1930), pp. 91–2.

Waugh, Evelyn, *Rossetti: His Life and Works* (London: Duckworth, 1928).

Waugh, Evelyn, *Decline and Fall*, 2nd edn (Harmondsworth: Penguin Books Ltd., 1937).

Waugh, Evelyn, *Vile Bodies*, ed. by Richard Jacobs, 4th edn (Harmondsworth: Penguin Books Ltd., 2000).

Waugh, Evelyn, *Put Out More Flags*, ed. by Nigel Spivey, 3rd edn (Harmondsworth: Penguin Books Ltd., 2000).

Waugh, Evelyn, *The Loved One*, 2nd edn (London: Chapman and Hall Ltd., 1965).

Waugh, Evelyn, *Brideshead Revisited*, 4th edn (Harmondsworth: Penguin Books Ltd., 1962).

Waugh, Evelyn, *Love Among the Ruins* (London: Chapman and Hall Ltd., 1953).

Woolf, Virginia, *The Waves*, ed. by Gillian Beer, 2nd edn (Oxford: Oxford University Press, 1992).

William Wordsworth, *The Prelude: 1799, 1805 and 1850*, ed. by Johnathon Wordsworth, M. H. Abrams and Stephen Gill (London: W.W. Norton & Co., 1979).

V   Secondary Sources (General)

Anonymous, 'The Euston Murder', *The Architectural Review*, vol. CXXXI, 782 (April 1962), pp. 235–9.

Armstrong, Isobel, ed., *Victorian Scrutinies: Reviews of Poetry 1830 – 1870* (London: The Athlone Press, 1972).

Armstrong, Isobel, *Victorian Poetry: Poetry, Poetics and Politics* (London: Routledge, 1993).

Bayley, John, *The Romantic Survival: A Study in Poetic Evolution* (London: Constable and Co. Ltd., 1957).

Bristow, Joseph, ed., *The Victorian Poet: Poetics and Persona* (Beckenham: Croom Helm, 1987).

Brown, Dennis, *The Poetry of Postmodernity* (London: The Macmillan Press Ltd., 1994).

Carpenter, Humphrey, *The Brideshead Generation: Evelyn Waugh and his Friends* (London: George Weidenfeld & Nicolson Ltd., 1989).

Carson, Rachel, *Silent Spring* (Harmondsworth: Penguin Books Ltd., 1999).

Chadwick, Owen, *The Victorian Church – Part II*, 2nd edn (London: Adam & Charles Black, 1972).

Chapman, Graham, John Cleese, Terry Gilliam, Eric Idle, Terry Jones and Michael Palin (with Bob McCabe), *The Pythons (Autobiography by the Pythons)* (London: Orion Publishing Group Ltd., 2003).

Cook, Olive, *The Stansted Affair: a Case for the People* (with a foreword by John Betjeman) (London: Pan Books Ltd., 1967).

Cunningham, Valentine, *British Writers of the Thirties* (Oxford: Oxford University Press, 1989).

Davie, Donald, *Thomas Hardy and British Poetry* (London: Routledge and Kegan Paul, 1973).

Dimbleby, Jonathan, *The Prince of Wales: A Biography* (London: Little, Brown and Co., 1994).

Eagleton, Terry, *Literary Theory: An Introduction*, 2nd edn (Oxford: Blackwell Publishers Ltd., 1996).

Ellmann, Richard, *Oscar Wilde* (London: Hamish Hamilton, 1987).

Ford, Boris, ed., *The Cambridge Guide to the Arts in Britain: 7 – The Later Victorian Age* (Cambridge: Cambridge University Press, 1989).

Freud, Sigmund, *Jokes and Their Relation to the Unconscious*, ed. by Angela Richards (Harmondsworth: Penguin Books, 1960).

Gardener, Helen, ed., *The Metaphysical Poets*, 4th edn (Harmondsworth: Penguin Books, 1985).

Gorman, George H., *Introducing Quakers*, 3rd edn (London: Friends Home Service Committee, 1978).

Hardy, Florence Emily, *The Life of Thomas Hardy: Volume 1 – 1840 – 1891*, 2nd edn (London: Macmillan & Co. Ltd., 1933).

Hardy, Florence Emily, *The Life of Thomas Hardy: Volume II – 1892 – 1928*, 2nd edn (London: Macmillan and Co. Ltd., 1933).

Harper, Duncan, *Wilts & Somerset: A Railway Landscape* (Bath: Millstream Books, 1987).

Hill, C. P., *British Economic and Social History 1700–1982*, 5th edn (London: Hodder & Stoughton, 1985).

Hoey, Brian, *Anne: The Private Princess Revealed* (London: Macmillan Publishers Ltd., 1997).

Hoggart, Richard, *The Uses of Literacy*, 2nd edn (Harmondsworth: Penguin Books Ltd., 1966).

Hynes, Samuel, *The Auden Generation – Literature and Politics in England in the 1930s* (London: The Bodley Head, 1976).

Jackson, Alan A., *London's Metropolitan Railway* (Newton Abbot: David and Charles (Publishers) Ltd., 1986).

Jauss, H. R., 'Literary History as a Challenge to Literary Theory', tr. Elizabeth Benzinger, *New Literary History* vol. 2 (1967), pp. 7–37.

Lieberman, Abraham N. and Frank Williams *et al.*, *Parkinson's Disease – The Complete Guide for Patients and Carers* (London: HarperCollins*Publishers*, 1995).

Levi, Peter, *Tennyson* (London: Macmillan London Ltd., 1993).

Lyotard, Jean-François, *The Postmodern Condition: A Report on Knowledge*, tr. by Geoff Bennington and Brian Massumi (Manchester: Manchester University Press, 1986).

Margolis, Jonathan, *Cleese Encounters* (London: Chapmans Publishers Ltd., 1992).

McLuhan, Marshall, *The Gutenberg Galaxy: the Making of Typographic Man* (London: Routledge and Kegan Paul Ltd., 1962).

McLuhan, Marshall, *Understanding Media*, 2nd edn (London: Routledge, 2001).

Millgate, Michael, *Thomas Hardy: A Biography* (Oxford: Oxford University Press, 1982).

Muggeridge, Malcolm, *The Thirties: 1930 – 1940 in Great Britain*, 2nd edn (London: Collins, 1967).

Olroyd, D. L., *Darwinian Impacts: An Introduction to the Darwinian Revolution* (Milton Keynes: Open University Press, 1980).

Parkinson, Neil, ed., *Poets and Polymaths: Special Collections at the University of Sussex* (Brighton: University of Sussex, 2002).

Pevsner, Nikolaus and Enid Radcliffe, eds, *The Buildings of England: Yorkshire West Riding*, 2nd edn (Harmondsworth, Penguin Books Ltd., 1967).

Punnett, Neil and Peter Webber, *The British Isles* (Oxford: Basil Blackwell Ltd., 1984).

Purdy, Richard Little, *Thomas Hardy: A Bibliographical Study*, 2nd edn (Oxford: Clarendon Press, 1968).

Radice, Betty, ed., *Who's Who in the Ancient World*, 2nd edn (Harmondsworth: Penguin Books Ltd., 1973).

Rice, Phillip and Patricia Waugh, eds, *Modern Literary Theory: A Reader*, 3rd edn (London: Arnold, 1996).

Rose, Kenneth, *King George V* (London: Weidenfeld & Nicolson, 1983).

Rubinstein, William D., *Twentieth-Century Britain: A Political History* (Basingstoke: Palgrave Macmillan, 2003).

Selden, Raman, *Practising Theory and Reading Literature: An Introduction* (Hemel Hempstead: Prentice Hall/Harvester Wheatsheaf, 1989).

Seymour-Smith, Martin, *Hardy* (London: Bloomsbury Publishing Ltd., 1994).

Stanley Gibbons GB Stamp Album, 2nd edn (London: Stanley Gibbons Publications Ltd., 1981).

Symons, Julian, *The Thirties – A Dream Revolved*, 2nd edn (London: Faber & Faber, 1975).

Tennyson, Hallam, *Tennyson: A Memoir by his Son, Vol. I* (London: Macmillan & Co. Ltd., 1897).

Thompson, Paul, *The Work of William Morris*, 2nd edn (London: Quartet Books Ltd., 1977).

Thorns, David C., *Suburbia* (London: MacGibbon and Kee Ltd., 1972).

Tindall, William York, *Forces in Modern British Literature 1885–1956* (New York: Vintage Books, 1956).

Ware, Dora, *A Short Dictionary of British Architects* (London: George Allen and Unwin Ltd., 1967).

Watson, J. R., *The English Hymn: A Critical and Historical Study* (Oxford: Clarendon Press, 1999).

Williams, David, *George Meredith: His Life and Lost Love* (London: Hamish Hamilton, 1977).

Whitehouse, Patrick, and David St. John Thomas, eds, *The Great Western Railway: 150 Glorious Years* (Newton Abbot: David & Charles (Publishers) Ltd., 1984).

Whitehouse, Patrick, and David St. John Thomas, eds, *The London Midland & Scottish Railway: A Century and a Half of Progress – LMS 150* (Newton Abbot: David & Charles (Publishers) Ltd., 1987).

Wraight, Heather, and Dr Peter Brierley, eds, *The UK Christian Handbook 2000/01* (London: HarperCollins Religious, 1999).

Betjeman Filmography and Audiography

Betjeman Filmography

Discovering Britain with John Betjeman. Random Films (for Shell), 1955 (26 films – Stourhead, Clifton Suspension Bridge, Avebury, Eastleach Martin, Great Coxwell Barn, Romney Marsh, Heaton Hall, Adlington Hall, Stystead Mill, Dashwood Mausoleum, Holderness, Bolsover Castle, Wellingborough, Hardwick Hall, Wakefield, Castell Coch, Chastleton House, Bolton, Haddon Hall, Stokesay Castle, Kedleston Hall, Merryworth Castle, Crofton Beam Engine, Abingdon, Burton Agnes Hall, Bradwell-Juxta-Mary)

John Betjeman Goes By Train. Dir. Malcolm Freegard. British Transport Films (in association with the BBC), 1962.

Marlborough. Prod. Jonathan Stedall. Television Wales and West, 1962.

Clevedon. Prod. Jonathan Stedall. Television Wales and West, 1962.

Malmesbury. Prod. Jonathan Stedall. Television Wales and West, 1962.

Weston-super-Mare. Prod. Jonathan Stedall. Television Wales and West, 1962.

Bath (I). Prod. Jonathan Stedall. Television Wales and West, 1962.

Devizes. Prod. Jonathan Stedall. Television Wales and West, 1963.

Sherborne. Prod. Jonathan Stedall. Television Wales and West, 1963.

Crewkerne and Chippenham. Prod. Jonathan Stedall. Television Wales and West, 1963.

North Lew and Swindon. Prod. Jonathan Stedall. Television Wales and West, 1963.

Sidmouth. Prod. Jonathan Stedall. Television Wales and West, 1963.

Bath (II). Prod. Jonathan Stedall. Television Wales and West, 1963.

Branch Line Railway. BBC, 1963.

Londoners: A Pity About the Abbey (written with Stuart Farrar). Prod. Ian Curteis. BBC, 1965.

Betjeman in Australia. Prod. Margaret McCall. BBC, 1972 (4 films).

Thank God It's Sunday. Prod. Jonathan Stedall. BBC, 1972 (2 films).

Metro-Land. Prod. Edward Mirzoeff. BBC, 1973.

Summoned by Bells. Prod. Jonathan Stedall. BBC, 1976.

Time With Betjeman (compilation and contemporary interviews). Prod. Jonathan Stedall. BBC, 1983 (7 films).

The Real John Betjeman. Dir. Marion Milne. Channel 4, 2000.

Reputations: John Betjeman – The Last Laugh. Prod. & Dir. Edward Mirzoeff. BBC, 2001.

Betjeman Audiography

John Betjeman: Poetry from the BBC Archives. Prod. Pat McLoughlin. BBC, 1994 (various sources).

John Betjeman: Summoned by Bells. Prod. Douglas Cleverdon. BBC, 1991 (first broadcast 1960).

John Betjeman: Recollections from the BBC Archives. Prod. Peter Hutchings. BBC, 1998.

Includes: *Desert Island Discs* (12 April 1975).

Speech at the Annual Dinner of the Royal Academy of Arts (1 May 1962).

A Sense of the Past (from *Scenes That Are Brightest*, 23 June 1968).

Trains of Thought (8 May 1953).

School and University (from *People Today*, 24 December 1959).

Cornwall (from *Scenes That Are Brightest*, 16 March 1969).

St. Mark's Church, Swindon (3 March 1949).

Let's Find Out (10 August 1962).

London Before the Motor Car (from *Scenes That Are Brightest*, 9 January 1968).

Tennyson as a Humorist (3 July 1950).

Public Image (from *Any Questions*, 23 May 1969).

From *Parkinson* (TV, 17 February 1973).

From *Thank God It's Sunday* (TV, 1972).

I Remember, 5 June 1962.

Index